CORRESPONDENCE OF ROBERT M. T. HUNTER 1826-1876

A Da Capo Press Reprint Series

THE AMERICAN SCENE
Comments and Commentators

GENERAL EDITOR: WALLACE D. FARNHAM
University of Illinois

CORRESPONDENCE OF ROBERT M. T. HUNTER 1826-1876

Edited by Charles Henry Ambler

DA CAPO PRESS · NEW YORK · 1971

A Da Capo Press Reprint Edition

This Da Capo Press edition of the
*Correspondence of Robert M. T. Hunter,
1826-1876,* is an unabridged republication
of the first edition published in
Washington, D. C., in 1918 as Volume II
of the *Annual Report of the American
Historical Association for the Year 1916.*

Library of Congress Catalog Card Number 76-75307

SBN 306-71257-1

Published by Da Capo Press, Inc.
A Subsidiary of Plenum Publishing Corporation
227 West 17th Street, New York, N.Y. 10011

Manufactured in the United States of America

CORRESPONDENCE OF
ROBERT M. T. HUNTER
1826-1876

TWELFTH REPORT OF THE HISTORICAL MANUSCRIPTS COMMISSION. DECEMBER 30, 1914.

WORTHINGTON C. FORD.
CLARENCE W. ALVORD.
HERBERT E. BOLTON.

JULIAN P. BRETZ.
ARCHER B. HULBERT.
WILLIAM O. SCROGGS.

CORRESPONDENCE OF ROBERT M. T. HUNTER, 1826–1876.

Edited by CHARLES HENRY AMBLER.

CONTENTS.

PREFACE.

The letters and papers here presented derive their value from the importance of the period (1826–1876) with which they deal. Except in so far as he represented and spoke for Calhoun's followers in Virginia, always more formidable than numerous, Robert Mercer Taliaferro Hunter (1809–1887) had little of claim to statesmanship or influence. Moreover, the period of his constructive effort was one of declining influence for his State and later one of civil strife between the great sections of the Nation. Although he served the public almost continuously during a period of thirty years, he held only a few positions of trust, most of his service being in the United States Senate. A chronology of his life would therefore tell little, and a brief biographical sketch instead may be helpful in this connection.

R. M. T. Hunter, familiarly known as " Bob " Hunter, was born at the homestead of his maternal ancestors, the Garnetts, in Essex County, Va., a county which, by the way, produced more leaders of influence for Virginia than did any other one county or small section of the State for the period from 1800 to 1860. To one at all familiar with her history the names of Spencer Roane, Thomas Ritchie, John Brockenbraugh, and the Garnetts (J. M., M. R. H., and R. S.) at once suggest themselves. Hunter's early education was received at the hands of his father and at the Rose Hill Academy, two and a half miles from his home. To this school he and his colored boy, Austin, walked every morning. Later he entered the University of Virginia, matriculating for its first session and becoming one of its first graduates. After completing his university course he took up the study of law with that famous teacher and effective apostle of State rights, Judge Henry St. George Tucker, of Winchester, Va. It was in this period of his preparation that Hunter met and married Mary Evelina Dandridge, a niece of Judge Tucker's wife and the reputed heroine of Philip Pendleton Cooke's " Florence Vane," a famous love poem.

After a short period (1835–1837) of service in the General Assembly of Virginia, and despite the fact that he had refused affiliation with either of the leading political parties of the time, Hunter was elected by the State rights Whigs to represent his district in Congress. To the great surprise of the Whigs he, with Calhoun and others, supported Van Buren's plan for an independent subtreasury; but, to the disappointment of the Democrats, Hunter voted with the Whigs in the memorable contest of 1839 between the rival delegations claiming the right to represent New Jersey in Congress. Thus he continued an unknown quantity in politics, but this fact made him available and the successful candidate for the speakership in 1839 in his second term of service. In the contests which followed between the rival factions of the Whig Party he showed a marked leaning toward the State rights element and was thus rendered *persona non grata* to the dominant faction. As he owed his election to the speakership largely to the northern Whigs, he thus failed of a reelection, being succeeded in that office by John White, of Kentucky. Moreover, factional differences between the Whigs of Virginia and a legislative arrangement of the congressional districts of that State, caused him to fail of a reelection to Congress in the election of 1843.

Notwithstanding these reverses, Hunter continued his political activities with renewed energy and purpose. The two succeeding years marked a period of great activity on the part of the State Rights Party in Virginia. It sought to place its idol, John C. Calhoun in the presidency. Hunter was the recognized leader of the movement and, as such, carried on a large correspondence with numerous local politicians throughout the Union, particularly those of the Tammany Society of New York City. As the campaign progressed and as Van Buren's hold upon the Democracy of the country became more and more evident, Hunter and others decided to abandon Calhoun's candidacy and to groom him for the presidential race in 1848. But they were unwilling to take this course without first securing some concessions from the dominant faction of the Democracy in Virginia. Accordingly a compromise was agreed upon whereby Thomas Ritchie, of the Richmond Enquirer, and other State leaders agreed to accept Calhoun's political principles, as a party platform, in exchange for an undivided support for Van Buren's candidacy for the presidency. Hunter and his friend, James A. Seddon, wrote the resolutions committing the Democracy of Virginia to the extreme State rights position. Thus a practically new political party was created, and Hunter and others had no hesitation in affiliating with it and being known henceforth as Democrats.

Under these changed political conditions Hunter was reelected to the House of Representatives in 1845, but James A. Seddon, Lewis E. Harvie, and a few others of the State rights faction of the Virginia Democracy interested themselves in a movement by which he was soon elected to the United States Senate. His term of service there began March 4, 1847, and continued to March 28, 1861, when he withdrew. In the Senate Hunter was a tireless worker of genuine accomplishments. For more than ten years he was chairman of its

Committee on Finance. Besides, he was personally responsible for some of the most important acts of Congress of his period of service, notably the Tariff Act of 1857.

Though a compromiser by nature and environment, he shared the aggressive attitude of Jefferson Davis and Robert Toombs regarding the property rights of slaveholders in the common territories. In this attitude he was continually spurred onward to action and assertion by Seddon and Harvie. Consequently he, Davis, and Toombs were frequently spoken of as the " Southern Triumvirate." By the country at large he was esteemed a man of " sturdy common sense, slow in his methods, but strong and honest in his processes of reasoning." In both 1856 and in 1860 he was prominently and generally mentioned for the presidency. In the Charleston convention Virginia cast her vote for him from the first to the last through forty-five successive ballots. When, later at Baltimore, compromise with the northern Democracy became impossible, it was Hunter who led the remaining Southern States in their decision to accept Breckinridge and Lane, already the nominees of the cotton States for the presidency and vice presidency, respectively, as the standard bearers of a united southern Democracy.

Though he made no public utterance urging or encouraging her action, Hunter willingly followed Virginia into the secession movement. He was one of the five delegates first appointed to represent her in the provisional government of the Confederacy, and he hastened at once to Montgomery, Ala., the seat of the new government. Soon after his arrival he was made Secretary of State of the Confederacy. However well Hunter might have performed the duties of a cabinet portfolio,[1] he soon expressed a desire to serve the Confederacy in its Senate. To what extent, if any, Benjamin's superior influence in Davis's cabinet or his own feelings toward Davis himself influenced his action would be difficult to determine. Nevertheless, he secured the desired election, but not without opposition, and continued a member of the Confederate Senate until the fall of Richmond. In this new rôle his efforts were comparatively unproductive of achievements.

Hunter never again figured prominently in the public eye but once, and that was in the famous Hampton Roads Peace Conference of February 3, 1865, in which President Lincoln and W. H. Seward represented the Union and Alexander H. Stephens, John A. Campbell, and Hunter represented the Confederacy. Before the conference took place Hunter was known to be sick of war and favorable to the inauguration of such negotiations as would bring peace on the best possible terms for the South. Nevertheless, he yet cherished

---

[1] Hunter was Secretary of State of the Confederacy from July 25, 1861, to February 17, 1862.

the hope of independence for the Confederacy. Therefore Lincoln's refusal to treat with it while in arms came as a sore disappointment to Hunter, notwithstanding the fact that the refusal was accompanied by promises of executive clemency. After the failure of the conference Hunter continued to press for peace and would not have been averse to a restoration of the Union. He even went so far as to offer to take the responsibility for inaugurating a movement looking to negotiations for peace. Under the circumstances, the South having resolved upon a last desperate effort, to which Hunter had committed himself in a speech at the African Church in Richmond, his peace activities only brought him into disfavor, causing Davis to lose confidence in him and Richmond to revile and ridicule her "conquered Senator." But the Union Army was already fast closing in on Richmond, and Hunter was soon forced to serve the Confederacy in an alleged traitor's prison.

After several months in Fort Pulaski Hunter returned to his home, Fronthill, Essex County, to eke out a living. Two years before his property had been singled out for destruction, and under the direction of Gen. B. F. Butler the work of vengeance was consummated. Thus, as the grip of needless poverty and the growing infirmities of age wrought their destruction in a life usually kind and cordial, Hunter came to express feelings of bitterness toward the North. Meanwhile he wrote articles upon the Confederacy, and in 1877 he engaged in an unfortunate dispute with Jefferson Davis over the Hampton Roads Conference of 1865. Beginning in 1874 he was treasurer of Virginia for a period of six years, and at the time of his death he was collector of the port of Tappahannock. Some time before his death he attempted to write a final and authoritative biography of the idol of his youth and the guiding star of his riper years in two Senates—John C. Calhoun. Though undertaken at the request of Calhoun's children, the biography was never completed, and those parts of the manuscript that have not been destroyed are disappointing.

Practically all the papers here presented are a part, and a small part, of a collection kept until recently in the old Hunter home at Fronthill. Fortunately the entire collection will soon be placed at the disposal of the public in the State Library of Virginia at Richmond. The letters and papers here printed and not to be found in this collection are indicated by footnotes. As a whole, the main collection, as well as that portion here presented, is markedly miscellaneous, embracing as it does letters upon a great variety of subjects and, for the most part, only those written to Hunter between the various sessions of the Congresses of which he was a Member. In fact, the subjects treated range all the way from local politics, internal improvements, and industrial enterprises to the larger topics of Indian wars, western land enterprises, the occupation of California, the organization of the Army, and the fixing of customs duties to national and even to European politics. It is hoped that the paucity of source materials for that period of Virginia's history immediately preceding the Civil War will be sufficient justification for the comparatively large number of letters presented herewith of almost purely local interest. They throw much light upon the political history of Virginia, especially upon the rival factions within the Democratic Party.

That these letters contain no single group or groups covering the whole or any considerable part of the period of Hunter's activities is regrettable. Of the letters and papers by Hunter himself there are only seventeen in the whole collection, and some of them are of minor importance. His letter of October 28, 1857, discussing various questions growing out of the proposed admission of Kansas, and that of December 10, 1860, upon the status of public affairs, are probably the most important of all those by Hunter himself. Of the others five were written in 1857.

Viewed from the standpoint of groups and writers the letters of James A. Seddon are probably the most valuable of any of this collection. Even the five letters from Calhoun (1842–1845), here printed for the first time, are comparatively unimportant. The letters from Seddon, ten in all, cover more completely than do those of any other of Hunter's correspondence the period before the Civil War. That of December 26, 1859, upon the probable effects of John Brown's raid is both interesting and instructive. Of the other groups of most value first place belongs to that from Lewis E. Harvie, who, though scarcely known beyond the borders of Virginia, did more probably than any one leader to keep both Hunter and his colleague, James M. Mason, in the United States Senate and to shape the policy of Virginia in many other matters. His letter of June 16, 1856, written shortly after his return from the Cincinnati convention of that year, gives an excellent expression of the radical pro-Southern position toward the North at that time. Other groups of letters probably most worth while are those by William O. Goode, Thomas S. Bocock, John Letcher, Francis Mallory, and George Booker. A single letter from Littleton Waller Tazewell, dated August 18, 1850, shortly before the death of that venerable statesman, is of interest and importance because of its detail treatment of the great compromise of that year.

For the most part the letters and papers here printed have been reproduced with all the peculiarities of the spelling, capitalization, punctuation, and paragraphing of the originals. Economy of space has made necessary a general exclusion of addresses, subscriptions, and signatures, and, in some instances, has excluded from the texts passages of a more or less personal nature.

This collection was undertaken at the suggestion of Mr. Worthington C. Ford, made while he was chairman of the manuscripts commission of the American Historical Association. He and the editor of this collection then thought it possible to locate and secure the use of the letters and papers of two or three prominent Virginians of the period immediately preceding the Civil War. We had in view the publication of a volume of source material for Virginia similar to "The correspondence of Robert Toombs, Alexander H. Stephens, and Howell Cobb," published as a part of the Annual Report of the American Historical Association for 1911. In the process of collection diligent effort was made to secure the letters of at least one prominent Virginia Whig, one prominent pro-Southern Democrat, and one administration Democrat of the Henry A. Wise type, but the effort revealed a great dearth of contemporary documents bearing upon the secession movement in Virginia. Many collections were destroyed in the Civil War period; Seddon seems to have kept no letter files; the correspondence of William O. Goode has disappeared; the letters of Thomas S. Bocock were destroyed in a recent fire; and other collections, such as the Wise and Alexander H. H. Stuart papers, are too fragmentary to be of great value. Harvie's disposition of his papers is regrettable. Believing that they contained incriminating information regarding the movers in secession, he ordered his vast collection destroyed immediately following the fall of Richmond. Thus we were forced, temporarily at least, to be satisfied with the present collection.

For his aid in securing the use of the Hunter papers, acknowledgment is due to Capt. Edward R. Baird, of Essex County, Va., and to R. M. T. Hunter's only surviving son, Mr. P. Stephen Hunter, also of Essex County. He resides in the old Hunter homestead and has kindly consented to donate his father's papers to the State of Virginia. In the preparation of the biographical sketch here presented the biography of R. M. T. Hunter, by Prof. D. R. Anderson, of Richmond College, was of most value. It was published in the "John P. Branch Historical Papers of Randolph-Macon College" (June, 1906). "A Memoir" of R. M. T. Hunter by his daughter, Martha T. Hunter (1903), was also helpful. Two short sketches of the life of Hunter were used; one by Lucius Quinton Washington in the "Southern Historical Society Papers," XXV, and the other by Theodore S. Garnett in the same publication, XXVII.

CHARLES HENRY AMBLER.

RANDOLPH-MACON COLLEGE,
    Ashland, Va., July 20, 1916.

CALENDAR OF LETTERS, PAPERS, AND ADDRESSES OF ROBERT M. T. HUNTER HERETOFORE PRINTED.[1]

1839. July 4. Address delivered before the Society of the Alumni of the University of Virginia. Charlottesville, 1839.

1841. ——. To M. R. H. Garnett.
Instructions regarding college work. Hunter: A Memoir of R. M. T. Hunter,[2] p. 85.

1843. June 16. To John C. Calhoun.
Calhoun's followers in New England; Charles Levi Woodbury; a proposed Calhoun organ in Virginia. Annual Report, American Historical Association (1899), II, 865.

September 19. To John C. Calhoun.
Discusses editors for proposed Calhoun organs for both Virginia and New York; Calhoun's prospects for winning the presidency in 1844. Annual Report, American Historical Association (1899), II, 881.

December 19. To John C. Calhoun.
A treaty for the proposed annexation of Texas; Calhoun to be made vice president; the presidential nomination conceded to Van Buren. Annual Report, American Historical Association (1899), II, 906.

1844. January 19. To John C. Calhoun.
Discusses Calhoun's refusal to permit his name to go before the Baltimore convention as a candidate for the presidency; a possible split in the Democratic Party of Virginia. Annual Report, American Historical Association (1889), II, 914.

February 6. To John C. Calhoun.
A proposed union of Virginia Democrats to support Van Buren for the presidency upon a State-rights platform. Annual Report, American Historical Association (1899), II, 927.

1850? ——. To their constituents.
An address of southern delegates in Congress. As Hunter's name leads all the signers he was probably the author. Washington, 1850. pp. 15.

1854. December 14. A discourse: Observations on the History of Virginia. Richmond, 1855. pp. 48. Washington, 1855.

1856. Address before the Democratic Demonstration at Poughkeepsie, N. Y. [n. p.] 1856.

1857. July 3. Address delivered before the two literary societies of the Virginia Military Institute. Richmond, 1857. pp. 59.

---

[1] For a list of Hunter's most important speeches in Congress see Bibliotheca Americana, VIII, 568.

[2] This volume by Hunter's daughter contains several letters and parts of letters from Hunter to members of his family.

13

1858. February 22. Address on the Inauguration of the Equestrian Statue of Washington. Southern Literary Messenger, XXVI, 167–184; reprinted Richmond, 1858.

1861. June 12. To Jefferson Davis.
>Offers advice in military matters. War of the Rebellion Records series I, volume II, 920.

September 23. To Hon. James M. Mason.
>Letter of instructions showing why the Confederacy should be recognized by England. Southern Historical Society Papers, VII, 231–241.

September 23. To Hon. John Slidell
>Letter of instructions showing why France should recognize the independence of the Confederacy. Southern Historical Society Papers, XIII, 455–466.

1863. December 28. To Joseph E. Johnston.
>The Mississippi campaign; expresses confidence in Johnston. War of the Rebellion Records, series I, volume XXIV, 1065.

1865. February 5. To Jefferson Davis.
>This letter is signed also by Alexander H. Stephens and John A. Campbell. It is an account of a conference between the signers and Abraham Lincoln. Messages and Papers of the Confederacy, I, 520. See, also, Jefferson Davis, A Short History of the Confederate States of America, p. 458.

May 11. To Hon. Edwin M. Stanton.
>Asks about his rights under the Amnesty Proclamation. War of the Rebellion Records, Series II, Volume VIII, 551.

1869. October 16. To James M. Mason.
>Discusses conditions in the South. Public Life and Diplomatic Correspondence of James M. Mason by his daughter. p. 568.

1874. ———. To His Excellency, James L. Kemper, Governor.
>Presents a plan for a constitutional currency. This was prepared shortly after he entered upon the discharge of his duties as treasurer of Virginia. Richmond, Virginia, 1874. pp. 9.

1875. June 30. Address to the Alumni of the University of Virginia at Charlottesville. Richmond, 1875, pp. 17.

1876. January —. A paper on the Origin of the Late War. Southern Historical Society Papers, I, 1–13.

1877. ———. To the Philadelphia Weekly Times. Discussing the Peace Commission of 1865. Reprinted in the Southern Historical Society Papers, III, 168–176.

December. To J. W. Jones, D. D., Secretary of the Southern Historical Society. A reply to a letter from Jefferson Davis regarding the Peace Commission of 1865. Southern Historical Society Papers, IV, 303–316.

1885. ———. A review of The Republic of Republics. Southern Historical Society Papers, XIII, 342–355.

CALENDAR OF LETTERS (1826–1876) TO AND FROM ROBERT M. T. HUNTER HERE PRINTED.

15

CORRESPONDENCE OF ROBERT M. T. HUNTER.

ROBERT BAYLOR TO R. M. T. HUNTER.

FREDERICKSBURG [VA.], *May 20th, 1826.*

DEAR ROBERT: Your highly acceptable letter of April 19th did not reach me until a few days past, in consequence of my having left Essex before it arrived at Loretto, with the proceedings at which office you are too well acquainted, to need to be told, that it was there permitted to enjoy "otium cum dignitate" for nearly a fortnight. That I had heard of Wars and accounts of Wars, assertions and contradictions, etc., respecting the Students of the University is a fact about which you were not at all mistaken but the majority of the reports have proved as groundless as malicious. Mr. Lomax told me yesterday that another blow-up as he termed it had occurred, which eventuated in the expulsion of one of the students, and the suspension of some three or four others. I hope however for the credit of our State and the prosperity of the Institution, that this may turn out as false as some others. Such reports though they be totally devoid of truth, tend materially to injure any Institution, and are doubly damning to those whose Reputations are not permanently established.

Mr. John Randolph has given us the pleasure of his company twice lately, in going to and returning from Richmond to Washington, on both of which occasions he amused us highly with his eccentricities of manner conduct and conversation. Had such capers been played up by any one else except himself or some kindred genius, they would assuredly have been viewed as the whims of a moonstruck madcap. One of his freaks was to continue his journey to Richmond in a few minutes after arriving here from the Steamboat Landing between eleven and twelve o'clock at night, because the fat Landlord (as he called Rawlins) had retired to bed and was not ready cap in hand to receive his lordship: and that too after declaring that he had not slept five minutes for seventy two hours. His companions were his servant Johnny, of whom he took occasion to make such honourable mention in the Senate in one of his late long winded harangues and a pointer puppy which he carried in his lap. He and Mr. Loyd from Massachusetts had some very sharp shooting in a late debate, wherein Mr. L[oyd] is said to have expressed a perfect willingness as far as he was individually concerned, to accommodate him with a repetition of his late amusement.

27

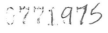

We have between ten and fifteen black legs as fellow inmates of our establishment, who have come on from different parts of the world to make ready for the Races which commence here on Wednesday next; who together with those that were here before their arrival, form as heterogeneous a collection of characters as I have ever met with. Our mess is composed of one Chancellor one Judge of the Superior Court several attorneys and doctors negro-buyers shoemakers gamblers of every description with many others. The Racing if any, will be very indifferent, in consequence of the value of the purse, which is too insignificant to induce the owners of fine horses to contend for it.

I expect to follow Mr. Lomax with whom I'm now reading, up to the University, the powerful inducements which you mentioned as tending to detain me in Essex to the contrary notwithstanding, and permit me to declare in sober seriousness that could my presumption prompt me to so daring and worse than useless a project, as to compete with you for that " pearl of great price " to whom I presume you alluded, my regard for you would at least induce me to act [Ms. torn] on the subject, and wait until my betters were served. Perhaps though the sidelong glances and bewitching smiles of some of the fair ones, who I understand resort in great numbers to enjoy the salubrious atmosphere of Charlottesville rendered doubly efficacious by the juxtaposition of the University, may have usurped her place, and induce you to speak of her with such apparent indifference. Whether that be the case or not you will no doubt be pleased to hear that she is well and never more interesting. All of your Friends were also well except Miss Fenton Garnett who is very much afflicted with the Rheumatism. Remember me if you please to Mr. Temple.

JAMES M GARNETT [1] TO R. M. T. HUNTER.

January 4th, 1838.

DEAR ROBERT: I am anxious to hear whether you found my letter, on your return. Not because there was anything in it, of which either of us need be ashamed; but because no man likes his private letters to become topics of public remark, without his consent. It was, (if I recollect), a free commentary upon the opinions and feelings expressed in your letter, and if Tom, Dick, and Harry were to get hold of it, might *possibly* cause those feelings and opinions to be misused by your political enemies. My anxiety, therefore, that my letter should not miscarry, is felt on *your* acc[oun]t, for *I* (like the Eels skinned alive) have become callous to newspaper attacks; nay, I have been fool-hardy enough to provoke them, as you shall see. The proofs will be sent to you under another cover, and headed,

---

[1] Representative in Congress from Virginia, 1805–1809 ; died May, 1843.

" Dialogue the second, between the two old political cronies." This, I am unreasonable enough to beg you to read, as it contains an attempt to answer your arguments in favor of public men becoming party-men. Not that I can believe it possible for *you* ever to become a party-man; but because I think you utterly wrong in the notion which you seem to entertain, that to be useful in public life, a man *must* join some political party or other. *This* I most confidently believe to be one of the greatest, the most fatal errors that any honest public man ever committed; and therefore I am painfully excited to prevent (if I can) a most beloved sister's son, whom I highly value, for his own merits, from adopting a creed which would paralise his own usefulness, and so far strengthen the damnable doctrine of political *Partyism*. Don't understand me as fearing that you will ever knowingly fall into party-ranks; but I much fear the effect òf your apparent belief, that all men must be either drones, or non-entities in political life, unless they will fall into these ranks, and be led or driven, as party-politics require. My own belief *is* and always *has been*, ever since I had a capacity and moral right to believe anything, that the entire stock of knowledge and power which any man possessed to contribute to the welfare and happiness of his species, might always be beneficially exercised, under our Institutions, without his attaching and binding himself to any party whatever, either in politics, morals, or religion. Such attachment and binding might appear, for a time, to increase his *power*, because it increased his popularity; but it would always prove a " penny wise and pound foolish " business. *This* is the all important, the vital fact of which it is indispensably necessary that all honest public men should assure themselves. As *party-men*, they *may* gain and exercise great personal influence; but it is an " ignis fatuos " which can not possibly delude those who understand its real nature; and the mischief is, that all who have been once led astray by the *false light*, will always hesitate to follow that which is certainly *true*, certainly of *heavenly origin*. Young men are prone to be Enthusiasts, old men to be Laxidos on all enthusiastic feelings. Hence the former generally overshoot the true center, as far as the latter undershoot it. What should a wise man determine between the two? He should take for his guide the maxim " *in medio tutissimus ibis;* " and adhere to it, too, in defiance of all party denunciations against " *trimmers, and fence men*." We must either adopt and act upon this belief, or we must utterly eschew the notion, that the *People are competent to self government;* and in the latter case we must sell ourselves to the Devil, (politically speaking,) as fast as we can. As I cannot possibly believe that you have a fancy for making any such sale, I address to you these remarks, merely to cheer you in your course, and to prevent your taking, what I consider a false view of your own powers to pursue it, with a fair prospect of success. Weigh the matter fairly, bestow on it your most deliberate judgment, and should your final determination be, that a man can do no good in Congress, unless he becomes a *party-man*, then "curse and quit," the moment your time is out. Nay, call down curses upon your own head, if you ever enter into public life again. But I must say, you have no just cause to make any such desperate resolve; and that you have rational ground for believing, that the People of the United States will yet learn to estimate the "*no party-men*" as their only true and best friends. I believe these men to be strong enough, if they would only understand each other, and act in concert, to make battle successfully against all the party-men of the Nation. The conflict would be arduous and long protracted; but to despair of its favorable issue, would be to believe that truth, justice, and virtue will never obtain the ascendancy in this World: and thus to think. is to discredit the word of God himself.

GEORGE FITZHUGH TO R. M. T. HUNTER.

PORT ROYAL, [VA.], *December 15, 1839.*

DEAR HUNTER: I have not seen one single whig to whom the nomination of Harrison is acceptable. Many already declare they will vote for Van Buren in preference, some say they will not vote at all, and the rest that they will vote for any body sooner than Van Buren and for that reason alone will sustain Harrison.

Excuse me for suggesting to you that this is a favourable opportunity for you to let it be known that you will under present circumstances sustain the re-election of Van Buren. Dont let it be known however *through me* but if possible through some states right Whig in your District who is likely to pursue the same course. It seems to me this course will at once place you in an easy situation, in which you may enjoy the fruits of a pretty wide spread reputation, acquired, perhaps, in part by the painful notoriety of your late neutral position.

Of course, I only urge you to express opinions, which I believe you sincerely entertain.

I have been tracking Bob Hunter lately. * * * He is so far every thing I could desire. I should be glad to hear from you occasionally, I am too busy to visit Washington. Present my compliments to Mr. Pickens and tell him I have instructed you to sustain him for speaker.

GEORGE FITZHUGH TO R. M. T. HUNTER.

PORT ROYAL, [VA.], *December 17, 1839.*

DEAR HUNTER: The mail rider brings us the news this morning that you are elected Speaker, and the first information which the papers contain, gives credence to the report. I am more elated and delighted than you can possibly be, for you may be somewhat depressed in thinking of the responsibility you undertake. I suppose now it will be more than ever becoming in you to say nothing about your preferences for president. You undertake in assuming the seat to act impartially, and you have a better chance of doing so whilst untrammelled by pledges to either party. The people too will think a neutral position dignified and becoming in a Speaker, which they would not tolerate in an ordinary member. I sometimes fear that Calhouns friends may run him against Van Buren at [the] next election, if they do, Harrison will certainly be elected. As an original question I should prefer Calhoun, but the only way to make him President is to wait till Van's eight years expire. I enclose a letter I had written yesterday, I do not give to *Mr. Speaker* the advice I gave to *Mr. Hunter.* You will excuse, I am sure my familiar mode of addressing you, as you know it does not proceed from want of the respect.

THOMAS HENRY [1] TO R. M. T. HUNTER.

(*Confidential.*)

WASHINGTON CITY, *January 2, 1840.*

MY DEAR SIR: My position on the Committees is to me a little mortifying. I do not profess to be worthy of much consideration; but you have undoubtedly placed me in a situation, the last but one on the last and least important Committee. Which will give occasion to political enemies to reproach me and to reproach my friends in the highly respectable district I have the honor to represent.

I shall feel more sensibly the taunts of enemies, because I was among the first, who broke away from the Marshalled forces of the Whigs, and sustained you to the end, for the highly honorable station you occupy. What still adds to, and makes my position more peculiar, was the manner in which the whig papers of Penn[sylvani]a and of my own district, approbated my course.

It may hereafter, be in your power to remedy, I will not say the wrong, but the injury you have unconsciously inflicted on me.

DR. FRANCIS MALLORY [2] TO R. M. T. HUNTER.

NEAR HAMPTON, [VA.], *January 12, 1840.*

DEAR HUNTER: For some months past I had almost given over talking or reading of politics and my papers by the dozens were filed on my table unopened. So that your election might for a season have escaped my observation, so seldom is it that I leave home except to officiate occasionally in the humble capacity of an attendant on

---

[1] Representative in Congress from Pennsylvania, 1839–1843; died 1849.
[2] A Whig Representative in Congress from Virginia, 1837–1843.

human misery. Indeed I am utterly secluded from the gay world and its noisy concerns. While in this state of existence an afternoons chat with a neighbor, both of us mounted on a rail, was broken in upon by a horseman in full gallop who had sought me out to communicate your good fortune. It proved to be our friend Booker and most happily did we converse over your distinguished person. To congratulate you at this late season would perhaps be out of place. I have for several days intended dropping you a Line but my old enemy, procrastination hovers around me closer than ever. Most heartily I rejoice at this unexpected tho' not undeserved honor. You have nothing to fear, but act out your part and the " just of all parties will sustain you." To speak on this occasion as I feel and think would, to one of your modesty, savor somewhat of deceit or flattery; and I can only repeat that I rejoice in your elevation and trust it is only the promise of still better fortune and more distinguished honors. Altho' I can understand by what means your election was effected I cannot at this distance from the centre of action account for some few votes, such for instance as that of Rhett and more especially Dixon Lewis on the last ballot.[1] The former you know is no favorite of mine. I have no faith in the soundness of his head or the honesty of his heart. Like most reforming gentlemen he is a selfish changeling. As sure as you live he will deceive some of those who now confidently calculate on his services. B. H. Rhett aspires to be a leader and will some day or other set up for himself. So soon as the weather breaks, for we have had a most severe winter, I will send you up some good oysters. By the way who brews your punch now that I am no longer an honourable? Does Mr. Speaker heat his water in a shaving can as of yore to fabricate this divine distillation and regale himself with an air bath in a sitting posture by the round table as was the case on a certain occasion which now shall be nameless.

I like not Calhoun's reconciliation (so far as I understand it) with V[an] B[uren]. He has reversed his position. The Whigs on whom at least he depended for support he has in a measure driven off. His recent quarrel with Clay, altho I think not at first the aggressor, was ill timed and will prove ruinous. If he leans alone on Locofoism he will find it a broken reed. The bulk of the Whigs begin already to look up to him as their man against Benton, and Clay's friends are true to him to the last. Besides Clay is broken down as a Pre[sidential] candidate and by some little management his party in the South might have been secured. But I pretend to no knowledge of these things and let them pass. As

---

[1] Robert B. Rhett voted for Francis W. Pickens of South Carolina; Dixon H. Lewis for George M. Keim of Pennsylvania. Benton, Abridgement of Debates of Congress, XIV, 3.

regards myself politically speaking I have no hopes or fears. Mr. Loyall, the Navy agent, is about resigning his office to become Pres[iden]t of a Bank in Norfolk. My friend Robertson would like to obtain it on acc[oun]t of a poor brother-in-Law who could fill the station of club and thus provide for a large family. He is every way fit for this or any other station. His politics too are right— that is he is *with us* on any subject. Holleman will strive to sustain a Betonian in the person of his friend Dr. Batten of Smithfield. Robertson is the Leading Whig in the district and on the score of policy the adm[inistration] would gain. He is an honest fellow— a perfect gentleman and my best friend. Can you withoutt prejudice to your position without violence to your personal feelings assist him? Trust me in the matter as a friend. Be candid for from the circumstances surrounding, you ought only to be governed. Be not guided by ordinary rules on such occasions, for I know, and I hope, I appreciate the delicacy of your position. I would not call you friend if I thought you could not act with the utmost freedom toward me. If you can properly act, consult with Pickens and my late associates and do what you can for me, but decide and act at once. Send T G Broughton and son and S. T. Hill of Portsm[outh], Va., a document now and then. They will be pleased. If you see or write to Mason tender him my best salutations. If Mrs. Hunter is in the city and young Mr. Speaker be pleased to present me to them with my best respects. Wishing you, Hunter, every honor to which your heart aspires and every happiness which a virtuous and independent mind can here enjoy I remain

[P. S.]—Sewart is in Washington. Poor fellow he has become a vagabond—one of the last acts of his political life was a deliberate and I fear a mercenary conspiracy against my election. I pity him and still more his destitute family. My friends name is Geo. H. Robertson.

THOMAS W. GILMER[1] TO R. M. T. HUNTER.

RICHMOND, [VA.], *March 11th, 1840.*

DEAR HUNTER: I have frequently during the winter desired to write to you and to receive a letter from you, as one watchman likes occasionally to hail and to hear from another in a dark night. I hope that nothing has occurred or will ever occur to interrupt for a moment that perfect and confidential familiarity which has so long subsisted between us. From all that I learn of you through the medium (a bad one, I confess) of the newspapers, I take it

---

[1] Governor of Virginia, 1840–1841; a Whig Representative in Congress, 1841–1843; a Democratic Representative in Congress. 1843–1844; appointed Secretary of the Navy, Feb. 15, 1844, and served until his death on the *Princeton,* Feb. 28, 1844.

for granted that we are now as nearly together in politics as we were
when I saw you last summer. Nothing that has happened here or
at Washington, I presume, can have shaken your steadfastness or
mine in the great principles to which we have both given evidence of
our attachment. But let this be as it may, though you are (without
design on your part) the speaker of the H[ouse] of R[epresentatives]
and though I in like manner have been appointed with the executive
of Virginia, you are still Bob Hunter and I am as I always was
your humble servant. We can never forget the Friar Tuck scene
of the Expunging winter here, nor should either of us desire its oblivion. I suppose the labors of your station have allowed you very
little time for correspondence and though I shall not be more re-
spectful than the governor of New Jersey was to you, I venture to
drop you a line, to say that I hope we may occasionally interchange
a thought and a word. Is there any hope that parties will ever come
back to the good old lines of honest differences of opinion as to
principles. For until parties do so, there is really little or no hope
that the government (in any hands) will. Are we always to see the
millions of freemen in our country, marshalled as the mere clans-
men of ambitious aspirants for the presidency? Many, I know, indulge the hope that after November next, there will be some more
definite and durable organization of political parties. I confess,
however, that I see little prospect for it. The radical fault is with
the press and that I fear is past remedy. I am, however, on the
outposts and can see but little of the chess board. You are at the
fountain head, and I have only to ask that when you have time and
can communicate any intelligence which you think would do good,
that you may drop me a line, not that I would have you write as a
letter writer from Washington, but that you may speak as one friend
should speak to another about matters of the highest public concern. We have been grasping our way onward; so far together.
I shall sink the partisan of course in my new vocation here. Indeed I have been little of one for some years past. The grease has
been scarcely worth the candle. If you don't find time sooner, writer
to me in the dry days.

HENRY A. TAYLOR TO R. M. T. HUNTER.

WALNUT GROVE, [ALA.], *May 25th, 1840.*

DEAR SIR: Excuse the liberty I take in asking you to forward me
the report of the Secretary of War and the bill for the improved
organization of the militia of the United States. Our loco foco
friends here will not believe that such a *report* emanated from the
Executive. The fire of liberty is aroused here and will continue to
burn with refulgent brilliancy I hope until the election of W. H.

Harrison to the Presidency. The cause of liberty, reform and re-trenchment is daily gaining ground here and I would not be sur-prised if the State voted for Harrison, tho' a dark cloud at present hangs over our *currency* and political horizon. Heretofore our polit-ical opinions have coincided and I regret very much that we can't agree upon the question of the Subtreasury as it is generally under-stood that you are an advocate of that measure "a sound currency for the Government and a bad currency for the people." Holding the high political station you do I can't expect you to express your views as freely as heretofore, but the people ought to know the politi-cal views of their prominent men, therefore as friend, and admirer of your private and public worth it would give me pleasure to know your views respecting the next Presidential election, if not incon-sistent with your notions of policy. Next Monday the Whigs meet at Tuscaloosa to nominate electors.

CHARLES C. BARNETT TO MEMBERS OF CONGRESS OF THE UNITED STATES.

To the Honorable, Members of Congress of the United States, in Washington City assembled, showeth that, your petitioner (a Citi-zen of the State of Va. and County of Montgomery,) being desirous that a law may be passed by Congress, authorizing, the treasury, (or some proper officer) of the United States to sell the lands, that were forfeited to the Government, under the law, assessing the Direct tax for the support of the late war, and taken in by the Government. There is a considerable quantity of mountain lands in Western Vir-ginia that would not command the taxes, at the sale for the collection of the same, that was consequently bought in by the Government; and from the fact that there is no law, (as I have been informed by the treasury) directing any disposition of the same, it would conse-quently after years be sold again for taxes by the state. My indi-vidual object is to get a title to a small piece adjoining me of 150 acres, that was returned in the name James Cunningham; this land in its present condition is rendered an annoyance to the neighbor-hood in consequence of its having water upon, and thereby, render-ing it accessible, for a dishonest man to settle, and live in part upon our stock in the range. I was appointed a kind of agent by the treasurer, with directions that I was not to make the Government liable for any expense, consequently without any title and not privi-ledged to expend money in any case, it would not avail anything. There is a good portion of mountain land in the same condition. I would therefore ask a law to be passed, directing the proper officer to convey this land to any person, wishing to pay the taxes, &c. You will be unable to obtain a list in Washington in as much as the papers were burnt in the Treasury building in 1833, but it can be obtained from the Clerk of the Eastern District of Va. &c.

And your petitioner will ever pray, etc.

JAMES M. GARNETT TO R. M. T. HUNTER.

LORETTO, VA., *January 12th, 1841.*

DEAR ROBERT: Altho' in one of your late letters, speaking of a National Society of Agriculture, you express the belief, that "*it would be of inestimable benefit,*" (I quote your own words,) yet it is evident, that your confidence in this opinion is like the dead faith of the christian, unproductive of works. For you express not the slightest inclination to contribute towards the production of this "inestimable benefit"; altho' nothing seems to me more probable, than its achievement, if only a few of our public men would unite in the effort. But I will say nothing more on the subject, since every argument I could urge in favor of it must be quite as familiar to you as to myself.

I thank you for the pamphlet which you sent me, signed the Kentucky Democrat. It is well written, and displays considerable ability. But, if he imagines, as he seems to do, that the diabolical party spirit which has so long been distracting our country, can be cured, or even much mitigated, merely by his new mode of choosing the President and Vice President of the United States, he greatly deceives himself. The disease is too deeply rooted, and fosters too many of our worst passions, to admit of any other radical cure, than the moral and religious education of our whole People, a circumstance about as likely to occur, as that two Sundays should come together. The Author appears to me decidedly wrong in another important matter; I mean his defiance of Mr. Webster and Mr. Clay to point out any instance wherein, either Gen[era]l Jackson or Mr. Van Buren has ever violated the Constitution of the United States. But enough of this for the present. I fear that neither the Kentucky Democrat, nor any other sincere friend to reform in our Constitution will ever live to see them. I perfectly remember, that we had quite as much talk about them, when Mr. Jefferson was first elected as we have now. But no sooner did he and his friends get well fixed in their seats, than talk all died away; and in a few months, ceased altogether. Heaven grant, that the same game may not be played again.

P. S. What has become of the Petition of our Agricultural Society?

JAMES B. THORNTON, JR. TO R. M. T. HUNTER.

RICHMOND, [VA.], *February 25th, 1841.*

DEAR HUNTER: On the receipt of your esteemed favour on yesterday, postmarked 22d, I wrote a long reply which upon more reflection I have determined not to send, because there is nothing in it requiring immediate action for your success or vindication, and I hope to see you the 8th [of] next month at my house, when we can more satsfactorily review the whole subject.

I will remark here, that the threat to expose your correspondence, was *not* contained in the letter which was the subject of much conversation between Mr. Wise [Henry A. Wise] and myself. When the gentleman to whom that letter was addressed mentioned it to me, I expressed surprise at the writer's taking ground against you having often heard him urge upon the Whigs to take you up. The reply was that a letter from you expressing your willingness to accept a nomination from the administration party in the District had put this individual openly against you, and that he had said at our last court, that " *he had a correspondence from you which would prostrate you in the District.*" I mentioned this to Mr. Wise in a long conversation on the subject of the letter aforesaid and he no doubt confounded the two. I also mentioned another conversation with another individual, in which allusion was made to another correspondence of yours in a similar strain. These things induced me to think as I said to Mr. W[ise] that you had not been dealt sincerely with. I must express my entire approval of the honourable determination exhibited in your letter to challenge the publication of your correspondence, satisfied as I am that it must result in your entire vindication. But in the present envious state of parties in our district I must leave the *policy* of doing so to a further interview with you. I hope you will make your arrangements to spend the night of the 8th with me at my house as it is not possible for me to have a full conversation with you in any other event.

ALEXANDER FLEET TO NORBORNE E. SUTTON.

MELVILLE, [VA.], *March 1st, 1841.*

DEAR SIR: I have been much mortified at the course of the Whigs towards our friend Hunter and did hope he would have rec[eive]d the nomination of the Convention at Millers. I thought with you that Ritchie and his clique only intended to alienate the Whigs from Hunter to prevent their nominating him, without having any intention of running him themselves, but I find now that they have voluntarily given up the opportunity of electing one of their own party and taken up Hunter with the avowed purpose of thereby breaking

down the Whig party in the district. Can our friend? Will he, permit himself to be used by that party for such a purpose? I understand it was stated at Croxton's Springs at their late Convention
that Hunter would accept a nomination by that party, that he was
no Whig, that he had never agreed to support a states right whig for
Congress. I am *confident* he never made either of the latter statements, and cannot but hope he will decline the nomination of the
party convention when he learns that the grand object they had in
nominating him was to destroy that party with whom he had so
long been fighting side by side, to bring back the government to the
old republican tract. It would be to me a most painful thing to be
compelled to go against Hunter but if he accepts the nomination
under these circumstances I shall consider myself absolved from all
obligation to sustain him notwithstanding I have heretofore solicited
him to be a candidate and intended to sustain him with all my
energies. I cannot but hope and believe that the Locos will be caught
in their own trap for there seems to be much more division amongst
them than the whigs. Braxton is a candidate and will be warmly
sustained by a portion of his party and I think if Hunter accepts
and Braxton holds on Corbin must be elected, I do not believe he can
get 5 Whig votes in this country under such circumstances and Braxton will get 10 times that number of the Locos.

GEORGE BOTTES TO JOSEPH A. SCOVILLE.

LITCHFIELD, [N. Y.?], *January 7th, 1842.*

DEAR SCOVILLE: Yours of Jan[uar]y 1st I have rec[eive]d but
have neglected answering it wishing to see West and learn from him
what would be necessary to establish a Press in this place. I have
not seen him but have had conversation with Deming about it, there
is a press here that was used for the Democratic paper, formerly
printed here that I think would answer, if it will it would lessen the
expense. It belongs to Mr. L. P. Burk. It could be purchased
with the tips and fixtures at a reasonable price. Perhaps it could
be rented. It would be necessary to purchase some new tips, &c.
I think that the whole expense for starting a paper here would not
exceed $800 or 900 Dollars. It would help the party in this Country
to have a paper here. Mr. Abernathy is Probate Judge of this
district and would give it his patronage which would be $6.00 or 8.00
per week which will help some. Deming is wide awake for the
Spring Election. Seymour and his connection are as usual asleep.
Mr. W. never moves for fear of ofending his political enemies. I
think that the friends of Mr. Calhoun are increasing every day. I
have given Deming a list of all the Post Masters in this country and
their Politics. I believe it is correct, have taken great care to find out

every one. You may depend upon my help to carry our country for C[alhoun] men this spring.

[P. S.] J. C. Smith has married a rich widow and remains idle, have not heard from him since last fall. You cannot expect much from him, he will make great professions but all that he wants is his own turn served.

B. S. HART [1] TO R. M. T. HUNTER.

NEW YORK, [N. Y.], *June 9th, 1842.*

MY DEAR SIR: Yours of the 7th inst addressed to my brother I rec[eive]d this day. I am in his confidence and at his request open all letters directed to him. He left New York yesterday (Wednesday) afternoon for the South and ere this reaches you, you may perhaps impart to him verbally the contents of the letter in my possession. I have no secrets in the scheme now maturing. I am decidedly for Calhoun and as far as any influence I possess will go, it will be exerted in his behalf. He is a great man, an extraordinary man. Second to none in the Union. And as a statesman stands out in bold relief among the great minds of this or any other country, whether of the *Present* or *Past*. He has moved in his own orbit and his course has pointed as true as the needle to the magnet by the past we will judge him. You observed to my Brother that caution was necessary. The advice is good. But he is a practical man and has an old and fearless head though placed on young shoulders. You need have no fear for his course. If energy, indomitable preserverance, fearlessness, nerve, and determined resolution have any peculiar attributes, then have you a fitting representative in one who I am proud to claim as a brother. Give my respects to Wood. Scovell I shall write to myself. Remember me to my brother and when you or either of your friends write to N[ew] Y[ork] I would advise them to seal their letters with *sealing wax.* The letter I rec[eive]d from you was as damp as tho' it had been a printed sheet fresh from the press. Villianry stalks abroad and will not stop at any means to obtain its ends even should it be by violating the secrecy of a private letter.

JOSEPH A. SCOVILLE TO R. M. T. HUNTER.

NEW YORK [N. Y.], *Monday, August 29, 1842.*

MY DEAR SIR: Your letter of 27th is in hand, all is explained, and no more need be said on *that subject.* I have been very busy all the morning in writing letters to various parts of the country—*on the great subject.* In addition I have wrote a call for a meeting of

---

[1] B. S. Hart, Joseph A. Scoville, E. G. B. Hart, and J. Francis Hutton were local politicians in New York City, who tried to organize a Calhoun party there.

merchants at the Exchange, and it is now out for signatures. If we get *enough*, it will go on, if not, we will stop it, for it is useless to make a failure in *any thing* or *any move*, rather it hurts us. I have been unable to see Godwin. As soon as I *do*, I will nail him so fast that he shall not move out of the traces. The more I see of Slamm the more I like him. He is heart and soul with us, and if it were not that he is so hard up, and so dependant upon Van Burens friends in these pinching times, he would be with us. As it is, I feel his helping hand in 10,000 ways.

I am on *nettles*, for fear I have "put my foot into it. Two of our friends have just returned from Bryant. They report that my article will appear *this* afternoon. They compromised matters with Bryant by allowing him to *strike* out all the " *Caustic* " and *names* of leading Van Buren men here. If Wright should discover that I wrote that article he will *kill me*, but he thinks I am fishing at Litchfield. The Article if extensively copied here and in the North will play *h—l* with Matty, for it changes the fight with Van Buren *from* Calhoun *to* Wright. I will make a raise and purchase a lot of the Evening Post and send to you for circulation. We had a caucus last night, and it was decided that I must keep in the back ground for Slamm says " we are not yet strong enough in the City, and if that an issue was made in the Committees *now* between Calhouns friends and the friends of Van Buren we should get licked like thunder " *wrote Lewis the reasons* for my sudden return to New York. Every thing looks well for us where I have been. I must go up to Albany this winter. The more I think of it, the more I am satisfied we must have some one there who is willing to devote his time, talents and *Situation* regardless of consequences, to the movement. I feel that I can do it better than any here. Stuart will I think go with me and I can make him do any thing. He is more of a Scholar than Politician, and I flatter myself I would keep him very busy if he is in my net. Jas. B. Nicholson—rich—mem[ber] of Gen[era]l Committee is out for Mr. C[alhoun]—wants to have me see Denman—the Editor of the Truth Teller about his course. I shall do so the first leisure evening. I shall try and get on a good footing with Bishop Hughes as soon as Mackay or Stuart come in town. I want to *feel* him. Ask Mr. C[alhoun] to frank him his two Speeches.

"to the Rt. Reverend
Bishop Hughes."

it will give me a wire to pull when we meet.

I see that we have got to go against Mayor Murphy—his partner Lott wants to go to the State Senate and Murphy to Congress from the Counties of Kings and Richmond *we are sure* of *Crooke* and shall support him. He is a true Calhoun man, *and does not want any thing*, for he got a rich wife, it is one of the courses of politics that you can not form a correct estimate of the sincerity of men in general, until you know what they want and I am afraid Murphy is disposed to make a tool of Mr. C[alhoun] to get influence with John Tyler, but your good judgement will point out to you the propriety of keeping on good terms with every man, high or low, rich or poor and *yet at same time* be on your guard, that they don't *fog you.* Don't leave Washington until you put me in train to go with "Life Speeches and Orations of John C. Calhoun." Hart says he is hard at work—will write you as soon as he gets your letter. I will see Mr. Edwards as soon as I get a moments leisure. Tell Mr. Lewis I am afraid of Mr. Wright. I don't dare write him until I *see* him and form some kind of an estimate of how I stand in that quarter. He will be on in a few days. I presume that by 1st Sept[ember] you will be away from W[ashington]. Until 1st Dec[ember] is 3 months. Now let us have some understanding for a separation if anything should turn up in the interval.

Mr. Calhoun's address I believe is Fort Hill, So[uth] Ca[rolina]. He had better continue to adhere to his rule about correspondence and if I should write him anything that requires an answer, let some of the members of his household answer them. What is Mr. Lewis address? Your own? Pickens? Saunders?—how does Genl. Keim stand now? I can now open a correspondence with the list of names in the West, as some of our members, Mc[1] for instance will be on hand for franks and it will not cost a fortune to them and me in the way of postage.

Hart says it is very important that we shall have an understanding in relation to movements up to Dec[embe]r.

P. S. I wont write Mr. Lewis for after all I have said he will feel bound to answer it—cost what it may.

JOSEPH A. SCOVILLE TO R. M. T. HUNTER.

SUNDAY NIGHT, 11 O'CLOCK,
[NEW YORK CITY], *Sept[ember] 11, 1842.*

DEAR HUNTER: Y[ou]rs of [the] 5th in hand. Hart will write you all about the Convention business. To-day I send you a *paper* which is to be kept buried in your own bosom. I have had my hands and heart full for a week. I assure you I have not been in my bed before 3 A. M. in that time. Our success will depend on your entire secrecy in regard to any thing you learn of movements here. *Do not,* let me beg of you to write a soul here. Your letters are shown and there is the devil to pay. Slamm, Hart, Crook, Hutton and self must be your only correspondents here. There are 10,000

---

[1] Either Samuel McRoberts of Illinois or George McDuffie of South Carolina.

reasons which I cannot explain why you must follow *our* advice. Morrell[?] is crazy, and is hurting us beyond anything you can fancy. Vache who will be our chairman for the Gen[era]l Committee has been to me to-day, and told me of Morrell's[?] damned impudence. Keep on terms with him for Gods sake don't write him. Will you write him something like this, *as a closer*.

"*Private.*" And he will show it to every man he meets. Mr. Calhouns prospects are very bright. The South will go for him. Every slave holding State will do so. *We are all of us prepared* to abide the decision of the National Convention. Do not mention this to *a soul. It is in the most sacred confidence.* I know Mr. Calhouns feelings. I am glad you are interested so deeply in his success. My position is a very painful one, and I must take care that I do not break down under my large correspondence. I am aware that you need no urging to do *your* duty. With our cause in such hands as it is, all will go well. I shall be forced to drop some of my correspondence. I cannot go through with it. New York city I think will go right and our friends there must now take care of themselves. I am well satisfied we shall embarrass you by giving advice. You do not need it. Watch Scoville and keep him straight. Hart I am afraid is gone over to V[an] B[uren]. Slamms paper will not come out for us, and we must do as well as we can " this or something similar will put Morrell off the scent until we get through our present embarrassment. Morrell has told every soul he knows, that Hart, Maclay, Slamm and self are Calhoun men. It kills us, and I am by no means sure that Hart is not defeated, and myself also, in consequence. Maclay has had to deny it, and Secor[?] has openly done so, and Morell to night spent the evening with Bob Tyler at *Grahams* house. Avoid him. If you do not, you lose the best friends for Mr. Calhoun ever man had. On Saturday I was with Slamm all day and raised money enough by begging to pay off his hands—$290 and have pledged myself to raise $5000 in 14 days, and to morrow I commence by doing it in $5 Bills. I had hoped you would have helped us some—but I have given it up. I tell you again and again—*we must have Slamm.* I will devote my time day and night until I beg borrow or steal enough to render him independent. The morning Post is a Speculation and Tylerism Customhouseism, and all are mixed up in it.

I enclose a Tammany note, what think you the call is for? Why to *nominate Van Buren*, and appointing a sub-committee to enquire into any secret organization for nomination. We are rallying our forces, and shall be licked *sure*, and this partly arises from Morrells going around town and saying *we were organized.* Stevenson is to offer the resolution. We shall prevent it passing, if we can, if not, we will make issue and raise the hue and cry that it is dictation and is an attempt made to crush the friends of *Wright, Johnson* and *Benton*!!

Hart is tied up. He dare not speak. We dont speak or walk openly in the streets any more, and he is obliged to say he goes for Van Buren. He defeated that infernal treacherous lying son of a gun, John Kramer and succeeded in getting Judge Fine (an uncle of Frank Huttons) a warm Calhoun man, elected President. Had it been known that Hart was a Calhoun man, his influence would have been killed and he could have done nothing. Don't, my Dear Sir, get angry at my frankness, but let me beg of you not to write any letters out of the Committee of 5, or if you do so, Dont for Gods sake let your correspondents know any thing we may write you. We want to get control of the organization of the Party, and this man or that man—who have no party standing—do us more harm than good. I am afraid I shall not be able to get away.

Jackson, Camp. Capt. George, Vaché, Ed Curtiss, Morrell, the Herald, Chas. Delevan, Graham, and any person holding office under Tyler are enough to defeat the best organized party under the canopy of Heaven. Dr. Vaché told me that Morrell had been to convert him! and says he " good God Scoville you had better tell Mr. Hunter to publish his letters at once." He showed Vaché letters *from you.* He ought to have his neck broke for daring to give a letter to that mountebank Ch[arle]s H. Delevan. He is the laughing stock of the community and " I took Tea with Mr. Calhoun " is all over town. I frightened him the other night told him to go Tyler as much as he liked, but so sure as I heard of his mentioning Mr. Calhouns name into a public meeting, I would have him mobbed. Lewis told him about me and others, and he has repeated it to every body. He owes me $500 he borrowed 5 years ago, thinks he does me good by talking about me, curse him.

Now my Dear Mr. Hunter don't get angry with me. I am writing like a slave—have to do it. I never say Fail and you have Friends here that money or office could *not buy.* There is Hart and Slamm— Vaché and Secor, but imprudence on *your* part may *destroy us.* You do not understand this, *but it is so* and if we leave Mr. Calhoun or his cause, it will be the fault of himself or immediate friends. But I am sure you will be cautious. I send you to-day our organization.[1] It explains itself you see how cautious and guarded *we* act. I would not have sent it, had it not have become actually necessary.

We dont care how much people talk—or who they may be, when we get control of the *party organization*, but until then they actually do us injury, because *our People* think that there is something rotten in Denmark when such men throw the first stone for Mr. Calhoun and regard it as flung *at* them instead of for them.

---

[1] See document marked copy.

[P. S.] Will you write Mr. Lewis, or send him my letter. I shall have to neglect him entirely and you also, but one of the 5 will write you. Wood and Moore are *opponents* in the 10th Ward district, am sorry, but think Wood can lick him.

Maclay is sure from the 6 Ward district.

McRean is sure from the 8 do—do.

Crook is same from Kings

You must do all you can to put the life in *progress.*

[COPY]

We therefore the undersigned mutually agree to act in concert and do all, and every thing most likely to ensure a majority of the People of the state of New York to select him [Calhoun] as their candidate in the National Convention and under existing circumstances, it having been deemed advisable by our friends to select as a Committee of Five to cooperate with Mr. Calhoun's friends in Congress and elsewhere and to advise and suggest to our Democratic friends in this city a proper and prudent policy and such a course of action as will best accomplish our mutual wishes, and as it is necessary that such Committee of Five should be prudent and confidential in their operations and plans, that the cause may be benefitted and not injured. We the undersigned comprising said Committee do agree to adopt and strictly adhere to the following Rules and Resolutions made for our guidance.

Rule 1. We will mention to no person, save those most interested (Mr. Calhoun and friends hereafter named) that there is *such* a Committee, as its main object would thereby be defeated.

" 2 No member of this Committee shall mention to others that any one of us is in favor of Hon. J. C. Calhoun.

" 3 Each member of said Committee shall correspond, superintend and direct in his *own name* and shall in no case make use of the name of others of this Body.

" 4 A decision of *Three* of this Committee in regard to any matter brought before them shall be binding upon all and adopted by *all* as their unanimous decision.

" 5 Our meetings shall be informal and held at each others houses, and we agree to meet on receiving a request so to do, naming the hour and place from any of the Committee.

Rule 6 Any request to be made to Mr Calhoun to take any step which may be deemed important to present our party views shall be signed by *every* member of this Committee.

In as much as great injury may accrue from a *too* general correspondence and our cause may be retarded thereby—and as our friends in Washington have no knowledge of the character, influence, or standing in the party of many persons who *have* and who *will* address them letters from hence.

.Resolved, That said friends be requested to be very guarded in such correspondence. If ignorant in regard to men who address them letters—that they may be requested previous to placing any confidence in such men, to write some member of this Committee to make the necessary enquiries, and inform themselves in regard to them and their motives and report thereon to said friends, and further that it is advisable that our said friends should endeavor thro us to bring such correspondents into harmonious action with the general or Ward Committee hereafter named, and in such correspondence as may be necessary with others, to be on their guard, and communicate no information in regard to *us* or our movements and to take no important step or advise any such without communicating the fact of having given such advice, the nature of it, and name of the party or parties, to some friend and correspondent in this Committee.

Rule 7 Such letters from said friends shall be held individually sacred and strictly confidential by the individual member receiving them, and he shall not be required to show them to this Committee.

" 8 No letter shall be addressed by any member of this Body to any person or persons save and except the Hon. J. C. Calhoun, D. H. Lewis, R. M. T. Hunter, and F. W. Pickens which shall contain any information, of the nature, manner, policy or extent of our movements, proceedings and organization which may effect us individually, or collectively or our party.

Resolved, That as we owe a duty to the gentlemen named in the above rule, to keep them fully advised of all our proceedings that they may be requested to keep such information—*Strictly Private*, and in no case to mention it to others, or even hint that the Calhoun party here are organized or in drill as we have to contend against members and old Hunkers of our own party men who have been drilled in the traces for years and our success will depend in a great measure upon our entire secrecy in changing their organization and Power quietly and surely into our own hands.

Resolved, That each individual of this Committee shall use and exert his influence and organize a General Committee for the City by selecting from *each* Ward *three* of the most influential and competent men who are *known* to be warm and trusty friends of Calhoun and in whom the utmost reliance and confidence can be placed.

Resolved, That such Calhoun men as are at present members of the " old mens General Committee at Tammany Hall " be made members of this Committee of 5, and further it is resolved that for the remainder we will select as above three from each Ward and such men as we are sure can be elected and sent down by the people as *their* delegates on the first [of] Jan[uar]y, 1843 by these means quietly used. On that day the Party Government of the City at Tammany will be in the hands of the friends of " Calhoun."

Resolved, That we will use our exertions to elect as Chairman of the above Committee the most able man and the most prudent and influential politician we can find in the party and residing in ꜱᴏᴍᴇ ᴡᴀʀᴅ ᴜɴᴅᴇʀ ᴏᴜʀ ᴄᴏɴᴛʀᴏʟ ᴡʜᴇʀᴇ ᴡᴇ ᴀʀᴇ ᴄᴇʀᴛᴀɪɴ ᴏf ʙᴇɪɴɢ ᴀʙʟᴇ to elect him to Tammany in January and that he be made to act at once and divide the said Committee into sub Committees and prepare for immediate and powerful action.

Resolved, That as soon as said Committees are ready and organized we will with their assistance organize a Young mens Gen[era]l Committee of five from *each* ward upon the same basis selecting from the young mens Gen[era]l Committee of T[ammany] Hall as members of this Y[oung] M[en's] C[ommittee] *all* who are in favor of Calhoun and be prepared by January to have the whole 85 elected by the People to Tammany Hall in Jan[uar]y next and by these means have possession of both General Committees.

Resolved, that we will carry out the above four resolutions so quietly that each Committee may be ignorant of any combination, or suspect our motives, or be aware that the other Committees are composed of Calhoun Men, until after the election by the people, or the means used, or persons forming *this* committee of Five.

Resolved, That this Committee shall use its influence individual and combined, *secretly* but *directly*, and indirectly thro' the influence of individual members of the two general Committees to place on each and every *Ward Committee* in the city a majority of Calhoun men, and further to use the same means to place on the nominating Committees elected to Tammany and also for *Ward* nominating Committees for each Ward, Calhoun men. And further in Candidates for Congress, Legislature, City offices and other nominations we will endeavor so far as is practicable and judicious, by fair means to procure the nomination of such men as are favorable to Calhoun, and further, that on our State Central Committees and all other prominent places and situations of power and influence we will endeavor to place such men as are favorable to Jno. C. Calhoun.

Resolved, That our Combinations shall be made *only* with the young and untrained Democracy and we will avoid aiding assisting or trusting men who have belonged to another Age and Regime as with the former we can carry them and our measures through upon a solid, safe and sure foundation. We scout the idea of expediency.

We will break down all the old party organization and trust our cause to new and fresh formation.

Resolved, That in every democratic meeting held in the city and County of New York, Richmond and Kings we will cause to be introduced Resolutions directly or indirectly favorable to Mr. Calhoun and keep him constantly before the Democracy.

Resolved, That each member of the Body shall use his exertions and cause articles to be written and inserted in every neutral paper in these counties—whether daily, weekly or monthly—favorable to Mr. Calhouns nomination.

Resolved, That our Secretary Mr. Scoville shall keep a copy for the the use of this Committee of every article published in this County affecting in any way Mr. Calhoun.

Resolved, That the secretary shall keep a list of every Democratic paper in this State, ascertain its preference, and it shall be our duty to make an influence bear upon said papers that will bring them into the support of Mr. Calhoun.

Resolved, That the Secretary shall keep a list of prominent Calhoun men, not on acting committees, their names No. and residences so that at a moments warning, we can make a rally and bring out our entire strength, and that assisted by us he shall probe the various cliques in the Democracy, their leaders, objects &c so that we can make the G[eneral] Co[mmittee] operate effectually upon them.

Resolved, That the Secretary furnish us with a list of the number of members necessary to be made—in the New York Dispensary to elect Trustees and control the appointments and political influence of the institution—and that a sufficient number of Calhoun [men] be made members (one at a time to avoid suspicion) to control the election of Trustees, so that the City can be districted as we wish, and those appointments and their influence be given to Calhoun men.

Resolved, That we aid and assist in circulating a Life of Mr. Calhoun in any form it may be published—by Books, Pamphlets, Almanacks, so as to make him and his claims a constant subject of talk among the masses both of the city and county.

Resolved, That we will collect a sufficient Fund to carry out our views and the same shall be placed in the hands of E. B. Hart who shall be and hereby is appointed Treasurer, and this resolve shall be kept in full force until we are in the ascendant in the Gen[eral] Committee who control the Funds of the party.

Resolved, That the Sec[retary] shall request our Calhoun friends in other States to furnish him for the use of this committee any papers in their state that hoist the Calhoun Flag and come out openly for him.

Resolved, That as soon as practicable suitable Delegates be appointed to traverse the State and open correspondence for the general Committee, and attend to such matters as will assist to bring our Calhoun friends into combined action and develop Mr. C[alhoun]'s strength in other portions of the State.

Rule 9, It shall be the duty of each of us to impress upon the minds of the members of the Committee and upon our *own* the absolute necessity of not "showing our hands" until we can do so *safely* and surely, that no one may suspect any organization until it is complete in all its details, and further to impress upon the minds of an active partizan the extreme caution necessary to be observed in all their movements and conversations, both in private with individuals and in public before members, never to attack Mr. Van Buren or speak ill of him, or show the slightest hostility towards him—to profess Van Burenism. And weaken him by pretending to defend his weak points, at [the] same time strengthen Mr. Calhoun by a weak attack on him or his strong points, until we know our *men* and their feelings.

Resolved, That the two members from Kings and Richmond shall organize the Calhoun party in their respective counties, as to make the party efficient in such a manner as they deem most advisable.

Resolved, That this Committee have power to increase their number to one from each Congressional district in this State, no one being allowed to become a member, except by the unanimous consent of all.

Resolved, That a copy of this paper shall be furnished by the Secretary to each member for his guidance and also copies to be sent to Mr. Calhoun, and Messrs. Lewis, Hunter and Pickens and that the original with our signatures attached be enclosed and sealed and placed in the hands of our chairman Levi O. Slamm, and that the same shall not be opened until Mr. Calhoun is nominated, and shall then be opened and destroyed in presence of two or more members of this Committee.

Original signed by Levi O. Slamm
E. B. Hart   N. Y. Cong.
Jos. A. Scoville   district.
P. S. Crooke   Kings and
J. Francis Hutton Richd. Co.

John C. Calhoun to R. M. T. Hunter.

Fort Hill, [S. C.], *30th September 1842.*

My dear Sir, I have been absent on private business for the last 10 or 12 days, and on my return, I found your two letters of the 5th and 12th instants on my table, which I hasten to acknowledge.

I regret much to hear of the severe illness of Mrs. Hunter, and hope ere this she has entirely recovered.

The affair at Shocco went off exceedingly well. Considering the short notice, the company was large, say 500 or 600, embracing the entire population for a considerable distance round, and many who had come from a considerable distance. All was well conducted, and terminated, as far as I could judge, to the satisfaction of all. I cannot conjecture what has delayed the account of the proceedings. I fear they have been waiting for me to write out my speech. I was pressed to do so, but gave no encouragement that I would do so; on the contrary expressly declined, that I did not think I would have leisure.[1] I am sensible of the difficulty you must feel in carrying on the New York correspondence. The jealousy among the leaders there is extreme, and great caution is required. Scoville is by far the most active and full of resources. I have had several letters from him, in which he presses me, as he has you, on the subject of my life. I think it important, that both that and my speeches, reports and communications, at least on the subjects that may bear on the coming contest, should be published; but it appears to me to be much more important, that it should be well done, than speedily done. The former would take some time. My own collection of speeches, and reports is very imperfect prior to the time I was elected Vice President; so much so, as not to be sufficient to make the necessary extracts for a satisfactory biography. Since then, it is full with one or two exceptions, which I hope to be able to supply in the neighborhood. I shall, however, with the materials I have get a friend next week to commence preparing such a biographical sketch as Mr. Scoville desires. I shall, I fear, be much interrupted by a busy correspondence and frequent visitors; but will have it executed as soon as I can. I will write to Mr. Scoville on the subject. More leisure may be taken to prepare a volume of my speeches &c &c for the press that I can take with me to Washington, if I should not have it completed before. The indications in N[orth] Carolina, as I passed through were as highly favourable as my best friends could desire. There, I think, can be no doubt of the State. The same may be said of Georgia, and from what I see and hear I should say of Alabama and Missi[ssippi]. I have had since my return a letter from a friend, who has been much with Mr. Polk, from that, I infer there is no understanding between him and Mr. Van Buren. This State is as nearly unanimous as it can be. As far as the indication goes every paper, Whig and all, will be in my favor.

E. G. B. HART TO R. M. T. HUNTER.

(*In strict confidence.*)

NEW YORK, [N. Y.], *October 5th, 1842.*

MY DEAR HUNTER: My time has been occupied to that degree as to entirely prohibit the continuing of my correspondence, in fact for the

---

[1] Following the adjournment of Congress Calhoun spoke on his return trip to South Carolina in both Richmond and Petersburg.

last six weeks I have been up to my eyelids in politics. And even now there seems to be "no rest for the *weary*," leaving me to suppose there is no probability of my being unrelieved until our elections are over, which take place in the ensuing month. I have got much to say to you, more than my time will permit. Wood has had an almighty struggle, in his district were Rosevelt, Allen, Ely Moore and Col. Hepburn. I think we shall succeed in effecting his nomination, but I have my fears of succeeding with any one in his district, there being so much excitement, between the friends of Moore and Wood. Monday is nominated from the 5th Dist[rict] and in all probability he will be elected. I am of opinion that he is strongly our friend. Moses G. Leonard of [the] 4th Dist[rict] will be nominated. His election is not looked for, as McKeon's friends are strongly disposed to oppose him. The friends of Leonard carried every delegate not leaving a look for John McKeon. In the 2nd [district] Henry C. Murphy is nominated. You will no doubt recollect him. I introduced him to you in Washington, as well as to Mr. Calhoun. He is a warm friend and I am happy to find the interest our boys have taken in his welfare has carried them through successfully. Rhett left here last week. I regret that my arrangements were of that nature as to limit my intercourse with him the ev[enin]g previous to his departure. Scoville, Secor and self had a long talk with him. Curtis is removing Whigs and rumor says placing the friends of Mr. Calhoun in their stead. I trust no understanding has been had with that political traitor. Should it be believed that such was the case the injury to us would be irreparable. I am continually falling in with friends to the cause, many make no hesitation in openly expressing their sentiments. In Huttons county we are all powerful and it is so admitted.

Now my dear Hunter, one word as to myself. I am about becoming an applicant for a lucrative office in the gift of this State, should we succeed in carrying it, and in order to ensure success, I have been obliged to keep myself free from suspicions of being connected with Mr. C[alhoun]'s friends in this city. Our friends here fully understand my position and certain am I were it known that I was warmly interested in the advancement of Mr. C[alhoun] a most violent opposition would be created against me, so as to put my chance entirely "Hors de combat." That would be done by the friends of Van [Buren], and in my own defence I have been obliged to follow their system of political tactics in order to undo the suspicion that has been attached to me. When at Syracuse I was pointed out by Dick Davis as being a Calhoun man, many of my friends interrogated me. And in order to effectually stop his tongue I took him a one side and told him some cock and bull story. I began by telling him that my being associated so frequently with the friends of Mr. C[alhoun] during my visit to Washington, created the belief that the object of my visit was for the purpose of forming a party in this State to favor Mr. C[alhoun]; that I went to Washington on business for Mr. Gilbert the inventor of a Floating dock, and in order to enable me to carry out the objects of my business there and place Mr. G[ilbert]'s invention in the light desired, I found that Mr. C[alhoun]'s friends upon enquiry possessed an influence which it was important for me to have exerted, and through them I succeeded in accomplishing what was necessary to place Mr. G[ilbert]'s plans on an honorable footing with others, that it was supposed that extraneous influences might be brought to bear upon the Sec[retar]y of the Navy so as to induce him to come to a decision, without giving my friend a hearing. And it was through them that a fair Commission was appointed to examine the models of the various applicants &c.

This quieted the man but since which I have understood that the same gentlemen has cautioned some of our friends to beware of the traitor. I make this explanation so that you may be able to fully understand me. And it is for your ear, in order to enable you to make the proper explanation should any of our friends suspect me. I have not heard from Lewis since he left Washington. Scoville is working hard for a nomination to the Legislature.

N. B. The Commission is in this city composed of Mr. Johnson, Humphreys and Capt. Kennon.

JOSEPH A. SCOVILLE TO R. M. T. HUNTER.

NEW YORK, [N. Y.], *November 21, 1842.*

DEAR MR. HUNTER: Your esteemed favor of 14th was duly rec[eive]d. The time is near at hand when you will once more come forth from your country retirement to mingle in affairs at Washington and I hope and trust ere the coming Session closes, that we shall be more settled than at present and on a sure footing for Mr. Calhoun.

In our late election we carried everything—Gov[ernor], L[ieutenant] Gov[ernor], 22 out of 34 Congressmen, all the State Senators save one, and 2/3 of the Legislature—much too large a majority, as it will make Mr. Van Burens friends sanguine and bring them out.

Mr. Leonard you will find *right*. It is a very awkward matter to ask a man a direct question as to his preferences, but you can form a pretty correct opinion from his associations and conversation. I am now a constituent of Leonards, having moved into the 8th Ward for the purpose of being sent down to Tammany Hall from that Ward, and to be able to get 2 more men friends to Mr. Calhoun.

Mr. C[alhoun']s son in law Mr. Clemson was here a few days since. I introduced him to about 500 Locos. We had supper at B[rook]lyn at which Murphy was present. He is *true*. I was alarmed at his

Van Buren associations previous to the elections and as deception is the order of the day here, I thought he might be one of them. I am at work from 8 A. M. to 12 P. M., negotiating and arranging our strength here, to bring it into combination. I get completely disheartened sometimes, get over it and go to work again. I am alone. Hart is hard at work to get appointed inspector of Pot and Pearl Ashes. He has 15 Competitors, from his own Ward *2*, beside himself. He is unable to help me any, in fact for the last 3 months he has devoted himself to this object and not a word has passed between us in regard to Mr. Calhoun. *Slamm* has deserted us, I am afraid, in *fact am sure of it.* Some time ago (when he found no money was coming, and that we were *too* poor here to do anything) he had a meeting of Vanderpool and several of Van Burens friends and they made up a purse and I believe he is independent now, in fact I have not been in his office for some time. I met him yesterday, and he asked me if I had done cursing him yet. I answered that I had felt hurt at his conduct for many reasons.

Chas. P. Daly is elected, a warm friend of Mr. Calhoun, and will do our cause more good than I could have done. Some time I will explain the causes of my defeat. I am glad I was defeated, for I am *too* poor to bear the expense.

Hutton is hard at work in his County (Richmond). Crook I have not seen for some time. Neither of these friends reside in the City.

This scramble for office breaks in upon our arrangements. Were it not for this, Hart and many others would be at work to carry the Gen[era]l Committee in Dec[embe]r instead of getting office. Gov. Bouck will probably make no appointments until after 20[th] Jan[uar]y, and our Committees are elected about 16[th of] Dec[embe]r. All our friends seem afraid to define their position. Hart wants to be remembered to you. I wish you would think well of some plan for a general organization throughout the Country. You are more of a politician than any other friend of Mr. Calhoun in Congress, and can readily understand the necessity of what I propose. I have written something of the kind to Mr Calhoun, and told him that I hoped you would head it, that there must be some one in Washington who could stand in the same relation to him, that Wright does to Van Buren, or rather did, and *I am not so sure but he does now.* To tell you frankly, it struck me very forcibly that there was very little of such a system as I have been accustomed to see in our State politics, and which is so essential to succeed in any great political movement. Now suppose for the next Session and thereafter you adopt some plan like this.

First, Yourself in Washington near Mr. C[alhoun] and when you can be assisted if necessary by Rhett, Lewis &c in what you will find **a** very arduous undertaking (at same time, it will bring you into intimate contact with many rising men throughout the Nation and will prove of great advantage to you hereafter in a political view.)

Second, The four following States or either of the *three* can give a nomination in Convention to any Candidate now in the field. They hold the Balance of power. Ohio capital Columbus. Pennsylvania capital Harrisburg. New York capital Albany. Virginia capital Richmond.

Select in each capital a prominent and influential man, either a member of the Senate or House, who is devoted to Mr. Calhoun and will devote his time and who will go into active correspondence and organize in concert with other parts of the organization hereafter named, and this to be done while his Legislature is in Session. And it should be your policy to follow out this System in every Legislature of every State in the Union.

Third. In each congressional District in the Union, there should be a Person of influence selected who has tact and experience enough to organize his district by Counties, Towns and villages. In arranging this, you must follow the new district system and where States have not districted, follow the old plan. Great care, caution and prudence will be required in the selection of such men, especially in the Northern States, as they will have a heavy duty to perform, they will be obliged to canvass thoroughly, find where public opinion exists in favor of Mr. C[alhoun], either in individuals or masses, in this way. Documents, Pamphlets, Speeches &c can be sent to every town and our Co strength can be solid, and as strength makes strength, every day will add to Mr. C[alhoun']s friends. You waste no time or energy, let individuals go to the devil, unless they are willing to get into the Calhoun traces. If an individual writes you, all you have to do is to refer him to his county or town organization, thank him and tell him to go to work. Everything will then go like clock work, all report to certain points, and to Head Quarters. If New York friends want to operate on Ohio friends we know how to go to work and do so effectually. New York, Phil[adelphia], Albany, Harrisburg, Columbus, Boston &c would be the most important points aside from Washington. Unless Friend Hunter some organization (General) is commenced, we cannot act with any Strength, and we may find when *too late* that we have been *trusting* to appearances, and *honest* public feeling, and have neglected the means to bring it out and render it available for Mr. Calhoun and such negligence has defeated him in his nomination by the National Convention.

As an instance of the effect of organization I inclose you 3 or 4 papers. In 1840 the party had *their* post masters, every post master (to save postage) was an agent, even for other men residing in their town to communicate with T[ammany] Hall. By these means

50,000 Documents could be mailed here and sent into every town or village. There is an immense field to operate upon, and if Van Buren becomes a candidate we have got to meet tact with tact, cunning with cunning, interest with interest, or say what you will, think as you will, we are beaten horse foot and dragoon in that convention. If that infernal fool John Tyler would wake up and see the hopelessness of *his* cause, or at least see that his *only* chance was in placing his partronage and influence for Calhoun, to break down Van Buren and give his appointments in this State to Mr. Calhoun or to such men as will work against Van Buren. Let every P[ost] M[aster] be an agent. We should have such an organization afloat as would break down Van Buren sure in his own State, and Mr. Calhoun need not appear in it, or Tyler either. Give me the means of being a Traveling Agent for the P[ost] O[ffice] with power and I only want 2 months and I would give him (or rather Mr. C) such an organization as would astonish little Matty. *He* will make a move yet that will *astonish* us, if we are not on our guard; *organization is our only safety.* Curtiss got back from Wash[ington] yesterday and it is reported and I believe it, he will not be removed. I wish Tyler would or could be made to appoint about 8, or even 5 men in that Custom House, I could do wonders with even those for I would make it a condition in 2 or 3 doubtful wards, that they should not be appointed, unless they carried some men I would name in their wards on the general Commitee for 43.

If Tyler would remove Curtiss or any leading office holder here, no one but a friend of Mr. C[alhoun']s must be confirmed by the Senate. Woodbury will understand this, his Brother in Law Barnes of Boston came to see me yesterday. I advised him to organize in every *district* in Mass[achusetts] and let W[oodbury']s friends do so in Maine and N[ew] Hampshire. Woodbury must go to work in earnest. I shall see him and have a talk this week. I want to see a display of his influence *not openly but quietly* by following my plan. *You* need not trust any man. You will get your opinions from the people in the most primary way, and you will know after the plan is in operation by many sources the feelings of the people in every State and how it can be increased.

9 Wards or 27 men (Calhoun) have to be elected to carry the committee and I need not express to you how great is my anxiety to do it, at any cost, it must be done, and if we succeed it will be the worst blow Van Buren has yet received. I shall await your first letter on your arrival at Washington with great anxiety. For we shall know whether Tyler is to be considered an Enemy or friend. He is our worst enemy as long as he pursues his present course, for it is abroad that he is friendly to Calhoun and he connives at it (Tyler) if it is not so. Mr. T[yler] *does not intend to throw* his

patronage to Mr. C[alhoun']s hands (for as to influence he has none) the sooner some means are devised to show that he is an Enemy to Mr. Calhoun, the better. It is utter ruin to allow things to remain as they are now, to have all the *odium and no benefit.*

Hamilton informed me yesterday that he had wrote you sometime since enclosing a letter Mr. Calhoun wrote him in 1830. That it would do great service to Mr. Calhoun to publish it. Nonsense, if it is published it will injure Mr. Calhoun, for it is dated 1830 and would lead the public to believe that A[lexander] H[amilton] was an *old* friend, and it identifies Mr. C[alhoun] with Col. H[amilton] and makes Mr. C[alhoun] to a certain extent liable for the political slips of the latter, don't publish it, it is *too* small game.

[P. S.] To avoid any mistakes I will number my letters and in replying say " recd No 1 a— h—.

JOSEPH A. SCOVILLE TO R. M. T. HUNTER.

PHILADELPHIA, [Pa.], *December 11, 1842.*

MY DEAR SIR: My remarks yesterday in regard to information to be acquired were not sufficiently explicit to satisfy my own mind, and I therefore enclose some questions that have suggested themselves to-day. You must, in dealing with northern politicians, *direct them what to do, mark out a course for them to follow,* and they will be sure to do so. In 223 Districts, averaging 3 counties or even 4 to a district say nearly 900 Counties in all, or 450 in the free States, and let this system once go into operation, and it is *perfectly practicable* and can be in full force by 1st [of] Feb[ruar]y, if you use the proper method to start. it, and what is the immediate result, not merely securing information to govern the future moves in Washington but if the person who receives these questions answers *one half of them,* after practical observations, and the work necessary to be done before he *can* answer them, you have achieved much. It carries home to the people, to the ground work, in every free state town and village, an excitement in favor of Calhoun. When for instance one state like Pennsylvania has a person of influence at work in combining the masses in every county not three weeks could pass before each one would be assisting each other without knowing it. These questions are a guide, a map and followed out, make unity of action. They point the policy of Mr. Calhouns friends up to the last Gun. One question then finishes the chapter, it is this " Can you not be elected to the National Convention as a delegate from your Congressional District? " And if the agents are clever politicians, they will be able to do it. And they will find, on Mr. C[alhoun']s strength, *they* are strong. The next question is in regard to the manner of communicating their Queries to our Friends. My idea is that it should be done by some of our friends, as private hints, and confidential, and not be given by you in your letters, or in no way, that can be traced to you, for you must not appear as the mover. It will not do for you to have to look ahead and Van Buren like never show your hand. I merely send you the Queries and you may use them as you see fit, there are men of course, particularly South, in whom you have unbounded confidence. I think it would be of service to have your Southern friends take part in the northern system of organization. It will be of service at the North to know that they are wide awake South, and have an interchange of sentiments and opinions between the various sections. This is the last letter I shall address you in regard to organization. Out of my last 10 letters you may find some hints, ideas, or suggestions that may prove of service, if so, I am repaid for my labor in writing them. I wish you to distinctly understand me. I have not wrote you so much and so often, from either vanity or the " Fun of it " nor do I feel that you are at all wanting in the necessary qualities to direct a great movement, or that you are not ably competent to carry it to a successful issue, far, far from this. But I feel interested. I dread being defeated and most of Mr. Calhouns immediate friends are Southerners and some how they do not *feel* the vast importance of a combination of interests and strict discipline and system in their party, and the more you have in your councils of able and experienced northern politicians who are true to Mr. C. the better and surer is our cause. My idea is that no stone should be left unturned, no efforts relaxed, and no hopes be entertained, until we have defeated the *old* party organization and it is prostrate, to work in every quarter up to the last moment for his nomination by National Convention, and if we fail, let the minority of that Convention be ready, there are not three men who can beat him, he will get more votes at the election than any other one, and will of course be one of the three to be elected by the House, and will be elected. This will show you the necessity, in order to have the latter event sure, to have your eyes on the Congressmen elected and to be elected, attention to them now *may save a state to Mr. Calhoun hereafter.*

Neither Martin Van Buren, R. M. Johnson, Cass, Buchanan or Benton are rivals to Mr. Calhoun. His Rival (and the only one he has to fear) is that man on whom the old party organization of 1828, 1832 and 1836 (or what remains of it) unite. *To day* they have strength enough to nominate a man in that convention, and their interest would lead them to unite on Van Buren. He has no strength, and is not to be feared save as identified with the old party and leaders that nominated him in 1836. If Mr. Calhouns friends can build up a stronger Organization in the North, assisted by his powerful friends in the South, the old organ[izatio]n is defeated and the whole kit of Democratic Candidates. People talk about Pennsyl[vani]a for Buchanan, the West for Johnson, Ohio for Cass, New York for Van Buren, the South for Calhoun and the probability of a division, stuff Martin Van Buren laughs at it (and so does Wright and will until his eyes are opened by finding his tactics are applied by Mr. C[alhoun']s friends north). *The old leven is there*, and altho they may vote scattering on the *first ballot*, yet on the 2d Ballot, Van Buren 138! I may be mistaken, but I hope I shall never see the experiment tried. No Mr. Hunter, the District System of Organization I have proposed in my last 10 letters, is safe for Mr. Calhoun, and it is sure, Mr. Calhoun cannot, must not, allow his friends in the Free States, [to] be obliged to compete with State Conventions to elect delegates to that Convention. Our defeat is inevitable in the 4 great States. Let the organization of his friends be based upon the simple system of districts, every district being a State of itself and nothing to do with other districts and in every District of the Union, let our friends act singly for him, no compromise, let Calhounism be well *planted* now in each district, and my life on the assertion: " May 1844 will see John C. Calhoun nominated almost unanimously by the National Convention."

I hope you will have given these letters (or rather the subject) your attention. I shall be happy to learn that you approve of it and I am then ready to off coat and go to work to carry it out.

JOSEPH A. SCOVILLE TO R. M. T. HUNTER.

NEW YORK, [N. Y.], *January 1, 1843.*

MY DEAR HUNTER: I feel gratified at the opportunity afforded me of introducing to your correspondence Mr. Edmund I. Porter. This gentleman is one whose friendship I highly value and I am sure you will entertain the same feeling when he becomes known to you. He was a valuable representative in the Legislature from this city a few years, and his experience in political matters and his advice and suggestions, you will find valuable and interesting.

Mr. Porter is a man of talent, a Lawyer by profession and capable of appreciating the greatness of character of such a man as John C. Calhoun, and it will not surprise you to learn that he has long been an admirer of the Southern Statesman.

I should long ago have given Mr. P[orter] a letter to you, had circumstances justified it, or had there been any occasion to do so, but the time has now come when Mr. Porter can be of immense service. In the late contest, Mr. Porter was elected a delegate to the Gen[era]l Committee from the 10th ward, 450 to 85! From his long services in the Democratic Ranks he will of course possess great weight with the members of that body, and you will learn from him every thing, from time to time that you may desire to know, and you may rely upon his tact and secrecy in such correspondence as may pass between you.

J. FRANCIS HUTTON TO R. M. T. HUNTER.

(Confidential.)

RICHMOND COUNTY, [N. Y.], *Thursday night,*
January 25th, 1843.

MY DEAR SIR: Our friend E. B. Hart has just returned from Albany and brings the most favourable accounts of the prospects for Mr. Calhoun. The old Conservative party and the new radical party are violently opposed to each other, and the success of the former in the Councils of the State will unite radicals in opposition. Dutchess County in Davis district have organized near 1000 Calhoun men and intend to nominate Mr. C[alhoun] about the 1st of next month. A delegation came to the City and were surprised to find our boys so well organized and they left here delighted and encouraged to persevere.

Scoville is in high spirits *to-day* and extremely active and useful but a most confounded grumbler. The proof sheets of Mr. Calhouns life are in the hands of Scoville and the work will shortly be published. Among our Irish adopted Citizens it will produce a great sensation. How go appointments.

E. G. B. HART TO R. M. T. HUNTER.

NEW YORK, [N. Y.], *February 13, 1843.*

MY DEAR HUNTER: I have just returned from Albany and finding a letter awaiting me, hasten to acknowledge its receipt. The pleasing intelligence it conveyed of Mr. Calhouns increasing prospects was indeed most welcome. You may now depend that your suggestion of "going to work" will be immediately attended to, and I trust you will ere long have ample proof that a second request similar to the one alluded to will not be needed. I have however not been inactive, and purpose in the course of this week to give you some evidence of it. Strong opposition to Bouck will soon be made. We have been deceived as to his firmness, he is disposed, to favor the "Old Hunkers." Young is no doubt Van, such is my impression based upon the opinion of others. In my next you shall have my views at length. There is one thing in particular for you to attend to, (as funds are somewhat essentially necessary to aid a good cause) and that is the pushing through of Gilberts Dock. With my best respects to friend Lewis.

Joseph A. Scoville to R. M. T. Hunter.

(*Private.*)

New York, [N. Y.], *February 16, 1843.*
12 o'clock P. M.

My Dear Sir: I leave for Hartford in the morning, you had better direct to me *there*.

I believe I can do nothing more than I have done about the work. I have directed Harpers to send about 20 of the *first* issues to various persons in W[ashington].

Manry has been with me all the afternoon and I have given him an account of how matters stand here. He is poor you know. I have told him to draw on me for whatever may be necessary to hire a Room, where the leading friends may meet daily to advise him.

I will write you fully from Hartford. Budy and self may go soon to Maine.

[P. S.] Currie will correct the misspelling in the next reams— seperation—adherance &c. Please frank and forward the enclosures. The letter for Stuart is a private one, not to be published. Give Lewis my address. Why dont he never write to me?

J. Francis Hutton to R. M. T. Hunter.

New York, [N. Y.], *February 18th, 1843.*

My dear Sir: I like to keep you advised of everything that comes to my knowledge calculated to keep you on foot as to the movements of the adverse interests to our cause. You are aware I suppose that Mr. Coombs (the gentleman Mr. D. H. Lewis is acquainted with by his political writings in favor of Calhoun) is in the Custom House, and of course assists in editing the "Union."

Now in confidence I say to you that the men most active apparently in the support of Tylers interest here, are well aware of the little chance there is for him in the coming contest for the presidency and all their efforts for Tyler will in future be subsid[i]ary to that interest of the Hon. John C. Calhoun. Mr. Coombs consults me daily on the policy for the "Union" to pursue and is desirous of now and then giving a dashing leader or two in favor of Calhoun in that paper but I have dissuaded him from that course while the name of Bouck stands at the head of that paper for the Vice Presidency. We are determined not to mix up the interests of Calhoun with that of our present Gov[erno]r, for the sins of the present administration are too weighty for us to carry and Bouck therefore must be a Van Buren man whatever his personal feelings may be for Mr. C[alhoun]. What is your opinion of this matter? Hart is at work collecting our strength for a meeting of the leading Calhoun men which I think will take place in course of next week. It is our intention of feeling such men as we cannot be mistaken in and when the Committee is formed you will be furnished with their names and with our wishes in reference to correspondence. There is a man in the Custom House by the name of Barbour an Englishman who states he has been written to from Washington to become an editor for a New Calhoun paper about to be established here, is this so? He is I understand an intimate of Morrells. The life of Mr. C[alhoun] will be out in a few days, so will the new letter paper for political correspondence bearing the vignette of the head and bust of Calhoun, on the right the banner of Free Trade low duties &c and on the left the time and manner of construing the Convention. Every mail will convey hundreds of these letters to all parts of the Union and accustom the people to think of Mr. C[alhoun] whether they choose or not.

Our friend Thompson is a host, he writes daily half a dozen letters to every man of any importance in the East, North and West urging them to move in favor of Mr. C[alhoun]. He showed me a letter from Robt. Dale Owen of Indiana in which it is stated that Mr. Calhoun has a powerful party in that State among the rank and file. Among my constituents there prevails but one opinion and in the city New York our strength is increasing daily, truly I think we shall see the triumph of principle over all party intrigues and John C. Calhoun the nominee of the Baltimore Convention.

[P. S.] While Curtis is in Washington is it not possible to induce him to make two or three appointments for Richmond County in which I reside?

R. M. T. HUNTER TO ———.[1]

(*Private.*)

[WASHINGTON, D. C.] *February 20, 1843.*

MY DEAR SIR: I am afraid that my last letter miscarried as you speak of yours being unanswered. Certain I am that I wrote the last and I do not mention this my dear sir by way of opening an account (for I hold myself always your debtor) but only to show you that I have not neglected you. I have been so overwhelmed with correspondence that I have been forced to forego the indulgence of my inclination to write many letters which would have been useful to the cause as well as agreeable to me. But to the point. We are endeavoring to get up an efficient organization—a central committee here. A central committee in each state whose duty it should be to get up a corresponding committee of four or five in each county. All this to be done silently. Our central committee here

---

[1] Use of this letter was permitted by Mr. W. G. Stanard, of the Virginia Historical Society.

is not yet organised. But in Richmond James A. Seddon is the ch[airma]n, Giles, Young and Greenhow are his coadutors. We wish to get up corresponding Calhoun Committees in each county. We may then acquire the means to concert action, to circulate documents, and to have 4 or 5 energetic advocates in each county. Some of these ought to attend each court and every public meeting. Amongst others I wrote Beverley Tucker to get himself appointed delegate from Jefferson to the State Convention and to organise Jefferson and Berkeley. I have not heard from him as yet. Will you write to him on the subject? He has ability, energy and is disposed to Calhoun. He may win a political position now which may tell in his after life. I was about writing to you when yours reached me. I see you are appointed to the Convention and I hope you will attend. Time is vital to us. A convention in May 1844 and 8 districts I believe will secure us. At any rate we cannot oppose a convention " per se " without being unchurched.

Right or wrong we cannot oppose a Gen[era]l Convention fairly organised and held in May 1844. The Richmond Convention will name an early day unless a strenuous effort is made by our friends. They must not name the place and time unless they are willing to give them. The Democratic papers (many of which I have sent to Seddon) are declaring for the principle of Rhett's pamphlet. The Dem[ocratic] party at Annapolis in Caucus have declared for a convention in May 1844. If we decided on this matter the ' prestige ' of victory will be with us and in my opinion Van Buren must give way before the canvass. Our prospects are bright and if the limits of this sheet permitted, I could give you many evidences of it. Michigan (we are informed) is with us. So of the Democrats in Arkansas, Miss[issippi], Louisiana, Alabama, Georgia, So[uth] Ca[rolina] and No[rth] Ca[rolina]. So in V[irgini]a we exert ourselves—So in Maryland. The New England Democracy we have good reason to hope is with us. In N[ew] York if the Convention be by districts we hope to carry 12 districts. In P[ennsylvani]a B[uchanan]'s friends prefer C[alhoun] as a second choice. Illinois we are assured by her senators is with us. Why then should we dispair? Let us work for V[irgini]a. The organization is all important. Can't you see Gordon on the subject. There are fine materials in Albemarle and Louisa. We are about to publish a *life of Calhoun* which we wish to circulate extensively and with which we desire to furnish all the corresponding committees. I will send you one of the sample numbers when I receive it. I will also send a prospectus to which Randolph might obtain subscriptions from the districts. The Harpers publish it. We shall make efforts to establish a press here if we can do so without open war and procure a competent editor.

We have also propositions from Richmond. But we should "observe" Ritchie a little longer. The organization must proceed.

Your essay I have not had time to read as yet. I will study it tonight and hope we may make a good use of it. My kindest regards to Mr. B. T. and to Randolph. I write in the House and I fear incoherently but you will be able to gather the general drift of our plans. I shall submit your essay to Mr. C[alhoun] before I act. He often speaks of you and requested me to beg you to be in Richmond if practicable.

JAMES BROOM, SEC[RETAR]Y (CALHOUN CENTRAL COMMITTEE) TO
R. M. T. HUNTER.

(*Private.*)

WASHINGTON, [D. C.], *March 4, 1843.*

DEAR SIR: I enclose you a Prospectus of a Newspaper, which the friends of Mr. Calhoun have selected to be the Central Organ of the Calhoun portion of the Democratic Party. The Spectator will continue to be published Weekly, as heretofore, until a month previous to the meeting of the 28th Congress, when a Daily Paper will also be issued from the same Newspaper establishment.

The Spectator will publish every movement relating to Mr. Calhoun's growing prospects, and the proceedings of his friends in the various sections of the country.

Its Editorial columns will be under the charge of an old personal as well as political friend of Mr. Calhoun. It is desirable that the Spectator should be circulated as extensively as possible; and means will be used to obtain Subscribers in every town in the Union. I am desired to send you a Prospectus for your own use, and also an additional number of 19, to be handed by you to well known friends. You will confer a favor by getting as many Subscribers as possible. Please give the same directions to those friends to whom you hand the other Prospectuses. They are numbered 250 to 255, 261 to 265, 254 to 260, 241 to 245, and you will be expected to see that said numbers are returned to Mr. Heart, eventually, whether any names are subscribed or not.

I send you, also, 50 Receipts for subscriptions, which I have received from the Publisher of the Spectator, Mr. John Heart. You will please account to him for the same, at the prices named in the Prospectus, as I have informed him of the number of receipts that I send you.

[P. S.] Please send a list of all the leading newspapers published in your State, Post offices and names, also mark the Calhoun papers.

JAMES A. SEDDON TO R. M. T. HUNTER.

RICHMOND, [VA.], *April 1, 1843.*

DEAR SIR: I was much gratified by the receipt of your last letter and should certainly have sooner replyed had not my time been wholly engrossed by professional engagements and the obligation of writing to many of our friends throughout the State. We have been ever since the adjournment of the Dem[ocratic] Convention greatly engaged in carrying out our concerted scheme of organization by the formation of Corresponding Committees in different Counties, through them we have circulated all the lives of Mr. C[alhoun] placed at our disposal and find the demand for them still increasing. To meet this we have written to the Central Calhoun Committee in Washington to ascertain on what terms a further supply may be obtained both of the "Vitae" and the Speeches. We already hear of the beneficial results which are following these steps. We are daily receiving accessions and are decidedly the Movement party. From various sections we hear of influential States rights men coming out with the decisive declaration that they will cordially unite with us in electing Mr. C[alhoun] but will not vote for Mr. V[an] B[uren]. Nothing of novelty or added force can be given to the arguments or views favourable to Mr. Van Buren, and his adherents have to encounter the distrust inspired by another disheartening Conviction resulting from his past defeat, while on the other hand the arguments in favour of Mr. C[alhoun] are daily waxing stronger in their impression on the popular mind and his friends are actuated by a zealous active and hopeful spirit. So far from being dismayed by the results of the late Convention they seem but to have been rendered more animated and determined. Such is our progress that were the [Richmond] Enquirer removed from our way to morrow I should have the most sanguine Confidence of carrying the State by a decided majority to counteract the insiduous hostility of that paper I am each day more satified that the establishment of a Calhoun Organ here is indispensible. Conducted with prudence it might avoid all collision with the Enquirer, which unless I mistake Mr. R[itchie] would dread and shun a quarrel, and thus all the benefits of an able paper on our side might be obtained without drawing down upon us the hostility and influence of the Enquirer. Through the imprudence of some of our hot neutral friends, a rumor has gotten out of the intent to establish a Calhoun paper and the Whig notices it this morning. This of course renders positive determination about the matter more necessary. Meantime however we labor under the natural reluctance to embark in the enterprise without some guarantee ag[ains]t serious loss, and are most solicitous to know how far the aid of our friends may be relied on. To test this at once and at the same time to enlist private interest in obtaining subscriptions, we have determined respectively to propose to *confidential* friends to *guarantee* such number of subscriptions as they think they can certainly obtain. I have offered personally to guarantee $100, or twenty subscribers at $5 each. May I venture to request that you will say whether you will be willing thus to stand Sponsor for subscribers and if so, to what extent, and also to apprize us how far others among your friends, with whom you can readily communicate will pledge their credit. We have ascertained we can commence and publish a paper twice a week for a year with 600 *good* subscribers at $5 each. This number we ought surely to command with ease but yet we are not willing to incur the responsibility without some previous assurance. I wish much that 30 men could be obtained at once to pay up for the Cause one hundred dollars each. I would cheerfully join the number and pay my quota in the part. I think too I might give the assurance that other members of our Committee will raise another hundred, as all would doubtless contribute except Mr. Greenhow, who will have to sacrifice so much in time that more ought not to be required of him. What say you to this matter?

I have invoked of late the action of our Committee here to promote the re-election of our Friend Mr. Goode and for that purpose have addressed to the Calhoun members of the Petersb[ur]g Convention, which assembles Tuesday a long and earnest letter urging his nomination if practicable. His chance is good, if the Calhoun men will not allow personal preference for Dromgoole to sway them unduly. I feel much interest in the matter on account of its effect both in and out of the State. From your own Canvass I hear animating and I doubt not just accounts. In Essex, you must strain every nerve for Wm. P. Taylor for I am satisfied the *pinch* of the contest with him will be *there*.

Please inform me of some Leading Calhoun men in the Northern Neck, our correspondence there is very limited.

J. FRANCIS HUTTON TO R. M. T. HUNTER.

NEW YORK, [N. Y.], *September 26, 1843.*

DEAR SIR: The Van Buren meeting after all the parade of names turned out a most miserable failure both as to numbers and effect, certainly 1/3 were Calhoun men 1/3 Johnson men, the remainder Whigs and Van Buren. I attended and counted around me 100, well known friends of Mr. C[alhoun]. There were not more in attendance than at our meeting and as to enthusiasm it would bear no comparison. Several gentlemen from the West have arrived in

Town to arrange with our Central Committee a plan of operations to carry out vigorously the Calhoun movement. We met last evening after the meeting in the park and it was truly gratifying to receive their congratulations at the result. The hand bill I sent you per post containing the names and occupations of the signers to the call, worked wonders and I trust you will have some thousand struck off for distribution in your State, that is if you cannot get it published. Of course it is not known that Calhoun men had any hand in it and must not be known. Our paper will be published in about ten days, send on as fast as possible all the subscribers you can obtain.

Send me the names of some of the first men in your State and N[orth] Carolina, Tennessee and Georgia. Our committee appointed last night a finance Committee, E. B. Hart, Treasurer, any funds in aid of the cause will be received and acknowledged by him, do what you can for us for remember we are without patronage. Robt. Tyler has been in town and complains utterly that the Charleston Mercury is making War on the administration this should not be. We want the post offices and must have them and by the course of the Mercury, Tyler may be driven off. Conciliation for a time is all important. The West of our State will move very soon to protest against the proceedings of Syracuse and elect delegates to Baltimore. The delegates from the West mentioned above have come to the city for the express purpose of carrying out our plans to effect the object of selecting delegates to Baltimore, simultaneously with the City. Action, Action is the word. We now are to every one friendly, the ball is fairly open and we must all press onward and victory is sure.

If any Southern gentleman comes North let us make his acquaintance. It will assist us in circulating pamphlets &c. We are conducting our movements now with admirable skill and effect. We know this for it *tells!* Ah! if we had only our present organization 12 mo[nth]s ago. Yet it is not too late, for the Van Buren men have by this delay of ours thrown everything in our hands and the men we most rely upon are fresh zealous, and stand high before the public, while the V[an] B[uren] men are led by old party hacks, and excite less enthusiasm than the Ex-President.

The Seventh Ward Calhoun association have a public meeting to-night. The fifth Ward next week, the 15th the week after. Richmond Co[unty] will follow the city movements and so on through the State.

The Corresponding Sec[retar]y, F. Byrdsall will write you as to our plan of operations, which if satisfactory we wish pursued through the Union.

JAMES A. SEDDON TO R. M. T. HUNTER.

RICHMÓND, [VA.], *August 9th, 1844.*

MY DEAR SIR: On my return to the city about a week since I found your considerate Letter awaiting me but owing to numerous pressing engagements which have accumulated upon me, I have been unable to return until now my grateful acknowledgements for your kind and prompt compliance with the requests I had ventured to prefer to you.

Altho' destitute of the letter from you which I had intended to rely on as my chief credentials, I was emboldened by my anxiety for Greenhow's welfare and my remembrance of Mr. Calhoun's uniform kindness to call on him as I passed thro' Washington and prefer in person the application which I wished you to second. The Noble Old Man treated Mr. Caskie who accompanied me and myself with his usual frank courtesy and altho' I confess at first he rather startled me by the gravity with which he heard the application, he soon threw aside all reserve and while expressing high confidence in Greenhow and great reliance on our Recommendation, yet explained his apprehension that from peculiar causes (all of which I ought not to entrust to the risk of letter) it might not be in his power to confer an appointment, which he was pleased to say, it would be no less gratifying to him to give than for the recipient to receive. He advised measures should be taken to secure the favourable consideration of the President (in which by the way I had anticipated his advice as far as practicable) and assured us his warm recommendation should be given in the event of a Vacancy. I had also the pleasure (almost the highest I can enjoy) of a free unreserved conversation with him at his rooms in the Evening, in which I was the attentive auditor to the most original yet profound views on the subject of Government I ever heard. He is a wonderful man, in power of analysis and Generalization, in originality and profundity of thought surpassing all that I had ever conceived of the power of human Intellect, and with the purity of his Life and the worthiness of his personal character as added to his splendid intellectual endowments, he stands forth preeminently the first of American Sages and statesmen. It is a burning shame in his day and generation that his powers and his virtues have not long since been placed in their highest sphere of development and usefulness.

But on this subject I shall run beyond my sheet, unless I check my course however grateful to my own friends. I intended to write you on another subject. Do you take the Mercury? If so, you will have perceived that our gallant friends of So[uth] Carolina, especially the younger and more ardent among them, burning under the course of the atrocious, heresys inflicted and threatened from

Federal misrule and abolition fanaticism are seriously contemplating an immediate resort to State interposition and in doing this, many are seriously assailing our Presidential Candidates and injuring our party in this State by giving countenance to what old Ritchie styles "the wolf cry of Disunion," now so loudly clamoured by the frenzied Whigs of this City. Mr. Calhoun I know and many others of the most experienced leaders in So[uth] Carolina I believe disapprove of these movements at this time and Juncture, and I am satisfied if our friends of the Palmetto State knew what serious embarrassment they were causing to their best friends here and how severely they were endangering Democratic ascendancy in this State (when moral influences were partially in their behalf is of the utmost importance and can only be hoped for in the event of our success in the Canvass) they would forbear for a while from rash resolves and harsh epithets. God knows I expect to be with them in sentiments and written avowals, perhaps even in open action, should the struggle which I seriously apprehend ever actually come, but I would pray that the cup might pass, and at least that it should not be pressed now to the distruction of friends who may prove most efficient in the hour of need. In the compass of a letter I cannot explain all the dangers and embarrassments which the course of our Southern friends now cause *us* here, but you will doubtless readily comprehend and appreciate them. My purpose therefore is to entreat you either to write alone (or join me in writing) earnest remonstrances to our So[uth] Car[olina] friends to pause awhile in their proposed action, and let us see the results of the Presidential Election and the course of the new incumbent. If I knew Elmore's name I w[oul]d write him for he seemeth to me both prudent and sagacious. If you would prefer a joint letter, pen it and forward it to me. I will readily sign whatever you write. Why are you not out in the Canvass? The question is often asked. I wish you would enter with all your soul when it hath for present good and for the sake of future. . . .

JAMES A. SEDDON TO R. M. T. HUNTER.

RICHMOND, [VA.], *August 19, 1844.*

MY DEAR SIR: Your two last kind letters have been duly received and for them my earnest acknowledgments are due. You must not however suppose I have been thus long remiss in expressing my thanks for the first. I found it awaiting my arrival from the North, and in a day or two thereafter, as soon indeed as the pressure of peremptory engagements consequent on my return would allow, I wrote you a warm letter giving some account of my personal conversation with Mr. C[alhoun] while in Washington and the impression it had made upon me. How or why that letter has miscarried I cannot conceive for it was actually deposited by myself in the office here. I feel some solicitude on the subject, for although I was fortunately prudent enough not to enter into particulars, because as I explained I was unwilling to trust to the accidents of the mail, I yet intimated matters which it would be well that no other eyes less friendly than yours should see. I trust the letter will yet come safely to hand. From my personal observations while in the city I was prepared for the turn of your last letter, which I regret far less for the disappointment of a family schism much cherished, than on account of the embarrassing circumstances with which it shows our distinguished friend to be encompassed. I can understand your self gratulation at not having been instrumental in placing him where he is. I always dreaded the measure and would have dissuaded too, but I little anticipated such a result. I doubt much if the position ought to be held longer. If it be, to all who know the truth the highest possible manifestations of self denying patriotism will be afforded. The Globe, in times back was not in such egregious error as I supposed and the little charity I was beginning to feel in a certain direction is waning fast into unmingled contempt. But enough of this. We will talk of it when we meet.

Another subject of my last letter was the menacing movements in South Carolina, which at the time seemed to trend pretty strongly to immediate nulification to which I felt assured Mr. C[alhoun] was opposed. Of such premature agitation I dreaded the effect especially on the agitating contest now going on in this State and I wrote to invoke your prudent counsels and friendly interposition with our South Carolina friends. Not however hearing from you at once I took the responsibility of writing pretty much on behalf of *our* wing in this State, alone an earnest appeal to Elmore (in whose discretion I felt high confidence) setting forth precisely our position views and principles here and the dangers which I thought a hasty course in South Carolina at this Juncture would entail on the whole Democratic party but especially the States rights portion of this and other Southern States. I have not yet heard in reply, but coming as it must have done when as I judge from appearances, more prudent counsels were beginning to prevail, I hope it will not be without beneficent fruits. The danger of premature action is I think for the present passed. Mr. Calhoun's influence, together with the advice of all the more distinguished leaders has for the present settled the storm. How long the calm is to continue I cannot say, but unless with the next presidential incumbent relief comes, for one I am prepared for action. The insult and injury of the recent iniquitious Tariff are unindurable, and to the [manuscript defective] with all republicans, as of old with the [manuscript defective] to your tents must be the cry. I do not however yet dispair. The Democracy if not undermined by treachery must prevail and then with Clay out of the way, the South will rite herself and the tariff must come down. What think you of the recent elections. To me they are encouraging. The contest will be close, but if the Whigs hold not the popular vote of 1842, when many of their voters did not come to the polls, is it not manifest the Democrats are even now advancing. I fear a little for this State chiefly because I believe there has been the systematic manufacture of Whig votes. All our energies are wanting. Why rests Achilles in his tent? Can't you take the field actively and at once?

JAMES A. SEDDON TO R. M. T. HUNTER.

RICHMOND, [VA.], *August 22, 1844.*

MY DEAR SIR: I received this morning your letter together with the Manuscript of your nephew and immediately called on Minor the Editor of the Messenger to obtain if possible the insertion of the latter in the next Messenger. Unfortunately the Ms. came too late for the Sept[ember] number which has been already fully made up, but Minor promised me to examine the article with a liberal eye and if he could possible reconcile it with his neutrality would insert it in the Oct[ober] number. Every effort shall be made on my part to procure its insertion, and should Minor object, I will endeavor earnestly to remove his Scruples. I believe great results are to follow in V[irgini]a from the publication of Mr. Calhouns life and speeches, provided only public attention can be called to them. This we must compass through the literary publications if possible, if not thro' the political and neutral press. Mr. C[alhoun]'s wishes will be an added spur to my own enthusiasm on the subject of this publication.

I have just received a letter from Elmore on the subject of the Carolina Movements. He represents them as hasty and unadvised, attributable to the imprudent zeal of Rhett and the heated feelings of Stuart but that through the influence of calmer counselors they have for the present been quieted. He refers to resolutions unanimously adopted in the Charleston Mercury as expressive of the true determination of the party in So[uth] Carolina. I have not yet seen them, but from Elmore's tone I have no doubt they are well considerate and judicious. Mr. Elmore desires to be warmly remembered to you. I have also heard today from Mr. Ritchie who was much pleased at your prompt interposition to stay the So[uth] Carolina excitement. We are all here on the alert. I start tomorrow for Accomac on an electioneering tour, and for the next four or five weeks I shall be pretty much given up to spouting. " Cui bono " it is hard to say but such is the duty exacted and for the future hopes of *our* cause I shall comply. Why are you not in the field. The Northern neck is especially in need of labourers and I wish you would take that vineyard for yourself.

ROBERT B. RHETT TO R. M. T. HUNTER.

[?], *August 30, 1844.*

DEAR HUNTER: I have rec[eive]d a letter written by you to Elmore, with your request that it be shown to me. You will doubtless ere this, have learned that Elmore is not in the "movement." That Holmes got into it, but was soon scared out of it, and that I alone must bear all the "anathemas" of my Democratic friends in and out of this little State, for presuming to "embarrass" the party by wishing to prepare the State to redeem her pledges, to protect herself from the treacherous and plundering policy of both parties Whig and Democratic. Now it seems we have some hope of righting the Government thro' the Democratic Party and Presidential Elections. You know how hard I have wrought in this line of policy. But I am done with it. The mean and treacherous move of the Democratic Party last session of Congress on the Tariff—the 21 Rule and Internal Improvements, has satisfied me that we of the South have no hope in their assertions; and those Polk born, equivocating letters to Kane of Pennsylvania have rendered him too dispicable in my estimation, to regard him in the least in my course. Nor have I any hope in the South generally. Virginia will have to intervene to prevent the only alternative which will bring back the Government from its rapid tendency to a consolidated despotism——disunion or reform. In this way the Union must be risked, to be preserved on the terms of its original formation. Virginia is too divided, and with her frontier position such bold councils will never prevail, and without it, in my opinion we will never drive back the Government to the limits of the Constitution. Look you Candidly do you expect the Democratic party of the North to give up a protective Tariff—or re-take position with us on the 21 Rule—or throw of the West to surrended internal improvements, which they revived at the last Congress? If you do, your organs of credulity must be astonishingly develloped; and out in defiance of all evidence and facts.

Expect no such results from them. They have given way and have given way forever to the foul and insulting interference of the Fanatics on the floor of Congress, and will go on plundering us to the end, by taxing us unrightiously and by appropriating the taxes. Such are my views, and of course I take no other faith from those who still go on shouting at the tail of the Democratic Party, only to have the glory of being crushed under foot, when triumphant, or may be to have the august privilege of placing a tool in power like Polk, who they can appropriate and weedle for their ends. My dear Hunter, I am sick and disgusted with the meanness and falsehood of the Democratic Party, whilst I detest the open, impudent despotism of the other. I will associate with the Democratic Party, but will not consent to follow it, have wearied with fighting [for] a Party which you must immediately turn round to oppose. We of the South will be ruined, unless we will act independently of both parties, against supporting what both parties of the North and South join to put upon us. As long as we regard either party, above our rights, they never will be redressed. If you would succeed tomorrow (in what I know is your earnest policy) make Mr. Calhoun President (which you will never do, unless he will be [a] tool) and surrender all the policy of his life) you would do nothing. So far as the rest goes it may be well But for laws in operation like the Tariff policy he would do nothing. Despairing of all their reasoning, I turn to this little State, and am striving at least to save her honour. She has declared she will resist the Tariff policy, in the Convention of 1833, and in the Legislatures of 1841 and 1842. I say let her go on. I have no doubt of the result, if this cursed spirit of President-making does not prostrate her. But if it does, and she is made in shame and dishonour to submit, I wish the world to see, that I have not counciled it.

As to all the outcry that I am seeking to distroy the Union, you know very well that there is no truth in it. I am seeking to put the Union on its true basis of the Constitution. I trust I appreciate the Union the Constitution has established as highly as any one. I hold the Constitution in politics as I do the Bible in religion. My object is not to destroy the Union, but to maintain the Constitution, and the Union too, as the Constitution has made it. But I do not believe that the Government can be reformed by its central action, and that we will have probably to risk the Union itself to save it, in its integrity; and perpetuate it as a blessing. If it brings us to a consolidated Government, it must be one of the worst forms of tyranny. Of course I expect to be called Disunionist, Mischief-maker Traitor etc. All men who have ever attempted to reform an evil, by strong measures, have had such epithets to bear. They do not much disturb my equnimity, being satisfied the liberty and safety of the South requires the strong policy I propose. That you and others differ from me I regret but I must nevertheless go on.

JOHN C. CALHOUN TO R. M. T. HUNTER.

WASHINGTON, [D. C.], *September 27th, 1844.*

MY DEAR SIR: I have entire confidence in the judgment and discretion of my friends in Virginia. Their position is one of great command. They have fought the present battle in Virginia. It has made them acquainted with the people and the people with them, and given them a stand and influence in the state, which, if they act together and be prudent and vigillant must give them its control.

From all I hear, I should think, Mr. Ritchie is well disposed. He ought to be treated with great delicacy and respect so long as there is any prospect of his acting in concert, all collision with him ought to be avoided. If he will go right take his stand on the old platform of the Republican party and put Virginia at the head of the South, all will go right.

I expect to leave tomorrow for my residence in South Carolina, where I shall probably spend the month of Oct[ober],. I have been much engrossed by the duties of my office since the adjournment of Congress. I have prepared in the time many and some of them very important dispatches. Our foreign relations, especially as it regards the South, have been much neglected by the Government for many years.

The general impression here, with our friends is, that Clay will be defeated and Polk elected. Indeed, it is regarded by the great majority, that it is almost certain. Although I do not go as far, I think the prospect is highly favourable to our side.

I have, I think, the pamphlet of Gov[ernor] Cass to which you refer, but it is among my papers at home. If I can put my hand on it after I arrive there I will send it to you.

Mr. Harris of your State (member of the last Congress) has concluded to take charge of the Spectator and intends to get and write the Madison[ian] with it, and give a new name to the paper, if he can obtain it on fair terms, as he thinks he can. It is our important movement. I think well of his talents and highly of his character, and do not doubt he will make an able and sound editor. He starts under highly auspicious circumstances and has a fair prospect of rallying a strong support. I hope our friends will give him liberal patronage.

JAMES A. SEDDON TO R. M. T. HUNTER.

RICHMOND, [VA.], *November 16th, 1844.*

MY DEAR SIR: The glorious work has been consummated and nowhere else more triumphantly than in the old Dominion. We have carried our candidate and defeated I trust forever Mr. Clay and his odious system of measures, but how far we have secured the

permanent ascendency of our own particular Creed, the old republican faith of V[irgini]a remains yet to be seen.   I would feign hope for
the best but confess I am not without serious apprehensions, to prevent the realization of which now becomes our peculiar duty.   The
hour has now come when the friends of Mr. Calhoun who wish to
take in time counsel together and prepare for whatever consequences
may await us should according to precedent meet here, and we are
even now thinking of fulfilling the trust imposed on us at the Charlottesville Convention and of appointing some time for our little
quiet convention.   Before doing so however we are most anxious that
full communication should be had by you the most trusted among
us with Mr. Calhoun and that you s[houl]d ascertain from him in the
fullest manner his views and wishes in regard to the action of his
friends in this State.   I very much fear that the lights are not at
present before him or us which will enable us to determine or act
prudently, but he is much more likely to have information in regard
to the real character, projected policy and proposed relations of Mr.
Polk than any of us possibly could, and besides his interests are to
be more affected and his judgment more to be relied on than those
of any other.   I think frank communication from him is indispensable and I fear it will entail on you the necessity of a hurried trip to
Washington.   Personal conference is so infinitely better than correspondence (however free) that I would recommend by all means such
a trip on your part before you meet us here.   We have not fully determined the time of our meeting here but think it would probably be
best to avoid observation, that we come together at the meeting of
the Legislature, when many strangers will be around.   If you think
that by that time you can visit Washington and return please let
us know, as it would most materially influence our appointment with
our other friends.   I have thought a good deal on our moral course,
and tho' it may seem strange, I confess the inclination of my mind is
that we s[houl]d now do nothing and practice that hardest policy
quiescence.   We will however have time hereafter to confer fully.

The Whigs here are more completely prostrated and crestfallen
than you can possibly conceive.   It is really pitiable to see their
sunken faces and to hear their gloomy predictions.   We have not
the heart to exult and rather turn to sympathize with and shun
them.   I am not without hopes that by the practice of moderation
and wise conciliation we may win some of the erring among them
again to our fold.   Little signs of a coming rangle among them may
I think be discovered and we may be the gainers of the result.   Lyons
I think almost sure and I do not absolutely despair of our friend
Brooke, w[oul]d indeed be an acquisition.   Botts must I think lose
ground, for gentlemen cannot easily wear his collar much longer.
Nothing has transpired about Jones' intentions except an indication

of a desire on his part to get out of the way in a manner which I for one will never consent to. Cox (a friend of Mr. C[alhoun]) but the immediate representative of Jones intimated to Harvie the other day that Jones ought to be made Senator next winter. Now on you all our hopes are placed and, devil take it, if we are to be defeated by such a trimmer as Jones, I have been endeavoring and so has Harvie, to get one or two Whigs instructed in your favor, and if successful in that we think we can defy Whigs and old Hunkers too. I have a good joke to tell you on Harvie. We had taken an oyster supper together and he returned to sleep with me. We sat up very late talking of Mr. C[alhoun]'s prospects and the difficulty to be apprehended from Silas Wright, who is quite a bugbear to Harvie's mind. Having retired, about the middle of the night I was roused by a groan and a loud call—" Seddon—Seddon " in most imploring accents. Starting I called out " Harvie what on earth is the matter." " Good God, (replied he), I am so obliged to you for waking me. I had such a nightmare, and I thought that D—d fellow Silas Wright was on my breast pommeling me." I had no one to join me in the laugh, but I have not thought of the scene since without one of Hawk eyes internal chuckles. Write me soon and let me know when you can be with our little squad of good and true men, all of whom are in the very highest spirits.

Dixon H. Lewis to R. M. T. Hunter.

Senate Chamber, [Washington, D. C.], *February 1st, 1845.*

My dear Hunter: I write to drop you a suggestion, to be followed just as far as your better judgement may deem it necessary. Newton has gallantly, I think, voted for the Texas Annexation. I understand he has drawn upon him in so doing the fire of the " Whig " at Richmond, and that he feels greatly in doubt whether he has not sacrificed himself with his own Party, without propitiating the Democracy. Now as you do not intend to run for his District, but are looking to the Senate, would it not be politic in you, to evince a disposition to give quarters to Newton for what he has done, and to hold out the prospect of still further putting down opposition to him, if he still continues to do better. A shrewd friend of mine who has canvassed with Newton, thinks it would have a happy effect not only on him, but on some of his friends in the Legislature who may help you in the election of Senator " Verbum sat."

I arrived here in good health on Monday night last after having been detained by repeated attacks of sickness. I am still weak but well. Are you coming to the Inauguration? I hope so by all means. I will try and get Elmore to come on, and we will have a general consultation about matters in future. On an occasion like that I want the Calhoun wing of the Party fully pledged.

JOHN C. CALHOUN TO R. M. T. HUNTER.

WASHINGTON, [D. C.], *February 14th, 1845.*

My DEAR SIR: I have just received yours of the 11th inst., and when I inform you, that I am not yet so far recovered as to be able to leave my chamber, I am sure you will excuse me for not writing before and the brevity of the present letter.

There is no foundation, as far as I know, for the rumor, that the Commissioner of Patents[1] is to be removed. I feel confident that he will not be removed before the present administration goes out, and I suppose that there is not certainty as to Mr. Polks views in reference to him.

There is at present no dispatch to be sent to Texas. The rule I have adopted is to send all dispatches by mail, except in extraordinary cases. Should there be one of a character as to require special messages, I will with pleasure present the name of Mr. Parker to the President for the place, but I do not think it probable, that there will be.

The fate of the Texian question is still doubtful in the Senate. Were it not for Benton's humbug move its success would be most certain. Nothing is yet known as to Mr. Polk's Cabinet arrangement. I think the probability is that he will form one of entirely new members.

JOHN C. CALHOUN TO R. M. T. HUNTER.

FORT HILL, [S. C.], *March 26, 1845.*

My DEAR SIR: I regret much, that I did not see you on my way home. I spent a day in Richmond and saw and conversed freely with all our friends, both in reference to my position in relation to Mr. Polk and his administration, and the course we ought to take in relation to the portion of the inaugural, in which he speaks of the Tariff.

Personally there is no hostile feelings towards him or his administration, on my part. It is no grievance to me, personally, that he did not invite me to remain, as one of its members. If he had, I would not have accepted, but on the condition of continuing until I had completed the Texian and Oregon subjects and that it should be announced, that I remained for that purpose, at his special request. Even then, I would have felt no little hesitation, with my impression in reference to the Composition of the Cabinet and the ground taken in the inaugural on the subject of the tariff. I hold the latter to be unsound, and the former unsafe, both in reference to the Tariff and the Oregon question. In the event of the failure of the negotiation,

---

[1] Henry L. Ellsworth of Connecticut, Commissioner of Patents, 1836–1845.

its influence will be thrown on the side of recinding the joint occupancy, the inevitable effects of which will be, the loss of the Territory
and hostilities with England. She is desirous of settling the question, and does not want war with us; but would encounter it boldly;
if we should, by rescinding the Convention, make it a question of
force, who should occupy it. If on the contrary, we hold on to the
joint occupancy, and England should not rescind it, the whole Territory must become ours by the natural progress of our population;
and that in a far shorter space of time, than the most sanguine calculate. It is indeed, the only way we can obtain the whole; and if
the influence of the administration should be brought to bear efficiently and in the proper direction, the publick sentiment might be
controlled in the West, and the whole Territory secured, even if the
negotiations should fail. Composed as it is, I have no hope that it
would. Thus thinking, I had no desire to remain, and felt rather
relieved, than otherwise, that I was not invited to continue. In the
interview, I had with Mr. Polk at his request, he treated me with the
greatest respect, which left nothing to disturb our personal relations.
Thus much as to myself.

As for the publick, it is for it to decide, whether Mr. Polk's course,
in reference to me, was right or wrong, and what indications it gives,
as to the line of conduct he intends to pursue. To it and my friends,
I leave the decision. It seems, indeed, strange that one who had been
forced into the office in reference to two important negotiations by
the United voice of both parties, and who had brought one to a successful close, as far as it depended on him, and made satisfactory
progress in the other, should without the slightest objections be superceded and that without leaving time to bring to a close, the duty that
he had thus far successfully performed, and to the performance of
which he had been unanimously called, but a short time before. I
must say, that I can see but one explanation, and that is, that I stood
in the way of the restoration of the old Jackson Regime, both as to
individuals and policy. The ground taken in the inaugural is nothing, but a repetition of Jackson's judicious Tariff in different language. There is not a man in the Cabinet, who did not continue
throughout a thorough Jackson man. If Virginia stands fast on the
issue, on which Mr. Polk was elected especially in reference to the
Tariff the scheme will fail; otherwise it will terminate in the overthrow of the party and the triumph of the Whigs. I explained
fully to our friends in Richmond the ground we ought to occupy in
reference to the portion of the inaugural, that relates to that important measure, in your pending Canvass. It will not do for us
to endorse it, on the one hand, or to come, at this time, into conflict
with the administration in reference to it. Either course would be
fetid. In order to avoid both, I suggested to our friends to admit

frankly in the Canvass, that ground, taken in the inaugural was not satisfactory; that to say the least it was ambiguous; but to add, that there was no ambiguity as to their principles; that they were in favour of a revised Tariff, with no discrimination, but on revenue principles, and with a maximum not exceeding 20 per cent; that is, in a word, in favour of the compromise. And to conclude by adding, if such was the meaning of the inaugural, they would give Mr. Polk a cordial support in carrying it out; but if not, they would be constrained to oppose his views, however, reluctant; and that they would leave him to explain his meaning by his acts at the next Session.

I do hope our friends have acted accordingly. On no other ground can we safely stand on this vital question. If we give away in reference to it, all will be lost. Texas, I regard as settled, unless there should be gross mismanagement, which will leave no other living question between the parties, but the Tariff and those connected with it. Our friends by taking the ground firmly can control Virginia, and that will the administration. Otherwise, everything will fall into confusion, and the Whigs rise permantly into power. Our course may be difficult, but it is a clear one. Let what will come, we must adhere to the issue on which we succeeded at the late election. Three fourths of the whole party are opposed to a protective Tariff, either indirect or direct. The movement of England towards free trade will greatly strengthen us, especially in the North West. To restore the old Jackson Van Buren party will be impossible. I kept no journal, while in the Department of State; but will, if I shall find leisure, put down in writing the principal occurances during the period.

I hope there is no doubt of your election.

JOHN C. CALHOUN TO ———.

FORT HILL, [S. C.], *May 16th, 1845.*

MY DEAR SIR: I entirely concur in the view taken by our friends, in their consultation in Charleston, as stated in your letter, with a single exception, that of travelling this summer. My impression after a review of the whole ground is unchanged, on that point; especially that of travelling this summer. Admitting it to be expedient, I am of the impression, it ought to be deferred until next year. To be still and quiet for *the present* strikes me as the proper course.

I will visit my plantation in Alabama to see my son and his family, sometime this fall. In that case I shall extend my visit to Mobile, N[ew] Orleans, and possibly Vicksburg and farther. Another year, if my friends shall think it advisable I will yield to their opinion to visit the North and West.

The first point at present is to develop in a proper way our determination not to yield to the dictation of a Convention, and through the office holders and office seekers, the rights secured to the people of the U[nited] States by the Constitutions to elect the chief Magistrate. For that purpose after full consultation by correspondence with our Virginia friends, a pamphlet ought to be put out, stating our ground and the reasons for it in opposition to a Convention. It should appear in Virginia and be prepared by Hunter, Seddon, or some talented friend there.

A letter from you to Scott, would put the thing in motion. On its appearance, the Southern papers should be out in motion to attract public attention to the subject and in due time, the Southern Review the Literary Messenger and Bronson's Review should contain articles, of which the pamphlet should be the subject. When the publick mind in the South is sufficiently [prepared] for it, then my friends if they should choose to present my name as the peoples candidate in opposition to the Convention Candidate may do it with success, provided they determine to nail the Colours to the mast. If we are resolute and determined, the office holders and office seekers will succomb. They are a compromising race. With them a half loaf is better than none; and prospect of success is better than no prospect. In no other way, be assured my friend, can we succeed. The mercernary corps will never permit power to be put in my hands, if they can elect another. That is fixed, but had rather see me elected than an opponent from whom they can have nothing to hope. That is the philosophy of the whole affair. We can only succeed by showing them, that I am the only man of the party who can be elected, which we can easily do if our Virginia friends choose to take the stand, early and firmly. Without it, establishing newspapers travelling and every other thing is in vain. Indeed if I am to travel I would greatly prefer to do it openly as the candidate of the people and the Constitution; and under invitation from them to meet them in that character. It would be far more respectable to do it in that than any other character.

Such are my views. If you concur, you can do much to execute them. Write at once to Scott, Elmore, Hamilton and such other friends at other points, as you may think judicious.

Elmore should call a small meeting of our friends in Charleston and place the subject before them in extenso, and organize a systematic movement beginning at a few important points, and address our friends in Richmond as the Organ of the meeting on the subject of preparing and issuing a pamphlet. What is wanted is action, action, action; quiet and still but wide spread and efficient action, among those you ought to unite. I would add Elmore of E. New Orleans and Redwood Fisher of Cincinnati. He was at Washington last Winter and is efficient and faithful. He may be fully trusted. He writes well and if you would put him in possession of the line of action, I have no doubt [he would] prepare an able pamphlet suited to the Western Meridian.

You are at liberty in your correspondence if you should think proper to use my name and give such extracts from what I have written to you on the subject as you may think proper. I particularly concur in the opinion of the Charleston meeting, that retirement for me at present, is the proper position for me. I have no idea, that the mission will be offered to me on the terms you suggest, it might. If it should it would be difficult to decline, although it would be very adverse to my inclination. There is but one possible reason which as far as I can see, should in any contingency force me into publick life at this time. The Oregon question might take a turn, that might make my presence in the Senate almost indispensable. War must not grow out of it. I know it need not, or rather I ought to say needed not. Polks inaugeral has greatly embarrassed the subject, as I apprehended at the time. I have no confidence in the administration in refference to the subject.

I did my best to put him in the right direction in relation to it before he delivered his inaugeral but as it turned out in vain. I fear if he is not overruled War will be [the] consequence, a War which must end in the loss of the territory and countless disaster to the Country. The government itself will hardly survive it. I have for years kept my eyes on it and what I have said is the result of deep reflection. He can I fear be only overruled by the Senate and not by that unless the South is true to itself. If my efforts [are] necessary to prevent so great a calamity as such a war, I must meet the responsibility as great as it may be.

MARCUS MORTON [1] TO HON. JOHN C. CALHOUN.

BOSTON, [MASS.], *February 16, 1846.*

DEAR SIR: Without my consent and against my wishes I was appointed Collector of this post. I at first determined that I would not accept the office. But the importunities of my friends including almost all of the most respectable democrats in the State who seemed to think I owed it to the party, and that my refusal would be a great injury to the party did much to overcome my first determination. Then the personal request of the President being added induced me to accept.

I had twice before refused the same office and I assure you that I deeply regret that I did not now follow the dictates of my own

---

[1] A Representative in Congress from Massachusetts, 1817–1821; governor of Massachusetts, 1840–1841, 1843–1844; collector of the port of Boston, 1845–1849.

judgement. The business is not at all to my taste and in any event
I will not long remain in it.

I may be allow to say that my appointment was most favourably
received by the whole community. And were the question of con-
firmations submitted to all the people of the State, or to the democratic portion of them, or to the Whig portion of them, or to all the
business men, or to the democratic portion of them, or to the Whig
portion of them, I should have no fear of the result under the *two
thirds*, or even a three quarter's rule.

An opposition however to my appointment has been got up but I
am confident I don't say too much when I say that it owes its origin
entirely to disappointed office seekers, either men who have been removed from office or disappointed in their applications. It is not
unexpected to me that this opposition is carried to Washington and
that efforts are being made by artful and indefatigable men to induce the Senate to reject my nomination. Now however unpleasant
the office may be to me, I assure you a rejection would be a source of
deep mortification to me. I have taken no steps to induce the Senate to make a favourable decision. I have no wish to do so. My
only wish is that they should obtain the truth. I have no correspondent in Washington. I have written only two or three letters
to any members of Congress during the Session. I hear objections
are made against me, but what they are I know very little except
what I get from that most uncertain source, letter writers for papers.
I therefore presume I have very little correct information of what
occurs in relation to myself.

It is said that very strong efforts have been made to induce yourself
and your Southern Friends to vote against me. I know not how
much truth there may be in the report. But our excellent friend
Col. Pierce of N[ew] Hamshire, attached so much importance to
it that he advised me to address you on the subject. In obedience to
his advice I now take the liberty to submit their remarks to your consideration. I may have been misled by the reports; but it is reported
that I have been charged with *Abolitionism, Nativeism* and *prejudice
against yourself and your friends.*

Abolitionism.

I should be glad to have my Southern friends understand my true
position on this subject, and I would willingly abide their judgment.
I admit in the outset that I am *opposed*, (if you please) *decidedly
opposed to slavery.* But I deny most emphatically that in any way I
ever did anything to aid or encourage the abolition party or the doctrine of abolition. I have never opposed any interference with the
domestic regulations and laws of the slave-holding States. They

alone are responsible for their principles and conduct as we are for ours. As a private citizen, as a professional man, and as a judicial and executive officer, I have exerted myself to secure to our Southern brethren a full and fair execution of the laws, in relation to their slave property. While I was at the Bar, a Virginian undertook to reclaim his slave under the U[nited] S[tates] laws. But he was resisted, indicted for assault and battery on the slave and thrown into prison. No member of the Bar would appear for him. I went forward, at the hazard and loss of business and reputation, procured bail for him and with the aid of my young partner carried his case through the courts and sustained the law against passion and prejudice. The decision may be seen in the 2 of Pickerings Rep[orts] Com[monweal]th vs. Griffith.

I have for a long time been before the public in a situation which exposed me to many calls which I was under the necessity of answering; and I have written numerous letters, perhaps a hundred on this subject, yet my oponents have found only two, and these private ones, which they thought would tend to support the charge. If they had produced the others, especially those written with more care for more public occasions, they would have shown that I always opposed the organization and movements of the abolition party and all interference with the municipal affairs of the Southern and all other States. If they will refer to my official acts they will find in them evidence not to support but to refute the charge. When I was Governor in 1840 and 1843 the two parties seemed to run a race for the favour of the Abolitionists, who held the balance of power in the State, and passed several very high toned abolition and Anti-Texas resolves, some of them unanimously. These, notwithstanding the strongest importunties of some of our leading democrats I refused to approve. And now, some of the men who blamed me for not signing them, try to involve me because at the request of the Legislature, I forwarded them to their destination, or rather the secretary did under a usage and an implied authority from me.

In relation to the two private letters refer[re]d to, only extracts are published. Whether these are correct copies, I have no means of Judging. I do not mean to be understood that I think there are any material alterations. But the parts omitted would show the occasions on which they were written and that they were private and confidential. The one to Whittier was written in answer to one received long before and to which an answer had been promised. I had made repeated efforts to convince the more honest Abolitionists that their measures defeated the very object they had in view. I desired to try that argument with Whittier, who is a talented and I believe a very honest man.

The letter to Eddy was written in very great haste and very late in the night. It was expressly asked in confidence and written in confidence. Had I deemed it possible that it could ever be published I should have taken care to use different language. You will at once perceive the difference between hasty unguarded expressions used to a confidential friend and language prepared to be seen by everybody. You are doubtless aware that the Eddy letter was published in violation of the strictest confidence, and on express promise.

It may have been stated that I signed the resolve to appoint Commissioners to Charlestown and N[ew] Orleans and a law to authorize marriages between whites and blacks. If so, I can only say it is *false*.

I defy any man to produce any proof that I am an Abolitionist or ever favoured the Abolitionists: There is not a prominent man in Massachusetts against whom stronger evidence cannot be produced. I have been misunderstood as well as misrepresented; and a strong desire to set myself right has carried me quite too far in these remarks. Yet had I time I might add many more circumstances in refutation of this charge. But I trust I have said enough. I close with the assumption that no patriotic Southern man will be influenced in his vote upon a man because he is *opposed* to slavery and no Northern man will be influenced against a man because he is in *favour* of slavery.

Nativeism.

No more unfounded charge can be brought against me than this. From the days of the Alien law to the present I have always been an advocate for Naturalization law and the rights of foreigners, and especially catholics. I have heard that some quotations from a letter of mine, have been circulated with a view to ruin an impression that I am unfavourable to the catholics. It is wholly untrue, I never was influenced against any man on account of his religion catholic or protestant. Few if any men ever went farther in favour of religious liberty and perfect equality of religious denominations. I might in proof refer to many of my printed opinions while on the bench.

I was called upon to recommend a man for a Post Master in North Bridgewater. There were two candidates. One I suppose a protestant supported by nearly all the democratic citizens of the town and by the county Committee. The other of whom I knew nothing was represented to me by respectable men to be an unfit person. They said he was extremely unpopular and as causes of this said that he was a catholic and a political trimmer. I knew the Inhabitants of the town were very calvinistic and could but infer that they would be very averse to have a catholic Postmaster, as the Gentlemen stated to me. I suppose the aversion of the people to the man whether founded on prejudice or reason, formed some objection to his appointment. I therefore repeated to the Post Master what had been told me not as facts known to me, but as what had been *said* to me. A reference to my practice will test my opinion in this matter. There are in the Boston Custom House *five* or six catholics, which they will admit is their full proportion. In my removals I have not displaced a single catholic. Strong objections were made to one but in my investigation of the subject, I assure you he fared none the worse for being a catholic. It was my intention not [to] let the mans religious faith have any influence; but if it had any it was not unfavourable to the Catholic.

It has been the policy of certain office seekers, who were removed by me or who imagine that their chance of getting office will be increased by my rejection, to represent that I have been influenced by our late presidential predilections. Those who circulate this story don't believe it and I know it to be untrue. A reference to facts will show its falsity. I have removed *eight* or *ten* officers who called themselves *democrats*. Every one was for what I deemed *good cause*. It was either because he was unfaithful or incompetent or of objectionable moral character. In removals or appointments I never inquired into any mans Presidential preferences; and did not know them except in a very few cases. In my removals I happened to discharge every Van Buren man in the office. And in my appointments I happened to include a portion of the friends of all the different candidates. Untill this charge I did not know the preferences of one third of the men in office. But I have since requested one or two Gentlemen to make enquiries; and they inform me that of the men holding office under me, a *large majority* were and are *Calhoun men.*

In my official course I have been on the most friendly terms with my predecessor and have to a great extent followed his advice, especially in reference to removals. And those who have made the greatest complaint and are now the most active against me were removed by his advice and from information communicated by him.

I suppose many things have been or may be fabricated of which I never shall have knowledge. I know how indifatigable and unscrupulous my opponents are. But I cannot excuse myself in going any farther.

JOHN TYLER, JR. TO R. M. T. HUNTER.

Friday evening.
RICHMOND, VA., [*January 15, 1847.*]

MY DEAR SIR: The vote in the House of Delegates, for Senator of the United States, has just drawn to a close, and I congratulate you, most cordially, upon the result. You have received *83* votes. There were three absentees. This ensures your final election upon joint Ballot.

I need not say more. The cause of Patriotism has triumph'd.

WILLIS P. BOCOCK TO R. M. T. HUNTER.

RICHMOND, [VA.], *18 January, 1847.*

DEAR SIR: Having waited long enough for the promised letter from your farm in the summer, the failure of which I excuse because you did not reach there till the interest of the *cropping* season had passed, I venture to say a word in the hope it will be duly appreciated. In the recent election of Senator you are not to infer that all the democrats in the legislature who did not at any time vote for you are bitterly opposed to you. Smith was the strongest man of all as a first choice. How it was between Jones and yourself I do not know. His friends thot him the stronger, but I am very sure some and I think not a few of them would have preferred you next to him and would have so voted in Caucus had you there proved stronger than Jones. Such has been my information since from one or more of their number. But the Jones men having gone into Caucus, (your friends and some others holding off) and being there largely outnumbered by the Smith men, were displeased with your friends because they did not go in, in order to suffer you to be decapitated and then to go to their aid and make a nomination of Jones. In the election under these circumstances the Caucus men went against you because they were bound by the Caucus, the Smith men because their friend was the *nominee* and the opposition made by your friends was manifestly to prove his ruin, the Jones men because your friends had saved you and they had lost their man, the McDowell men at first because though generally not bound by the *Caucus* they hoped to build up a strong position for their man out of the ruins of the party organization which they saw at every discharge tumbling more and more heavily around them, and afterwards because the little fabric they attempted was demolished before it could be raised, the party men because you were not the party candidate, the I dont like to say, hunkers because your friends were Calhoun men, and·all because whigs were voting for you. After the election there was no indecent exultation on the part of your friends, or outward signs of bitterness on the part of those who were beaten. And since while some are talk[ing] to us very violently, some seem quite subdued and others profess to be rather pleased than otherwise because they say they preferred you to Smith and are glad that Smith is killed off. Woolfolk, whom I am far from disliking, swears the whigs are a better party than the Calhoun party and doubtless would say, I think I heard him say so, that he would go for both in preference to any of the *clique*, because, as he stated, Smith has done more good to the democratic party than any man in the State, and Botts next.

The result of what I have to say is that while there may be exceptions you are not to look upon the democratic party in the legislature as hostile to *you*, or as doubting your democracy. And the why I say it is that possibly in moments when you are alone it may be a subject of regret that so many of your political friends are found holding out against you as if particularly hostile to your elevation. I do not think the opposition was aimed at you *personally*. It was a compound of the ingredients I have mentioned with perhaps some others. I hope and believe the effects and consequences will be beneficial, but come what may your friends will not regret the course they have taken or shrink from its responsibilities.

After two or three weeks, if you can come without inconvenience, I think a visit to this city would not be disadvantageous nor disagreeable.

R. S. GARNETT TO R. M. T. HUNTER.

CAMP NEAR MONTEREY, MEX[ICO], *January 30th, 1847.*

MY DEAR COUSIN: I have just seen by the papers which reached us to-day, that a bill has been introduced in the lower house by Mr. Haralson[1] to raise an additional regiment of Dragoons and nine of Infantry to serve five years or during the War. I take it that this is to be a regular force; and I need hardly add that I should be much gratified, and much obliged to you, if you could succeed in securing me promotions in any one of them, should the Bill pass both houses. What are your opinions as to the permanency of this additional force? Will it be retained after the War, or in case of a reduction, will it stand an equal chance with the regular force now in service, of being retained. This latter was the case with the officers in the reduction of the Army after the termination of the last War with Great Britain, and it would seem fair to expect such a course in this case.

As the increase is so great, I should like, if possible, to get the rank of a major particularly if it should be in the Infantry. My preference is, of course, for the Dragoons or mounted service, but should the number of applicants for that corps, greatly decrease my chances for high ranks, I would fall back upon the Infantry. The recommendatory letters which were in the hands of General Jones during my application for a Commission in the mounted Riflemen, are now in my possession, but as they produced so little effect on that occasion, I have not deemed it worth the while to forward them again. Should they be necessary, they can be forwarded at once. If necessary, please advise me on this point.

---

[1] A Representative in Congress from Georgia, 1843–1851.

The army is earnestly hoping that Congress will adopt the suggestions of the Secretary of War in regard to the additional major for each regiment and the *retired list*. The army is almost paralysed by the imbecility of its old officers—men who have already worn out in the service the ordinary energies allotted to mankind and Congress could not possibly pass at this time an act which would more essentially benefit the army than that establishing a retired list, and in saying this, I feel safe in adding that it is the uniform opinions of the whole army.

What has become of that *bronze medal* that we were to receive from Congress? I think it died a natural death in the Senate. Will it be revived this session? If it should, for God's sake, give it a lift, for I assure you I had rather wear one of those stars on my coat, than to receive a half dozen of those empty brevets. And in this feeling I believe, the army generally agrees with me.

We also see by the papers that the President is meditating the appointment (if authorized by law) of a "Lieut. General" to Conduct the War and a "high Commission" to treat for peace. Gods! what "a fire in" Genl. Scott's "War." This is more, I expect, than he bargained for when he left Washington, and may probably cause him after taking a "hasty plate of soup" at Vera Cruz to return. The Genl. (Scott) has played the devil with Genl. Taylor both in front and "rear." He has withdrawn from the Command of the latter upwards of 9,000 men, and has left upon this line (from Mondova to Tampico) but 5,000 volunteers, and a few regular artillery and cavalry, while we have a force of 25,000 Mexicans in our immediate front. If Santa Anna possesses the smallest degree of energy we are certainly now at his mercy and if he omits this opportunity of striking a blow, he deserves to fail. With all respect to the "bone and sinew" of the country, I should dislike very much to go into a general battle with volunteers alone. They have not, and justly I think, sufficient confidence in their officers and as soon as one man runs, the rest follow to see what the matter is. We have already lost, in front of Saltillo, a party of some 90 mounted men under the new order of things, and God knows what may be in store for us a few weeks hence. A remarkable fact about this whole matter is that although General Scott left Washington on the 18th of November for this country, General Taylor has not yet received from the War Department any notifications that General Scott has been authorized to call upon him for troops, a period of more than two months. General Taylor is, of course, much annoyed at this treatment and quite at a loss how to understand it. He leaves this place to-morrow for Saltillo, near which point his H[ea]d Q[uarte]rs will be established.

HENRY A. WISE[1] TO R. M. T. HUNTER.

RIO, [BRAZIL], *May 12th, 1847.*

MY DEAR HUNTER: Y[ou]rs of Feb[ruar]y 8th was rec[eive]d in the last few days. Whatever I may have said in my letter to Mr. Calhoun or any one else, I wish you to understand that I did not mean to "count you out" of the list of my friends; and, though I would have been glad to have heard from you more frequently and fully, yet I was too well informed of your good offices in my behalf to doubt for a moment that you have been warmly one of my best friends in my absence, and I justly acquitted you of all blame for not reporting regularly what you had done for me, when it was enough that you *had done* all that I could expect or require. I thank you sincerely, and as the Lord liveth and will allow, I will repay. The affair with this Gov[ernmen]t has now become serious, and as you are to my heart content one of my own Senators in Congress, and as another friend too is your colleague from Virginia, I desire to inform you both fully of the exact posture of our relations with Brazil. Three causes have existed, each sufficient in itself, for my rupture with the Imperial Gov[ernmen]t.

1st. I have earnestly endeavored to snatch our flag away from the uses of the Brazilian African Slave-trade.

2ndly. I have urged with pertinacity claims of our citizens to the am[oun]t of a million nearly, the most of which had been grossly neglected for 20 years, and some of which were never presented at all until the time of Mr Calhoun in the Dep[artmen]t of state and my time in the Mission.

3rdly. I have firmly protected our citizens resident here against the barbarous assaults and false imprisonments of a corrupt police whose constant practice is to extort bribes from foreigners under the cloak of keeping the peace.

Under the latter head was the case of L[ieutenan]t Davis of the Corvette Saratoga. I wont bore you with its details. It was a gross outrage and insult. I acted decisively and promptly. Suffice it to say that the Pres[iden]t and Sec[retar]y of State sustained me, as they have ever done throughout my mission with effect. This case occurred on the 31st of October. On the 15th Nov[embe]r and 2nd Dec[embe]r, 1846, the days of the festas for the baptism of the Imp[eria]l Princess and for the birth of the Emperor Dom Pedro II, Comdre Roupeau declined to interchange salutes. This excited the most inflamed ire of Imperialism. Appropos enough, just as my dispatchers were going home informing our Gov[ernmen]t of the Davis affair, the President's letter to the Emperor was coming out congratulating him on the birth of the Imperial

---

[1] Wise was minister of the United States to Brazil, 1844–1847.

Princess. It found me prostrate on a bed of sickness. On the 18th
of Feb[ruar]y I was well enough to address the Min[ister] for
F[oreign] Aff[ai]rs, Barad de Cayru, a note saying I was instructed
to present in person to H[is] Majesty this letter of the Pres[iden]t
of the U[nited] S[tates] and asked when I could be allowed the
opportunity of doing so. The reply on the 25th was that H[is]
M[ajesty], the Emperor would not receive the letter at all from my
hands until he heard the result of the Davis affairs at Washington;
but the Minister of F[oreign] Aff[ai]rs w[oul]d receive the letter
at my hands. To this I returned what I deemed a most proper
reply: abided by the decision of my own Gov[ernmen]t and declined
to present the Presid[en]t's letter to any one but the Emperor himself. On the 10th of April the decision of the Pres[iden]t and
cabinet at Washington was rec[eive]d here. The Emperor was
absent on a northern tour. I waited and reflected maturely on my
course and on the 21st of April addressed to the Minister for
F[oreign] Aff[ai]rs the following note:—after informing him that
I had rec[eive]d the decision of my gov[ernmen]t, I said:—" Whilst
the undersigned cannot but be gratified that his own course has been
not only approved but complimented by the Pres[iden]t of the
U[nited] S[tates], he, at the same time, feels more deep cause of
congratulation, on account of the public good of both countries,
in the happy result that " the controversy " (quoting from Mr.
Buchanan) " has been settled after explanations from the Brazilian
Gov[ernmen]t through their Minister at Washington, which were
entirely satisfactory to the Gov[ernmen]t of the U[nited] S[tates]."
The Pres[iden]t, through the Sec[retar]y of State, has informed
Mr. Lisboa that " the whole occurrence, so far as the U[nited]
S[tates] are concerned, shall henceforward be buried in oblivion;"
and, he has said to the Undersigned " that he relies with confidence,
the " amende honorable " having been made by Brazil, that " his "
conduct towards the Brazilian authorities will be guided by a desire
to restore harmony and promote friendship between the two countries whose mutual interests are so deeply identified with each other."
The Undersigned will, assuredly do all in his power, not to disappoint this just and flattering confidence of the Pres[iden]t, and he,
at once, tenders to the Imp[eria]l Gov[ernmen]t every disposition
to conform cordially to this friendly instruction, and to enter upon
a new interchange of kindness and civility. He regrets that there
was any occasion for misunderstanding; and, with a view to remove
all causes of ill feeling for the future, he reminds Y[ou]r Ex[cel-
lenc]y that there are many matters of business and of etiquette now
pending between the Court of Brazil and this Legation. He had,
months before October last, requested to be recalled: that request
is likely soon to be complied with, and in the meantime, he is in-

structed especially to procure the payment of the indemnities due to the Citizens of the U[nited] States, which have been so long pending. And he, therefore, again brings these claims to Y[ou]r Ex[cellenc]y's serious consideration &c &c, &c." On the 3rd inst H[is] M[ajesty] the Emperor opened the Session of the Gen[era]l Legislative Assembly and announced in his speech that the Davis affair was *not* adjusted, and that the Senators and Deputies might rest assured that it *should* be concluded in a manner comporting with the National dignity. On the 26th of Ap[ri]l he had dismissed Mr. Lisboa from the diplomatic corps for making an "amende honorable" to our Gov[ernmen]t. On the 4th inst the Min[ister] for F[oreign] Aff[ai]rs sent me a note by order of H[is] M[ajesty] saying that he having disapproved of the act of his Minister at Washington, he considered the settlement of the affair still pending between the two Gov[ernmen]ts, and in the mean time the interruption of H[is] M[ajesty']s relations with me would continue. I made no reply and shall make none to this note until the arrival of my successor, Mr. Tod, and have so informed Mr. Buchanan. And I have ventured to suggest to the Cabinet that *now*, more than ever, a bold and decisive course is required on their part.

The very insolence of Imperialism has prevailed in the Councils of Brazil respecting this affair. They have recalled Mr. Lisboa, for reason of a proper apology for both outrage and insult to the U[nited] States. It behooves the Pres[iden]t, then, to decline receiving any other Minister as long as the act of Mr. Lisboa is disapproved; and he is bound to recall the Min[ister] of the U[nited] S[tates] at this Court, for the reason that the Emperor refused to accord customary privileges to their Min[ister] now here on account of acts approved and applauded by his own Gov[ernmen]t.

To-day, the 13th, the Barad de Cayru Min[ister] for F[oreign] Aff[ai]rs has come out with a long relatonio (report)* to the Legislative Chambers of the whole affair. His Synopsis is a most *garbling lie*, to say the least of it. I shall wait patiently for Tod and demand my pass ports and tell him plainly what he ought to do. Thus, this affair, small in its beginning, not bigger than a man's hand in the horizon, has assumed serious importance in its present phase. It is no longer the bare imprisonment of a L[ieutenan]t and three Seamen. I beg you to call for the whole correspondence up to the meeting of the next Congress.

We expect Tod in July. I desire very much to return home and find no fault with the Pres[iden]t's course towards me as I understand it out here. On the Contrary I am his debtor, and "I will repay." You know, I don't know that you do, how far I would go now to make Mr. Calhoun, Presid[en]t, but I regretted nothing so much as his note about Mr. Ritchie. That was unlike him. On his own acc[oun]t I was exceedingly sorry. If we cant get Calhoun, what shall we do? You need not answer this, I shall be off hence as soon as possible. I shall look well around me when I get home.

JAMES A. SEDDON TO R. M. T. HUNTER.

RICHMOND, [VA.], *June 16th, 1848.*

MY DEAR SIR: For my long silence, I fear I have no better excuse to proffer than that I am confoundedly lazy and have not been able to summon energy enough to grapple with the great difficulties and embarrassments of politics in which you are naturally absorbed. That I shake off habitual indolence now is rather due to the claims of friendship than to any interest on my own part in the vexed questions of the times. Our common and very gallant young friend, Caskie,[1] finds himself since the Baltimore nominations in an embarrassing position. Having been actively instrumental in the introduction and adoption of the resolutions known as the Virginia platform, he feels himself specially pledged not to swerve from their committals but to carry them resolutely out. At the same time he is, I believe, thoroughly convinced that true policy and the best interest of the South will be eventually subserved by active support being granted by the State Rights men in this State, in the coming canvass to the Baltimore nominees. Their is no doubt whatever in my own opinion that such is truly the case in respect to the party here but I am even more clear that it is especially important to Caskie's own prospects, now and remote that in the coming contest he should not observe an unprofitable neutrality but cast himself vigorously into the meter. He has not however been able positively to satisfy himself that he can honestly and conscientiously after the declarations of the V[irgini]a resolutions take this active part. Under these circumstances, it has occurred to me that possibly by a visit to Washington, he might obtain either such information in relation to Cass, real opinions or such insight into the state of parties and their relation to the subject of our Southern Institutions as to remove his scruples and start him with a clear conscience on the right track, and considering as I really do, his prospect very seriously dependant on his course *now*, I have advised him by all means to go on and have full and frank conversation with you and other friends. Do try, if it be practicable, to satisfy his honest scruples and endeavor to make it the interest of some of Cass' confidential friends, if they honestly can, to reveal his position satisfactorily. I am earnest about this, because apart from a general and cordial wish for John's advancement, I in common with many others look to me [him] specially just now as the best and most available opponent of Botts

---

[1] John Samuels Caskie, a Democrat of the strict construction school; represented Virginia in Congress, 1851–1859.

next spring. I have eschewed utterly, having no taste for a reputation of popular gratitude, and can and will not if I can help it be a candidate. I honestly believe that John is the most popular and available candidate but be that as it may with my resolution, he is the only one who. can run with a chance of success. Neutrality in the present canvass would of course preclude his selection and on this account, you see the importance of his being satisfied. Rely upon it, if he can be placed in Congress he will do good service to the South and the State Rights party and he must not be lightly sacrificed.

For my own part I have no difficulty in supporting Gen[era]l Cass on the score of the slavery question. I am inclined to think him very trusty if not exactly right on the territorial question and his position, affiliation with and to Wilmot proviso men and passed course give me abundant security that the South will be safe under his presidency. Indeed, as Caskie will more fully explain to you, I think the events of the times are combining wonderfully to aid and strengthen our Southern Institutions. I feel more secure about them than I have for years past and that security will I believe be much more certain by the election of Cass than Taylor. In all other respects except one Cass is decidedly to be preferred. That one is his western Radicalism about our foreign relation, which amid the whirl of revolutions abroad may be very complex and delicate. I distrust him on this I confess, but suppose I must gulp it down and hope for the best. The responsibilities of the presidency will do much to sober and steady the excesses of a man especially cautious and perhaps bound—at least I trust so.

You must and I suppose will support the nominee. Indeed in your position no alternative exists unless you wish to resign. You would have no Constituancy and no recognized position. Some pain I know must be experienced by the position thus forced on you, but I rejoice to think it the last dilemma of the kind to which you will be exposed. Neither you nor I can affiliate with the Whigs or give them the aid of our forbearance. I wish our friends in S[outh] Carolina would think and act with us, but if they cannot, for God sake invoke them not at this critical time to form even the most transcient alliance with the Whigs. If they do, permanent annexation will be the inevitable consequence.

MAXIMILLIAN SCHELE DE VERE [1] TO R. M. T. HUNTER.

FRANKFURTH, [GERMANY], *June 23d, 1848.*

DEAR SIR: The great kindness which you have of late as always shown me, encourages me to make the following communication

---

[1] Maxmillian Schele De Vere was born in Sweden, 1820, educated in Germany, and came to America in 1843. In 1844 he was made professor of modern languages in the University of Virginia, where he served continuously for 50 years. He died May 10, 1898.

which I beg you to consider simply as a proof of my desire to show you my sense of such obligations.

At Paris I found Mr. Rush most completely indifferent to the movements of Germany and heard there at the Prussian Embassy that Mr. Donelson as well as Mr. Stiles were not inclined to leave their post and to go to Frankfurth. Here however I find things in a far more interesting and advanced state than I expected. By means of former connections and the kindness of the American consul I obtained access to their provisional Parliament as well as to the person of their distinguished president, Mr. von Gagern.[1] At an interview which I had this morning with him, he declared with his usual frankness that he felt confident, an overwhelming majority in the Parliament would at the taking of the question, which will be some day next week, decide in favor of a constitutional monarchy. He himself does not believe that this resolution will be accepted by Germany without a civil war; he considers however even this as a better state of things than the anarchy which would inevitably follow the declaration of a Republic. The Central Power, also only a provisional power until the first regular Parliament shall have fully digested a written Constitution is to be vested in either one or three persons. Mr. v[on] Gagern and both, the rights and the Centres are in favor of one and this the Archduke John of Austria, a man of openly proclaimed liberal views, extremely popular where known but not known beyond his little Tyrol and one who has as yet given no guarantees for his capacity to rule a German Empire in such times with wisdom and energy. Others wish a Triumvirate, adding to this prince an old but much esteemed Prince, William of Prussia, uncle of the King and a Prince of Bavaria.

Only the extreme Left desire a Republic. The present body, most commonly called German Parliament is thus elected. The provisional fifty men in Frankfurth established and proclaimed the necessity of such a body to give Germany a constitution. The different governments, compelled by the force of public opinion and domestic revolutions agreed to it, published laws of election and sent their delegates. These now hold that they have to treat not with the German nation as such but with their respective governments. Hence the Central Power also is not to be elected by the people but appointed by the sovereigns of Germany. It is to last only until a final settlement of all constitutional questions; they consider however this latter business so important, requiring so much reflection and time, how German! that a second provisional Power is required.

Among their Committees is one for Volks-wirth-schafts; this is subdivided into several branches one of which has for its special task the agreement on leading principles for a united system of commerce

---

[1] Heinrich Wilhelm August Gagern, 1799–1880.

for all Germany. At the head of this Sub Committee is Baron Roenne, whose departure for Washington seems to me, in spite of his own wishes, very certain. They have a decided majority in favor of a general system; measures have already been agreed upon to reconcile the interests of the sea-shore towns like Hamburg &c who wish for free trade with those of the manufacturing districts like Westphalia &c who seek protection in a tariff. The Zollverein is here at least considered as having, historically, fulfilled its duties and to be superseded by a German Verein. This I understand to be a most momentous question for the United States; Ras. Roenne has been selected for the Union as most conversant with the interests of both countries and will naturally drive a very hard bargain. It is in this view principally though not alone that the absence of an American agent is most deeply regretted by all who have an interest in our country. Col. Mann does not understand or speak German and is in so bad health as to be prevented from attending any meeting. The American Consul is very old and by gout chained to his arm chair; thus as anxious as unable to do his duty. Mr von Gagern has repeatedly expressed his hopes that at least, when the Central Power is established, which *may* be in two weeks, a representative of the U[nited] S[tates] will be here to give countenance to poor Germany and to take care of the interests of his own country.

The American name, I am glad to find, has never stood higher, everywhere are works and pamphlets in bookstores and on centre tables on our Institutions, and almost every orator points to them as a glorious example.

If I found in France most unequivocal mobocracy and the Republic considered, even by men like Lamartine and Thiers, only as a " pis aller " and the only means to preserve momentarily peace and order, I am truly grieved to find Germany so generally unprepared for a Republic. Republican and Demagogue are identic and both contain a strong mixture of Communism and Fourierism. They are lost in Theorems and debate for days on the true meaning of a republican head at the head of a constitutional Monarchy! The members of the Right proclaim from the rostrum that they are proud to be called by their sovereigns " their faithful loyal subjects," the Left proclaim the necessity of decapitating all sovereigns and of the slaughter of some thousand human lives before order can be restored.

War with Russia is everywhere considered inevitable. The damage in Bohemia has been fearful; more fearful is, that the Emperor of Russia is expected to avail himself of this opportunity to protect the Slaves in Germany and thus to interfere. Russian troops are along the Eastern frontier within an hour's march. Some hope that such a war, a common calamity, would best unite all Germany; others fear the Radicals might avail themselves of the necessity to demand

more than would be desirable. It is in every respect a fearful crisis
for the whole Continent and poor Germany seems now also to be
destined to be the heart of Europe which feels most and suffers most,
whilst on its vast plains, where all momentous questions for Europe,
from the Huns to the Reformation—War and from Frederick 2 to
Leipsic have been decided, a new and fearful struggle is decided.

You will, I hope, pardon this uncalled for letter. Should you or
any of your friends have a wish to hear of what is doing and what is
contemplated in Germany, I would be most happy to furnish such
information as may be in my hands. A letter addressed to the care
of the U[nited] S[tates] Legation in Berlin, will always reach me.

RICHARD BROOKE GARNETT[1] TO R. M. T. HUNTER.

NEW ORLEANS, [LA.], *December 28, 1848.*

DEAR SIR: It is with great reluctance that I trouble you on a subject which does not come within the sphere of your duties, but without further apology I will lay the matter before you, and leave you to
judge of its propriety.

It is doubtless known to you that quite a number of officers of the
army have used political and other influences to get brevets for
services during the Florida and Mexican Wars, and I know in *some
instances*, where they were not very deserving of this honor. Now
as this has become, (I am sorry to say), rather a general practice and
those who have too much delicacy *to ask for compliments*, see themselves out stripped and ranked by their less scrupulous companions,
I think it but right to put in a word for my friends who belong to the
former class.

Neither of those for whom I would make interest are from our
state, (You see I do not intend to bring in a very formidable list,
there being but two), and therefore have no particular claims upon
you, yet when you have heard their cases stated, I hope you will be
kind enough to exert yourself in their behalf. If you find that it
will not be in your power to act in this matter, will you at least be
kind enough to bring it to the notice of their Senators or representatives, who may be induced to take the necessary steps to secure the
object in question.

The first officer I would mention is 2d Lieu[tenan]t, A. D. Nelson,
son of Dr. Nelson, of Maysville, K[entuck]y. We were classmates at
West Point, graduated the same time and entered the same Regiment
the 6th Infantry. He has now been *seven years* and upwards in the
army and by bad luck has reached no higher grade than that named
above. This, however mortifying and discouraging, does not entitle

---

[1] A brigadier-general in the Confederate army; killed in action at Gettysburg, July 3, 1863.

him to a brevet, but it does to some commiseration, and when I add that he served under Gen[era]l Scott during the whole of the campaign of the Valley of Mexico, led a company at the battles of Churubusco and Molino del Rey and behaved gallantly on both occasions, as I have heard officers of his own and other regiments say, then I confidently believe and hope he may obtain some advancement for his services. Such has been the slowness of his promotion that he is now ranked by officers who have graduated several years after him, and indeed by some who were never at the military academy and that entered the army during the last War. He was also grievously disappointed last fall when a vacancy had occurred among the captaincies, and he confidently expected to succeed to his 1st Lieutenancy, when Major Woods, who had left our Regiment to accept a majority in one of the New ten Regiments, was put back at the reduction, when peace was declared. The other is Robert P. Maclay of P[ennsylvani]a, who belongs to the 8th Infantry, with the rank of 1st Lieutenant. He was wounded at the battle of Rescaca de la Palma and his name placed on Gen[era]l Taylor's list of brevets, but by some oversight was left out.

I have observed it to be a universal custom during the Fl[orid]a and Mexican War to confer brevets on officers who were wounded in battle and indeed other officers of Maclay's Regiment, who were struck by his side were brevetted and he overlooked. It is due to both of these gentlemen to say that they have no knowledge whatever of my intention to endeavor to enlist influence in their favor. I will conclude by stating that an *intimate acquaintance* with both of them, warrents me in assuring you, that no honor which may be conferred on either of them will ever be tarnished by any conduct of theirs, and also, that I will always feel extremely obliged to you for whatever trouble you may take in this affair. Dr. and Mrs. Hitchcock passed through N[ew] O[rleans] a few days since, with their little daughter. All were well. Lilly is a very sweet and interesting child. The "Asiatic Asphyxia" (as the doctors call it) is prevailing to considerable extent in the city but is confined chiefly to the lower orders. Many citizens, and nearly *all* the visitors have left town which makes it look very gloomy for the season. I manage to keep cool in spite of the panic. Gen[era]l Brooke is at Pensacola, whither he went on a tour of inspection. He will remain I expect until the cholera abates.

I am sorry to learn from home that your health had been feeble, but I hope it is restored by this time. Remember me kindly to your wife and the rest of your family if you please.

THOMAS RITCHIE TO R. M. T. HUNTER.

(*In confidence.*)

WASHINGTON, D. C., *April 30*, [*1849?*].

DEAR SIR: I am certain beyond the possibility of a doubt, that the Clique of John C. Rieves & Co. are artfully and mischievously employed in cancelling the present contract for the Public Printing, in order to participate in the profits of the work at the old profitable price. I have no doubt that Benton's Resolution is the opening of the attack, and Wentworth of the House, a man of no principles, is engaged in the same combination. It is Benton, Van Buren, John C. Rieves, and the Free Soil Interests vs. the Washington Union.

John C. Rieves is the man, in conjunction with Mr. Blair of whom Heiss and myself purchased *bona fide* the whole establishment of the Globe out, in 1845, for $35,000, all paid. Yet such is his faithlessness, such his voracity for money (though he has realized that reasonable profit of his own, for 120 to 150,000, Dollars, and though he has now two profitable jobs annually with Congress) that he is artfully to chase us out of this work in the most insidious manner.

I state these facts frankly to you, presuming so much upon your friendship, as to defeat this unhallowed and dishonorable trick of John C. Rieves.

If I have mistaken our relations, destroy this note, and I will never trouble you again.

[P. S.] You may show this note to Butler, or to any other Senator in your sound and personal discretion.

THOMAS AP C. JONES TO R. M. T. HUNTER.

The wants of California immigrants considered and means for supplying them suggested by Commodore Thomas ap C. Jones, Commander in Chief Pacific Squadron.

SAN FRANCISCO, [CAL.], *December, 1849.*

At the close of the second season of the *Golden harvest* of California, and after a thorough examination of the great question of demand and supply needful to sustain the present, and rapidly increasing population of California, I venture on some suggestions based on personal observation, having during the past summer visited several of the Gold-Diggins, and traversed the Vallies of the Sacremento and San Joaquin, from Benecia, via Feather to Juba river, and from the latter, via Bear Creek, American, Consemna, Makolennes, and Calevera, to Stockton, and thence *Livermores* Ranches, through the valley of the Monte Diablo to Martinez, on the straits of Parquines *opposite to Benecia.*

The present population of Upper California is estimated at 150,000. I do not think it is so great, for although the inpouring has been incessant by every avenue of approach during the year 1849, many who arrived from Oregon, the Pacific Isles, and the South American States, have returned again, and not a few from our own Atlantic States have gone back; many 'tis true will return in the Spring with largely increased numbers, so that it is more than probable that the population of California at the close of 1850, will quadruple its present number, which I set down at this time in round numbers to 100,000, exclusive of Indians; consequently provision has to be made for the subsistence of 400,000 inhabitants in the State of California for the year 1851, and for three fourths of that number for the approaching year 1850.

With the exception of fresh beef, and a very scanty supply of potatoes and other vegetables, the inhabitants of California, be their number large or small, must at least for two or three years to come, and I may say, for all time to come, that is long as (the placers) continue to remunerate the Diggers, as shown by the exports of 1849, or until Negro slavery to till the soil is admitted in the State, Californians must depend upon foreign supplies, not only for bread, but almost every necessary, as well as all luxuries of life. Supposing all the ships employed in the California trade to average 3,500 barrels burthen, and that each white inhabitant of California consume annually one barrel, or 200 lbs. of flour, which is too low an estimate when we consider that 7/10 of the population is composed of able bodied robust *young working men*, then we have employment for 114 ships to supply bread alone; and an equal number will at least be required to supply salted pork, which must also be imported. Then for groceries, dry goods, furniture, and all other necessaries of life, for lumber and houses, tools and implements, machinery, &c., &c., there will be required some 400 more, making an average of near 800 ships of 350 tons burthen for the year 1850 and of at least 1000 or 1500, for 1851.[1]

As regards the Ocean carriers nothing is to be feared, the ships and produce of all the world will pour in their contributions; but how, and by what means three millions of tons of goods, and articles of first necessity are to find their way from the *One Port of Entry San Francisco* to the consumers on the Sacramento and San Joaquin rivers, and their numerous tributaries, and from thence to Miners

---

[1] Since these estimates were made reference to the custom-house records show, that between April 12th, 1849, and January 29th, 1850, 805 vessels, exclusive of Steamers and Men of War, measuring 284,238 tons, entered at San Francisco, and from which 39,888 passengers were landed. During the same period about 4,000 by steamers and a like number from Mexico, Lower California, Oregon, and overland from the Eastern States added, and we have the aggregate 88,000 immigrants between the 12th of April, 1849, and 29th of January, 1850, may safely be set down at 120,000. [Note in original.]

along the base of the Siera Neveda is a question of the gravest importance, and one upon which, in my opinion the Executive and Legislative branches of the General Government cannot bestow too much consideration, as *action, prompt,* and *efficient action* at an early period of the present Session of Congress *can* alone provide the ways and means, by which the Miners of California may be supplied with the necessaries of life, for the next, and succeeding winter.

Reference to the annexed Memoir marked A "The Bay of San Francisco and its Harbors" will show that the only Port of Entry authorised by law on the coast of California, San Francisco, is *not the best* nor even a convenient nor safe Port for discharging cargoes, and the accompanying notes "*New York of the Pacific* re-visited" marked B. will further show conclusively that above the Straits of Pasquines there is no practicable, convenient navigation for *sea-going ships;* consequently *San Francisco* the present port of Entry, and Benecia on the North side of the above Straits, must divide the Ocean trade of California.

The former Port with all its natural defects by reason of *adventitious* circumstances will always supply the Eastern Arm of the Bay of San Francisco, and the Vallies of San Jose and San Juan, while all goods to be consumed in the great Basin of the Sacremento and San Joaquin, and the Placer which stretches along the Eastern limits of that Basin from the head waters of the Sacremento to the rivers Stanislaw, Goualame, and Mercedes, will be transhipped from Benecia by river Steamers to Sacremento City 90 miles up the Sacremento river, and to Stockton equally distant on the San Joaquin, and from there principal rivers, Depots at no very distant day, by Rail roads into every hill and "*Renagon,*" from which gold may be dug, or, was here.

A correct map of California will show that from San Francisco to Sacremento City via Sutters-fort through the Bays of San Francisco and San Pablo, through the Straits of Parquines, Suisun Bay and the river Sacremento is about 130 miles, and nearly the same distance to Stockton.

By reason of rough water and strong currents in the Bays of San Francisco and San Pablo, none but stanch steamboats of good power, can with certainty or safety *carry* cargoes through those stormy Bays, consequently boats best adapted for the Bay, could not ascend the rivers higher than Sacremento City and Stockton; nor can any boats so employed compete successfully with like boats plying between the *river depots and Benecia,* seeing that Benecia is 35 miles nearer to Stockton, and Sacremento City, than is San Francisco, and situated on the Straits of Parquines, avoids all the dangers, delays and inconveniences of navigation as well as the delay and expense attending the trans-shipment or landing of cargoes at the inconvenient Port of San Francisco.

The saving of 30 miles of distance in each passage is *60 miles each trip*, is not the only, nor the most important advantage Benecia has over San Francisco as a Port of Entry to supply the inhabitants of the Mineing districts.

The accompanying Memoirs already cited show the natural advantages, and disadvantages of both places. Since those observations were made, the 1st Class Steamer Senator and several of smaller size, brought out in pieces, and put up at Benecia, and other places have been put on the Bay and rivers. All but the Senator have disappointed their owners, and so far as navigating the Bays, and for want of power to stem the circuit of the rivers, have proved failures. The Senator a boat of great power, but too long (240 ft.) and drawing too much water (9 ft.) can only make two trips per week, *carrying full cargoe* between San Francisco and Sacramento City, stopping only 15 min[utes] to land passengers at Benecia; the same boat plying between Benecia and Sacramento City would with equal ease make three trips per week, allowing an entire day for receiving and discharging cargoe at each place. This difference of time is not so much owing to the difference of distance (35 miles) as from the difficulty of navigation presented by Suisun Bay which renders day light necessary to pass through in safety with the smallest sized Craft.

Benecia situated on the confines of Suisun Bay, vessels from thence bound up, would need only an hours day light to take them clear of the *Shoals*, then the navigation is free, and the rivers may be run with safety during the night.

. Descending Steamers will leave Sacramento City in the night, with time enough only to reach Suisun Bay by day-break, and will land passengers at Benecia always in time for *early breakfast*, so that between those two points, men of business will travel by night, and without the loss of a single business hour, but to continue on to San Francisco must ever make a large encroachment upon the day, and after arriving at San Francisco, there will be no time to transact business in season for a return boat the same day. Consequently the business man must remain over night at San Francisco, and expend the next day in returning or waiting for conveyance back to Sacramento City, thus showing that what may be done between Benecia and Sacramento City without the loss of a single business hour, will generally require two days, and three nights, between San Francisco and Sacramento City. This must always be the case with the transportation of goods, and is strictly true as regards travelling.

From these facts let.us look to the effect upon trade, but particularly upon the cost of supplying the consumers out of whose pockets, after all must come, all costs charges &c. Here then it is shown beyond all contradiction, and beyond cavil, that if one freight steamer can make two trips per week between San Francisco and Sacremento City, a like Steamer can with equal certainty make three trips per week between Benecia and Sacremento City. It follows then as a natural consequence, that the tri-weekly steamer can afford to carry freight and passengers at much lower rates than a Semi-weekly vessel of like capacity and expense, the difference I set down at about one third; and in reference to the points compared it will be all of that. The average rate of freight between the Port of San Francisco and Sacremento City for the year 1849, will show a cost of three dollars per one hundred pounds or $6 per barrel of flour, or an equivalent in bulk or weight.

Assume then that the demand for the supplies of the Sacremento Basin for the year 1850, of every description should not exceed 1,000,000 barrels in bulk at the present rate of freight from San Francisco to Sacremento City, the freight alone between these two points would be $6,000,000 whilst between Benecia and Sacremento City the same amount of goods, with equal, or greater profits to the carriers might be trans-shipped for $4,000,000 *showing a clean* saving of $2,000,000 to the *consumers*. Doubtless the competition will ere many months greatly reduce freight on inland transportation, but many years must pass away before a barrel of flour, or salt provision, can or will be taken from San Francisco to Sacremento City for much less than three dollars, but it matters not how low freight may fall, since it is manifest that however low transportation may be between San Francisco and the Upper Depots of the San Joaquin and Sacremento rivers, *Benecia can always afford transportation 33¼ per ct lower than San Francisco.*

Tis true that San Francisco is two hours nearer the ocean, than is Benecia, if that be deemed any advantage, it is entirely balanced by the *Superior harbor of the latter.* Ships once moored at Benecia are perfectly secure against any, and every wind; and even now as little as is generally known of the comparative merits of Benecia and San Francisco, ship-owners in Boston and New York will deliver freight at Benecia at lower rates, than at San Francisco, because they have no difficulty in effecting insurance at the usual rates, to discharge at Benecia, *whilst no insurance office* in England or the U[nited] States will sign a Policy for any vessel to lay at San Francisco.

The question again occurs, how, and by what means is the immense amount of imports into California to find their way to the consumers in the interior of the country? this is a question which Congress alone can solve. At its last Session little was known of the actual condition of California, nor of her wants, or means of supplying those wants. Another year has cleared up many doubts, and brought much light to bear upon the subject, the most important of which is, the inexhaustible Mineral wealth of California. Not only is that true as regards the inexhaustible store of gold, but silver and quick silver are of the richest quality, is known to abound in many parts of the territory, convenient to navigation, *and the entire dependance of the Miners upon distant countries, for all the necessaries of life.* The true and natural solution to the above question, will be found in the principles of free competition in trade and commerce.

Why compell immigrants from the States, who peril their lives, and exhaust their means in crossing the icy barriers which seperates the Eastern States from California's Gold-field, to pay *tribute* to the amount of Millions of dollars per annum, for the poor priveledge of using an unsafe, and inconvenient Port of Entry, when there are in every respect, better, and more convenient Ports, *nearer the consumers,* only requiring an Act of Congress to make them Ports of Entry. Abolish the Monopoly now enjoyed exclusively by the Merchants and Land-holders in San Francisco not, however, by closing the Custom House in San Francisco *that by all means should be continued,* but not as at present *the Only Port of Entry* on the entire coast of California. Why should the inhabitants of Monterey, Los Angeles, San Diego, &c &c be compelled to perform a voyage from the Lower Districts of California to San Francisco (requiring more time than a voyage from Europe to America) to buy goods, when the Ports named above, are far safer, and more convenient for commerce than San Francisco.

Again for several months in the year the rivers Sacramento and San Joaquin are navigable up to *Sutters* or Sacramento City and Stockton for vessels not drawing more than *9* or *10 feet water,* that is the Draft of our fine Stanch-fast-sailing Fore and Aft Schooners which ply at all seasons between the Northern, Eastern and Southern states. Several of these vessels have already found their way out here, and are now employed as regular traders between San Francisco in the transportation of vegetables, building materials &c. &c.

During the past winter and summer the Miners in the diggins suffered much from the Scurvy caused by scanty supplies and the almost total absence of the ordinary culinary vegetables, such as potatoes, onions &c &c. That disease is still prevalent in the country. Ought not all such necessaries of life for a limited period at least, be admitted into California free of duty? The average price of Irish-potatoes, at San Francisco for the last 6 months has exceeded $12 per bushel, sweet-potatoes, onions &c 50 per C^t higher. Why not permit such vessels to carry on a direct trade between Sacramento City, Stockton, Benecia and all the world, *without paying tribute,* and heavy tribute too, as I have before shown to the *adventitious town of San Francisco.*

The remedy for the evils which I have faithfully portraied, and for no other purpose than to invoke relief at the hands of those, *who, Alone can* provide for the general welfare, will be found in establishing Benecia, Stockton, Sacremento City including the new town of Boston, seperated from Sacremento City by the American river as Ports of Entry, the former on a footing of equality in every respect with San Francisco or any other Port in the Union; that done the grand and main difficulty of supplying the Miners will nearly vanish, but for the accommodation of the sea-coast, and Southern districts the Ports of Monterey and San Diego now Ports of *delivery only,* ought also to be made Ports of Entry open to foreign trade.

The zeal and apparant urgency with which I recommend the extension, but immediate extension of commercial facilities on the coast of California, may appear uncalled for by those not familiar with the country through which every necessary of life for the subsistence of the Miners (numbering this day not less than 50 or 60,000) has to be transported from the river Depots over extensive plains for 30, 40 and even 60 miles, which plains or Tulies are under water from Nov[embe]r till March, and passable only by Pack animals from March till June, and when wheeling becomes practicable in Midsummer, the pastures by reason of drought are so parched, or exhausted, that Draft animals are unable to draw heavy loads, and are maintained, when fed on grain, at a cost too high to name.

Barley the chief food for Draft cattle and Horses employed in transporting provisions, and goods from the river landings to the Mineing districts of California is derived from *Chile,* the ruling price of which at Stockton and Sacremento City is $8 per bushel; suffice it to say that I saw teamsters turn their cattle out to grass in Sacremento City last July, rather than haul provisions, at 25 cents, per pound 30 miles over good roads to *Mormon Island Diggins* 50 cents per lb. being the usual rate of transportation in good weather. $2 per lb i. e. $400 per barrel has been paid this present winter 1849 and 50 *for transportation from the Sacremento to Colema 60 miles.*

Thus it will be seen that from June to Nov[embe]r, five months comprises the season for transporting all supplies from rivers across the Tulies to the various *Gold-diggins;* and hence the imperious necessity for prompt action in the premises, for unless *Benecia,* and the river Ports above named are opened as Ports of Entry by the 1st of June 1850 it will be too late for foreign vessels to clear for these Ports in time to send forth their cargoes in season for the winter of 1850 and 51.

The rains set in this year 1849, on the 10th day of October. The fall of water was copious, and in a few days communication for transporting heavy articles between the rivers and Mines, was entirely suspended on most of the routes, and over such as were at all passable $1 per lb, was paid for transportating flour 30 or 40 miles, for which flour the *Consumers* in the *Mines* paid $2 per lb; pork sugar, &c &c, as well as the few other necessaries of life that could be obtained, in like proportion.

By an accurate calculation I find to victual 150,000 persons one year, with the full Navy-ration, the contract price of which is 20 cts per man per day, cost $11,714,400 to which add freight at $20 per ton, to transport the same, say from New York to California (in 469 ships of 300 tons) $2,816,000, added to cost of ration, make up the sum total of $14,530,400, for subsistence alone for one year, for 150,-000 persons *on the Navy-ration.* To this heavy amount for coarse provision must be added for articles of luxury, and necessity, even to Houses, fuel &c &c in bulk, and cost certainly three or four times as much more, consequently to subsist clothe, and shelter 150,000 inhabitants in California for the year 1850, it will employ at least 1400 ships of 350 tons each, and the cost and charges of the needful supplies delivered at the Port of San Francisco will not be short of $52,500,000, to which add at least $8,000,000 more for transportation from the Ports of Entry to the Mineing districts; this estimate of $8,000,000, for inland transportation is based upon the supposition that San Francisco *will not be the only Port of Entry* to foreign trade within the Bay of that name and its tributaries.

If the inconvenient adventitious and unsafe sea-port of San Francisco should be continued by law, as the only Port of Entry, through which the Miners can receive their supplies Oceanwise, then one third, or one half more may be added to the foregoing $8,000,000, for *inland transportation.*

Neither the Anchorage, nor the land about San Francisco is sufficiently capacious for half the commerce now entered there.

The average distance from ships to landing places exceeds half a mile, and level space on shore for Ware-houses is so contracted, and the cost of landing, and storeing goods so enormous, and the danger from fire so imminent, that two thirds of the goods now in the country, are still afloat in the Harbor.

To this already overcrowded state of the Port, add all the ships to arrive in 1850 and the inconveniences and expenses already so justly complained of attending the delivery, and trans-shipment of goods at San Francisco will be still further agrivated.

Moreover it is well known to all persons acquainted with the state of commercial operations in the Port of San Francisco, that owing to the crowded state of the Port the system of transshipping cargoes without landing them, the Revenue of the U[nited] States is defrauded probably at least one half, at any rate to an amount greatly beyond the necessary expenses of all the Custom-houses, the creation of which I have suggested.

Not one of the objections above stated against San Francisco, apply to the Sea-port town of Benecia, where the shores are bold and the largest Merchant-ships lay alongside the natural bank at all seasons of the year, in perfect security.

RESOLUTION.

Resolved, That a committee of five be appointed to ascertain who amongst the Southern members are willing to unite in an address to the Southern people advising firm, prompt, and manly opposition to the Wilmot proviso in the event of its being applied by law to the territory acquired from Mexico south of 36° 30′ and that the said committee be empowered to call a meeting of the Southern members when in their opinion it is proper to do so.

The committee will consist of Messrs. Hunter, Johnson of Louisiana, Rusk, Berrien, and Foote

> JEFF[ERSO]N DAVIS
> J. C. CALHOUN
> S. W. DOWNS
> R. M. T. HUNTER
> A. P. BUTLER
> D. L. YULEE
> H. V. JOHNSON
> D. R. ATCHISON
> THO. J. RUSK
> WILLIAM R. KING
> H. S. FOOTE
> BEN FITZPATRICK
> J. D. WESTCOTT
> W. K. SEBASTIAN

JOHN H. McHENRY [1] TO R. M. T. HUNTER.

HARTFORD, KY., *21st February, 1850.*

MY DEAR SIR: Perhaps you may almost have forgotten the individual who now addresses you, and who retains a vivid recollection of the many meetings and pleasant greetings he had with you when he had the honor of being an humble member of the committee of which you were chairman in the 29th Con[gress].

At the risk however of being entirely forgotten I have concluded to drop you a line if it be only to ascertain the fact.

Since we separated you have been busily engaged in the Senate of the U[nited] S[tates] aiding in the councils of our Nation, while

---

[1] A Representative in Congress from Kentucky, 1845–1847.

I have been mostly engaged in the practice of the law riding over hills and vallies, swamps and waters as duty or necessity might require. Last year I was elected a delegate and took a part, an humble part, in forming a new constitution for my own native state. Except this I have been wholly disengaged from politics. I have been looking with deep solicitude at the course of events since I left Congress and have seen nothing to change the opinion which I expressed to you in a conversation during the pending of the three million bill or just before I do not now recollect which, " that the Mexican War was gotten up by the abolition raving of the then Cabinet to get a large scope of territory to make free States out of and to surround the slave States entirely to get back what they were pleased to term the balance of power which they said they had lost by giving up half of Oregon " and advised you if possible to put a stop to the war before the rank and file got into the secret for if you did not the devil himself could not do it, that even Giddings and Culver would come in if they found out what it was for. You told me that you and your immediate friends were doing your best but were powerless, but if I would only keep Garrett Davis from throwing in his d——d resolutions of warning, which were calculated though not intended to bind the party together, that you thought you could possibly do something. I have often thought of this conversation and wondered if you had any recollection of it. Things that have occurred since have indelibly impressed it upon my memory.

In looking about for the causes of the Mexican war, I believed those assigned by the particular friends of the president were some of them insufficient and some of them unfounded and therefore I looked round for some reason to satisfy my own mind, and could find none but that. I named it to several of my friends and colleagues but could find none to agree with me. I formed the opinion first from reading Morey's instructions for raising Stephensons regiment. I thought the intention was to settle that regiment on the southern border of whatever land we might acquire and thus form the nucleus for a settlement from the free states immediately on our southern border and thus prevent· a settlement from the slave states, by slave holders at least· within the bounds of the newly acquired territory. Upon due consideration of all that has happened since that time do you not now think that I at least guessed well if I did not form a correct opinion?

In my canvass for delegate last summer I had to encounter emancipation in all its forms and triumphed over it. The leading men in this country are with the south but they are also for the Union and do not look to disunion as a remedy for any evil. They will " fight for slavery but die by the Union." As to the boys up the hollows and in the brush who form a considerable portion of our country they are not to [be] relied on in any contest against the Union. In a contest about the Union they would be willing to have the motto of the first soldiers of the revolution " Liberty or death "—but in a contest about slavery they would be a good deal like one Barney Decker who was about to have a soldiers badge and motto made and when the lady who made the badge asked him if he would have the same motto hesitated and then replied " You may put "liberty or be crippled." I am afraid the boys will say "slavery or be crippled." For God's sake try and settle all these questions of slavery if possible and let us not dissolve the Union.

But if we have to write like Francis the 1st to his mother, " Madam all's lost but honor " let us do it with this and we will have the approval of our own conscience without which a man is nothing.

RICHARD RUSH TO HON. J. M. MASON.

SYDENHAM, [PA.], *March 12, 1850.*

Accept my thanks, my dear Sir, for the copy of Mr. Calhoun's speech you were so good as to send me. I have read it with deep interest. Pages 7, 8 and 9, deserve to be considered by the whole country—more, I fear, than they will be. To the three first paragraphs on page 10, the allusions to Washington are beautiful, logical too, as it strikes me. But I will stop specifying, my marks being on almost every page. It is a very powerful speech, and I think very patriotic.

I beg you to offer my friendly respects to him. I rejoice at the improvement of his health. I regretted my inability to see him when in Washington lately, except once. I should have been truly glad to hear him converse on European affairs; the more, as I found myself agreeing with him on the little there was at one time for him to say when I visited him.

RICHARD K. CRALLÉ TO R. M. T. HUNTER.

[?], *March 23, 1850.*

MY DEAR SIR: Since we parted I have run the subject of our conversation through my mind, with some anxiety to reach a just conclusion. I said, perhaps the word should be, *prophesied* when you first took your seat in the Legislature, and before I knew you personally, that you were destined to become the most influential man in the State. This, I have repeated a thousand times since in *public;* and no man likes to be proved a false Prophet. So that, as the matter concerns me particularly, you will excuse my freedom of speech.

As to the general line of your proposed argument I feel no difficulty. The constitution, the just rights, and the honor of Virginia mark this deeply and broadly. We cannot surrender an inch South of 36½ degrees. It would amount to absolute submission.

The rank and file of neither of the two great Parties in the State are prepared for this; and if they were, no high-minded man can concur with them. Next to this, we must hold the *States* responsible for the delivery of our fugitive slaves. The compact was made with them, Congress is only their joint agent. For this we must hold them bound in the *first place*, and for two reasons. *Such is the compact*, and substitute of Congress must be unavailing, without their concurrence. No act, whatever be its provisions, can be carried into execution *against* the popular consent; and the effort will but "*film the ulcerous sore.*" This contest must be between the States themselves; and it ought to be waged with zeal and determination. I care not to rule in the aid of Congress, it must be ineffectual, and can only serve to postpone the issues which must finally come to be tried between the States themselves. What power has Congress to enforce the execution of its acts in this respect? None whatever.

Next, we have a right to demand that this agitation shall cease in the *Common* Halls of Legislation. This is the cancer that is eating into our vitals. We are daily paying for abolition appeals out of the common treasury. Take strong grounds against this. The *right* of petition, has nothing to do with the subject; and they who urge it know it well.

These are the main points. I have urged them years ago, and time only confirms me in the belief that we cannot safely yield an inch on them. I have spoken to no man on the subject. They are the oft printed conclusions of my own judgment.

As to the general tone of your argument, it cannot well be too high, so that it be announced in moderate but firm language. The present is a peculiar juncture; and its certain results will be to *make* or *mar* many fortunes. A truly great mind cannot fail to make itself to be felt. The issue is clearly submission or a stern maintenance of right, and in this instance *right* involves security. All temporary expedients must fail, and their failure will involve the ruin of many. My well considered opinion is, that, on the points mentioned we cannot yield any ground, no, not an inch. As to Mr. C[alhoun]'s view in respect to an amendment of the Constitution, that might be passed over. It goes rather to the philosophy of our system, than to its present practical operation which has thrown up the present issues. These last are the urgent issues; and we must deal with them as they are, and by themselves.

As to the matters, which may be regarded as *extraneous*, yet bearing strongly on the issues themselves, it is, in my view of the highest importance to sustain the Southern Convention, as a *means of preserving the Union*. In this view it has not been sufficiently pressed. Such only can be its legitimate purpose, and in that view no Southern man ought to object to it. As a deliberative, a consultation body, its expediency is called for by the highest consideration.

In respect to the matter we discussed in the Committee room on yesterday, would it not be advisable for you or Mr. D. *casually* to speak to the gentleman we referred to? Something useful might come out of it, while no evil can so far as I see. Keep the name of the gentleman *South* entirely to yourself.

It is after midnight, and I will tire your patience no further. I write in great haste, and conclude with this admonition, " *Stand up for old Virginia at all hazards, whose cause is just, and leave the consequences to God.*"

WILLIAM O. GOODE [1] TO R. M. T. HUNTER.

BOYDTON, [VA.], *March 29, 1850.*

DEAR HUNTER: I write to impose a little labour upon you, or rather I should say, trouble, but not more, than under a change of circumstances, I would cheerfully encounter for you. You know, I file and preserve in the form of a Book, Speeches, which well discuss, great political topics before Congress. I have procured a pamphlet copy of your very fine speech on the Austrian question. I thank you for delivering that speech. I wish you would send me, pamphlet copies of the speeches of Mr. Berrien and Mr. Webster, on the Slavery Question. And I should like to have a copy of Sewards Speech, if you think you can send it, without violating the Law against the circulation of incendiary publications; and even if you dread to encounter such a penalty, I promise not to inform against you, as I really want the speech, to enable me to contemplate the whole extent of this fearful subject.

If I were in Washington at this time, I would do what I never have done. I would call on Daniel Webster to pay him my respects. I know very well, he would regard it as a matter of the utmost insignificance even if he thought of it at all, but I would do so for my own gratification. I feel for him now, a higher respect than I ever did before, and more than I thought I could cherish for the greatest, the ablest, the most dangerous advocate, of the broadest construction of our Federative Compact—the Con[stitution] of U[nited] S[tates]— a Compact, which he calls Government, Government, invested with the highest attributes of Sovereignty, and for which, he challenges my highest allegiance. But it appears to me that this Slavery Speech, has established a claim to my gratitude. It could only have originated in a patriotic heart. It could only have been expressed by a generous mind. If we except, every thing which refers to Cali-

---

[1] A State rights Democrat and a Representative from Virginia in Congress, 1841–1843, 1853–1859.

fornia, and the allusion to the appropriation of Federal Money, to the deportation of Free Blacks (which he designed as a liberal concession) I should be happy to have carried out, the eloquent suggestions, of his eloquent discourse.

I sincerely hope, there may be speedily evinced at the North, a determined purpose of adopting and acting out these suggestions. Such a manifestation would be hailed with general joy at the South. So far as I have been able to observe and to form a conjecture of public sentiment, there is an obvious reluctance to take the initiative, but yet a firm, determined fixed purpose, to defend and maintain our social rights, and our political equality. It would be a fatal error on the part of the North, to mistake prudence and caution, for doubt and timidity. They may rely upon it, the subject has been *painfully* considered, and the *decision unalterably made.* If the North shall fail to exhibit a spirit of Moderation and pacification, before the Nashville Convention shall be holden, no human sagacity can foresee the consequences. That body will consist of men, for the *most part anxious to preserve the* Union, but firmly *resolved to save the South.* The safety of the South is the leading, the prevailing object, and the predominant idea. In the examination of their perils, and the consideration of their wrongs, the most temperate debate will glow with animation, and moderation itself, will kindle into rage. Who shall control their conclusions, or give law to their acts? Whatever their action may be, unless marked by *tameness*, it will be sustained by the Southern mind. In the beginning, there may be some diversity, but it will soon come to pass, that, contending Parties will vie with each other, and contest the supremacy of acrimony against the North. We will turn from the contemplation of this melancholy condition of things. With a heart all Southern, and a mind, painfully impressed, by the cruel wrong already suffered, and the flagilous outrage held in reserve; with a resolution immutably fixed, I yet pray the Genius of Webster may prevail, to save the Union, and give peace and harmony to the Land.

I must rely on your generosity to protect me against the charge of presumption, in venturing to allude to such a topic.

Present me affectionately to Mason. I thank him for the many public documents which he has sent me. Tell him, I claim as a matter of right, a copy of every speech, made by you or himself, in the Senate, and which shall reach the pamphlet edition.

I pray you to offer to Mr. Calhoun, assurances of my highest respect and kindest regard. I devoured his late Speech and thank him for the copy he sent me. I called a few days since on an old friend, a cankered Hunker, who, in dispite of the kindest relations between us, has perversely persecuted me through life, as a Nullifier Disunionist and Worshiper of John C. Calhoun. He met me with the exclamation "I acknowledge Mr. Calhoun is the greatest man now living. He has made it all as plain as day, why did we not see it before?"

This cankered Hunker is prepared to rush to any extreme. What is the madness of the North. I beg your pardon, Hunter. I know you rarely read more than one paragraph in a letter. You note that a bore if it contain three lines. You will read the last of this as it mentions our illustrious friend.

[P. S.] Can you spare time to write me, what *you all* wish *us all* to do. Snow 5 Inches on 25 March.

JOHN R. THOMPSON TO R. M. T. HUNTER.

RICHMOND [VA.], *9 April, 1850.*

MY DEAR SIR: Feeling deeply impressed with an unaffected and painful sense of the great public loss occasioned to America and to mankind by the death of Mr. Calhoun, I am anxious that some fitting eulogy on his character and public services should appear in the Southern Literary Messenger. While the grief of his personal friends is yet fresh, and the general sorrow pervading the country unabated, such a tribute might be most worthily performed without discussing his political opinions or offending persons of opposite views with any reflections on his party attachments. I need scarcely say, sir, that I know no one so well qualified, by long and intimate acquaintance with the illustrious dead, by congeniality of sentiment and study, and by facility of elegant and finished composition, to undertake this labour of love as yourself. I am sure that you would willingly do me a service and I am equally certain that you would yet more gladly render to the memory of your noble and lamented friend that tribute of affectionate remembrance and admiration which is so proper over his closing grave. May I not ask then that you will furnish for the Messenger an eulogy on Mr. Calhoun? If you accede, be good enough to inform me at what time I may expect to receive the Ms, if, you decline, pray make my best regards to your friend, the Hon. Mr. Seddon or to your nephew, Mr. Garnett, and ask, in my behalf, such an article from one of them.

WILLIAM O. GOODE TO R. M. T. HUNTER.

[BOYDTON, VA.], *April 20, 1850.*

MY DEAR HUNTER: I live five miles from our Post Office. The other day I despatched a letter to Mason and the servant returning brought me your letter. I reply promptly, because I have an interest or an object in doing so. Before I heard from you, in my letter to Mason, I expressed my apprehensions as to the effect of Webster's

Speech, and I also gave it as my opinion, that if *Eastern Virginia* be not fully represented in the Nashville Convention, Foote will have contributed efficiently to such a result. At the opening of the Session I was greatly pleased with his bearing. There was something in his notice of Mr. Calhoun's speech, for which I found myself at a loss to account. I hope it susceptible of explanation consistent with his own honor and the highest interest of the South.

From Webster's speech we gain at least the weight of his authority against the Abolitionists, Free soilers and Agitators at the North. And we have his acknowledgment that the South has suffered great wrong at the hands of the North. We have his authority and influence also on [the] Fugitive Slave question, and on the future admission of Texas States. These appear to me, to be objects, not unworthy of consideration. But they are no equivalent for present, positive legislation. They afford not present nor permanent relief for which we must rely on our own virtue and which can only be secured by unanimity and concert in the South. The Nashville Convention is the present available agency through which to secure concert and unanimity, and my chief object in writing now; as it was in writing to Mason, is to induce you to urge the Virginia Delegation at Washington to stimulate their friends in their several Districts. The time is short, and I fear it is almost too late, but much can be done. So far as I am informed Amelia, Nottoway and Dinwiddie in Mr. Meade's district have taken no action. He might procure it in time, or the District Convention might be postponed long enough to afford time. The same remark may be made in nearly all the Districts. I myself should have taken an active part long ago, but for considerations which I would not hesitate to explain to you in a personal interview. The chief injury to the South, resulting from Webster's speech, is the hesitation it has occasioned. This has given courage to all who wavered in their resolution or who were secretly opposed to the measure. And it is possible that an opposition may rally in the South on the California issue supported by the plausible popular arguments connected with that subject.

I have another motive for this letter. I expect to attend a District Convention 8 May, suppose a thin meeting, and suppose Virginia meagerly represented at Nashville. What will be best? Consult with our most reliable and judicious friends and write me fully and frankly.

I say nothing of the death of our lamented friend. I know not what to say. It were impossible to express what I feel.

(P. S.) I offered a suggestion to Mason which I will repeat to you though I presume it had occurred to both of you. I said to him that in my own opinion, even the compromise 36° 30′ was almost disgraceful to us, but public opinion must be consulted and something given up, for peace and tranquility. Suppose 36° 30′ can not be had. Would it do to take or offer Sierra Nevada from 42 as Eastern boundary of California down to near the Southern termination of the range as indicated on Fremont's Map, thence right line to St. Barbara about 34° on Pacific? This would give us a line to the Pacific and may be useful in the future. "*The State*" of Deseret has asserted this boundary for herself according to a writer for the Enquirer. And that *fact* may possibly aid to support an argument for such a proposition. The suggested line would give to California, perhaps the most beautiful geographical conformation in the Union. It's present delineation is a hideous deformity. But all is a mere suggestion without opinion.

WILLIAM O. GOODE TO R. M. T. HUNTER.

[BOYDTON, VA.], *May 11, 1850.*

DEAR HUNTER: I have to thank you for the copies of the speeches which you have sent me. Seward's "*Execrable*" is at hand! Your own speech had been eagerly read before I received the Pamphlet, and read I assure you with pride and satisfaction. In this part of the State, it is esteemed, the best effort which you have made. My individual opinion might accord equal merit to previous labours but I was proud of the last speech. The position which it assumes and to which you particularly directed my attention, I regard as indisputable, and resting at the foundation of the Social Compact. The *Property* of the Citizen is subject to taxation, and as an equivalent for this right surrendered to Society and by the Citizen. Society guarantees protection to property. They are just as much recognized equivalents, as Military service and protection of *persons*. *We feel* that the Federal Government exercises the power of Taxation, and we know of no political arrangement or process of just reasoning by which it can claim exemption from the obligation to protect. Property subjects itself to taxation and claims protection as an equivalent. The right to tax and obligation to protect are reciprocal terms and will only be controverted by those who would dispute the first principles of the social system. When I had written thus far I was interrupted and did not resume until my return from the District Convention. I wrote you a short and hasty note from Lawrenceville. I was called out in Convention before the Election of Delegates. I expressed the opinion that the Compromise projected by the Senate Com[mittee] as shadowed forth in the Newspapers, would be distructive of the South, that the South surrendered all and secured nothing. I supported this opinion by examination of the Subjects of Compromise, but expressed my readiness to take a compromise approved and recommended by Southern Members of Congress, because I trusted them as honorable men who would not sacrifice the honor of the South and property of the South.

I said in substance, California would be admitted with her present boundaries, not designed to be permanent, but contemplating a division and future erection of two free States, whose character was to be determined by the Casual Agency and usurped sovereignty of the present Adventurers, designedly fixing boundaries to include *all* the Land suited to Slaves &c. And I deprecated subjecting any part of Texas to future jurisdiction and action of freesoilers. I spoke perhaps more than an hour and awakened opposition to me. My election was opposed on the ground of my Ultraism and alledged desire for dissolution, which allegation is gratuitous. I do not desire dissolution. I expressed the apprehension, that California and the Territories in *one Bill* might command [a] small majority of the Senate without the Wilmot [Proviso]. In the House, they would be separated. Cal[iforni]a sent back to Senate, would pass without the Territories. After which Territories would be subjected to Wilmot [Proviso] or neglected. I lost nearly all the Anti Ultra Vote. I received nearly all the Democrats present with some Whigs. I lost [the] greater part of Whigs with a few Democrats. Petersburg was not represented (Meade's residence). All the Counties were represented.

I want you and Mason and Seddon, Meade and others to inform me fully of the prospect before us and furnish me all necessary documents. I shall prepare to leave home by 20 Inst. *if necessary.* I shall be delighted if the necessity can be superceded. I am obliged to be a little troublesome. You must talk with our friends especially those mentioned above and write me fully and immediately and tell them especially Seddon and Mason, to do so too. I write in great haste, shall be exceedingly occupied for ten days. Do let me hear from you forthwith.

[P. S.] I expect to be in Rich[mon]d 20th Ins[tan]t: to go Southern Route.

WILLIAM F. GORDON [1] TO R. M. T. HUNTER.

ALBEMARLE, [VA.], *July 2d, 1850.*

MY DEAR SIR: I rec[eive]d your letter accompanied by the Prospectus of the "Southern Press" and a number of the Papers. I enclose you $10 as a subscription of the triweekly paper. I have no doubt it will greatly subserve the Interests of the South. I thank you for your complimentary notice of my share in the Nashville

---

[1] An early advocate of secession; represented Virginia in Congress, 1830–1835.

Convention, and am happy to think that it will, in your opinion, make a profound impression. Confusion must be worst confounded by the *usurpation* of New Mexico, and the evident interference of our Slaveholding President, and yet I can perceive no real Difference between the Case of California and New Mexico. These events must hasten the Catastrophe to the South, the admission of these territories as states and the rejection of 36 30 Degrees as a Dividing line fills our Cup of humiliation to the brim. In the "argument not yet exhausted? when shall we stand to our Army?" Will neither legislative or Executive Despotism arouse us? Will not both combined? I cannot look on these events, in any aspect, but a designed insult and indignity to the whole Slave holding States. For one I am not willing to bear it. I am ready for resistance whenever the insult is consumated by Congress. So I hope will the whole South. The Nashville Convention is to reassemble in six weeks after the adjournment of Congress.

If anything is done by Congress, inconsistent with the rights and honor of the south, would it not be well for the Southern Senators and representatives to address their states and constituents on the occasion? It would have a powerful effect on the states and on the Convention. Unanimity is not to be expected, the pure and bold public men must lead, and I doubt not any course recommended by them, or a majority of them would be our guide. The more decided the better for me, for I think this *protracted insult* of Congress and the Executive, on refusing our clear constitutional rights, provocation enough to justify the strongest measures; and unless they are acknowledged during the Session I hope decisive resistance may be made. I have been contemplating in my solitude, how to work out the problem. I should follow our revolutionary example, that of Virginia. I would take our present Federal Constitution for the Southern States and put it into operation, as soon as a sufficient number of States would secede, this would simplyfy matters, would pervent confusion, as the officers of our *Southern Republic*, would at once understand their duties, our *Sub Treasures*, are all ready, we should only shake off the northern states, as we did the King of England, (for they have oppressed us far more than our Old Mother England ever did) and have our government in full and immediate Vigor without the Delay of Forming a New Constitution, which, however we might do at our leisure. This mode recommends itself, by the example of the illustrious ancestor of your Colleague, who formed our Virginia Constitution. Present to him my best respects.[1]

---

[1] This reference is doubtless to Senator J. M. Mason of Virginia and to George Mason, author of Virginia's Bill of Rights.

WILLIAM P. DUVAL[1] TO R. M. T. HUNTER.

AUSTIN, [TEXAS], *August 13th, 1850.*

DEAR HUNTER: I transmit you the Gover[nor']s message to our Legislature. The people of this state are camly determined to take possession of the Santa Fe country. There is no noise or violent excitement about this subject. When a people know they are rightfully protecting their own dignity and honor and have determined to do it at every hazzard it is pretty certain they will effect their object. The first hostile gun that is fired in this contest disolves the union. Every southern State will stand by Texas. Hers is the common cause of the South.

Your course in the Senate does honor to your State and yourself. As a Virginian I am proud of you. We have heard here the compromise bill has failed. I rejoice at the fact I had hoped it would have been so amended as to place the South on an equality with the North, but it could not be so formed, and less than equality, would disgrace the South. Our Governor's message speaks the voice of this state that you may rely upon, and his views will be carried out by the Legislature. Virginia will have to head the Southern confederacy. She has arms for herself and two [other] Southern States, and if the union is broken, we will save the North all further trouble with California and New Mexico, for we will take them to our exclusive use.

(P. S.) If Taylor had lived our Union would have vanished as it certainly will if Mr. Filmore pursues the same policy. Such a President as poor Taylor was and such a cabinet as he had would in four years ruin any nation that has, or ever exist[ed]. He had not one statesman in his cabinet, they all were mere time serving politicians from remote circumstances, in all great nation affairs.

LITTLETON WALLER TAZEWELL[2] TO R. M. T. HUNTER.

NORFOLK, [VA.], *August 18th, 1850.*

MY DEAR SIR: Upon receipt of your kind letter of the 10th Inst[ant], I immediately commenced such a reply to it as I thought you wished to have and I myself best approved. I soon discovered, however, that my inclination had imposed upon me a task surpassing my physical ability to perform; and I was so constrained to desist. The attempt has been renewed several times since, with no better success. Age has so dimed my sight and stiffened my fingers, that I now write with much difficulty and generally with some pain.

[1] A Representative in Congress from Kentucky, 1813–1815; later moved to Texas.
[2] One of the early followers of John C. Calhoun; representative in Congress from Virginia, 1800–1801; Senator in Congress from Virginia, 1824–1832; governor of Virginia, 1834–1836.

Hence, nothing but absolute necessity induces me ever to touch a pen. But in the pleasing hope, that by complying with your request I might give you some proof of my continued respect, esteem and confidence, and feebly disburthen my own mind of the sad forebodings that sometimes oppress it, I forgot the infirmities of age and commenced such a letter as I have described. I wrote *con amore*, but I had not proceeded far, when I was obliged to acknowledge to myself, that altho' the spirit was still willing the flesh was no longer able to aid it; and with some mortification, I reluctantly abandoned a subject, which, in my mode of treating it, threatened to expand into a volume.

I was a little consoled under this compulsory abandonment of my first design, by reading in our newspapers, that while I had been writing most of the subjects I was discussing were no longer open questions (as the lawyers say) but had passed into *res judicatae*, so far at least as the body of which you are a member is concerned. Mr. Clay's Compromise Bill had been rejected as a whole, altho' many of the parts of which this whole was compounded had been approved by the Senate. The votes by which these results had been brought about, show so clearly the motive power that had produced them, as to leave no doubt upon the mind of any, I suppose, that what remains will meet with like approbation. Therefore, to continue the discussion of questions already decided, and so decided too, would be a labour painful to myself and quite profitless to you. I will not deny myself the pleasure of saying to you, however, that I concur with you entirely in every opinion you have expressed and in every vote you have given in regard to any and all of the several subjects involved in the so called Compromise Bill, so far as these votes and opinions are known to me. In saying this, I believe I express the sentiments of a very great majority of the Citizens of Virginia. But, my friend, while you and your Colleague may both rest assured that the course you have pursued meets the cordial approbation of a very large proportion of the people of Virginia at present, neither of you should flatter yourselves with the hope that these opinions will be permanent here.

Throughout the U[nited] S[tates] patent causes have been silently operating for some time past to produce a radical change in their Government; and the future action of these causes must be greatly aided and facilitated by the measures recently adopted by the Senate. It was my purpose, at first, to enumerate these causes, to trace them to their sources and to show to what results they must inevitably lead, even if not designed to produce such effects. But, as I have said, I am no longer able to perform such a task. I can give you only a birds-eye view of the principles the Senate has asserted, in some of their votes, of the practices they have established to serve as precedents for themselves and their successors hereafter, of the influence these precedents must have upon the destiny of the U[nited] S[tates] both abroad and at home, and of the cause that has effected all this mischief. I am not able to complete the picture, but must leave it to you to fill up the outline.

By the admission of California into the Union, under the circumstances existing when she presented herself, the Senate have decided that the unknown dwellers and sojourners in a territory recently conquered, while they are still subject to the strict discipline of a military rule, may, without even asking the permission of their Conquerors, put off this rule, erect themselves into a sovereign state, appropriate to their own use such part of the conquered territory as they please, and govern it thereafter as they think proper. That for such acts of mutinous insurrection and open rebellion against the legitimate authority of their conquerors, instead of meeting the censure and punishment which existing laws denounce, they shall be rewarded. Provided they will take care to insert as a condition in their Organic law, that none of the slaves belonging to the citizens of one half of the states of the Union shall ever be introduced within the limits they have chosen.

By the purchase of a large portion of the territory admitted to belong to Texas, which purchase the Senate have authorized to be made, they have asserted the doctrine that it is competent to the Federal Government to buy up the whole or any part it may wish to acquire of one of the Confederated States of the Union.

By the proposed annexation of the territory to be bought from Texas to a portion of the conquered country of New Mexico, the narrow limits of the latter will be expanded into a territory of a respectable size, many of the free citizens of Texas will be degraded into territorial subjects of the Government of the U[nited] S[tates]; and when to escape from this state of vassalage, they shall hereafter ask to be admitted into the union like California, you may rely upon it, that this boon will be refused, unless like California they will exclude all Southern Slaves from their limits, by their Organic law.

The Statesman must be deficient in political sagacity, I think, who does not foresee that all the nations holding territories adjacent to the U[nited] S[tates] must feel anxiety for the safety of their dominions, when such principles if not openly avowed are acted upon systematically by the Government of the U[nited] S[tates]; and that the portion of the great family of civilized nations can regard with indifference the effects of these new doctrines interpolated into the public law.

Of their effects upon the slave holding states of the Union, I have neither space enough left to express more than a brief remark. These states have long accustomed themselves to regard the Senate of the U[nited] S[tates] as the only body upon which any reliance could be placed for the conservation of their political rights and interests. They will now see, I suppose, that this was mere delusion; that these rights and interests have been wantonly sacrificed by members of that body in whom they had good reason to repose confidence; and like the dying Caesar, struck down at the foot of Pompey's statute by the daggers of pretended friends, they may well cry out *et tu quoque Brute.* It is neither necessary or proper for me to say any thing now as to the course which, I think, they ought and will adopt under present circumstances. The measures which the Senate have recommended and sanctioned by their votes have not yet received the assent of the other Departments of the Government; and altho' to indulge the anticipation of any different result in these quarters may be hoping against hope, yet while a single chance remains, however remote it may be, prudence would seem to indicate that the slave holding States should abstain from any hypothetical declaration of their purpose. Whatever that purpose may be, I am sure it will not be influenced by any craven fears, and so far as Virginia is concerned, I hope it will be worthy of her character. For my own part, whatever that purpose may be I will abide by it. I have often invoked my God to witness the solemn pledge I willingly gave to be " faithful and true " to her; and when I forget the sacred obligation of this vow of allegiance, may that God forget me.

Accept this long letter, (which I have written with difficulty) as a testimonial of the high consideration in which I hold you, I commit it to your discretion, to be used as you please, provided always that it shall not reach the newspapers. Altho' I have no·care to conceal any thing that I have ever thought said or done in my whole life, yet I have ever felt a morbid horror at becoming a subject of notoriety.

ROBERT SELDEN GARNETT [1] TO R. M. T. HUNTER.

St. Louis, Mo., *September 27th, 1850.*

MY DEAR COUSIN: On my arrival at this place yesterday I heard a rumor to the effect that there was a strong probability that Congress before its adjournment would raise one or two additional regiments of Dragoons for Western service.

I now write to request your kind offices for procuring for me the appointment of *Major* in one of these Corps. You are fully·aware of the importance of this promotion to me, and I need not therefore say anything to you on that head. I make this application upon my

---

[1] As a brigadier general he took command of the Confederate Army in western Virginia in June. 1861 : killed at Carrick's Ford, July 13, 1861, while leading his troops.

own character and services as any other officer would do, yet it may be a matter of some weight with the administration to understand the relations that existed betwen the late President and myself; and although I consider that my standing and services in the army, fully warrant me in seeking this advancement, I feel safe in saying that in view of my position on Gen[era]l Taylor's personal staff, Gen[era]l Fillmore would be fully sustained by his party at least in giving me the position now asked. I presume you are well acquainted with Mr. Crittenden and Mr. Steanst, and I beg that you will make these facts known to them. To the former gentleman, I shall write directly, but with Mr. Steanst I have no acquaintance whatever.

I shall address Col[onel] Davis and Gen[era]l Jones on this subject, as well as Mr. Conrad, but your assistance will be highly important to my interests, and if convenient, I beg to invoke it. Had Gen[era]l Taylor lived I feel satisfied that this promotion would have been given me unsought, and it was in consequence of expecting some such occasion as the present that I had refrained while he was alive, from annoying him on this or kindred subjects.

To Col. Davis I am personally and fully known and I beg that you will confer with him, should you be able to give this letter any attention. I am perfectly willing to undergo any amount of hard service for any length of time, if I get this promotion.

I beg to hear from you as early as convenient. Please direct to me at Fort Leavenworth, Missouri.

SIR HENRY LYTTON BULWER [1] TO R. M. T. HUNTER.

WASHINGTON, [D. C.], *October 1, 1850.*

DEAR SIR: Will you allow me to remind you of the conversation which we lately had in regard to the emigration of negroes from this country to the British West Indies. I shall be very happy to receive from you any advice or suggestions with regard to carrying out such a plan, provided you consider it feasible.

ELWOOD FISHER TO R. M. T. HUNTER.

WASHINGTON, [D. C.], *October 22, 1850.*

DEAR SIR: Yours is received and I herewith send the letter of Mr. Tazewell. You will see how it was mutilated while in the hands of the printer and against my orders, but I have saved every article of the precious paper.

As to Georgia the indications are unfavourable. The tone of the resistance press is not so good as it has been. Elsewhere there is no change, unless in Charlestown, V[irgini]a and in Rockingham [County, Virginia] where by the way you were expected. I got a

---

[1] Minister from Great Britain to the United States.

letter from Bedinger last night who says that Mason made a capital speech at Charlestown, and that it was well received, and that all the Democrats are with us, and the Whigs opposed. The proceedings however have not yet reached here.

By the way that truest test of the state of affairs, the subscriptions to the Press are not coming in so rapidly as immediately after the session closed. The members have either done nothing—or done it in vain. My opinion is they have done about nothing, that is so very customary with them.

You see Filmore has surrendered to Seward, submission is the order of the day.

ELWOOD FISHER TO R. M. T. HUNTER.

WASHINGTON, [D. C.], *October 29th, 1850.*

DEAR HUNTER: Your second favour was received enquiring after the first which had already been answered, and I presume you receized the Tazewell letter, as safely as it came from the hands of the Visigoth printer.

The news for the last few days looks better from the South. The Georgia papers have better tone, and our friends claim to be strong. I learn to-day that Toombs has written here that Georgia can be saved for the Compromise if the North will only behave itself, a thing that the North wont do more and more every day.

Wagner of the New Orleans Courier has retired, and the paper goes more with the South. In a card he publishes he ascribes his retirement to his devotion to the Union which was too great for the proprietors of the paper. I suppose we have to thank Soule and Barton.

Doherty (Judge) of Georgia, Whig and the man on whom all the Whigs but seven united for Senator at the last election instead of Dawson, has come out for resistance.

The Mississippi papers look pretty well.

I have written over to New York about your nephew, and if possible will get him a place. Soon as I hear will write.

(P. S.) Cabell is elected by decreased majority.

JOHN B. FLOYD [1] TO R. M. T. HUNTER.

RICHMOND, [VA.], *November 8th, 1850.*

MY DEAR SIR: I was absent when your letter of the 9th ult reached the City, and I have delayed an answer to it until now for the purpose of consulting with some of our friends upon the subject. I am pleased with the idea of sending our free people to the Brit-

---

[1] Governor of Virginia (1849–1852) ; a member of Buchanan's Cabinet (1857–1861).

ish West India Islands, nor is it by any means a new one to me. I had a conversation twelve months ago with some gentlemen upon the subject; but we made nothing of it for the want of information; and being equally ignorant of the sources to procure it, let it drop. I would take it as a favor confered upon the state if you would ascertain of even the British Minister distinctly the terms upon which his Government would take them, and the condition in which they would be placed upon their removal to the Islands.

We to be sure would part with them very willingly upon any terms, but this information is necessary to render their co-operation hearty. If advantageous terms were offered I do not much doubt, but that they would all emigrate in the course of a few years. I should be very much pleased to render every facility in my power to the conservation of the project.

SIR HENRY LYTTON BULWER TO R. M. T. HUNTER.

WASHINGTON, [D. C.], *December 19, 1850.*

MY DEAR SIR: I am very much obliged to you for your kind letter and attention to the subject which I brought under your consideration when we last met.

The communications which I had received from my Government at that time inclosed some correspondence from a resident at Jamaica, stating his belief that the House of Assembly of that Island would be disposed to offer small grants of land to immigrants of color, and to defray a portion of the expense of their transit from the United States.

This person moreover stated that he believed that many slave proprietors in this country would be willing to manumit their slaves if they were sure of being able thus to dispose of them.

Her Majesty's Government however, expressed no distinct opinion on these subjects; but requested me to obtain information as to the feeling of the slave proprietors of the Southern States, with respect to giving liberty to their slaves, and with respect to sending negroes who had received their freedom, to any foreign country where they would be sure of good treatment, observing that if the substance of the correspondence forwarded to me were correct, arrangements might probably be made for receiving such persons as those alluded to, in the British West Indies: and by another communication received, I was instructed to ask for any farther information I might require from H[er] M[ajesty]'s Gov[ernmen]t in order to deal practically with this question. In reply to the above mentioned communications, I stated that I did not think that emancipation of negroes for the purpose of their emigration to the West Indies would be carried to any great extent, but that I did believe that there was a disposition on the part of the Slaveholding states to get rid of their present free negro population and I observed that I should endeavour to ascertain from persons well qualified to give me an opinion on the subject, the regulations under which such an arrangement could be made, whilst in the meantime I suggested that if the Colonies in question passed any law securing a tolerable existence to free negroes emigrating thereto, such a law would obtain attention here; and that it was probable that the Legislature of the Southern States would adopt measures for facilitating the egress of the free portion of their colored population.

In this position the question now remains, Her Majesty's Gov[ernmen]t probably waiting for farther information from me; and such information I should very much desire to obtain from you.

Indeed I would observe that before I could make any suggestions to you on this subject, I should have to refer again to Her Majesty's Gov[ernmen]t, which would have to refer to the authorities at Jamaica, and on receiving their opinion, would have again to communicate with me, when the proposals would have to be discussed here and if any alterations were then necessary, further proceedings of the same dilatory character, would be required: Whereas if you could furnish me with a plan for some arrangement that would suit you, this would immediately receive the attention of Her Majesty's Gov[ernmen]t and that of the Legislature of Jamaica; and either be settled at once there or if any modification were necessary, transmitted thence hither, and arranged between us in a very short space of time.

Will you therefore consider of this matter and come and dine with me here on the 29th inst. (since I may be absence during the holidays) at 6 o'clock in a quiet way, and we will then talk over and come to some determination with respect to it?

GEORGE F. THOMSON TO R. M. T. HUNTER.

NEW YORK [CITY], *February 3, 1851.*

DEAR SIR: There is much interest felt here among the merchants, as well as those engaged the business of storing goods in Bond in reference to the action Congress will take (if any) on the Ware Housing Bill. The two existing systems, the one a Government affair, the other Private have been so long and thoroughly tested that not a shadow of doubt exists that the private Ware Houses are in every respect superior and are by the Merchants preferred.

The Government system entails an annual expense upon the Treasury in this City alone, of nearly or quite $100,000. While the Private ones, Bonding mere goods, are not one cent expense to the Treasury. I have been some time engaged in this business but the constant annoyances we are all subjected too must if continued ruin us. The two systems cannot exist together unless we are allowed a fair competition with the Government. This is all we ask. Give the Merchant the privilege, and surely it is [a] right one, of Bonding his goods in *any* duly authorised Bonded Ware House and we are perfectly willing to take one chance of success even with the Government for a competitor.

But as affairs are now conducted there is no fairness, no justice. We are under very heavy expenses, give heavy Bonds for the faithful performance of the trust pay over $3. per diem or $1095.00 per an[num] to the collector for the officer in charge, and yet much of the time he, the collector, refuses to allow the merchant to place his goods in our charge. These private stores are prefered by merchants for many reasons. They are at different points of the City, therefore more accessible to business men. There is more accommodation and better care taken of his merchandise. It is for the interest (the strongest of incentives) of the Storekeeper to do so. The charges are less, and Insurance is only about one half of that charged in the Government stores. All these amount to a very heavy percentage on an invoice of goods, the merchant therefore naturally makes his arrangement with the private stores. He arranges as to prices, takes out his Insurance, or possibly he already has a policy, and then goes to the Custom House to enter his goods for said store but is quietly informed that he cannot place them there. They must go into the Government stores. Such is the operation and you can readily understand the effect. It is ruining those who alone should have the business (I mean private individuals) entailing an expense of $100,000 on the Government. The truth is it is a very small business for the Government to be engaged in, that of storage! Why not carting? The stores should be leased and the Secretary is censurable for not having complied with the law of the last Congress authorising him to have them on or before the 1st of Jan[uar]y last. No *real* effort has been made. They would to day if put up at auction bring nearly as much as are paid for them by the Gov[ernmen]t stores along side of the large U[nited] S[tates] Bonded store on Broadway, and also in front of them rent for *more* money. But the truth is there are some 50 or 100 more, good positions probably, connected with these stores and so long as the Government pay their expenses why have the stores! If they are to be continued as Gov[ernmen]t stores, then we wish that our formidable opponent be compelled to play fair. Let there be no forcing goods in these stores against the wishes and interest of the merchants. Give us fair and open competition, guard us against having forced upon us, to protect the interest of the Government! too many cousins, nephews and the like, as Custom House officers and thus eating us up, and we will Bond all the goods that may offer to better satisfaction to the merchant, *with more safety to the Government* and save to the Treasury a large am[oun]t annually. The system should be extended to three years at least, why not indefinitely? Duty Bonds cancelled when goods are destroyed by fire or otherwise, but why give Bonds for duties at all while the Government possesses the goods, are they not sufficient receipt for duties?

It is certainly to be hoped that a Bill with such a similar feature may soon become a law and no one is more capable of effecting this result than yourself.

HENRY A. WISE TO R. M. T. HUNTER.

RICHMOND, [VA.], *February 13th, 1851.*

MY DEAR HUNTER: There was a meeting of the Democracy here last night. To describe its tone and temper no one could undertake, except to a person who was present but uninitiated. There is to be another meeting held next Monday night and a Com[mit]tee of 12 is appointed to prepare subjects for consideration. I am at the head of that Com[mit]tee. Nothing can or will be done. Why? the hares are squatting under the nose of the Ritchie hounds. Ritchie has to get his *printing contract* through Congress before he will allow anything to be attempted for the conciliation of State Rights Democrats and for the uniting of North and South Democrats. That printing Contract pervades, in under-current, every pulse of action here. By it we were sold out to the Compromise, by it Bayly was carried to downright treason, by it Ritchie is bound and by him the Democracy of Virginia is held in durance vile. Are we to let him put us in his pocket? You must trust to me to save "hooks and lines" here and I appeal to you as a Senator and patriot never to allow that contract to be consummated unless Ritchie will sell us to ourselves back again. We must hold him by the *printing bill.* Don't let it pass either house until you have beat him to terms. You can do it.

WILLIS P. BOCOCK TO R. M. T. HUNTER.

RICHMOND, [VA.], *13th February 1851.* .

MY DEAR SIR: Permit me to introduce to your acquaintance my esteemed friend Col[onel] Fuqua, a member of the Convention of Virginia from my old county of Buckingham, and a good and true democrat and southerner. He is one of the signers of the "Ebony line" letter and to him I refer you for his views with this only remark that whatever he may say you cannot better satisfy him than by Strict adherence to the principles that should guide a V[irgini]a Senator. Tell him what I have said.

I have no doubt that the signatures procured to that paper are in the main attributable to the influence and popularity of Beverly Tucker and Kennedy. They were over here and gave a supper *to that end.* Besides that a friend of theirs Hon. Mr. Chilton of Fauquier presented and when necessary pressed it on the members of the Convention. His good nature, their facility and a general and growing desire in V[irgini]a for some plan to remove the free negroes accounts for the number of signatures. While it was in Chilton's hands and after it had been presented to me I spoke of it in [the] presence of one or two members of [the] Convention. One of them I remember said he had signed it thoughtlessly and would go and have his name taken off. I have not had an opportunity to converse extensively on the subject, but I am decidedly of opinion and will add such is Goode's opinion, that you and your colleague should act upon the lights before you without reference to these signatures unless the more deliberate wishes of the legislature should be communicated.

I hope after 4th March and when you have paid a short visit home and seen the State of progress on your farm, unexampled in your experience as a farmer, you will come over to see your friends here and make yourself very agreeable to members of the Convention, but especially to the members of the Legislature.

A message for T. S. Bocock if you see him. The Whigs of his district in Convention assembled have, without any other name being before them, nominated the Rev. John Early D. D. as the Whig Candidate for the district. Harvey Irving is furious on it, and opinions are various as to the strength of the nominee. It is rather a formidable move, but in my opinion not invincible.

Mr. Wise is attempting to make a platform for the democracy in Virginia. A meeting was called last night perhaps you saw or heard of the call in the Enquirer. It was well attended. Mr. Wise moved for a committee, and I understand read resolutions. The Committee was appointed to report to an adjourned meeting Monday night next. I learn I am one of the Committee, I did not remain till they were named. The resolutions which Wise read take the ground of attachment to the Union and the rights of the States &c, submission to what has been done and opposition to dissolution for that cause, compliment to Pennsylvania and a promise, *the other democratic states concurring,* to sustain such candidate for the presidency as she may name, with an invitation to her to designate a candidate. He is of opinion there is a design to put Cass on us again whom he wont vote for. [He] is I believe for Buchannan, believes a national Convention Nomination impracticable, and thinks the Whigs will beat us unless we take the platform of Union from them. What think you all? I wish I could hear from our friends in Washington on the subject in time. This movement makes little favor here as far as I can gather, and is not agreeable to my own notions.

R. M. T. HUNTER TO GEORGE N. SANDERS.[1]

March 27, 1851.

DEAR SAUNDERS: I was in Richmond when your letter reached Garnett. By the way it went first to the army hands. M. R. H. Garnett is the name of my nephew. The other is M. Garnett and a *whig.* So note the distinction when next you write. By the way I see you still talk of that dinner. If gotten up it would be owing to nothing but your personal address, not to any hold which I have there. And if gotten up it would do harm. Trust my judgment for this matter at least. In all that you say in relation to the new Editors of the Union I concur. That is to say I concur as far as I know Donalson, but my knowledge of him is very slight. He is not for "the ticket" as you call it. At least I do not believe that he is. I heard Douglass well spoken of in Richmond. Gen[era]l Chapman is ardent. I did not hear what were the leanings of the Speaker Hopkins.

CHARLES MASON TO R. M. T. HUNTER.

ALTO, KING GEORGE [COUNTY, VA.], *April 5, 1851.*

MY DEAR SIR: The subject of a Southern Convention, has become a topic of very great excitement in our County; and owing to the unfair report of the proceedings of our second, joint meeting (which has been charged on the chairman) a good deal of angry and desultory discussion has ensued. The question has, unfortunately, assumed a party character here, and an effort is being made to stifle the independent action of the friends of a convention, on the ground, that we ought to submit to an accidental majority against us. We do not feel the force of any such obligation, either morally or politically, and do not intend to yield. Although we shall be too late to unite with the district convention to assemble at Tappahannock on the 10th, yet we can confirm the action of that meeting. We shall call a meeting for our general muster, and I will be greatly obliged to you, if in your power and not subjecting you to too much trouble, to fortify me with documents to sustain our position. I want evidence to show how many Southern States have recommended the Convention; and to controvert the assertion if I can, *that six of them have, in their legislative capacities, gone against it,* that Tennessee, herself, has refused to allow it to meet within her borders. If these States have done so, of which I have seen no evidence, I would

---

[1] This letter can be found in the Library of Congress.

be glad to be informed what is the ground of their opposition, and whether they are not Whig States? I want moreover to show what portion of the people of Tennessee are opposed to its assembling in Nashville. I have to contend singly and alone against my brother, who is a practiced speaker, and Col[onel] Taylor who is a loud talker, but our party [will] go for it, with great unanimity. Fitzhugh spoke at our last court, but not in good taste, and with little effect. Newton is warm for it, and I learn is open in his denunciations of the administration; so are Washington and Garnett of the same county, and I am looking forward to no distant day, when Westmoreland will become a member of the Democratic family of Counties. I sincerely wish the meeting of the Convention were not so near; the people are just beginning to wake up to the importance of the question. I would give a great deal to have you among us for a short time; we want some potent voice and lofty spirits to rouse the sleeping energies of the South to a sense of their danger. If we can not see you personally, I should be glad to have a letter from you, of such a character as you may deem prudent and politic to read at our meeting. I am sure it would do a great deal of good; but if you think otherwise, of course no use will be made of any communications, you may honor me with.

R. M. T. HUNTER TO GEORGE N. SANDERS.[1]

LLOYDS, ESSEX [Co. VA.], *May 9, 1851.*

MY DEAR SIR: You will be surprised to hear that your letter has just reached me. The mail comes here from the North but twice a week and it is irregular at that. No man can appreciate such a compliment more highly than I do and I wish to act according to the advice of my friends but they differ as to this matter. The same mail which brought your letter brought also one from Douglass. Confidential it was but there are no secrets from you. He advises me to decline, but to visit New York without parade during the summer. In the same letter he speaks in the highest terms of the skill and judgment with which you manage affairs. He himself I think is one of the coolest observers even when he himself is concerned. that I ever saw. For myself I do not mean or wish to be obstinate. You know what my opinion has been all along. But I suppose and hope I shall soon hear from you again. Your report of progress is encouraging beyond any expectations I have ever had. I think that Douglass will take well in this state.

P. S. If Bev[erly] Tucker is in New York when this reaches you please tell him I had intended writing him by this mail but upon considering [?] the day of his sailing I found the letter would

---

[1] This and the following letter are in the Library of Congress.

probably not reach him. I regret this very much as it was an oversight on my part.

R. M. T. Hunter to George N. Sanders.[1]

(*Private.*)

Lloyds, Essex Co. [Va.], *June 20, 1851.*

My dear Sir: I found your second favors here upon my return and I avail myself of the first mail to reply to them. I am under many obligations to you for your kindness and for the skill and address with which you have managed matters. The affair of the Herald I think will do neither good nor harm. The moment you mentioned Westcotts name I understood the whole matter. You ask me what is the cause of his dislike to me? I know of no cause and was not aware that he had any dislike to me. In truth I do not believe that he either *likes* or *dislikes* me or cares one cent about me. He has a natural propensity for mischief and delights in making a sensation. He could indulge these propensities better by the course which he pursued than by following your suggestions. This I suspect is the key to his conduct unless there is somebody in New York whom he wished to annoy. Mr. Jefferson said of Burr that he was like " a crooked gun " and no one could ever tell where he would shoot. The same may be said of W[estcott]. The best way is to let him alone. He will be satisfied with what he has done unless somebody pursued it further.

I am glad that you are satisfied with my letter. I was afraid you might think I did not attach sufficient importance to your wishes which was far from being the case. But after weighing the matter well it seemed to me most prudent to decline. But enough of this subject. What does Donelson mean by his constant praises of Web ster? Is he bolstering him up to give him strength enough to *divide* the whig party or is there an alternative in which he contemplates the possibility of supporting him. Scarcely the latter I should think. But there must be some object. Pray let me hear from you when you have leisure. Have the North Western papers said any thing of my letter? Where is Douglass and what is he about?

P. S. I will write you a letter in relation to Cushing. He would make a capital selection.

Richard K. Crallé to R. M. T. Hunter.

Raleigh, N. C., *November 28th, 1851.*

My dear Sir: Detained here, for a few hours, waiting for the Stage to take me to Fayetteville on my route to Columbia and Charleston, I fulfill a purpose which I designed to have done before I left home.

The first volume of Mr. Calhoun's Works is now published, containing his views on Government, and the Constitution. It is so inconvenient for me to attend to the publication of the remaining volumes, in *South Carolina*, that I propose, if it can be done on fair terms, to change the place to Richmond. Nash and Woodhouse are anxious to establish an extensive Publishing House in this City, and I [am] desirous to get their works to commence with.

Now putting aside the question of real or individual interest, I am quite sure they would undertake the publication of the remaining volumes, as well as a large edition of the present, if they could have some assurance that they. would not sustain an actual loss. To provide against this they propose to go on to Washington to consult with some of Mr. Calhoun's old friends in regard to the probabilities of a subscription on the part of Congress.

Now on this point, I wish to speak to you in all frankness. I am confident that the work now published must, if not generally, exercise a powerful [influence] on public opinion throughout the Union. It cannot be otherwise. A few, and these prominent Whigs, to whom I have loaned the single volume I have, have openly and publicly declared that its views and arguments are unmeasurable. A similar declaration was made to me by a leading Whig in New York, who had the Proofs last Spring.

The work on the Constitution will do more, I verily believe, to build up the Republican Party, and preserve the Union, than any, and all other causes combined. All that is necessary to effect a great and radical change in public sentiment in regard to State Rights is, to give this Work a wide circulation. Congress, or even the Senate (of which he was so long a member) might do this. But you know the inflexible opposition which Mr. Calhoun ever entertained to this miserable traffic on the part of the Government, in the papers of dead politicians one of his last injunctions to me was, never to have his Papers put up at auction in the Capitol; and his family have since strictly enjoined on me not to violate his wishes. I mean not to do this, but there is a difference, a wide difference between offering the manuscript to Congress on sale, and a subscription on the part of that body to a work or works published by myself or by any one else. In the latter case Congress does not become the *owner* or publisher, but simply the *purchaser* of so many copies, to be used as it may deem proper. So important do I regard the circulation of this Book, that I would willingly tread thus far on the injunctions of the Author, should such an arrangement amount to this. It does not strike me, however, in this light. The Library Committee will, of course order one or more copies. The *use* will be for the *public*. The *principle* involved in the two cases is the same. At least, it so appears to me. True, the family of Mr. Calhoun will be benefitted in proportion to the number of copies sold. This is *incidental* and applies to the author or proprietor of every book. I can not, and ought not to be indifferent to this, tho' *they* seem to be; for they were perfectly willing to present the manuscripts *gratuitously* to the State of South Carolina, if it would see them faithfully and properly printed and published. This I would not consent that they should do. They are not more than *scantily* independent; and I was unwilling to see the literary labours as well as the public services of their Father pass to the Country, without some compensation. In what I now write I have consulted with none of them, but act upon my own responsibility. It seems to me that Congress ought to subscribe for a large number of Copies, and through the members to distribute them amongst the people. Will you give me your opinions on the subject at your earliest leisure. You can consult with other friends; and let me hear from you, if possible, on my return to Richmond, say Tuesday the 9th of next month. It will be important for me to have them at that time, as it might facilitate my arrangements with Nash and Woodhouse. I write in haste as the stage is at the door.

JOHN RANDOLPH TUCKER TO R. M. T. HUNTER.

WINCHESTER, [VA.], *December 24, 1851.*

MY DEAR SIR: I thank you for putting Mr. Guyer in the trail of the facts I enquired for.

Have you spoken to Foote's Resolution? And what position have you taken? I presume the same with Mason.

I hope your election is safe. Is there any danger of Bayly, or of Wise? Which have you any reason to look to as an opponent?

One of my delegates said to me to-day he would like to have *my* *advice* before going to Richmond. I of course told him I would like to *confer* with, not to dictate to, him. I think in this section we will have things all right for you. I heard favorable news from our Senator who has been somewhat doubtful to-day through his brother, who said, if he did not go for you, he ought to be turned out. He said he did not think he would fail you, that he was certain you were his choice unless Bayly were preferred by him. I shall write to him and set matters right as to him. In Jefferson I learn all is well. In Hampshire I know it is. Here in Clark, Warren and Page I am quite confident.

I wish you a Merry Christmas. We hear flying rumours of the Capitol Conflagration. Do you go home at Xmas? If not why not come here for a day?

I was glad to see your movement about the message. Your position is favorable and a good move on the Free trade pound would strengthen you immensely in a party point of view.

JAMES A. SEDDON TO R. M. T. HUNTER.

RICHMOND, [VA.], *January 18th, 1852.*

MY DEAR SIR: On my return last night from a visit of some days to the country, I was gratified by the receipt of your cordial letter. It has given a spur to the resolution I had entertained for some two weeks, ever since from my return from the South, to write you, and which I have been prevented from executing partly by my shameful habit of procrastination, and partly by the wish to give more satisfactory intelligence than I then possessed of the prospect of your reelection. I am personally pretty completely removed from politics, and have moreover, but one object of keen lively interest, and that is your reelection. *That* I have told all my friends in the Legislature from my return could and must be effected. At first there were much doubt and distrust on the part of your friends. They did not know whether to press a speedy election, whether to go into Caucus or not. My opinions and advice were decided, have the election at the earliest day and go into Caucus too, even if you risk something. I did not however believe they would. On my return last night, I was much gratified to learn, the day of election had been fixed without any appearance of overpressing on the part of your friends for Thursday next. I have been all the morning circulating with your friends among the members. I find them I rejoice to say all hopeful, most confident and some absolutely certain of the result. You know I am not sanguine in disposition and would not on any account form hopes to give a keener edge to coming disappointment. Yet I think I can do more, than bid you be of good cheer. I believe you may feel almost safe. Our friends have concluded they are strong enough to risk a Caucus without danger. I advise it by all means and the sooner the better. It will probably be held to-morrow night.

The only competitor seriously talked of is Wise and really he is not proposed by most of those who urge him. They want to reward him for his course in the Convention and get him out of the way for Western Competitors for other Honor. *They* have no thot save for the man. Wise makes a great mistake in not being more generous and true to his ancient friendships. He ought not to oppose you and I can't help hoping, if he knew how affairs really stand, he would not. At least, I hope such is the fact and advise all our friends to take that for granted and urge it on his Western supporters. In that way, I hope bitterness toward him will be avoided and yet good done in inducing *his* friends to come to your support. I want you elected, by a Caucus to purge all past objections, by a vote so nearly unanimous as to give to your past course the fullest indorsement, to your future prospects the most auspicious impulse. All this I believe and trust will be effected.

It may be well for some friend in the Legislature to have the authority to express your opinion ab[ou]t the Compromise as *a fact accomplished*, but let him be perfectly trusty and be even then cautious. Concurrence in Mason's late speech, or in Johnson's late message on this point might be ventured. Beyond I should be careful to go. The Compromise, curse on it, both in inception and accomplishment is perilous ground to every true Southern man. I eschew the thing in thought heart and deed as much as an honest man may.

Your friends in Congress from V[irgini]a may do some good by writing doubtful persons in their delegations, but I do not think much remains to be effected that way. I am rejoiced to hear they so generally approve and sustain you. It is a just reward and honors both you and them. Remember me cordially to my old friends among them and altho' I don't enq[uire] after them I warmly sympathize with them.

W. R. Nicholls to R. M. T. Hunter.

Mount Hope, Baltimore, [Md.], *January 18th, 1852.*

My Dear Sir: I avail myself of this occasion, to address you, a few words, from this agreeable, and romantic portion of the good democratic portion of Baltimore County, and I am glad to refer you with so much pleasure, and with a high sense of pride to the message, of the present Chief Magistrate, Gov[ernor] Lowe, and to state, that much [more] of the present, prosperity of this State, at this period arises, from facts, and arguments, and by the wise, and liberal policy pursued by those who are found to be sound on matters of State Rights, than those who are in no way governed by the true prosperity of the people. Hon. John C. Le Grand will succeed J. A. Pearce and I presume we will be able to send a good and sound man, in the place of T. G. Pratt, the people of Maryland endorse the sentiments of the people, of Virginia, and I hope to see you returned to the Senate, and I am glad to see the high, and liberal tone, of the message of Gov[ernor] Johnson of V[irgini]a, on the topics of education, and internal improvements, finance, though I did not calculate upon his election of Governor. However the old Dominion must and will take the lead in many matters. We will be able in this State to send in company with Judge Le Grand, Henry May, Esq. both to the Senate, at the present time it is not very important, but I will state the fact, and I think the documents, will prove it, that Gov[ernor] Pratt in 1844 went into office under the popular name of one of the defeated Candidates, for the Presidency and that his financial statements, have proven not correct, and consequently, on the subject of slavery his views are, and must be obnoxious, to many of the people of this state, while at the same time his colleague was flattering Gen[eral] Jackson by his report as chairman of the Committee, that voted to refund the fine imposed on him at N[ew] O[rleans] in 1814. This State has of late years, been more or less, influenced by renegrades from the *Jackson party*, such men as these, and their noble companions, Reverdy Johnson, and John P. Kennedy. I understand their political characters, and intend to show that they are, unworthy, and the means they have used, to advance themselves to the pinnacle of political distinction has not been strictly in accordance with the doctrines, or the tests, of true republican principles, though they have imagined themselves, secure. You will find before long that they will receive a rebuke from the people. Johnson is popular with some, but there is a strong, and lasting impression, on the minds of many of prejudice and I do not believe he can be elected, while Judge Le Grand is a candidate. He is a gentleman of very high qualifications, and for learning and integrity of character is regarded with much affection by the people.

I have much pleasure in being able, to speak of the many improvements of the day, and the great and rapid strides this section of the state has given and encouraged both in the higher branches of commerce, navigation, manufactures and agriculture, and the improvement in her historical pages. She has given new, and an increased attraction. They have a very large, and interesting library both in Balt[imore] and Annapolis and there is a gentleman of some celebrity as a writer, who is about to give us a sketch of the earlier history of Chestertown, when things under the reign of *Carroll* I believe if not Lord Calvert, have some what changed their nature, to the present day. Carroll was born in 1737, at Annapolis, at eight years of age sent to France to be educated, and at the age of twenty he commenced the study of law in London, and returned here in 1764. This is the land of a Wirt, and the home of that eminent man Pinkney, and the plain cabin, of that pure, and gifted genius and one of the men that, in mind and oratory, was the theme of wonder, and admiration, whose eloquence in the Senate house was such only as in the days of a Patrick Henry, have witnessed, for Wirt was a self made man, and was by nature destined to be a great and mighty orator, his style was melodious, sweet, argumentative and at times irresistible, fascinating beyond conception or the powers of a description. I hope you will pay me a visit, and in company with your friends, Judge Butler of S[outh] C[arolina], or Holmes, if you come to the City of Baltimore. I will give you a real Maryland and Virginia welcome, bring Mr. Rhett also. When you see my friends in Georgetown Ould and Caper-

ton bring them along. You cannot help finding M[ount] Hope if
you start from the Eutaw House in Baltimore that street will bring
you out here. I shall trouble you to send me a copy of the reports
of Committees of Commerce, Navy, Finance, Manufactures, and a
copy of the report of Patents, for 1851, and a copy of the Constitutions and a copy of such documents as you may think instructive and
of interest to me, which I shall preserve and keep for future reference, shall take very little or no part, at present in the active strife of
a political campaign, but to an old acquaintance and a friend of the
Carolina patriot and statesman, I have been induced to make these
requests.

What are the prospects for appointments in the Navy? I shall
be glad if you would take sides with Mr. Geyers and advocate the
retrocession of G[eorge]town to M[arylan]d soon after the discussion on the Navy reform, and fix on a day and make it the special
order. Ould and Caperton can impart to you all the details, give to
Geo[rge]town, a district and seperate county of itself not as an ap-
pendage to Montgomery. Col[onel] Joseph N. Fearson, the great
and disinterested champion of democracy, and whose ancestors in
Baltimore in 1812, at Balti[more] proved themselves, worthy sons
of a good and glorious cause, is to be the Candidate for the office of
Mayor of Georgetown in February, when I hope the salary will be
raised to $2,500 per annum, and that you will introduce a bill in the
Senate for lighting our town, with gas, and improving the streets.
We have had a fine and deep snow. And we are likely to have a long
winter, the sleighing is very fine, we have a great deal of beauty here,
the theatre bills announce a new star in the person of Lola Martz &c.
Should you want any good and accurate scribes for Committee clerks,
we can furnish you with two. You will be welcomed, and I shall be
much pleased to see you in this good and hospitable state when you
can find leisure to pay us a visit. Excuse all mistakes, and all or
what may be errors.

LEWIS E. HARVIE TO R. M. T. HUNTER.

APPOMATTOX DEPOT, AMELIA CO[UNTY, VA.],
January 19th, 1852.

DEAR HUNTER: I am very solicitous to procure an appointment as
Cadet, for my second son Jno. Harvie, in the military Academy at
West Point. My only chance of getting him in is as one of the appointments by the President. I have written to Mr. Mason on the
subject and desired him to show you my letter. I would not write
to you because I thought about this time you would be annoyed by
your election. Since I wrote I have been to Richmond and learnt
(with sincere gratification as you will believe) that your success

was well nigh certain. I have concluded to write to you and let you understand that I am much interested in procuring this appointment, hoping that you will interest yourself in it and aid me as far as you can. I do not know what step to take and hope you will let me know. This boy has as I am informed by his teachers a considerable talent for Mathematics which I wish cultivated and this is one among various reasons why I wish him sent to West Point. It has been suggested to me to state to you (what I should certainly not have thought of but for the suggestion) that he is a grand nephew of Maj[o]r Ja[me]s Eggleston who served as Lieu[tenan]t in Lee's Legion during the Revolutionary war, and was afterwards elected to Congress, from this District. As you know he was a gallant officer and highly respected as a citizen and Public man. His Great Grand father Col. Harvie, was also an active Patriot during the same struggle and a member of the V[irgini]a Convention in 1775 and 76. He was afterwards in Congress and signed the Articles of Confederation in 1778, and was then made Register of the Land Office in V[irgini]a, showing that his services were appreciated. I mention these matters with reluctance and only because I have been urged to do so. I hope you will forget I have done so unless they can be made available in favouring this appointment. I am sure that Holliday, Edmundson, Caskie, Bocock, Strother, Meade and Genl. Millson will aid me if I know how to use their assistance. I am under the impression also that I may be able to procure the intervention of Genl. Scott and Mr. Crittenden on account of others and not myself. My main reliance tho' is on you and Strother and I shall expect you to work for me as I would under similar circumstances for you and him. If I can't get him in this year I would be content to get him in the next. Let me hear from you as soon as may be.

GEORGE F. THOMSON TO R. M. T. HUNTER.

NEW YORK [CITY], *January 28, 1852.*

DEAR SIR: It is exceedingly satisfactory to the commercial interests of this city that you have called in the above resolution[1] for information in ref[erence] to the expenses of the Gov[ernmen]t Ware Houses. If the great inconveniences and unnecessary expenses to our merchants could also be reached by resolution it would throw much further light upon the subject. But what I desire to suggest is that you will also call for the number and expense of the private Bonded Ware Houses (exclusive of cellars for liquors). This

---

[1] The resolution referred to as having been offered by Hunter requested the Secretary of the Treasury to inform the Senate of the number of public warehouses then used by the Government, their location, period of lease, the terms of the leases, and the amount expended upon them for labor and other purposes.

would seem to be necessary in order to arrive at a correct understanding of the whole system and it is information our collector
can readily firnish. It will be found that while their private Bonded
stores are Bonding quite as much property as the Government stores,
equally safe and more convenient to the merchant, they are [at] no
expense whatever to the Treasury, in fact the Government derive
unjustly, a small revenue from them for the collector hires his officers to attend them for $800 p[e]r an[num] and collects from the
owner of each store $1095.00 p[e]r an[num] leaving a profit on each
store to the Government which is paid monthly by each owner of a
store $295. p[e]r an[num]. There are in this city 12 or 15 of these
private Bonded stores (exclusive of cellars which I do not include).
There are other private stores owned by merchants used for Bonding their own goods exclusively in what I think it will be found are
not placed upon the same footing as those stores in ref[erence] to
which the owners make the Bonding of goods a regular and legitimate business. I mean in ref[erence] to the amount paid for the use
of the officer. It is difficult to understand why a merchant who
uses a store for this purpose exclusively for himself should pay any
less for the Gov[ernmen]t officer than he who uses his store for
accommodation of many merchants. The Bonding system is one
of immense benefit to our merchants and commerce generally but
it requires a thorough overhauling and placed on a more liberal
footing excluding as much as possible all Government interference
and making it as far as possible a private interest, subject alone to
such simple regulations as will insure safety and security. The
convenience and safety of the private stores are universally acknowledged and preferred by our merchants. Suits are constantly brought
against the Government for goods lost from the Government stores,
but none so far have ever been lost from the private stores to my
knowledge.

JAMES A. SEDDON TO R. M. T. HUNTER.

RICHMOND, [VA.], *February 7, 1852.*

MY DEAR SIR: For some days past, I have been suffering serious
inconvenience and confinement from my vexatious complaints (of
which I have a score) and consequently have been prevented from
either acknowledging your friendly letter to myself or communicating my views upon the interesting points suggested in your confidential letter to our friend Goode who in pursuance of the leave
allowed him submitted it to me. My opinions are worth very little
indeed, especially now that my thoughts and feelings are so little
given to political subjects but such as they are, will ever be most
sincerely and frankly at the services of a friend so highly valued as
yourself. I agree with you readily as to the position and duty of

the Southern Rights (or as I prefer the States Rights) party of the South in the coming presidential struggle. Personally I should have preferred a separate organization and action on their part and 18 months ago, when I still hoped their spirit and their strength might prove equal to their zeal and the justice of their cause, I should have advised that course. Now however it is apparent, their *cause as a political one is lost* and thus separate action would be more than preposterous—would be suicidal. The cursed Bonds of party paralized our strength and energy when they might have been successfully exerted, and now as some partial compensation must sustain and uphold us from dispersion and prostration. In reviewing the past I am inclined to think the great error we committed in the South was the uniting at all in council or action with the Whigs. Their timidity betrayed more than treason. We should have acted in and through the Democratic party alone. Certainly that is all that remains to us now to do. We have and can maintain (within certain limits of considerable latitude) ascendency in the Democratic party of the South and probably controlling influence on the general policy and action of the whole party in the Union. The *Union* party, par excellence, we can proscribe and crush. What miserable gulls the *Union* Democrats of the South find them, and I am inclined to think the *Union* Whigs will not fair much better. "Woodcocks caught in their own springs." Of both for the most part, it may be safely said, they were venal or timid-knaves or fools and most richly will they deserve disappointment and popular contempt. The Southern Rights men by remaining in full communion with the Democratic party will be at least prepared for two important objects—to inflict just retribution on deserters and traitors— to sustain, it may be, reward friends and true men. I go for the States Rights men making themselves the Simon pures of Southern Democracy—the standard bearers and champions in the coming presidential fight.

Now as for the candidate. We must exclude Cass and every other such cats paw of Clay and the Union Whigs. We must have a candidate too who will carry the Middle States or rather on whom the Democracy of the Middle States will rally. Too many factions prevail in those states to allow any prominent man among them to unite all the Democracy. Besides they are peculiarly wanting in fit available men. It is rather farcical to be sure to those who know to insist on Douglas as most fit. The best man for the Presidency and yet I have for more than than a year thought it was coming to that absurdity. On many accounts I concur with you in believing he is our best chance and that we had better go in for him at once and decidedly, making our adhesion if we can [be] conclusive of the nomination. You know I have long thought better of his capacity than most of our friends, especially the Judge and he is at least as honest and more firm than any of his competitors. I should be disposed therefore to urge him.

As to the vice presidency, I am strongly inclined to urge the continued use of your name, unless your personal repugnance is insuperable. I can readily understand your present position to be more acceptable to your personal feelings. I think it the most agreeable position under the Government, but ought not other considerations to weigh seriously. There is the chance of the Presidency by vacancy, not much perhaps but still to be weighed. There is a certain niche in History to all time which to a man not destitute of ambition *is an object.* There is to your family the highest dignity and respect attached to the Vice Presidency in popular estimation. In this last point of view, is not something due too to your State. Southern States can hardly longer aspire to give Presidents. Whatever belated honors are to be cast on them must be through sub or direct stations and of these the Vice Presidency is the first.

These considerations I think should prevail and I suspect would, if some personal feelings reflected from the general estimate of your friends in regard to Douglas and a just estimate as I know and feel it of your own subornity did not make you revolt at a secondary position on his ticket. You may too fear that the influence and estimation of your character among the true men of the South might be impaired by this sort of a doubtful alliance with Northern politicians and schemers even of the most unobjectionable stamp. All these considerations are not without weight with me. I feel them to the full as much on your account as you can well do yourself, and yet I think *they* ought not to control. *We* must be practical as politicians and statesmen to be useful—a high position—good—a position of acknowledged influence and confessed participation in the administration ought not to be lost to the States Rights men from over refined scruples and feelings. As Vice President, I believe you could and would have great influence in the administration and that influence might prove of immense value to our cause in the South.

If however your objections personally are insuperable, I am too truly your friend to *insist* on their reliquishment. We must then look out for and obtain the next best of our school, who is available. I should not advise as you suggest J[ohn] Y. M[ason]. He is not strictly of us—is too flexible—too needy and too diplomatic to be fully relied upon. I fear we should have to go out of our State, unless Douglas could be content with Meade or with Goode himself. Bayly might have done but for his desertion, which has lost all old friends and gained none new. Jefferson Davis would be the best if he would accept. If not, what would be said to Gov[ernor] Chapman of Al[abam]a. He is I think a true man. Excuse an abrupt close. I have exhausted my only paper.

[P. S.] My best regards to the Judge and Mr. Mason. Write whenever you have a spare hour to bestow on a friend.

RICHARD RUSH TO R. M. T. HUNTER.

SYDENHAM NEAR PHILADELPHIA, [PA.], *April 3rd, 1852.*

MY DEAR SIR: My thanks for your Report on a change in the coinage, which I have not failed to read. The subject, as it has always appeared to me, is not an easy one to manage. In reading upon it, I have sometimes been ready to give up; and the most skilled in it are, after all, prone to end in guess-work, which they prefer to call " approximation." You are aware of this I see, though handling the whole matter very well.

I fully go with you in your most material point, the *proportion of currency to production.* What harm can arise you ask (page 9) from any probable increase of the precious metals, if both are allowed to swell the volume of currency? Your just answer follows. To my view, your closing sentences of the paragraph on page 7 are equally sound. An enlightened manufacturer in England once said to me that England could supply the whole world with manufactures. China included I asked? Yes he replied, " and another planet toboot, as large as our globe, if we could only open a market in another. *Markets* are all we want." He assumed that modern machinery gave England a productive working power equal to a population of three hundred millions. This is about the calculation of the Prince Joinville in his novel pamphlet, when he said that steam would now give to one French sailor the power of twenty. If this be anything like good guess-work, *production* must be greatly ahead of currency in the world. I confess I should rather be disposed to say, (to go on a little with guess-work,) that if the yield, annually of the precious metals were five times greater than it is at present, or than it is all likely to be for years and years to come, it would still lag much behind production, and therefore be insufficient to produce the best results upon the wealth comforts and prosperity of communities. I observe that our minister in London, Mr. Lawrence, no bad guesser I should think on such matters, appears under no apprehension of a surfeit of gold from California. Your bill may lead us to expect silver change enough for our present wants; and I hope that the principles of your well-matured and carefully drawn Report may lay the foundation of more extensive good, by helping to keep down, under the authority of such a senatorial document, all fears among us of the metalitic currency ever becoming too over-abundant, though the California mines, with those of Australia in addition, should yield far more than they have ever yet done.

I received your cordial acknowledgment of the 9th of February of one of my antiquated Treasury Reports. I always visit Washington with pleasure, being sure to meet with so many there to make it agreeable; but it seems to me that, just now, only *two* classes of persons have any business there; our Legislators and our President-makers!

EDMUND W. HUBARD[1] TO R. M. T. HUNTER.

SARATOGA, [VA.], May 8th, 1852.

DEAR HUNTER: I received your very able and valuable report on " a change in the coinage," and was highly delighted with this, and other evidences contained in the proceedings of the Senate of the manner, as well as distinguished talents with which you discharge the various duties of your high station. I have often said, that intellectually as well as in points of character, I thought you more resembled Mr. Madison than any other person. In some respects I think you will prove his superior. Madison in the abstract was sound, but he lacked either the elevation of character or the firmness of purpose to carry out his convictions. He gave to expediency what was due to principle. Without going beyond my candid convictions I may add, that I deem you will prove him superior in this respect.

If the health of my Family will permit I wish to attend the Baltimore Convention.

For various reasons I decidedly prefer Buchanan. In our section as far as I can learn he is the choice of more than 40 to 1. In our District Convention we thought it improper to express our preference or instruct our Delegates. But we adopted a resolution approving of the *two thirds rule* in making our presidential nomination. As an evidence of fairness, delegates were selected without reference to their *personal* preferences. All that was desired was that the popular will would be reflected, let that be as it might. Thos. S. Bocock was appointed and Wm. C. Flournoy and others not agreeing with a decided majority. I might add not with one in 20 in the District Convention. We are dead against Genl. Cass. He cannot be elected. We will take any other Democrat rather than him. He cannot carry V[irgini]a. Many leading Democrats declare they will not vote for him if nominated. He stands in the same relation to our party that Genl. Scott does to the Whig. He has talents, but with all is deemed more of a demagogue than statesman. His strong proclivity to ride both sides of a sapling argues unsoundness or over ambition—either way he is not trust worthy. Besides he has had his day. The Demo-

---

[1] Representative in Congress from Virginia, 1841–1847; resided at Curdsville, Buckingham County.

crats will settle down in favor both of one Canvass and the one term principle for the Presidency. Besides I am opposed to taking Senatorial Candidates and wish the Baltimore Convention to adopt a resolution excluding all holding office, from the field of selection. We must go to *private* life positions for our candidates for President and vice too. If we go to Congress for our candidates as well as for instructions as to whom to cast our votes, why Congress will soon absorb *all* the *powers* as well as all the *honors* of our republic. This policy unless averted will corrupt and revolutionize our government. The Executive must in inception, election, and action be distinct from Congress. Let the Congress indicate Candidates, which is tantamount to an election, the next step will be for the President to humble himself to his *real* master. Thus the judiciary will also fall under the influence of Congress. Then a congressional majority will decide and continue the fate of the country. I am opposed to all this. I want the President in *all* respects independent of both branches of Congress. The country people are daily becoming more disgusted with Congressional President making. That man will stand highest in the public estimation who keeps above all such extra official dictation. While the South held all the high *honors*, in truth got *all* the *benefits* of our government, they have fattened and grown strong upon the substantials, while we are starving and growing weak upon honors. Now I am for a change. Give me sound and reliable Northern or free State men, and so far as I am concerned they may enjoy *all* the honors. We want the real solid benefits of government and if they have the honors, it will be the most powerful motive with their aspirants on both sides to keep down the slavery agitation and also to so make the machinery of government as to rebuild the south. I look upon high honors as incompatible with sectional aggrandizement. We cannot get both at once. When the south held the Posts of honor, she had to throw all the crumbs of government to conciliate distant support. Now give the free States the honors and then they will do justice to gain our confidence and support, for without the slave state vote in Congress no Executive can honorably or properly administer the government.

I had rather see Buchanan, Marcy, or Douglas, or Dallas, or R[ichard] Rush by a great deal than Cass, under the latter [I] look upon our defeat as *certain*. With either of the others we may succeed. Cass is too much mixed up with all this Kossuth movement, and too strongly inclined to elevate himself not only above all our Diplomats, but above the wise policy upon foreign affairs of Washington and Jefferson to be trusted at this juncture. I look upon our Foreign relations at this time, as the most important point to guard in making our selection of candidates. Democratic measures are in the general to obtain either under a Whig or Democratic rule. But *justice* to the slave states, and a wise and peaceful Foreign policy is what we need. On neither of these points am I willing to confide in Cass. As for the Union and the upstart constitutional expounders from Tennessee, they had better put things in the ascendant at home, before they assume the leadership for the Union. That is either a Whig State, or else the least *sound* of any of the Democratic slave states. The Union is a high toned *Federal* organ but unlike other Federal papers, it does not seem to be *aware* that it is so. Now the Democratic editor from Tennessee is but little short of our former Globe editors from Kentucky. What one did for knavery, the other is doing for folly. I am opposed to being doctrinated by such chaps from the *New* States. The Union was clearly for Cass from the start, and all the time. Genl. Cass on a recent occasion went out of his way to laud Genl. Jackson and especially his *proclamation*. He is the advocate of *compulsory* democracy, and dead against the *voluntary* system. He would establish the inquisition, if the Union would suggest it, or the alien and sedition laws. Should he be elected the country might look out for the most high handed measures, all proved by the editor of the Union to be in accordance with the doctrines of Jefferson, Madison, and Jackson. May the Lord deliver our party from the hands of the quacks of Tennessee and Michigan.

To change the subject, I stick closely to my planting and farming, take no part except to vote in politics. We have a son and daughter which I shall train up for a match for some of your children. You and lady are as great favorites with my wife as your humble servant, and she often says she is in favor of Mr. Hunter over all others for the presidency. Of all things we would be most happy to see you and Mrs. H. and all the under fry here. The South Side Railroad passes by me as near as Farmville twelve miles distant. In about twelve months it will be open to Farmville and a few more months to Lynchburg. Then, my dear sir, there will be no valid excuse for your not visiting this part of the state. If you will come, I will take, or go with you any where here abouts. Pray give my best respects to Judge Butler, Atchison, Douglas and Mason and believe me as ever with highest regard and consideration.

G. H. CROSMAN, MAJOR OF VOLUNTEERS, U. S. A., TO R. M. T. HUNTER.

PHILADELPHIA, [PA.], *21st May, 1852.*

DEAR SIR: Although I have not the pleasure of your personal acquaintance, I cannot refrain from expressing the gratification I feel at the prospect of a reform in the settlement of Disbursing Officers' Accounts; which I infer from the recent Debates in the Senate upon this subject and from your remarks.

I have been a Disbursing officer of the army for about 25 years; most of which in the Q[uarte]r Master's Dep[artmen]t; and I call upon you, therefore, my dear Sir, from an *intimate and practical* experience, that the *evils* you are desirous of correcting, do not wholly or even chiefly lie in the direction you have been led to believe. The whole system requires re-modeling and reforming; and until that is thoroughly done, by proper legislation, neither Congress, the President, or the Disbursing Officers, can ever know correctly the Expenditures of the Government under any head of appropriation or balance their a[ccount]s.

Officers of the Army generally render their accounts with much promptness to the Treasury; but it is impossible, under the present system, for the Auditors and Comptrollers to be equally prompt in their settlement of them; and while the law is sufficiently stringent upon the neglects or omissions of the Disbursing officers, it takes no notice of the delays and omissions at the Treasury. I have, myself, had ac[count]s there, waiting settlement, for nearly *three years;* and frequently for one and two years at a time; much to my annoyance and regret. The death of the Disbursing officer, under such circumstances, is always attended with serious consequences to his family, and Bondsmen; for after such long delays, it is often impossible, and always difficult for his Executors and friends to get a settlement, by removing the objections of the Auditors by proper explanations, which the officer alone could do.

In France they have the proper system for settling military accounts. An Auditor, called "Commissary of ac[count]s" always accompanies the Head Quarters of an Army, in the field; and the accounts and vouchers of all the Disbursing officers are promptly audited *on the spot*, under *the eye of the Com[man]d[in]g Gen[era]l.* The Disbursing officer can, then, meet the enemy next day, with no pecuniary cases upon his mind. Not so with us; why lie, I have been all day engaged in chasing Indians, in Florida (and we caught some of them too) with $90,000 worth of "Mr. Haguer's 'Poetry," suspended vouchers of mine, in my saddle Bags; and then Vouchers, (all of which were suspended for mere informality, requiring, perhaps, evidence on some of them that Mr. A. B., or Book keeper and Clerk in the House of Messrs. C. D., was legally authorised to sign a receipt and receive money for the firm) had actually accrued two or three years previous, upon the frontiers of Missouri Arkansas and Louisiana—more than a 1,000 miles distant. Judge, then, my dear Sir, with what feelings I entered the swamps in pursuit of the enemy the following day! Here was $90,000 we suspended, in the settlement of my ac[count]s at the Treasury; and without long explanations, which I alone could give, would never be passed to my credit. In a moment that power might be taken forever from me;

and with a beggared family, and ruined Bondsmen, and perhaps, even a *tarnished reputation*, my military career would thus have ended most ingloriously. In the name of Humanity and Justice then let this State of things cease and determine. Enquire into this matter, and you will find many such cases as I have here suffered.

I have, myself, disburned Williams of the public money; but, from the causes I have stated, always with fear and trembling for the settlement, which I knew would be so long postponed. Unless yourself and other gentlemen examine one of our long complex Quarter Master's ac[count]s, you can have little knowledge of the difficulties in the way of their prompt settlement under the present system.

I hope, most earnestly, that a Committee of Congress will be appointed to examine thoroughly, and report upon the present mode of settling ac[count]s at the Treasury. Let the facts appear, that the public may know where the fault lies. If a Disbursing Officer has neglected or violated his duty, in any respect, let his name appear, and he be brought to trial. But I fancy the fault, mainly, will be traced to a vicious system, and incompetent Clerks in the Treasury Department. Young gentlemen of political influence have too often usurped the places of men [of] clerical ability—practical working Clerks, who understood their business, and did it faithfully and steadily.

I beg you to excuse the liberty I have taken, in writing to you this long letter, and attribute it to the real and sincere interest I feel in the subject; and the anxiety I share, in common with my brother Officers, for some "*radical reforms*" in this respect. As the Chairman of the Committee on Finance of the Senate, and the attention you have evidently given to this matter, it is confidently hoped and believed you will be able to bring forward some adequate remedies for the present evils, and the vicious system of settling ac[count]s at the Treasury of Army officers at least.

GEORGE BOOKER TO R. M. T. HUNTER.

(*Private.*)

BALTIMORE, [MD.], *June 7th, 1852.*

MY DEAR SIR: I am very sorry I had it not in my power to have seen you before I returned home, but it was impossible for me to leave this place sooner, and now my engagements compel me to go home immediately.

Last evening I had an interview with Wise and said among other things "Wise have you been speaking unkindly of Hunter? What is the matter? No. did you say you would not vote for Hunter for President? Geo. Booker I would crawl on my hands and knees to make Hunter President." I shall say no more for the present. You know the man and his manner.

I have thought it proper to say this much because circumstances and the zeal of some of your friends might have given to this matter a very different coloring. You and Wise shall not quarrel if my feeble voice can prevent it. Listen to no idle rumor. Wise is your friend. I know the fact.

A Southerner to R. M. T. Hunter.

(Private.)

RICHMOND, [VA.], *June 14th* [*1852*].

DEAR SIR: I beg to call your attention, to that portion of Judge Conrad's speech in the Anti-Fillmore Convention of New York, which is enclosed. (You will find the whole speech in N. Y. Herald of 13th.)

I write to you as a true friend of the South, to know what is the South to do. Are her statesmen looking ahead and preparing for contingencies? As this letter is anonymous, you are not bound, I admit, to treat it with any consideration. I ask only to free my own mind of thoughts which press painfully upon it, and to leave them with those who can best judge whether they are of any value or practicable. The question is this—Cannot the South form an alliance, either with England, or some foreign country, which will protect her from the threatened aggression of the North? Look ahead, and do you not see a storm coming from the North which must dissolve the Union? Ought we not then to look ahead, ought not the Southern leaders to meet together and confer, and sound the governments of England, or other foreign powers, to see what can be done in such a contingency? You are one of the few men, I believe, not eaten up with selfish ambition. Strike a blow, then, I entreat you for the safety of the South. Would to Heaven that the South would stop talking and go to *acting*. Imitate the *forecast*, the *practical* character, and (as it has become necessary to fight the devil with fire) the subtlety of our sectional enemies. *It strikes me, that it would be a good stroke of policy, and a most holy and righteous retribution*, if we could form a treaty with England, giving her certain privileges in *the cotton trade and vast navigation, in return for which, she could stand by the South, and crush the Free Soilers between Canada and the South States.*

RICHARD ROWZEE TO R. M. T. HUNTER.

TAPPAHANNOCK, ESSEX CO., VA., *August 2nd, 1852.*

MY DEAR SIR: The Federal press and party are circulating a charge against Genl. Pierce, the nominee of the democratic party for the presidency, to the effect, that he, in a speech delivered at New Boston

23318°—18—VOL 2——10

in December last, expressed himself in such terms as to leave no doubt of his abolition principles. Whilst the charge has been denied in the democratic papers, several democrats are doubting as to the course they shall take in the presidential election, and some I fear, will withhold their support to the democratic candidate, if they do not give in their adhesion to the federal one, all of whom may be saved to the party, if they can be convinced of the falsity of the charge. I know of no other way better to convince them than a statement of your opinion in relation to it. I therefore write to ask you to inform me whether you believe or disbelieve the charge. I with those who are doubting the course they shall pursue, have fears, that I should not have had, but for the circulation of this charge, which if true, would be destructive to our interests, and which can not be quieted by News paper publications, in which I have but little confidence. I am now an old and private man, having surrendered all my public trusts and duties under the old Constitution; anything therefore that will give me some of the passing events of the day, will be an amusement and gratification to me. You will therefore, if you please, send me the patent office reports for 1850–51, and any that may be of a later date, with any document that you may think will interest and amuse an old man in retirement. I trust you are in the enjoyment of health, and that that inestimable blessing may be continued to you through a long life to be devoted to your family and country.

R. M. T. HUNTER TO RICHARD ROWZEE.

WASHINGTON, [D. C.], *August 9th, 1852.*

MY DEAR SIR: I regret to learn from your letter that there are democrats in our county who hestitate in relation to voting for Pierce and King upon the suspicion that the former entertains "abolition principles." You ask my opinion in relation to this charge. I have no hestitation in saying that I have never given this charge the least credence. Gen[era]l Pierce's course upon this subject whilst he was in Congress was such as to have made it highly improbable that he could have uttered any such statement. The charge too has been denied by persons who heard the speech at New Boston, first by Messrs. B. F. Ager and James M. Campbell. The certain respectibility and credibility of these gentlemen have been vouched by Mr. Norris, a Senator from New Hampshire, and Messrs. Hibbard and Peaslee members of the Ho[use] of Rep[resentative]s from the same state. These are gentlemen of the very highest standing, men whose word no one can doubt who knows them. The statement of Messrs. Ager and Campbell has been sustained by more than one hundred persons who were present when the speech was delivered and who have published a document to that effect. But in addition to all this an editorial of the Union for which I presume Genl. Armstrong is responsible states that he has seen a letter from Genl. Pierce himself denouncing the charge as being "*grossly false.*"

It seems to me that this evidence ought to satisfy any unprejudiced mind. I may add that I was a member of the Ho[use] of Rep[resentative]s whilst Gen[era]l Pierce was in the Senate and had some opportunities to observe his course. The result of these observations was a conviction that he was one of the most reliable politicians upon this subject of slavery of all whom I knew in the non-slaveholding states.

JEFFERSON DAVIS TO R. M. T. HUNTER.

PALMYRA, MISS., *August 22nd, 1852.*

MY DEAR SIR: This is to introduce to you Jno. W. Smith of Washington City and to request your good offices in obtaining for him some appointment about the Capitol or public grounds. I spoke of him to you when I had the honor to be associated with you on the Com[mittee] of public buildings, and we joined in recommending him for the place of watchman on the Capitol grounds, to which he was appointed by the then Commissioners but removed by his successor.

Among the many claims to your consideration of matters of public importance he has very probably been forgotten. I will therefore say something of him to induce you to make further inquiry. He is a Virginian, and his wants led to my acquaintance with him in the winter of 1845. I found him in bad health destitute of means and with a large and helpless family. R. J. Walker gave him temporary employment as a messenger in the Treasury Department. His good conduct secured him continuous employment and would have led to his promotion if the Democracy had remained in power. In anticipation of his dismissal by the Whigs I sought for him the post before mentioned. My acquaintance with him enables me to say he is honest, attentive, and a man of good heart and sincerity of purpose.

I am sure you will never have cause to regret any service you may render him, at least it is my good fortune to remember the assistance I afforded to him and his family with as much satisfaction as I derive from any similar event in my life. It will always give me pleasure to hear from you and to be remembered by you as your sincere friend.

JOHN W. DUNCAN TO R. M. T. HUNTER.

MILLEDGEVILLE, GEORGIA, *October 23rd, 1852.*

MY DEAR SIR: I have just had the pleasure of reading, your speech, delivered some time ago in Richmond, and I assure you, I have rarely seen a clearer and more conclusive exemplification of true democratic principles and policy, than is contained in it. If it is published in pamphlet form, I wish you would be good enough to send me one or two copies. I am very glad, that you took the opportunity of giving your opinion upon two subjects, that seem now to form a prominent portion of the democratic creed, but which, you boldly and ably repudiate as most dangerous to our best interests. I mean Johnsons measure for giving away the public lands known as the Homestead Bill and the new doctrine of "Intervention." Either of these principles would destroy the best party on earth, and are certainly antagonistic to the recognized views of the "Virginia School." By the way was John Randolph a pupil of that school or an excrescence upon it. In what light is he held by its true disciples?

I suppose you begin to think by this time, that the politics of Georgia are perfectly inexplicable. The truth of the matter is we have a few leaders here, who are determined to sacrifice everything, even Pierce's election, to their own personal feelings. I told you when I saw you in July last in Washington, that I did not doubt, we should roll up a handsome majority for Pierce in Georgia. I then believed, that the elements of the democratic party, which had for a time been separated would harmoniously unite, but I am grievously disappointed. After the Baltimore Convention Gov [ernor] Cobb's friends held a separate meeting, and nominated a new Electoral Ticket, and thus put the democracy at defiance. The Whigs refused to sustain Cobb and went off into two wings, that of Scott and Webster and he soon began to see the anomalous position which he occupied, and he withdrew the ticket of Electors, composed one half of Whigs and the other of democrats. But he had carried his friends so far he found it would be more difficult to bring them back. So he began to beg and entreat, but alas! the door was shut in his face and there he now stands at this eleventh hour a miserable suppliant at the threshold of the Party with none even to pity or reverence him.

His friends in the highlands of the State have again put out another ticket for Pierce and King, the effect of which will be to distract the Party and prevent the popular vote from being cast for our Candidates. We therefore expect that the Legislature must be specially called to unite the knot which the politicians have made. So much for York and Lancaster.

I see that Botts, the notorious nocturnal companion of Tyler, has been pledging your State to Scott. Don't you think he ought to be indicted? I look upon this as a slander upon the good old dominion that never once was known to "flush" in her devotion to democracy.

I look upon Pierce's election as an absolute certainty, and then I have no doubt we shall have the government conducted on sound democratic and economical principles. What do you think about it?

FRANK G. RUFFIN TO R. M. T. HUNTER.

SHADWELL, ALBEMARLE CO., [VA.], *November 2nd, 1852.*

MY DEAR SIR: I know not if a man retired as I am from politics and never very active or influential in that field has a title to ask a favour even at the hands of one of his own strait sect; but as I speak not in my own behalf but for another I have ventured to approach you on the subject.

I learn, but not from himself, or by his agency, that in case Mr. Pierce shall have been elected, my friend, Gov[erno]r McDonald of Georgia has been mentioned in his own and some other contiguous states as a suitable member of the Cabinet: and it has been suggested that your influence would avail in getting him into that position. I need not mention to you how true he has been to the rights of the South and that he is not more of a disunionist than you and I, that is to say, as the lady remarked of Wilkes, "he does not squint more than every gentleman ought to." But I may say, what his retiring disposition and rare modesty may have prevented your knowing, that he is a man of marked ability, of wise moderation, of Roman firmness, of devoted patriotism, and of the loftiest public and private character. Every drop of his blood pulseth in accordance with Southern rights; and had every Southern man been as wise, as prudent, and as firm as he we should not now have to mourn the surrender of those rights?

I presume from Cobb's activity, that he is after some such post. You know *him*. Ought such a man, *dead in his own state*, except perhaps for purposes of mischief, to supplant him whom I propose, and thus rise one step higher towards that office which he has sought by betraying not only his own section, but the very principles which he *proposes* to maintain? Would it not be a step gained that the President of the Nashville Convention should aid the deliberations of Mr. Pierce?

GEORGE BOOKER TO R. M. T. HUNTER.

(*Private.*)

ELIZABETH CITY CO., NEAR HAMPTON, [VA.],
November 5th, 1852.

MY DEAR HUNTER: I wrote you in June a short note from Baltimore immediately after the adjournment of the Convention, to which I rec[eive]d an answer in a few days. I write now to acknowledge its receipt and to say that I have had several very free conversations with Wise since. He speaks of you in the kindest manner and does you ample justice, meet him with the cordiality of former days and all will be well. I know that he loves you and desires your friendship, nay thinks himself entitled to it. I pray God that nothing may ever occur to separate you.

Franklin Pierce from present indications will receive at least 270 of the electoral vote—the vote of every Southern State. We believe, an awful beating, this indeed. He is indebted to Virginia for his *Crown*. Well who from our State must go into the Cabinet? You say "I have nothing to ask and shall ask nothing from the incoming administration for myself." Do you intend to say that you would decline any offer? I ask the question because I frequently heard you spoken of and the wish expressed that you would accept the Treasury if offered you, indeed I have been asked if I thought you would accept. I had not thought much upon the subject, and had no wish about it. The only desire I have upon the subject is that you should exercise your own judgment and be where you can be most useful.

The Treasury will be the great leaver to work for reform 'tis very certain, and I hope to see some Southern man of the right stamp at it. Your present position is a commanding one and one from which you can better be heard by the nation, perhaps too it is nearer to the succession. Well if you shall come next after Pierce I shall not despair of the republic.

The last time I saw Bayly he told me that you would be the next President, that *he* intended to make you President. " You be d——d you can't get back to Congress yourself, and you talk to me about making Hunter President." " When and how come you so fond of Hunter. You always loved Hunter better than you love me." " If it be true can't you account for it very, very easy. Hunter votes right always—You only occasionally." Booker it is impossible you can doubt my fidelity to the South you must have confidence in me. " Confidence sir is a plant of slow groth as Mr. Pitt said." I like Bayly very much. We have been friends a long time, and I have tried very hard to forgive him. I withheld from him my vote the last time he was a candidate. It was painful to me to be obliged to do so. He does not understand his position, does not know how much ground he has lost. I doubt if he can ever recover. In saying this much do not understand me as doubting his fidelity to you. I do not, no, I believe him sincere. In the event of your taking a seat in the Cabinet Bayly and Wise will both struggle hard for your place in the Senate, the former I am certain cannot succeed the latter may, perhaps will. I know of no really formidable competitor in the East.

I am interrupted and must conclude before I had finished all I had to say.

HERSCHEL V. JOHNSON[1] TO R. M. T. HUNTER.

MILLEDGEVILLE, GEORGIA, *November 8, 1852.*

MY DEAR SIR: I cannot forego the occasion to congratulate you on the signal triumph of the Republican Cause. I had hardly expected ever to see the day that a man North would be found in whom the South could safely confide. I confess the future looks brighter to me; and if Pierce will redeem to the letter the pledges that are envolved in his past history, may we not confidently hope that a check will be given to the progress of fanaticism and the rapid strides of federalism? Will he not execute the Fugitive Slave law? Will he not maintain inviolate the Tariff of 1846? Will he not stay the hand of prodigality which has been wasting our public domain for corrupt purposes? Will he stand by the S[tate] R[ights] men of the South or will he countenance, give aid and comfort to the craven submissionists, who under the false clamor of *Union, Union,* have assisted the abolitionists in robbing us, of our rights in the Mexican Territory? Will he fold his hands and permit Cuba to pass into the power of England? These questions now, force themselves upon S[tate] Rights men with the Cogency of practical importance, and I believe Pierce may be trusted upon them all. else he never could have had my support. What think you, now the battle is fought and victory won?

We in Georgia feel a deep interest in the fate of the S[tate] Rights men of the South. If Pierce shall throw himself into the arms of the Cobb and Foote class of Politicians, by selecting from them his Constitutional advisers, his administration will be denounced in advance. I do not know how you feel in Virginia, but it will not be quietly submitted to in Georgia. We are expecting here that he will invite you to the State Department and you must not decline. You have many warm friends, in Georgia who are expecting to use you in 1856.

My Dear Sir, if Pierce should advise with you, let me beg you to deal most candidly with him in relation to the expectations and position of the true State Rights men of the South. He must not strike us down, we have had a hard fight, and without our aid he could neither have been nominated or elected.

If your time will allow drop me a line. I want your observations on the present and prognostications of the future.

HENRY A. WISE TO R. M. T. HUNTER.

ONLY, NEAR ONANCOCK, [VA.], *November 10, 1852.*

MY DEAR HUNTER: Inclosed is a letter from one of the most worthy of men I know in the world, Dr. Jesse I. Simkins of Northampton.

---

[1] A Senator in Congress from Georgia, 1848–1849; governor of Georgia, 1853–1857; candidate for the vice presidency on the Douglas ticket, 1860.

He needs what he asks and yet is no beggar though he is earnest in his appeal to *me* and through me to *you*. He is one of the *purest* and most intelligent of men and has any number of backers and any amount of family influence in and about Norfolk. There, he will not be considered an intruder and he is just such a politician as you should delight to promote and put in places of usefulness and influence; and his appointment would probably be more acceptable to aspirants in Norfolk than would be that of a more immediate rival in the Town. I bespeak for him your influence because he asks me to do so. He seems in a previous letter to make the mistake of supposing mine will be something, and in this the greater mistake of imagining that "to me you owe a heavy debt of gratitude," I claim none such and don't mean to be so understood in sending you his letter so saying. The majority for Pierce is so unwieldy that the effects of factions are to be apprehended.

R. M. T. HUNTER TO JOHN W. FINK.

(*Confidential.*)

LLOYDS, ESSEX CO., [VA.], *November 15, 1852.*

DEAR SIR: I received this evening your letter and a number of your paper containing a notice of myself. For the feeling which prompted both I am really and greatly obliged to you. I shall reply frankly but confidentially to you in relation to your enquiries. I have said to some of my friends that I desired no place in the cabinet and *greatly preferred* my post in the Senate—such are still my sentiments. But I do not desire to make any such public declaration, because it might savor of presumption to decline a place before it was offered and when perchance it might never be tendered. With these impressions I do not wish my friends to urge me for any place in the cabinet, nor do I wish to make any public declarations either directly or indirectly upon the subject.

Of course this is only for your own eye.

JOHN W. FINK TO R. M. T. HUNTER.

WARRENTON, [VA.], *November 17th, 1852.*

DEAR SIR: We wish to urge your claims in the Star as Secretary of State, but learn that you have said, you would not accept any cabinet appointment, which I suppose is mere rumor. I should [like] to have your views on the subject, which shall be confidential. We will in this weeks paper bring your name forward, and if you would accept an appointment press your claims.

We intend to urge your claims as our next candidate for the Presidency, and think a place in the cabinet would make you more prominent before the next Convention. If I did not think so I would prefer you to remain in the Senate, as I do not believe your place can be filled.

R. M. T. HUNTER TO HON. H. V. JOHNSON.

LLOYDS, ESSEX CO. [VA.], *December 2nd, 1852.*

MY DEAR SIR: I received your letter after it had performed its circumnavigation through various post offices of Virginia and write to thank you for it. I only wish that I could give you more than my speculations upon the interesting subjects to which your letter alludes. I know nothing with certainty as to the future course of the President elect. I guess that his feelings are all on the side of State rights, perhaps not so much so as that of state remedies. I also believe that his natural inclinations are towards economy and simplicity, but whether his grasp will be comprehensive enough for the party and the people whom he is called to lead I know not. I most earnestly wish that he may prove equal to the place. Much will depend upon his cabinet. In regard to which I will say at once that I do not look to a place in it. I have no reason to suppose that one would be offered me and if it were I would much prefer my place in the Senate. I say this in confidence because it is a subject on which I could not speak except to a friend. I should think that he would hardly commit such an impudence (to say the least of it) as to take up Cobb, in preference to such a man as yourself for example or those State rights men who really fought this battle for him. I have no right to suppose that he will consult me but should he do so I would give him my opinion pretty frankly as to the claims of the States rights men of the South. They constitute I presume a large majority of the Democratic party South and should Pierce begin by throwing them off it would be a sorry commencement of his administration. I should not be surprised if he threw his patronage to some extent amongst those Union men for the purpose of harmonizing his supporters but he would hardly venture to take up Cobb to the disparagement of the real and efficient leaders of the Democratic party South.

What he will do I know not. But surely he will consult the wishes of the Democratic party in the South of which the major element is undoubtedly composed of State Rights men. When I get to Washington I shall be able to form a better estimate of the probable course of events and will endeavor to keep you advised should you desire it. I must say however that I think there are breakers ahead upon the subject of our Foreign relations. The Cuba question is one of great danger to the South. It must be managed with *patience* and address. We want peace for the sake of opportunities (if for nothing else) which it will afford us to make an effort to decentralize the government, or rather to avert the tendencies of centralization now so manifest in the course of affairs. War has already given a dangerous impulse to this tendency and a speedy recurrence of such an event might be overwhelming to us. Cuba annexed peacefully and as it now stands would be of great service to the South and the Union. But Cuba with War and a general emancipation of slaves would probably get up a contest for us both at home and abroad which would be more dangerous to the South than any through which we have yet passed. Do my dear Sir consider this matter well. More than once the Democratic party has unadvisedly committed itself so far upon those questions of War or peace as to find it difficult to extricate itself from embarrassment. In this extrication the disagreeable portion of the service generally falls upon the South. We may go into these committals as a unit but the party generally comes out of them with a chism. Let us beware how we tread. The States Rights party of the South constituting as it does so large a portion of the Southern Democracy may wield an immense influence for good if it will be guided by prudence. It cannot afford to risk much upon experiments until it has consolidated itself upon sound principles at home and taken a position from which it may exclude unwholesome influences abroad.

I shall always be gratified to hear from you and have your suggestions, there is no quarter from which I should value them more.

Regarding Virginia Land Bounties.

The matter involved in the construction of the Act of Congress of August 1852 may be stated in a few words:

Mr Hunter on the 12th of April 1852, under instructions from the Virginia Legislature, introduced a Bill in the Senate, appropriating 850,000 acres in scrip, to satisfy Virginia military Land Warrants. This estimate, was based upon the statement of the Register of Virginia which declared that it would probably be sufficient to satisfy all the Bounty Land claims, which had been formally adjudicated and allowed by the authorities of Virginia, before the 1st of March 1852, the date from whence her act of limitations barring all further military Land Bounty claims went into effect.

Mr. Hunter's Bill was referred to the Committee of Public Lands, and on the —— day of June 1852, another Bill in place of it, was reported by the Committee, accompanied by [a] Report p. 240 which struck out the appropriation uniting the issue of Scrip to the amount of 850,000 acres, and left the amount indefinite to the end, that all the Bounty Land claims which the authorities of Virginia had adjudicated and allowed as above set forth should be fully paid and discharged (see W. C. Underwood's Report)

In as much, as the Virginia Act of limitations, proscribing every Land Bounty claim which had not been adjudicated before the 1st March 1852 by the constitued authorities of Virginia had thence gone into effect, a Proviso was incorporated in the Bill, that it should be taken as a full and final settlement of all Bounty Land claims of every description due by Virginia to her officers and soldiers in the Revolutionary War.

The Bill was in due course called up in the Senate and was passed. When the Bill came to the House, and was referred to the Committee of Public Lands, it was discovered that the provisions of the first Section contained either a clerical error, or a technical omission as follows: The Bill, which was based upon the Report of the Committee No. — referred to, and was intended as a full and final settlement of all Land Bounty claims adjudicated and finally allowed before the 1st March 1852, and to relieve Virginia from all her liabilities therein, had made provision only for those Warrants in the payment of Scrip which were actually *issued* by Virginia before the 1st March 1852, and left those Warrants *allowed* as aforesaid and before that date wholly unprovided for though Virginia was as much bound to pay the one class of Warrants as the other.

To remedy the error or omission, the Bill was amended in the House, so as to embrace both classes of Warrants, that is to authorise the issue of Scrip, upon Warrants *issued* before the 1st of March 1852 and those allowed in the manner stated before that date, and in that form it passed.

With that Amendment, it came back to the Senate and was passed 31st August 1852. The Amendment consisted in the additional words " or allowed " after the word " *issued* ", so as to read all Warrants " issued or allowed " before 1st March 1852 by the proper authorities of Virginia, this embracing as intended both classes of Warrants.

The construction now put upon the act by the Secretary of the Interior is that the words " issued or allowed " are synonymous and authorise the issue of Scrip *only* upon those Warrants which were *issued* before the 1st March 1852, leaving the Warrants *allowed* before that date wholly unprovided for.

The Secretary of the Interior in his annual Report, asks for the passage of a law to relieve his doubts in the premises, and so as to conform to the history connected with the passage of the Act, which upon every rule of equity he thinks should be granted.

HENRY A. WISE TO R. M. T. HUNTER.

(*Private.*)

ONLY, NEAR ONANCOCK, VA., *April 16, 1853.*

MY DEAR HUNTER: I thank you for yours of the 11th. I did not expect you would be able to tell me any thing definite. I have nothing in the world to complain of in these people. I stood aloof, they called me to them and were very kind in wishing to know my wishes, fortunately I had none and they were indefinite except in strong expressions that they would wish me to serve the administration. I cautiously avoided telling them what I did want or rather that I did want nothing. The Pres[iden]t was specifick in saying he would obey any request in respect to my son. Now that is what I have most at heart. On that subject I have written to Cushing and Buchanan expressing the wish for him to be Secretary of Legation at St. James! As to myself, let them alone, give 'em their own way for the future. Move not another inch further than you have gone in my behalf, for which I thank you. The President told me expressly that, if I said so, Robt. G. Scott should have the Consulate to Rio. I declined the appointment on my say so, but requested leave for Scott to communicate with him himself which he gave. I wrote to Scott and gave him instructions, Bedinger I tried to assist. There is a mistery in the Buchanan affair. He has kept in the dark until the last minute. But for me I doubt if it would have been tendered him. He seems miffed and close. I care not a fig who goes to France. Don't you distrust Cushing too much or at all.[1] You don't know all and I am not at liberty to tell you the key to his apparent bewilderment. P[ierce] told me expressly he appointed him at my instance and Cushing knows it. He is grateful and true but timid as a hare and has a nice game to play. Give him space and dont disturb his work, it will come out right, he is a worker and must be strengthened by *you* all you can. He has more heart than he shows, but you must get at it quietly or it will flutter out at the window. *He is my friend* or I am a fool. He was deceived or mistaken only about Dr. Garnetts little place. Matters have not taken direction yet. The Cass party have certainly most of the loaves thus far. I tell you there are unseen influences at work. I am watching them and the first mole I see above ground I'll catch for you. Moles cant live in our soil. That is the reason patronage weakens every administration, as it has done in my time every one except one. Jackson openly patronized his known friends and that made him troops of them.

---

[1] Caleb Cushing was appointed Attorney General in Pierce's Cabinet. This is probably the appointment to which Wise refers.

Bayly wants his brother-in-law made our Surveyor of the post. I am to the incumbent, Dr. Bagwell, situated as you are to Col. Garnett in Norfolk. I hope he may be retained but he is a radical Whig and I can say nothing. A rascal, Saml. C. White, Tully tells me, tried to impose on you for this place. The Democrats here had rather Bagwell was retained than White or Melvin either appointed. If Bagwell is turned out I wish that poor shoe-maker, Revell, to get the place.

ROBERT SELDEN GARNETT TO R. M. T. HUNTER.

WEST POINT, NEW YORK, *November 5th, 1853.*

MY DEAR COUSIN: Before Congress meets and you become pressed with business incident thereto, I wish to mention a matter to you in which it may fall within your power to be of some service to the Army. I allude to the organization of the Committee on Military Affairs in the Senate. The point is to have any man in the Senate placed at its head in preference to General Shields.[1] As long as he continues at its head the Army can expect nothing at the hands of Congress. We are abundantly satisfied of Gen[era]l Shield's friendly intentions towards us. But he appears to have no weight or consideration in the Senate, and is disposed to be led about by the staff and other idle officers about Washington City. The wild and conflicting schemes which he proposed in rapid succession during the last two sessions of Congress fully show this. A little knowledge is said to be a dangerous thing, and Gen[era]l Shield's military knowledge and experience is precisely of this sort. It can be well spared. Under his auspices two of the most unequal and unjust laws that Congress has ever enacted with regard to the Army, were passed, and we have no desire to have any more of the General's Military experience. We have nobody to urge as his Substitute, the best men being already at the head of more important Committees. All we ask is to get rid of Gen[era]l Shields and ditto of Weller.[2]

I trust that you have not relinquished all hope of establishing a Board of Accounts. I have had some experience in a small way in this matter, and I am fully satisfied of the inadequacy of the present system of adjusting Accounts with the Gov[ernmen]t, or rather of not adjusting them for half of them never will be settled.

My best regards to all at Fort Hill.

---

[1] James Shields, a Senator in Congress from Illinois, 1849–1855; from Minnesota, 1858–1859; from Missouri, Jan. 24, 1879, to Mar. 3, 1879.

[2] John B. Weller, a Senator in Congress from California, 1852–1857; governor of California, 1858–1860; minister to Mexico, 1860–1861.

McCULLOUGH AND CO. TO JAMES A. BAYARD.

WILMINGTON [DEL.], *March 29, 1854.*

DEAR SIR: We have taken the liberty of enclosing you herewith a memorial, which we shall esteem a great favor, indeed, to have referred to the proper committee, and we have sent a similar one to Mr. Riddle.[1]

Our reasons for presenting this petition are that under the Tariff of 1846, English Galvanized Tinned Iron is permitted to come in at a duty of 15 per cent. Whilst Common Sheet iron not galvanized is chargeable at 30 per cent duty. The English manufacturers, of this article, by a very simple and cheap process, tin their iron before galvanizing it in order to bring it in, under the duty chargeable on Tin Plates, (which is 15 pr. centum) thus saving this difference in duty, and after its Importation into our own country, disposing of it as *Galvanized Iron.* By reference to the Act of 1846, you will readily observe, how the law is thus evaded, and by the present recommendation of the Secretary of the Treasury Galvanized Tin or Galvanized Tinned iron, is placed on the *Free list.*

This, if effected, you will perceive, would paralize the efforts of our own Manufacturers in this country as the chief and intrinsic cost is embraced in the value of the *Iron* itself, prior to Galvanizing it, and this, proposing to be admitted free, will then give the foreign manufacturers, the entire trade of this article in the United States.

We have, within the past eighteen months, commenced the manufacture of this article, in this city, and with the advantage of the same protection and duty that is now chargeable upon common sheet iron, not galvanized, we fully believe, that we would then be enabled to compete, successfully with the Foreign (English) makers. As we think, the article is destined to be brought into very general use, in our own country, relying with the above advantage, in connection, with its own intrinsic usefulness.

We inclose you herewith a sample of the article manufactured by ourselves.

JESSE D. BRIGHT[2] TO R. M. T. HUNTER.

MADISON, IND., *September 2d, 1854.*

DEAR HUNTER: Yours of the 15th ultimo with letter in behalf of Mr. Lyle is received and for which accept my thanks.

Several of our Papers have come out in favor of your Bill, but not as plainly and pointedly identifying you with it, as they might and

[1] George Read Riddle, a Representative (1851–1855) and a Senator (1864–1867) in Congress from Delaware.

[2] Democratic Senator in Congress from Indiana, 1845–1862, when he was expelled for having, in a letter to Jefferson Davis, recognized him as " President of the Confederated States."

ought to have done. I have this day written two articles on the subject, one for the " Madisonean " and the other for the " Democratic Platform " published at the Capitol. I will see that they go into the Cincinnati and Louisville papers, and that they are generally copied into our County papers. Tucker shall be furnished with copies. Nothing was done in reference to the Military reservation up to the time I left Washington. I wrote Wilson last week on the subject but have not as yet received a reply. I also wrote Mr. Cameron to-day about it.

Letters from Robertson and Rice speak in the most flattering manner of the property of Superior. Robertson says he is selling Lots rapidly and at fair prices. For fear that I could not get off this Fall, (on account of our elections which are forcing me into the Hustings) I sent my nephew Michael S. Bright Esqr. up to Superior last week, and if there is to be a Partition, he will be present and see fair play. I gave him all the particulars, he is smart and I will guarantee, look after your interests, Dawson's, Corcoran's, Douglass' and mine closely. I may go up myself about the 20th of this month, I certainly shall, if I find my friends will not complain, at my leaving the mongrel mixed up political Canvass going on here now. I am afraid my friend from the signs, that the Free States (Indiana included) are lost for the time being to our Party. *Iowa has set a significant example.* Dodge stands not the least chance of a re-election.

The title Bonds I forwarded for the signature of Robertson, has not yet been returned, when they are you shall have yours. It will be all right.

Speaking in the open air, this warm weather is more than working on the "Appropriation Bills " with Gwinn [1] thrown in, to oppose.

By the way I have information which satisfies me *he cannot be re-elected*, and for which God and the Californians be praised.

Glad to hear from you whenever you can find time to write.

JAMES HUNTER TO R. M. T. HUNTER.

CAROLINE COUNTY, [VA.], *September 12, 1854.*

MY DEAR SIR: I have not written to you before, because I have been intending to come down to Essex every week for a month past; and now, that I find I cannot come, I wish to write to you about our business in Western Virginia.

Mr. J. W. Manry did not go to Kanawha—his daughter was sick at the Springs and prevented his making the trip. His brother R. H. Manry tells me he was very anxious to go out there and is still disposed to take an interest in the coal enterprize. While Mr. Manry

---

[1] William McK. Gwin, United States Senator from California, 1850–1855, 1857–1861.

was at the Springs, a gentleman named Carrington of Charlotte County went out to examine the property with the intention of taking a share if he was pleased with it and he said, that if he became interested, Mr. Charles Bruce and one or two others would like also to take shares. You are aware that we have not yet secured the property and that we have to make a payment to Edwards on the 1st of October to secure his portion of it. When I saw Phil Dandridge, he said he throught he could induce Edwards to extend the time of this first payment to the 1st of November. I shall write to-day to Phil to endeavor to obtain this extension of time.

Phil writes me that we can get Hill's land upon the terms we proposed, 50 cts per acre, by paying $2000 instead of $1500 cash. I will write to him upon this subject also. Barton Morris will advance this payment to secure an equal interest in the tract, and I believe it is understood, that all the other parties consent to his being admitted to an interest in that particular tract upon that condition.

I saw a letter yesterday from Phil to R. H. Manry, written from Kanawha and in reference to our operations at the Old Dominion Company. He writes in great spirits, and mentions that those coal lands are attracting a great deal of attention.

I wish very much to know whether you intend to visit Nicholas this Fall, if you do so intend, I would like to know at what time you will go, as I am anxious to accompany you. And if you do not intend going out, I must see, that we may have some understanding concerning these lands. I refer particularly to the Hansford and Edwards tracts of Coal land and the Hill tract.

During October we must come to some decision about them.

It is possible that Brooke will sell his interest in the agency in all these lands for an advance of $8000. The purchasers will be John W. Manry, B. W. Morris and Charles W. Coleman. If the sale is made, it will be made this week. They are willing to give that sum for it, but it is not certain that he will take it. Do not mention this, as in the event of his declining to sell, it would be as well that it should not be known, that any such thing was intended.

DAVID R. ATCHISON [1] TO R. M. T. HUNTER.

PLATTE CITY, [Mo.], *March 4, 1855.*

DEAR HUNTER: The Elections in Kansas came off on the 30th ult, the pro slavery ticket prevailed every where as far as heard from, by overwhelming majorities; we stormed Lawrence or New Boston as it is called; The Abolitionists did "hang their guilty heads," now let the Southern men come on with their slaves 10,000

---

[1] A Senator in Congress from Missouri, 1843–1855.

families can take possession, of and hold every acre of timber in the territory of Kansas, and this secures the prairie. Missouri will furnish 5000 of the 10,000; and the whole State will guarantee protection. We had at least 7,000 men in the territory on the day of the election and one third of them will remain there. We are playing for a mightly stake, if we win we carry slavery to the Pacific Ocean if we fail we lose Missouri Arkansas and Texas and all the territories, the game must be played boldly. I know that the Union as it Exists is in the other scale, but I am willing to take the holyland.

You never saw a people better up to the mark than ours. It was hard to get up but now the only difficulty is to keep within bounds. When the returns are all in I will send them to you. You will no doubt see your humble servant held up by the Abolition press as a Bandit, a ruffian, an Aaron Burr, dont believe a word of it. I have saved hundreds of their necks, and kept their cabins from being burnt to the ground; there was not the least disturbance where I was present, and that was on the Nemaha, elsewhere in a few instances the hickory was used upon the most impudent of them.

LEWIS E. HARVIE TO R. M. T. HUNTER.

March 5th, 1855.

DEAR HUNTER: I shall direct this letter to you at home, supposing you to be there. I did not write about the proposed organization, for after reflection I came to the conclusion that it was at this time impracticable. The difficulty grew mainly out of the fact that there were two Democratic papers in Richmond, each struggling for the lead and one of them not to be trusted. It would have been impossible, I think to have entered into the arrangement without the knowledge of that paper and still more difficult to get its sanction. Moreover the Enquirer is a Wise paper par excellence, and would have wanted some one that would not have answered. I was afraid to move lest I might do mischief. The time will come when it can be done and then it must be done. If we succeed in this election (and we shall) we will have the control of the party, unless we are thwarted by which I fear, but which must be risked. If however you think after reading this that it is better to go on, say so and I think it can be done. You had better take your part in this canvass, at least in a National point of view, suppose you make a Demonstration here on the Southside. If you are willing I can have you invited spontaneously. Wise is so busy he won't be able to come home and I think it would be well to give the canvass in Virginia a somewhat less personal cast than it has been made to appear. Don't understand me as urging this, I am only suggesting it. If you don't like it, tell me what you do like so that I may help. I thought I was done with Politics and personally I am, but I will help you at all times as you know. Moreover I believe that we are to have a row with the North, and when that game is to be played, you may always set me down as one. To get the South straight Know Nothingism must be overcome and *you* ought to say so and *help to do it* at once. I wish I could see you. Cant I meet you sometime in Richmond or Fredericksburg? If so name your time and place.

To come to other matters. Did you do anything for my boys? I feel very mean to be plaguing you about them, but as I told you once before, you are the only person that I do plague about my personal matters.

I got a letter from Lieut. B. W. Robertson of the Army asking me in case of an increase of the Army to solicit your aid in getting him promoted to a Captaincy. He says he has been on duty with only the intermission of a few months since he left West Point, and that he has seen much service, which is evident from papers on file in the Department &c &c. He is a very worthy young man from this County and I expect a good officer and if you can help him I would be well pleased. At all events he wrote to me to ask you and therefore and because I would be glad to further his wishes, I have done so. Write to me as soon as you can.

Lewis E. Harvie to R. M. T. Hunter.

March 17th, 1855.

My dear Hunter: Your letter and enclosures have been received and immediately thereupon I wrote to Capt. Meigs accepting the offer, which is all that I wish, saving the fact, that I think, and so I am sure does John, that he is qualified to discharge the duties of a higher grade than the one he will hold. If this should be the case however Meigs will find it out soon enough and if not it is best as it is. I shall also write to Professor Bache to remove any feeling that he may have about his withdrawal, and to express my obligations to him. It is said that the way to make a man an enemy, is to do him a favor. If so, and sometimes, it is, I ought to become a very bitter enemy of yours. All I can say, or at least all I will say, is that I don't just *now*, think that the proverb will ever apply to me.

What is to result from the Know Nothing nominations? And why should I have thought of Patton in connection with that ticket, just after writing the preceding paragraph? Sometimes, tho thank God not often I doubt my kind. Change of Party for good reason, is the evidence of high moral principle, but for *greed* or mere self it is degrading and vile, and unfortunately, when done by men high in the confidence of their community, it is demoralizing and utterly destroys confidence. This it is, and not the belief that so cold blooded an act of prostitution and treason, for a *consideration* either of money or place, can strengthen this Hivmaphrodite party, that makes me deplore this act. The ticket is strong and was the work of master workmen. It carries on its face tho' too plainly the object for which it was made. Flournoy, for the old Whigs, Neals for the Northwest and the old liners and Patton for the Chivalry and to give weight, for its ability. Men and not measures on their part. The Union of men of all parties. The hope of office extended to all from the Constable to the President. Let our cry be Principles not mere Trust in the People, open discussion Pledges given before trusts are confided. We will beat them I have faith, if I had not I should well nigh despair, not only now but for the future. If we can stand up and maintain this fight and beat this movement in Virginia I feel that our institutions will be sound if not may God have mercy on us, for on him alone must be our reliance. I have as yet seen no flinching here, our men are true and hopeful. The Whigs are however either of the Organization 'or aiding it. I still think you should throw yourself into the fight, heartily zealously and proclaim the consequences of defeat to your State, whose Representation will be listened to and whose statements must carry weight.

JAMES HUNTER TO R. M. T. HUNTER.

March 20th, 1855.

MY DEAR SIR: The Messrs Barings of London have taken the agency to sell the. Virginia State Stock. Mr. R. H. Manry of Richmond is of all the Citizens of that City, best qualified to attend to such business as the Barings may have in that City in connection with that business.

It has occurred to me, that you might in some way aid in securing him this sub-agency from the Barings, and if you can do, you will do both him and myself an especial favour.

The Presidents of all the Banks, all the State officers and all the principal merchants of Richmond will unite in recommending Mr. Manry as a fit person to attend to such business as the Messrs. Barings may have in Richmond in transfers and collection of interest &c &c in the City of Richmond.

JOHN L. DAWSON [1] TO R. M. T. HUNTER.

BROWNSVILLE, [PA.], *June 2, 1855.*

DEAR SIR: I have just received your favour of the 26th ult. To-morrow morning I leave for Detroit to meet Gov[erno]r Bright by

---

[1] Democratic Representative in Congress from Pennsylvania, 1851–1855, 1863–1867.

arrangement, and from thence we go to "Superior." I will with
pleasure attend to the suggestions contained in your letter, and will
write to you from "Superior." I have heard nothing special from
there since the adjournment of Congress.

The troubles in Kansas have attracted much attention here and
I fear will give trouble in the end The Whigs, or rather the opposition to the democracy, *fatten* on these difficulties and are determined
to make the most out of them. I am glad that you succeeded so well
in Virginia, she is a better battle-field than Pennsylvania.

With my best wishes for your success.

Isaac Edward Holmes [1] to R. M. T. Hunter.

Charleston, [S. C.], *8th June, 1855.*

My Dear Hunter: Some weeks since I rec[eive]d y[ou]r letter and
thank you for y[ou]r efforts in behalf of my brother. I seldom ask
anything and rather opine, that my *last request* is made. I sincerely
congratulate you on the success of the Virginia Election. I feared
the result, and believe the victory truly auspicious. If the Know
Nothings had succeeded, if the Frontier State of the Southern Confederacy had "*given-way*" our institutions would have been placed
in great hazard; as it is, "They are by no means safe." Fanaticism
never goes-back and for the first time in our history, abolitionism
has the ascendant in Congress.

I see that Senator Wilson has declared, That henceforth no Slave
owner, or pro-slavery man shall be President. As the Democratic
party are a minority in the North, and as the entire South will most
probably act as one man in the next Election, it is essential that we
have a Southern man for our Candidate. The sooner we make up
the Issue, the better. If we are to be in a hopeless minority, and the
Slave States to remain "*in statu quo*," We must share the fate of the
British West Indies. Not only will slavery be abolish[e]d in the
District, but in the Territories. Not only additional Slave States be
excluded, but free ones made Ad Libitum until the constitution is
altered and the entire labour of the South be destroyed. This cant
be termed *speculation*. The effect is as sure as the result of any
cause can be. It is my sincere desire that the Union may be saved,
but its salvation depends upon the next Presidential Canvass. Virginia must lead off. There should commence an active correspondence between the politicians of the Old Dominion and the Leaders
of the Northern Democracy. Before we go into a Caucus we should
have a distinct understanding upon all the leading points. Otherwise we should have only a Southern Caucus, irrespective of parties,
and proceed to an ulterior organization. I hope Wise may pursue

---

[1] A Representative in Congress from South Carolina, 1839–1851.

the true course, and "*entrenous*," I hope that his ambition may not be so stimulated by his late Triumph as to aspire to the purple. Virginia ought to give the President. Her position at this time is potential, and amongst her own people there should be entire unanimity before going into Caucus. Remember that the nominating Caucus will meet during the next Session of Congress, not a Twelve month hence. I am not a politician, but I deem the times so pregnant, that, if alive next Winter, my efforts shall be given to prepare the Southern mind for the Presidential Election. South Carolina, whilst she keeps in the rear of Virginia, must nevertheless be represented in the Caucus. She must no longer be isolated. Thank God, the Cuba question seems settled for awhile. It promised much distraction, and I employed my pen, for the first time these many years, in the endeavor to show the Southern States that the acquisition of Cuba was not to their benefit. One of my pieces or letters was transferred to the National Intelligence. I am writing you from the sick Chamber of Mrs. Holmes who has for a long period been confin[e]d to her room. Alas with little prospect of a recovery. I hope that y[ou]r own family are well.

THOMAS A. GLOVER TO R. M. T. HUNTER.

NEW YORK, [N. Y.], *June 23, 1855.*

MY DEAR SIR: Desirous of urging, most strongly, upon you the necessity of your coming to New York to participate in the celebration of the Anniversary of the Young Men's Democratic Club I cannot but write you again upon this subject, having addressed you some days since from Baltimore.

This celebration is one of much importance at this time, and if successful will have much weight upon the results of the coming campaign in our state. A campaign that must decide the position of New York in 56, whether she will stand among her Sister States, supporting the time-honored principles of the National Democracy or whether she will be found aiding and abetting, giving vigor and sustaining the treasonable combinations of Whiggery and Know-Nothingism, Abolitionism Maine lawism, proscription and Priest craft.

To aid and direct the Democracy of our State, in reestablishing her power, and asserting her supremacy we must look to Statesmen from beyond our geographical boundaries. Men who dare assert the majesty of the laws and whose courage and devotion has sustained the Republic in obedience to Constitutional enactments.

Within ourselves we have few, if any such men. Their alliances their preferences and their prejudices have lost them the confidence of the people and if the Democratic Masses of our State are to be united it must be through their reliance upon the young and untainted men of our State, advised, counselled and directed by the bold, vigorous minds of Southern men.

To ensure a co-operative action of the North and South to restore confidence and to complete their success the Democracy must profess and practice a common faith, vigorous in combatting error, valiant in vanquishing a Common enemy, they must adopt the principles of the early fathers of the Republic, they must go back to first principles they must stand where Washington, Jefferson Monroe and Jackson stood, pledged to sustain the Constitution of the nation, and pledged to sustain the individual rights of the States. Protecting themselves from assault from wishing and guaranteeing as just and an equal protection to their Sister States. And sir, we feel now, in our State that the hour is propitious that the Democracy of our State are prepared to take a conservative yet positive position upon these issues, and your coming among us at this time, will do much towards the speedy consummation of this result. We earnestly and cordially invite you. We offer you a sincere and cordial welcome to our city and cannot but hope you find your engagements such as to permit of your acceptance. We have also addressed Hon. M. R. Garnett and from the urgent manner of Mr. Wise as expressed in his letter to him I presume he will come.

ROBERT SELDEN GARNETT TO R. M. T. HUNTER.

FT. MONROE, VA., July 8, 1855.

MY DEAR COUSIN: Your kind letter of the 25th Ult was misdirected to me at New York and did not overtake me at this place until a few days since. I am truly obliged to you for the frankness and liberality with which you have given me your views in relation to my proposed marriage. I do not understand you as fully approving the step under the circumstances, and fully appreciate—perhaps indeed even concur with you in your doubts as to its wisdom. I need hardly assure you that I had rather have had your approval of it than that of any relation I have. I owe so much of my professional services and advancement to your kind exertions that I have felt it to be a sort of duty I owed you to speak with you freely and fully on the subject. I should have only felt too happy if the step could have met with your unqualified approbation, yet my own judgment told me that it would be unreasonable to expect it. I sincerely hope, however, and believe, that as time rolls on I shall be able to show that I have not made after all so great a mistake as would appear to be the case at first. In comparing my own case with that of hundreds of other officers of the army, the advantages appear to me to be all on my side. There are 86 majors in the Army. Of this number about *8* are bachelors. The rest are married men; many with large families and some even grand-fathers. In most of these cases, these officers married while in the subordinate grades of the Army, with small pay and when they and their families were consequently subjected to many inconveniences from which my rank will now entirely exempt me. Yet many of these people have lived very happily, have educated and established their children well as they could, and express themselves content with their present and past life. Many of these officers too—indeed the most distinguished in our service—acquired their professional reputations as married men, and that too when they married as subalterns—such for instance as Taylor, Worth, Lee, Smith, Mansfield, Huger &c &c. Marriage does not appear to have affected in the slightest degree their activity or efficiency. This was a point upon which I reflected much before taking this step and upon which I have but few apprehensions.

My rank in the army has freed me from many of the onerous and confining details of company, and subaltern duties. My movements are not now so much controlled by the movements of a particular line of men. I am much less subjected to that constant change of station so inimical to the comforts of married life in the army. I shall as a general thing henceforth, be in command when I go to my post, and will thus have the power and means of securing to myself many comforts &c. of which, as a Capt[ain] or Subaltern, I would have been necessarily deprived. I cannot believe that my professional prospects or standing will be injuriously effected by this step. Indeed I think that they may be materially improved, for what I most desire now is to have two or three years of quietness at some remote post where I may devote myself without interruption to professional reading and study, and I truly believe that I could do so much more successfully as a married man than as a single one. My own doubts and anxieties, however, lie in quite another direction. Life in the army is more precarious than in any other walk or pursuit of life; and an officer ought not perhaps to calculate upon living the usual term of years and then dying of old age. The obligation then to provide for his family for the future in case of his death is more urgent and imperative upon a married officer than upon other men; and as Miss Nelson is poor, I feel the full weight of this obligation in my case. Had I only to guard against disease I might perhaps safely calculate upon living long enough to do, as hundreds of other officers have done with fewer advantages than I have— viz, to lay up a respectable competency for my family in case of my death. This I confess is a point upon which I feel the greatest anxiety. During my life unless I should be ejected from the army, and this is improbable, I shall have no fears as to my ability to secure to her all the comforts she can reasonably desire; but it is a very painful reflection to me to think that I may be killed off and leave her in straightened circumstances—with nothing but my name. For this reason only, it has always, been my desire, if married at all, to marry a lady with some means of her own. If I felt certain that I should live 10 or 15 years longer, I should feel no anxiety on this subject, for with the increased pay and rank which I cannot help from acquiring in the meantime I feel confident that I could secure her against such a misfortune. A great many of our officers who have married with small pay and in the lower grades have managed to put away money and to live comfortable some have become independent and even rich; and it seems to me that there must be something radically wrong about me, if I cannot, with my rank and advantages, now do the same.

JESSE D. BRIGHT TO R. M. T. HUNTER.

SUPERIOR, WIS., July 29, 1855.

DEAR HUNTER: I have been here for the last eight days, and am now about starting home, before doing so, I take time to redeem my promise to you, and say a word about this place and your interests in it, which I have examined closely during my stay. This place has advantages infinitely beyond any other on the Western and Northern Lakes. It must outstrip Chicago within the next 20 years, you can sell your interests here for Twenty five Thousand Dollars. Several sales of quarter and half shares have taken place here since I came at this rate cash paid down. There is about 500 people here now, and improvements of all kind going rapidly forward. There is about 50 Houses up, and they are building at the rate of one per day. I have much more to tell you when we meet, than I have time to write now.

JOHN L. DAWSON TO R. M. T. HUNTER.

BROWNSVILLE, [PA.], August 10, 1855.

DEAR HUNTER: I reached home on last evening having left "Superior" on the 6th instant. I was delighted with my trip—the beauty of the *Town site*—its advantages and the absolute certainty that it will be a *great town*.

It is the prettiest situation for a City that I have ever seen. The rivers and the *bay* are unsurpassed for their natural beauty, the bay or harbor however requiring some dredging and the entrance to the bay requiring the construction of a *pier* to protect the channel. The country in the vicinity of the place is rich and will make a fine agricultural district. The whole thing is a *decided hit*. The *minerals* in the vicinity are also abundant and rich.

I have a map for you, with your lots coloured. I got a young lawyer to do the work but had the *numbers* carefully compared by

Mr. Clarke, Newton's chief clerk. I will send you the map by Adams Express if you will designate the place and route.

I cannot advise you to sell any of these lots, time will add *greatly* to their value. So impressed was Gov. Bright and myself with the prospects of " Superior " that we acceded to a proposition of Mr. Newton to *pay* off the notes given to Mr. Corcoran, say about $20,000 and take lots for the same, about 456 lots.

I send you a no. of the Superior Chronicle containing a letter written by Mr. Mitchell, one of the Editors of the St. Louis Intelligence descriptive of the place and its advantages.

I have declined as you have doubtless seen by the papers, the appointment of Governor of the Territory of Kansas. I hope to have the pleasure of seeing you some time this winter at Washington and can then tell you all about " Superior."

I await your answer concerning the shipment of the map.

JOHN L. DAWSON TO R. M. T. HUNTER.

BROWNSVILLE, [PA.], *August 25th, 1855.*

DEAR HUNTER : I received your letter of the 20th instant this morning and have just shipped the box containing the map of " Superior " to the care of Gallaher Young & Co., Fredericksburg Va. I sent it from here to Pitts[burg]h to G. W. Cass who will forward it to you by Adams Express. The numbering of the Lots begins on Robert-son Avenue : *Odd* numbers on the right, *even* numbers on the left. This reference will enable you to ascertain without difficulty the *Nos.* of your lots.

There was no map prepared, showing the general division. I had one coloured for you and one for myself by which I could distinguish your lots and my own. Gov[ernor] Bright had one also prepared, showing his lots. I consider your lots as of equal value with our division. The most valuable lots at the present time are these on Second Street, for the reason that nearly all of the improvements are on that street. The value of the lots will depend upon many future contingencies which no man can foresee, but at present I am of opinion that the most valuable improvements will be upon Left Hand river and between said river and Hollinshead Avenue. The Piers have not yet been divided. Quebec Pier is the only one improved and is in a good position. The next two piers below Quebec, and between it and Left Hand, will be still more valuable. The most of the lots and blocks will be ready for a final division this fall. The Superior City to which you refer as mentioned in Newtons advertisement is the *Town site* for which we are contending. It embraces 320 a[cres] and is *very valuable.* It is important that we establish our right to the same. Newton has taken a good many releases from the pre-emptors and will persevere, until he gets *all*. Bright seemed to think this of no consequence, but I urged him to procure *all* if possible. I sent you a "Superior Chronicle" containing a letter written by a Mr. Mitchell from St. Louis descriptive of the Town and its advantages, which I presume you have received. Mitchell bought a considerable interest and secured a pre-emption to 160 a[cres] in the vicinity of the town. His statements are to be relied upon. I repeat that is the prettiest site for a large City that I have ever seen. Its position geographical, commercial and political is great, and it is destined to be a great place, and no mistake. The *pier* will not cost more than 20 or 25 thousand dollars, and but little dredging will be necessary to make the harbor a good one.

What say you to the Canadian or British project of a ship canal directly to connect Lakes Huron and Ontario via Lake Semcoe and the Georgian Bay avoiding the circuit of Erie, Detroit River and St Clair and Flats and a great portion of Lake Huron, curtailing about 900 miles of Distance.

In politics I fear there is trouble ahead. The Southern Statesmen must act with great discretion and aid the democracy of the North in heading the Common enemy, headed by Chase Seward and Co. The free soilers and abolitionists will not unite with the K[now] N[othings] and I therefore believe that we can elect our President. It is of the greatest important to you as well as to the party and the country that you take good care to have your *friends* from *Virginia* and elsewhere in the Cincinnati Convention. If the nomination should go South, the vote of Virginia will go far in giving it the proper direction. In a word it is an important movement and requiring our whole attention.

JOHN L. DAWSON TO R. M. T. HUNTER.

BROWNSVILLE [PA.], *August 26, 1855.*

MY DEAR SIR: In my letter of yesterday I omitted to answer your inquiry whether the proprietor of "Superior" would be reimbursed by Newton with the original investment. The debts of the company are now paid off and I believe that Newton has bonds and claims for lots already sold to the Am[oun]t of about $60,000. The reserved lots yet undisposed of number about 1200 to 1400 together with the Hotel and *all the piers.* He has determined to put under contract another large Hotel and to cut and clear out the streets. I am satisfied that the Lot holders will profit by such improvements. Newton will be in Washington this winter and will report in full. I am not fully advised in the matter to answer your inquiry. I have shown you the ability of the Company to reimburse if such should be deemed the best policy. I believe however, that a judicious expenditure of the money in the improvement of the wharfs, streets &c would pay better than a division. I refer you however to Newton when you see him.

I have not seen the article in Blackwood to which you refer. I have written to Pittsburg to Mr. G. W. Cass to hunt it up and send it to me.

WILLIAM L. JACKSON [1] TO F. W. COLEMAN.

RICHMOND, VA., *September 5th, 1855.*

DEAR COLEMAN: I received a letter from Lyons to day. He suggests that a letter from Hunter will be beneficial. You can procure said letter. Hunter knows me personally and by reputation. He is aware that, owing to my efforts there was no division in the delegation of the Northwest at his re-election to the Senate. I was selected to make the nominating speech in the House of Delegates.

I am on my way to St. Mary's Pleasants County, Virginia and leave this letter. Any efforts of yours in my behalf will be gratefully appreciated. If it becomes necessary during my absence you can consult Col. Drinkard.

A. D. BANKS TO R. M. T. HUNTER.

PETERSBURG, [VA.], *November 23rd, 1855.*

MY DEAR SIR: For the past ten days, I have been in Richmond and while there have had frequent conversations with influential democrats from all Quarters of the State. It affords me pleasure to communicate the agreeable fact that Mason's re-election is already *un fait accompli. There will be no opposition.* The movement against him has signally failed and about the first business of the session will be his triumphant re-election. This you may confidently rely on. The attempt of which we spoke at Richmond on the part of certain gentlemen to head a feud between your friends and Wise's will also fail. Many ardent admirers and advocates of Wise have assured me that you were their second choice and that none would be more ready than themselves to frown down and discountenance any efforts at fomenting rivalry and dissatisfaction. Some of them express a determination early in the session of the democratic State Convention to introduce a resolution to the effect that the Virginia democracy have no choice between their two Prominent chiefs who have been named for the succession but will support either with cheerfulness and alacrity, leaving the fortunate one of them to be selected by the National democracy of the Union. This argues a better feeling on the part of Wise's friends than we had good reason to expect, and it is in fact all that we could ask of them.

---

[1] A political leader of local influence in western Virginia, now West Virginia.

I shall see you in Washington next week and should like to have a full and free conference with you on the future. We can then better understand the current and its course. Douglas' Position cannot be known too soon.

By the way my friends intend urging my name for the House clerkship I can lose nothing certainly while if a fortunate train of circumstances should conspire to place me in the Position it would be a most desirable place. Being the only person at present named from the South I ought to get quite a respectable vote. The Examiner and Enquirer here both voluntarily offered to support me warmly. Present me kindly to Garnett.

JAMES HUNTER TO R. M. T. HUNTER.

RICHMOND, [VA.], *December 3, 1855.*

MY DEAR SIR: I have merely time to write to you to ask you to see Mr. Bright and represent to him that it is indepensible and absolutely necessary in perfecting the Papers to organize the Kanawha Coal Company that his name for the present should remain as one of the Stock holders. After the Company is organized he can make such disposition as he pleases of his stock. Please attend to this at once and write to Mr. E. T. Morris and mention, that you have made this arrangement with Mr. Bright. I forgot to mention that it is necessary that Mr. Morris should know the name of Mr. Bright's wife in drawing the papers.

JAMES A. SEDDON TO R. M. T. HUNTER.

ST. JAMES, LOUISIANA, *December 3rd, 1855.*

MY DEAR SIR: Your letter only reached me in this outside world a few days since. Its confidence and kind consideration for my uninformed councils have afforded me sincere gratification. You may have many wiser but no truer friends, and so entirely conscious am I of the warmth and disinterestedness of my own regard and so confident of your just appreciation, that I feel privileged to use the utmost candor and frankness with you. It is plain to me there is imminent danger of jealously and discension arising, if not between Wise and yourself, at least between your respective friends and adherents, and in consequence the loss of the favorable contingency of elevating a true Southern States Rights man to the Presidency and adding another Chief Magistrate to the illustrious roll our State can now boast. Wise is clearly in a false position. While unconscious of the full eclat of his State triumph and the commendation it would afford to a certain class of lookers out for new stars in the political fermament to put him up for the Presidency, he, animated both by gratitude for the recent exertion of yourself and your friends in his behalf and by old relations of kindness, committed himself decidedly in your favor. Since, circumstances and the flattery of friends have deluded him and kindled ambitious aspirations that to one of his nature are but too seductive.

Wishing however to be an honest man, he can not forget or disregard wholly his promises in your favor, yet being so ambitious, he can not entirely reconcile himself to the preferment of another from his own section and state over him. He therefore compromises with himself by the persuasion that neither can be elected and casts around for chances to strengthen himself in the position.

This I take to be the true state of the case, although perhaps not fully realized to his own mind. Now this will never do as it will inevitably defeat you both *now*, which is all either can be secure of, and which is indeed a rare contingency not likely to recur speedily. Open rivalry is hardly more fatal than the open position taken by either of you, that no Southern man or Virginian must now be nominated. It is dangerous to have, even more fatally in our state, the peculiar feelings and jealousies which really render it impossible to run with success a Northern man, and the absence of which in the South gives her the preference of a nomination. All this is clear to me, but how to anticipate and avoid the evil is the rub. I confess I am very much at a loss, but I can imagine two minds and natures, as magnanimous and generous as I know yours and hope Wise's to be, might pin to the level of a noble understanding even in relation to such a post of honor and usefulness as the Presidency, and in a personal interview put matters on some bases satisfactory to the friends of both. I think indeed Wise ought to and with a just appreciation of the circumstances of his position and of the times I hope would at once withdraw all pretensions on his own part, and engage with characteristic zeal and energy in urging you. This is perhaps rather to be hoped than expected, although I confess I am not without some anticipation that recent elections at the North may have forced on his mind his original impression that a Northern man can not be nominated. Besides Buchanan, who is the only Northern man to whom past committals can justify him in adhering in preference to you, is wary and prudent and may not wish to run the gauntlet of an ineffective struggle for nomination. With the Session of Congress too Wise will drop more from public notice and you become more prominent. National politicians, who must and doubtless do prefer you, will then be more influential than during the recess in molding and guiding public opinion and Wise may be awakened from his temporary delusion. Should however this not prove the case, would it not be possible for you and himself to leave the question who shall be supported by V[irgini]a in the nominating Convention to the arbitrament of two or more mutual friends, who might quietly enquire and determine the relative strength of each and select the stronger. Or should this be impracticable, might you and he not have an understanding that neither should take the least measure to influence the action of the State or the selection of delegates to the Convention and that when assembled, their choice should determine, the one not preferred at once to withdraw and cast all his influence in behalf of the other.

By one of these or some kindred mode, growing discentions so distructive to the chances of both and so discredible and weakening to the Democracy of our State will be aviated, and what will please me scarcely less, the petty malice of Floyd and Smith with all their yelping pack will be frustrated. I can not answer your enquiry as to the motives of Floyd's peculiar animosity to you, but presume it had origin in some imagined slight to his overweaning vanity, while he was Governor and not infrequently in Washington, or perhaps in a desire thro' you to strike at Mason whose seat he has the folly to aspire to. The Examiner alone gives any venom to his sting but while hurtful to both him and yourself if disunited is impotent against your united strength. I wish much I could see you or be in V[irgini]a this winter and think it probable I may return in February. I shall be a deeply interested spectator of events and watch with delight your culminating star.

This climate agrees with me better than the more vigorous North and I enjoy it even the monotony of a French neighborhood and plantation life. I am busy making sugar and hope with it to sweeten the sour portions which the ill fortune of delicate health commends to my lips. Do give my cordial remembrances to Mr. Mason and Judge Butler and any other of our old political associates who may dain to bear in remembrance one who at heart has the merit of valuing his section and his friends.

———— ———— TO R. M. T. HUNTER.[1]

SENATE CHAMBER, RICHMOND, [VA.],
December 12th, 1855.

MY DEAR SIR: May I trouble you to obtain for me information which I see no other mode to arrive at; or, if that be troublesome to you, to put me in correspondence with some one who can furnish it?

I am told that, by recent legislation, the Banks of South Carolina are prohibited from discounting notes and bills, on time, payable out of that State, until all good paper offered, has been discounted.

I wish to know if the fact is so; and what the result is practically; if time enough has elapsed to show it. Some complaint is made of the Banks of Virginia that they give, in their discounts, the prefer-

---

[1] This letter seems to have been from a member of the State Senate of Virginia.

ence to bills and notes, payable to the North, over the domestic bills and notes. They make something in exchange, on such paper; the funds being found in N. York or elsewhere Northwards, where paid. If such preference is given it results, not only in an improper discrimination between the merchants of the different classes, but disadvantageously to the trade of our cities; thus, flour, or manufactured tobacco, is brought by a N. York merchant, who pay, for it, in an accepted bill drawn on him. This bill is discounted by our Banks, for our manufacturer of flour or tobacco. By the time, the accepted bill matures the New York merchant has sold the flour or tobacco, and gotten the proceeds to pay for the purchase. The result is that, with the aid of the Virginia Banks and Virginia capital, New York gets the benefit of the trade, in our main staples.

We lose not merely the use of the money, while the bill is maturing, and which is wrong; for, New York ought to pay, not in credit, but, in money for our staples. But it transfers the shipping from our merchants to those of New York; if the bill, accepted by the Northern merchant, is discounted by our Banks, when the same bill, accepted by one of our own merchants would not be discounted. It seems to me therefore that the subject of prohibiting the loan by our Banks on paper, that has some time to run, payable out of Virginia is a fit subject of inquiry at the present session. And as it is always dangerous to experiment in banking, it is desirable that we should have all the lights, before us, which the experience of our Sister State furnishes.

I have lately troubled Mr. Goode with a commission, concerning the same subject of inquiry; and as the minds of our representatives must be much harassed with the *amount of legislation dispatched* by them *daily*, I dislike to trouble him more.

I am sure you will pardon the intrusion.

(*Copy.*)

S. M. PETTENGILL CO. TO JOHN T. RUSSELL (PUB[LISHER] OF [THE] ARGUS).

NEW YORK, [N. Y.], *December 25, 1855.*

DEAR SIR: We have been applied to by gentlemen of high standing and respectability who desire to promote the nomination of Hon R M T Hunter of your state and Augustus Schell Esq of this city to the offices of President and Vice President at the Cincinnati Convention requesting us to enquire of you if you could admit into your columns as editorial, articles advocating their claims. Please inform us by *return mail* if you would do so, and if so your rate of charge per line or column for a series of them. Please consider this confidential.

JAMES HUNTER TO R. M. T. HUNTER.

CAROLINE COUNTY, [VA.], *December 27, 1855.*

MY DEAR SIR: I have received your letter, with Mr. Mason's letter enclosed concerning the manufacture of oil from coal. I have written to Mr. Robt. Brooke to send you parcels of splint and Cannel Coals, which I suppose you can submit to the chemist at the Patent Office for a trial of their properties.

I have delayed writing to you, because I was in daily expectation of seeing John Morris, who is now somewhere on his way from Nicholas [Now a county in West Virginia], and I wished to give you the latest news from that interesting region. But he is not yet come and I will delay no longer. John has been in Nicholas for three months past and writes in very good spirits about the land and the prospects ahead.

So far as I can judge, from what I have seen of the members of the Legislature I am confident that a Bill can be passed at this session which will secure the improvement of the Kanawha. But, Muscoe will give you the back information on this subject. I hope you will agree with me, that Muscoe should not lose the opportunity which is now offered him of obtaining the credit of the passage of the Covington and Ohio Rail Road Bill. He can pass it or defeat it, as he may choose. If he decides to give the Bill all the weight of his influence, he will have done the best he can do for the State and he will make himself the strongest man in Virginia.

Arthur Lewis, who has charge of the Hill lands, was with me yesterday. He is very much pleased with the Hill lands and also so much pleased with the Kanawha Coal Company that one of the first things he did when he returned, was to buy a quarter interest, and he now wishes to buy another quarter (Mr. Bright will have no difficulty in disposing of his share).

Lewis says with regard to the Hill lands and the lumber business— 1st That he has on the margin of the Gauley River as good Cannel Coal as there is in Kanawha County—that by the expenditure of $200 he may make the Gauley River navigable for boats carrying 150 tons or 4000 bushels to the Cov[ington] and Ohio Rail Road opposite Gauley Bridge. That the Cannel Coal on the Hill land is the most Eastern Bed of Cannel Coal; and when the Cov[ington] and Ohio R[ail] Road is finished it will be sent East. He also says that he can sell several thousand acres of the land during the next year, if we desire it, at from $1.50 to $2.00 pr. acre, but he is opposed to making the sale so far as his vote will go as one of the parties interested.

With regard to the lumber, he says, that he will hire ten (10) good hands and that with that force he will saw and deliver between the first of the year and the 15th July 312,000 feet of lumber—that during the latter part of June and July he will fix the Dam and the forebay and then will have power to run a gang of three or four saws and will saw during the balance of the year at least 800,000. That the 1,112,000 feet of lumber (2 in. stuff) is worth at the mill $20 pr. thousand—which is equal to $22,240 and that all his expenses will not exceed $6,000, which would give a profit of $16,240. He says that by the 1st of 1857, he will be fully prepared for the business and that he expects to work his mill the whole of that year and that he will saw at least 2½ millions of lumber. He went through all the calculations very carefully with me, and my opinion is that it is very probable that he will accomplish what he promises for the first year (1856) and as certain as anything can be that he will do all he says after the first year as long as the timber holds out. He says that the cost of carrying lumber from the mill to Charleston does not exceed $2½ pr thousand, this from his own experimental knowledge.

You will see Phil [Dandridge] in Washington and he will explain to you about the Kanawha Coal Company. He and others from Kanawha, state that so soon as the Improvement of the Kanawha River is secured the Front Coal Lands along the River will advance at once to $100 pr. acre.

GESSNER HARRISON TO R. M. T. HUNTER.

UNIVERSITY OF VIRGINIA, *Janury 21, 1856.*

MY DEAR SIR: I received to-day the "Report of the Patent Office on Agriculture, for 1854," which you have had the kindness to send me, and beg you to accept my thanks for this favor.

It is right, at least my feelings tell me so, that I should apprize you that I have finally decided to leave the University, to seek some better means of support. Whether I shall be able to complete my arrangements to leave at the end of the present session, I cannot say, positively, but I hope to effect this, which is my object.

I have a large family, and at the present and past years enormous prices of living, I cannot make ends meet, am spending the little I had laid up, and would presently be involved in debt. I have bought a farm four or five miles from Charlottesville, on the E[ast] side of Monticello and a little South of it, and intend to open a school for boys. My friends think I can get pupils enough to enable me to make a living and help me to pay for the farm. The step is a very hazardous one, perhaps; but I cannot see that I ought to hesitate to make the effort, while I still have some remaining energy and strength, to make some decent provision for my family, at least to supply them a home in case of my death.

The place I have chosen for my school is retired, in an excellent neighborhood, remarkably healthy, and with abundance of good land both for other purposes and for grazing. And I hope, from my large circle of acquaintances in the South, to be able to get pupils. Should it come in your way to procure me pupils, I hope you will feel justified in recommending my intended school. I shall commit myself wholly to the work of teaching, having entirely competent aid in the mathematics and other subjects which I do not profess to be master of, taking charge myself of the Classics and some subordinate matters.

MUSCOE R. H. GARNETT[1] TO R. M. T. HUNTER.

RICHMOND, [VA.], *February 5th, 1856.*

MY DEAR UNCLE: The Kanawha River bill passed this morning, waiving the State's lien on the tolls, so as to authorise the Ja[me]s Riv[er] and Kan[awha] Co[mpany] to issue 7 per cent bonds ($320,000) to improve it according to Fisk's plans. I congratulate you on the result. There is a prospect of selling (through Latham to N[ew] Y[ork] parties) one half of the Old Dominion Co[mpany] at the rate of $150 per acre. This would net me about $2,000 for one-half of my interest therein; don't you think this would be a bad bargain for me?

My report is at last made; it kept me so closely at work I had no time to write you but the brief note of last week. Yet I have been attentive to your interests. Directly after closing that note, I had a long interview with Charles Irving; he is thoroughly and warmly with us, and we have (at Harvie's advice) taken him into our confidence. This exchange is very important, for it gives us a voice in the Examiner wing of the party. He has been making strenuous efforts on Hughes and Floyd. I learn that the former seems amenable to reason, and might, perhaps, be changed or rationalized, but for Floyd; but the ex-Governor is blind with resentment. He resents the late Senatorial election and thinks you interfered with Pierce against him. Irving says he said Douglas told him so, but this is confidential. Can it be true? Kenna is trying his hand on him, and though with little hope, does not despair. With Floyd, our affairs would be easy. Kenna is for you, as you know, but he is too much for a combination with Pierce; if I understand him aright, he wants us to indicate our willingness to vote for Pierce first, with a view of securing P[ierce]'s friends to you. Do you think Kenna reliable? Irving has sent an excellent leader to his paper coming out for you. He has gone up to Danville to secure that paper, and Clemens thinks he can get the Wheeling Argus to come out. The Dem[ocratic] Recorder has already closed. Mallory

---

[1] A Representative in Congress from Virginia, 1856–1861.

will get Irving's editorial favorably endorsed in Norfolk, and the Valley Democrat and Lexington Star must be made to follow suit. Banks promises to republish and endorse in his paper; but at first he hesitated on the plea that it was impolite to alarm the friends of Pierce by pushing you just now. I cannot but think that, as Meade says, Banks has an axe of his own to grind, and the hope of getting into the Union effects him. I don't think he will be worth anything to you, if he gets there, though I believe he really prefers you.

Harvie, Mallory and a few others have a consultation with me tomorrow night for purposes of organization. Harvie has written for Booker to come up and we are to have a frank talk with Wise. What do you think of asking the Convention on the 28th to endorse you? I fear the attempt may be very dangerous, but Mallory and Harvie are disposed, if we conclude we have the strength to carry. And there are some fair arguments in favor of it, other states are disposed to go for you, but are held back by the reports of division and weakness in Virginia. It is supposed here that our friends in Washington expect an expression of opinion by that Convention. Shall we attempt it, or shall we trust to quiet organization in the Districts, and such demonstrations of public opinion through the press, as we are arranging? This is a difficult question ahead of us.

The members of the Legislature are much divided and very many undertermined. We have nobody who can efficiently work on the South well; we think Henry Edmundson could do much, if he would come down and spend a week here and be active. Cant he be persuaded to do so?

I deeply regret the Tucker business, both for its personal effects and for political reasons. Your friends here sustain you, but the Examiner has already opened its batteries and begins with a lie by saying that Forney is elected. Beverly [Tucker] himself has given colour to this charge by the assertion that Forney is still in the Union and that Stidell has pledges from the President that Forney shall be kept in. The affair cannot permanently injure except in that aspect, but if the President has cheated you, it may be very injurious. You owe it to yourself to see that Forney is excluded, and checkmate the fraud, if attempted.

WILLIAM O. GOODE TO R. M. T. HUNTER.

BOYDTON, VA., February 21, 1856.

DEAR HUNTER: I have just reached home safe and sound—having accomplished the journey with no other discomfort than such as is inseparable from a wearisome travel. At this moment the temperature is mild—but little of snow or ice visible and every thing decidedly vernal. Of course we are backward in farming operations, and the remaining supply of cow food somewhat scant, but we hope to get through without loss.

In Petersburg I saw Meade and Banks, who explained to me the action of the Public meeting there, and assured me that two thirds of the Committee expressed a preference for you, and yet they reported resolutions complimentary of Pierce and Douglas without including you; and which Meade says he has explained in a letter to me now in Washington. I would have preferred they had felt no occasion to explain. But both Meade and Banks thought there was no doubt about the sentiment of Petersburg. I shall endeavor to get back to Rich[mon]d on 28[th], but fear it is doubtful. Much judgment and discretion are required as to the propriety of bringing forward Resolutions of approval or preference. Meade, I think, is inclined to attempt it even if there be risk of failure. I attach greater importance to the selection of Delegates by the District Conventions, and hope to secure Harvie and Meade or Banks. If necessary I would go from Washington to attend our District Convention to secure that delegation, and if we can accomplish that and do as well in the other districts all will be well so far as Virginia is concerned. I found all well at home. For myself I feel better than I have since the first of December. I find this note has spread over two pages and I should be alarmed if I did not know it to be quite scattering. With affectionate regards to Mason and the Judge, and kind remembrances to the servants.

EDWARD KENNAN TO R. M. T. HUNTER

(*Confidential.*)

WHEELING, [VA.], *15th March, 1856.*

MY DEAR SIR: I arrived here on Thursday morning on my way home, but resolved to spend a few days in ascertaining how events were progressing. I have seen nearly all the leading men (except Judge Thompson, who is out of town, and Clemens who has not yet reached home.) there seems now no decided preferences. The impression has prevailed that Buchanan was the strongest man, that is could carry more northern states, than any other, and hence a leaning to him, I have had repeated conversations with Chas and Jno Rupely. The latter the Argus Editor, the former whilst he expresses a personal preference for you he thinks that should the North desire Buchanan they should have him, as a means of securing northern support in the coming contest after that, then you would be his choice. I am satisfied there is no moving him from this view at *present*, evidences of B[uchana]n weakness at the North or discensions in Pennsylvania would do it effectually. The importance of securing C[harles] R[upely's] cooperation is increased by the probability of his being one of the delegates to the Cincinnatti Convention. The contest will be between him and Koonts a decided Buchanan man with whom I had a long conversation on the subject this afternoon. I have in a quiet way done all I could to aid in Rupely's election. I talked matters over with Jno. Rupely the Editor. I sent you an Argus to day, The Editorial of which gives you the result. I also wrote the President, for Rupely remonstrating against the withdrawal, of some public printing from the Argus to give it to the Winchester V[irgini]a [n] as it is rumoured here it was designed to do. Should it be done, then Buchanan's interest will be greatly strengthened here. Clements whilst popular has no transferrable strength. Thompson is on the bench and takes no part. The Mountain Counties send a delegate it is supposed, Mr. Neeson of Fairmont, an intimate friend of Kidwells but who has been recently appointed by Mr. Wise, a visitor to the University ! ! ! It is almost quite · certain he will go, so Kidwell, rather uncertain, he *is all right*. It is said Kidwell can control the appointment of the delegates of the mountain counties. I think on the whole, things look favourable here but decided changes can be effected by industry, attend to *sending documents*, here some good ones to Chas. Kidwell and Jno. Rupely, Editor of the Argus also Koonts, *Loving*, Clark of Circuit Court. Get a list from Kidwell, You have no idea I am satisfied of the good that can be effected in this way. *You neglect it*. The Editorial in the Argus I sent you, was intended to recall the public mind to the old issues, and at the same time, to prevent the withdrawal of the printing from that paper. I send you a copy of a letter received by Rupely some time since, it explains itself. Should *Bright get wind of such a movement* I need not tell you what the consequences would be; It was given me for your ear, but to be used confidentially. Take care, the same proposition may not be now in progress of arrangement, between Mr Wise's friends and Schell's to be brought forward *at the Eleventh* hour. Beware of the New Yorkers' they are dangerous. I shall perhaps stop a day at Columbus, and will communicate anything I may learn of interest. They say here that John Martin, has no considerable influence, although exerting what he has for Wise & Co. Taylor County in my Electoral District is in Kidwells Congressional District, you had better see K[idwell] and ask him to interest himself in inducing a delegation to our Distirct Convention, favourable to me or have me appointed *alternate*. I think it is Taylor County. He can see by looking at the Counties. Has Edmondstone attended to Nicholas County? Depend upon it if you lose Virginia, it will be the cause of the supineness of your friends.

ISAAC E. HOLMES TO A. P. BUTLER.[1]

CHARLESTON, [S. C.], *17th March, 1856.*

MY DEAR BUTLER: I have rec[eive]d y[ou]r letter and speech.
The best speech you have made and y[ou]r notice of Atchinson was
admirable. I shall write a notice of the speech and y[ou]r remarks
upon Atchinson, whose devotion to the Southern cause is above all
praise. The South are not awake, and my own opinion is very decidedly, that the North will carry their point. I have looked for
the success of the Emancipation Party ever since I was in Congress,
and believe that henceforth the Battle will always be in their favour.
The hostility of Rhett to you, flashes out in the Mercury on every
occasion, and even y[ou]r remarks in a letter upon the Convention
draws down his *ire.* A man is a Prophet save in his own *Country,*
and whilst you are acquiring a fame and influence wide as the Union,
efforts are making to dwarf you in the State of y[ou]r Nativity.
You may look down with scorn upon their efforts, few men have
firmer friends in So[uth] Carolina than yourself.˙ The next Presidential contest will be severe. My opinion is that the election will
fall upon The House. Events will transpire before this Session
closes to bring forth more decided manifestations of the management of Seward and it will require all the *Tact,* and Knowledge of
under-currents, on the part of our friend Hunter to counteract his
inclinations. I know little of what is passing in the City, my time
is devoted to Mrs. Holmes and my books and the study of *philosophy*
of which I stand in great need. I have read more in one year than I
have done in ten previous ones, but I have to submit to fate. I often
think of the Mrs. and the happy days spent with you *all.* You know
that I am a great admirer of Hunter who I believe has more wisdom
than falls to the Lot of even distinguished Persons, and I regard
Mason as a man of sound sense, and an accomplished Gentleman.
Atchinson must be missed by *you,* but he is well employed at home.
We are in a revolution of which he is the Master Spirit and in the
event of conflict, I doubt not will distinguish himself as the Champion of the *South.*

Walker at Nicaragua will shortly settle the question of the Musqui-
toe Kingdom, and it may well be left to him to battle with England—
who will assuredly crush him, and his great Army, whilst they will
embrace the opportunity of settling the vexed question of the *Pro-
tectorate,* with Nicaragua and leave us free to disentangle ourselves
of the Monroe Doctrine. Depend upon it, France and Britain will
unite in any efforts necessary to keep the United States from pos-
sessing the South American States and thus bringing them, as portions of Mexico, already are brought under the influence of our Do-

---

[1] Andrew Pickens Butler, a Senator in Congress from South Carolina, 1846–1857.

mestic Commerce. Suppose the Philobusteurs were to take Mexico—Central America, and the other American States South of the Isthmus. They would annex them as Texas was to this Confederacy, and thus the entire commerce of America with New York would be in our hands to the exclusion of Foreign shipping. The first cause which led to the Revolution of the Spanish American provinces, was the jealousy of G[reat] Britain at this very exclusive trade between Spain and her possessions. Miranda's, agent [of] Mexico, expedition was sustain[e]d by England, and it was her apprehension of this *evil* of exclusive Commerce which incited Mr. Canning to give us notice of the designs of the Holy Alliance to restore the Colonies to Spain, and which led to the Monroe *Doctrine.* I confess, I dreaded at one time the result of the difficulties about Nicaragua. A War with G[reat] Britain w[oul]d ruin the Southern States, but enough, regard to the Mrs.

CHARLES MASON TO R. M. T. HUNTER.

ALTO, [VA.], *March 18, 1856.*

MY DEAR SIR: You would be amused to learn some of the manouvres which have been resorted to in our state to secure the nomination for the presidency. *You stand no chance* in such an intriguing age; and the truth is I have lost confidence in every body. A man who, some months since, told me he could and would make you president, if I am correctly informed, is now throwing every obstacle in the way of such a result. His own ambition may be an apology, but if it be true that he has countenanced strange combinations there is no excuse for him.[1] I can scarcely believe what I hear from Richmond and I say nothing of my own knowledge, for I have been confined to my room for nearly three weeks, with a violent cough which prevented me from attending the convention. The resolutions of our little meeting here, every body understood was a preference for you and your name was not mentioned because we thought it would do more harm than good.

The plan pursued by our convention was a proper one, to express no preference, for any body of men who go into the National Convention tied down to a name, must have an up hill road to travel. I saw the disadvantage Mr. Buchanan labored under by such a course in the last convention. There was an omission, however, in our friends not instructing our delegates to cast the whole vote of the state as a unit. They sh[oul]d have gone further and instructed them to vote always for that son of V[irgini]a who was presented to the convention, by other states and receiving the largest vote.

---

[1] Probably Henry A. Wise, who was then governor of Virginia.

We were very near having our vote scattered in Baltimore by the Floyd party, which would, at once have broken the moral force of Virginia's strength and defeated a nomination.

DAVID M. STONE TO R. M. T. HUNTER.

OFFICE OF THE JOURNAL OF COMMERCE,
NEW YORK, [N. Y.], *March 25th, 1856.*

DEAR SIR: I believe I had the pleasure of meeting you once, but waiving any claim to old acquaintance, I avail myself of the kind introduction of Mr Cisco, to say a few words in regard to the proposed modification of the Tariff.

The Manufacturers at the North and East believed for many years that the old Whig party was the only organization which cared a button for their interests, and that a high protective tariff was essential to their salvation. The more sagacious among them have at last opened their eyes, and finding that the hot-house system is not conducive to a healthy growth, are anxious to try the free-trade method of struggling for life in the open field. The only real difficulty in the way of this, is the tax upon raw materials, which the manufacturers of all other countries are allowed to import free, or at a merely nominal charge. The free-trade party tried in Walker's time to secure this, but the opposition was so wedded to the principle of protection, that it was found impossible to obtain a majority for it. Our woolen manufacturers, especially, need such legislation as shall take off the restrictions which a blind policy has formerly imposed upon their raw material; and thinking men in all sections of the country, without distinction of party, have advocated the measure of relief proposed. I have written, within the last eighteen months two pamphlets upon this subject, which have been widely circulated, and the response from solid men in all parts of the country, has been in favor of the scheme. I think that I have shown conclusively that it will benefit the wool growers quite as much as the manufacturers, and my views have been approved by a very large number of leading agriculturists and farmers. I rec[eive]d a long letter from Gov[ernor] Wright of Ind[ian]a some time since, assenting to my views, and confirming my opinion that those who control public sentiment at the West are with us on this question. Mr. Houston of Al[abam]a consented to this, last session, and at my suggestion, placed wool and many other raw materials in a schedule at a nominal duty; this bill passed the House, but failed in the Senate for want of time.

The measure is likely to be opposed, however, by those politicians who have heretofore been the most clamorous friends of the manufacturer. Greely hesitates not to declare, privately, that it shall not pass this session, but must be kept back for use in the next Pres-[identia]l Campaign. Seward has sullenly agreed not to combat it openly, but as I learn from some of his own friends who have been on to Washington, on purpose to see him, he will prevent its success if he can without personal exposure. James of R[hode] I[sland] has drawn up his bill based on free trade in raw materials, but in order to effect his reelection, has levied the duties on other impor-tations far too high. I send, herewith, a leading article from the Journal of Commerce of Saturday, commenting upon his scheme. Our merchants here are becoming impatient that a plan against which so little can be said, should meet so many delays. The manu-facturing interests have been closeted at Boston, and feeling more than ever absolved from party ties, are fastening their eyes upon those Conservative Statesmen who are known to be honest, to see if now that there is an opportunity to do something for the pros-perity of the country, without building up one at the expense of an-other, they may not find help in some whom they have not been accustomed to regard as friends.

Mr. Guthrie has been highly applauded for his services in repeat-ing and enforcing the recommendations of Mr. Walker upon this subject, and there needs but a voice to be heard above the din of fac-tion upon the floor of Congress, to draw the hearts of all the Com-mercial classes into one channel. Where shall we look but to you? Standing midway between the North and South, ever on the side of right in the past, and (if the signs of the times be true) to be still more largely trusted in the future, who so fit a spokesman for the public of all sections in this crisis as yourself?

Mr. W. W. Stone of this city (with whom I can claim no connection notwithstanding the name) a member of the firm of Lawrence, Stone and Co. one of the most respectable domestic houses in the country, and intimately connected with Eastern Merchants and Manufac-turers, visits Washington to-day. He has been an earnest advocate of this revision of the Tariff for several years, and would like to con-verse with you in regard to it. He has formerly acted with the Whig party, but in the present unsettled state of political affairs, feels no party responsibilities, and has, I am sure, the welfare of the country at heart. He will speak to you more at large of the state of feeling at the East from which you will see that I have not written unadvisedly.

CHARLES LEVI WOODBURY TO R. M. T. HUNTER.

BOSTON, [MASS.], *April 1st, 1856.*

DEAR SIR: I send you a copy of the French Tariff whose promulga-tion has reached here in the last mail. In the pendency of the pro-posed revision of our own, the new position of France, possesses much

[of] importance. Our constitutional and treaty limitations necessarily make the task of revising a tariff, full of perplexity and requiring mature analysis.

With all the aid the Treasury Department have furnished to the experience of Genl. James,[1] there are some features in his otherwise able bill, which are based on principles that cannot be justified in the free trade school of Statesmanship. There is a living faith in popular opinion eventually rendering to a patriot and a statesman the acknowledgment of his merit and forecast. You are beginning to experience this in the North. It has happened to me several times within a few weeks, conversing with leading merchants and manufacturers of this section, to hear from their lips those acknowledgments with regard to yourself that none of our party could ever have expected.

The policy you have advocated is now successful and the manufacturers here, express their unqualified confidence that you can arrange a revision of the tariff which would be absolutely satisfactory to the South and agreeable to the North. From the known accordance of my views with your policy, it could not have been intended I should withhold these expressions from your knowledge.

In my judgment the time has come when the tariff may be set on a permanent footing of low duties and equitable adjustments. To reaffirm at this juncture the cardinal principles of the advalorem and foreign valuations, to establish the free trade policy on the admitted basis of its general welfare and to reduce the unnecessary and enormous revenue now derived from customs, would carry important consequences in the political world which none can better estimate than yourself. I should not write thus frankly, did I not presume you were occupied with the proposed revision. The confidence all these great interests repose in you make this a happy moment for your effecting permanent good, and with your permission, it would give me great satisfaction to aid in bringing the interests here to that communication, which would possess you of their views, and show that they approved this question in a spirit of concession heretofore unknown to them. Allow me to renew the expressions of my sincere esteem.

FRANCIS MALLORY TO R. M. T. HUNTER.

NORFOLK, [VA.], *April 13, 1856.*

DEAR HUNTER: Since my return home I have been so unwell that I have had no opportunity of mixing extensively among the people though so far as I can learn you have gained much in this

---

[1] A Democratic Senator in Congress from Rhode Island, 1851–1857. He was elected as a protective tariff Democrat.

district. Buchanan's popularity is based on that of Wise whose friends have sought to make the impression that he (B) is the strongest man now before the people. This causes the timid and time serving to represent themselves as preferring Buch[ana]n. Wise has lost all power in the East save among his Eastern Shore men and such as they can influence. The Eboshin and Fendum have done their work effectually and two or three appointments made in this place within a few weeks past have given great dissatisfaction because they were taken from among the Eastern Shore men in preference to residents. Buck's [Buchanan's] is only a reflection of Wise's popularity and to dissipate it is no difficult matter. The idea that to insure success for the Cincinnatti nominee he must be from the North has been industriously circulated over the South, and this has been the chief weapon of the W. and B.[1] men. Let something be done in the right quarter to cause doubt of its truth and we can carry every Eastern district. Give me a program for operations and I will carry it out. If you wish an open demonstration made I will have it started here or in some county. How are you and Pierce now? Would it be safe to make one for him as the choice of the Northern candidates, if so would [it] whip the office holders into measures? But as to this I will not move till I hear from you. Banks sends me word all is right above—that is in the upper part of the district. Simkins, Wise's friend, is proud of the Demo-[cratic] Associations but the selections was not plain because of the jealousy over here about Eastern men. He talks of resigning, if so a *Hunter* man will fill it. The election was no test but was owing to the personal popularity of Simkins. Tell me what I can do and I am ready to act.

I may be in Washington in 10 or 12 days. Pierce promised my son a commission in the army, the first vacancy last spring or sum-. mer but I have not troubled him since. He was disposed to confer it then but *Davis* defeated me. Pierce felt and expressed some compunction for his move against me as Navy agent and wished to make amends in this way. I care nothing for it myself but the boy (now 22 years old) is anxious for it. He was educated at Lexington and would make, so says Col[onel] Smith a fine officer. He seems to have no turn for anything else but he is well behaved, handsome and brave. He had much better marry a rich girl but he seems to prefer fighting Indians at $40 per month, and being a wilfull boy he must have his way. Is there any chance? Some forty vacancies have occurred within a few months. But I started to write you about other matters and did not design to trouble you with my small wants.

---

[1] Wise and Buchanan men.

[P. S.] How would it do for me as an old Fillmore man to come out in a letter assigning reasons why I could not vote for him and giving reasons also for my preference for others. If this would be politic give me an outline of my platform—who I should war upon—who pray—and how far to go in either case. Is not Millson[1] against Pierce? I should think so from questions he put to me the other day.

ROBERT SELDEN GARNETT TO R. M. T. HUNTER.

POST AT MUCKLESHUTE PRAIRIE,
NEAR STEILACOONE, W. T., *April 20, 1856.*

MY DEAR COUSIN: By the time this reaches you the excitement growing out of the Cincinnati Convention will, I presume, have somewhat subsided. I need not tell how much I hope it may find you the successful man in the struggle that may occur there. Should however this be not the case, I hope you will console yourself with the reflection that there is yet sufficient time ahead for your turn.

It was my intention at an early day after my arrival in this country to post you up thoroughly on the origin and merits of this war going on here with the Indians. But I no sooner landed than I was packed off to this outpost where I have been unable to see any intelligent or disinterested man who could give me the information I wanted. Nor have I been able to meet any hostile Indians in action or otherwise and learn from them their own accounts of their difficulties. Indeed it is in this respect that I conceive one of the greatest blunders of the whole business has been committed, for I have been unable yet to see any one who can give me an intelligent and consistent account of what the Indians regard as the cause of the war, and as its object, and upon what terms &c they desire. We in the Army are campaigning and fighting here in the dark. Without understanding the cause or the object of the war, and consequently without the means of knowing what are the best means to bring about a peace. Most of the whites say it is dissatisfaction with the treaties made by Gov. Stevens. If so instead of going to War on the subject, and, attempting to teach them a lesson on adhering to treaties which will cost us some millions of money, why not send for them and learn what features of the treaty are distasteful to them, and if reasonable why not let them have what they want as long as it does not interfere with the just wants and safety of the settlers. I am told the Indians complain that by these treaties they are required to live upon small reserves incapable of subsisting them and their animals in their mode of life. That the Indians [?] have been located upon lands badly situated, indeed so much so that the whites can't use it, with no prairie or pasture lands for their animals and

---

[1] John S. Millson, a Representative in Congress from Virginia, 1849–1861.

no clear lands for their potatoes &c; and that if they are all crowded upon such small ill-selected spots they must starve to death.

If there is truth in this, and no one has tried that I know of, to see the hostile Indians to ascertain whether this be so or not, it is in my opinion a just cause not only of dissatisfaction and complaint but of war. We cant expect men to change their habits of life, the habits of their race, or to starve to death quietly merely to satisfy the wild schemes of white men. If this be true I can see no reason why they should not have larger and more suitable reserves given them, particularly too since they have relinquished by these treaties more lands than will be sufficient for the settlers of this country, at present rates, and for the next hundred years. In making this concession to them we should be giving them nothing more than humanity demands us to give them, and which common justice should never have permitted us to take away from them. But you will gather from the enclosed newspaper slips something of the merits of the question at issue between the authorities here. From all that I can learn I am well satisfied that this War has been *very unnecessarily* brought on by Govr. Stevens' treaties. Not only by the ill judged provisions of the treaties themselves, but especially by entering into treaties with them where the wants of the country (in my judgment) did not require anything of the sort. As bad fortune would have it I am told that *this treaty*, out of the large number which he made on his Quixotic pilgrimage in the interior of the continent where no white men will settle in the next 300 years perhaps, was the only one which reached Washington City in time to be confirmed by the Senate during the last Congress, and is now the law of the land. I am satisfied that if this were not the case and I had the power from Mr. Pierce to annul and destroy Stevens' treaty I could establish a permanent peace here in six weeks and not fire a rifle, a peace by which the settlers should be safe from danger, and not checked in their settlement of the country. And I would make no concession to the Indians which any practical and reasonable man could find fault with.

FRANCIS MALLORY TO R. M. T. HUNTER.

NORFOLK, [VA.], *May 11, 1856.*

DEAR HUNTER: I have just returned from a visit to my old (Hampton) county and hope things will end there as we desire. Booker is warm in your favor and out against Buch[ana]n talking publickly of his Tariff vote in '42 and Missouri Compromise opinions. I shall attend the convention there on next Thursday and so told Booker who seemed much pleased at my promise. I shall be an outsider but will try my best. Drop B[ooker] a Line the *moment* you get this. It will encourage him much. Your letter to him had a fine effect.

He is fond of you but has been much courted by Wise. High minded
honorable and brave as he is these little attentions are always agreeable especially to a country gentleman living a secluded life. He still
praises W[ise] but thinks him out of the question this time. I want
you to ask him to go and say you will leave him to act according to
his own judgment content with any action he may take &c. Wednesday the convention for the Norfolk district comes off. But for the
Wise men who still look to W[ise] as residuary Legatee of B[uch-
anan] we should have no difficulty. No one is opposed to you but the
idea is afloat that B[uchanan] is the strong candidate and as office
here controls every thing they profess preference for him because he
is as they think the strong man. Simkins has softened down very
much and so has Blow. If either of them go from the lower end I
have a strong hope of getting him right. If they get in their men I
will work day and night to operate on them and if I can wield a
little influence in Washington I may succeed. I have just had a conversation with Simkins the Leader of the Wise party here as to the
proceedings in Portsmouth and he *asked me to draw up the resolutions* (this of course confidential) and state his positions: 1st Compliment Pierce and endorse his admin[istratio]n, 2d support nominee
of Cin[cinnat]i Convention, 3d Express no preference, 4th Leave
delegates free to act according to circumstances. We shall carry a
true man I think from the upper counties and will at least divide the
district.

I told Banks to get old Frank Rives (who he says is all right) to
work on Boykin of Isle of Wight and Atkinson and he writes me
that it has been done. *Boykin wants office* and is slippery. He is weak
in intellect and his attachments by no means stable. He wants to go
as a Delegate. I cant advocate him but I know, I think, how and who
can manage him. He is more tractable than Blow or Smith. The
son I can do nothing with. He wanted the Collectorship here and is
sound against Pierce. He will make a hard fight for Delegate but
we have quietly operated against him on the ground, that the Elector
comes from Portsmouth, Smith's place of residence and that she is
not entitled to [a] Delegate and none of the Norfolk City Delegation will support him. Pierce's office holders give us no aid whatever. They are afraid to take position. When I was Navy Ag[en]t
I ruled my party in the District and so could Loyall have done, but
he is effete, selfish and timid. Sawyer has no power, even with his
subordinates. Will the above positions (I mean the resolutions) suit
you or would it answer to make an issue for Pierce direct. The result
would be doubtful in as much as the floating vote in Conventions
generally sides with the moderate party whether they be so in fact
or in fraud. Drop me a line the *moment* you get this and draft me a
resolution or two. You need not be afraid of my indiscretion. You

fellows in Congress did not know me half as well as I did you. If I talk at random sometimes, so also can I be silent and prudent when there is necessity. If I had *position* in the Line or on the staff I could win the victory here. If I can do any good I will speak at both Conventions. I care not who gets the nomination for Delegates I mean to commence operations on him and if it be any but Smith (who hates me) I hope to succeed. I am far from giving up the fight for these ten districts for none will be pledged or committed.

Send me the names of your friends in *Gloucester* that will be in Hampton that I may know who to approach. My Brother Chas. K. Mallory, a lawyer, residing in Hampton is a warm and active friend. It will be hard if him and Booker acting together can not carry things to suit us.

Tell Muscoe our inspection law has so far put a stop to slave stealing in lower Virginia. It works beautifully tho' the Senate did it much damage by its amendments. I have got things quite snug for him in the lower end of his district in view of Bayly's departure.

My son has just returned. Many thanks for your kindness, and please thank Pierce for me.

If you wish me to hear from you before the Conventions meet, write the moment you get this, which is nearly as hard to decipher as your own. The Baltimore Boats leave in the afternoon and arrive here next morning. This you will get Tuesday morning. If the positions in the resolutions suit you, telegraph me in the words "All right," if not "make an issue direct for P[ierce] or H[unter]" as the case may be and sign it. T. M. provided you cant mail your letter by the 1 P. M. [boat] for Baltimore or 1½ P. M. or that which carries the mail through to Norfolk which can be known by enquiring at the City p[ost] office. If the vote of V[irgini]a depends on these two districts I dont think you have much to fear let things take what shape they may just now. It is easier to vanquish men in detail than attacking numbers. I shall act as we Doctors say "pro re natu."

FRANCIS MALLORY TO R. M. T. HUNTER.

HAMPTON, VA., *May 15th, 1856.*

MY DEAR SIR: According to promises I proceed to give you an acc[oun]t of the proceedings of the District Convention which met here to-day and have just adjourned. Every County in the district was represented and the Convention was respectable both in numbers and talent. At 12 O'clock the convention was called to order in the spacious ball saloon of Dr. Banks' delightfully located Hotel which he had kindly tendered to its use.

As the proceedings will soon be published in the leading public journal of the State, I must content myself with giving a mere synopsis of what passed without going into particulars.

Jno. W. Catlett Esq. of Gloucester with Eleven Vice presidents, and Mr. Hope and Mallory of Hampton, as Secretaries, was chosen as the permanent officers of the Convention. During the absence of the Committee on Organization, our Elector Wm. B. Taliaferro Esq. entertained the Convention in a very pretty speech of half an hours duration. It is the intention of Major Taliaferro to canvass the district after the nominations at Cincinnati, and as you will of course have an opportunity of hearing him and judging of his oratorical abilities for yourself, I will only say that he is a good looking man and of pleasant address. Conl R. C. Claybrook the talented delegate from Northumberland in the last legislature also spoke, and made a very happy effort indeed. He is a fine popular orator, and as he is quite a young man I should not be at all surprised if before a great while, he is called on to play a prominent part in the politics of this district.

Mr. Catlett on taking the Chair returned his thanks for the honor conferred on him in a neat and appropriate address which I hope will be given to the public by the accomplished Secretary exactly as it fell from his lips, for it was full of sound Southern sentiment patriotically expressed.

The rules of the house of Delegates were adopted for the Gov-[ernmen]t of the Convention and also a resolution " that whenever a sealed vote should be called for, each delegate should give his proportion of the aggregate Dem[ocratic] vote cast by his County in the last Election for Governor." It was generally understood that the Convention would not attempt to express a preference for any one of the distinguished gentleman whose names have been so prominently spoken of for the Cincinnati nominations; then, judge of our surprise when a gentleman from Williamsburg, Mr. Causnan offered the following resolution, which caused no little stir and a perfect war of words: " that while this convention do not intend to instruct their delegates to the Cincinnati Convention, yet the nomination by that body of their distinguished fellow citizen H. A. Wise Esq. for the first office in the gift of the American people, will be highly gratifying and meet with the cordial approbation of the people of this district." I believe I give you the very words of the resolution; I am certain you have its pith and *marrow*. Mr. Causnan accompanied his resolution with a short speech, citing the action of the late convention in the Essex District which expressed a preference for Senator Hunter, as a reason very cogent to his mind, why this district should pronounce for Gov. Wise. A gentleman from

Gloucester I think, moved to lay the resolution on the table, while another moved its indefinite postponement. A long debate ensued in which a good many silly and common place things were said. Mr. Seawell of Gloucester however, made a very sensible speech; he said—"that Mr. Wise *might be, probably he was*, the choice of a majority of the District, yet he had no hesitation in saying that he would receive *fewer* votes and a less cordial support than any other man the Cin[cinna]ti Convention might nominate; that such a resolution ought not to pass unless as the unanimous sense of this Convention, which could not be; that the strong opposition to it would rob it of even the semblance of a compliment and destroy that moral effect which it was intended to convey."

It is a great pity that the overzealous friends of the Governour did not heed these words of wisdom. A Sealed Vote was called for. The friends of the resolution were taken all aback, and no little feeling manifested in certain quarters, by the vote of Accomack, *two* of her delegates voting *for* postponement and *two* against. The fate of the resolution was doubtful, but when the Secretary announced that 1002 had voted against and 1227 for indefinite postponement, the sensation throughout the convention was most profound. Chagrin and mortification were depicted on many countenances. Noses, to use a vulgar phrase, had been counted in the morning outside of the Convention and it was thought the resolution could be carried and certain Wise workers intended to do it against all opposition. A member immediately arose and offered the same resolution, substituting the name of Senator Hunter for that of Gov. Wise. Amid the noise and confusion around me I could not hear the remarks he made, as he spoke in a low voice. At this point there was a struggle for the floor. Mr. Custis of Accomack however gained it, and moved the indefinite postponement and took occasion in strong and nervous language to define his position, " he had voted to postpone the first resolution because he regarded it as an apple of discord calculated to mar the harmony of the Convention and the Convention had acted wisely in disposing of it as they did—he was unwilling to express a preference for any man although he had a decided choice. The delegates to Cin[cinna]ti should be left free and untrammelled. He was willing to trust to their discretion and good judgments. Virginia could not decide between her distinguished sons and present that unity of sentiment and action in which consisted her great moral power. To attempt such a thing would produce discord at once, and realise the fable of the Kilkenny Cats; if either Mr. Wise or Mr. Hunter should receive the nomination at Cin[cinna]ti the first move in favor of either must come from some other State, and when that was made, their good old mother would be prepared to follow."

These sentiments met with general favour. The resolution was then unanimously postponed.

At this stage of the proceedings a general anxiety to go into the election of Delegates to Cin[cinna]ti was manifested, but Mr. Cary of Hampton insisted on explaining the reasons that influenced the Convention in their late votes, and offered a resolution to this effect, "that the Convention was opposed to the expression of a preference for any one, feeling perfectly satisfied that the Cin[cinna]ti Convention would give us no other than a good and true man, whom we could all most cheerfully and enthusiastically support." This is the substance though not the language of the resolution. Now after a session of nearly four hours, the real business for which the Convention met, commenced, viz—the Selection and appointment of Delegates to the National Convention. Geo. Booker Esq of Elizabeth City, who has served on former occasions in 1848 and 1852 at Baltimore, and who seems to be a general favorite, was elected on the first ballot by a nearly unanimous vote. On the 3rd or 4th ballot M. W. Fisher Esq. of Northampton, was chosen as the other delegate. And Conl. R. C. Claybrook of Northumberland and Jno. Seawell Esq. of Gloucester were appointed alternates.

Here the scene became very interesting; each one of the Eleven Vice Presidents were in turn, called out and delivered themselves of short, pithy speeches, abounding in humour and happy hits. The Convention adjourned after returning thanks to the Democracy of E[lizabeth] City for their kindness and hospitality. A most sumptuous repast was spread in the basement of the Hotel for the Convention, abounding in all the good things of this life. Champagne *poped* toasts were drunk, and speeches made, it was literally a " feast of reason and a flow of soul."

At night the good people of Hampton and vicinity met at their Court House, and were highly delighted by speeches from T. Cropper Esq. of Norfolk, Mr. Weaver of Accomack, and Jno. Seawell Esq. of Gloucester. Mr. S[eawell] is generally regarded as one of the ablest lawyers in the district, and is a fine speaker. He is very much like our friend L——. The best feeling and spirit pervades the Democracy. They are confident every where of a splendid victory, eclipsing all past victories in November next. Hoping to meet you soon, when we will talk all these things over and many more.

GEORGE W. THOMPSON [1] TO R. M. T. HUNTER.

(*Private.*)

[WHEELING, VA.?], *May 24th, 1856.*

DEAR SIR: I have had a somewhat desultory correspondence with my old friend Linn Boyd.[2] He thinks it likely, he will be put in nomination for the Presidency by Kentucky. I do not think he has much hope beyond this. You are his first choice when his claims are disposed of. I wrote him last week a letter intended to satisfy him, that the danger was in the nomination of Douglass whom he very cordially dislikes for various reasons, and that his true policy was to get the nomination from K[entuck]y and to hold on to it until Buchanan and Pierce were out of the way, which I think will soon be the case and then to give the fruits of the game to you. He has no respect for Mr. Buchanan and a decided hostility to Pierce and Douglass. His choice after you would be Rusk.[3] But I hope he can control the K[entuck]y delegation and if he can I think it most likely that at an early stage of the game he will go for you. I deem this important as our own state from the division which exists will be measurably impotent in the Convention and as their is a growing jealously of our influence in the nominating Convention by Ohio and other states. I cannot but think that most of the south must take you in preference. The state-rights party all over the south must prefer you, if there is any reason in mens preferences, before any other man named either north or south and I have been inclined to think that the Pierce movement was for your benefit only. But I intended only in this note to write you in relation to Boyd and to suggest a cautious movement on the part of your confidential friends towards Boyd's K[entuck]y friends in Con[gres]s. The manner of this approach I cannot suggest for I cannot anticipate the actual condition of things which may make it proper or improper. If I hear that Boyd himself is at Cincinnatti I will go down myself if it is possible for me to leave. Russell is for Buchanan first from choice. He is for you on the second. Neeson I understand personally prefers Pierce, but *must* go for " Buck," but " Buck " and Pierce being pitted and killed by the same operation he will then I think go for you. But we will soon know the result.

---

[1] A Democratic Representative in Congress from Virginia, 1851–1852.
[2] A Representative in Congress from Kentucky, 1835–1837 and 1839–1855 ; twice elected Speaker of the House, 1851–1855.
[3] Thomas Jefferson Rusk, a Senator in Congress from Texas, 1845–1857.

ERASTUS T. MONTAGUE TO R. M. T. HUNTER.

WASHINGTON, [D. C.], *June 9th, 1856.*

DEAR HUNTER: I presume you have heard ere this of the action of the Cincinnati Convention and its utter abandonment of most of the great cardinal principles of the Democratic party.

I have never before despaired of the Republic but I confess that since ascertaining the nominee and reading the platform and addendum, I have but little hope for the future. The constitutional party have been basely sold for the contemptible consideration of office, and what is most humiliating our *hitherto* honored state seems to have taken the lead in the treacherous proceeding. It is true some of our friends resisted. But in my judgment they should never have yielded but rather have withdrawn with a protest. From all I can learn, there was a perfect understanding between the friends of Mr. Buchanan and the Internal Improvement men and Fillibusters that if elected he should favor all their wild and unconstitutional measures. That Virginia should have contributed to such a result is too bad to think about.

I returned on Saturday but deferred writing till today that I might inform you whether the Senate would do any business of importance this week and I learn that nothing will be done for a fortnight except making speeches for home consumption.

Judge Butler has the floor for Thursday next, in reply to Sumners abusive tirade. The Judge is still alone Messrs. Mason and Goode being still absent.

But few of the members of the convention have returned. I have seen but one, Houston of Alabama. He is quite as much dissatisfied with their proceedings as I am.

ROGER A. PRYOR [1] TO R. M. T. HUNTER.

RICHMOND, [VA.], *June 11th, 1856.*

MY DEAR SIR: We are to have a ratification meeting in this City next Friday night; and I write to entreat a speech from you on the occasion. Your presence is absolutely indispensable, not to the interests of the candidates, but to the fortunes of *our* wing of the party in the State. You will understand me without further explanation. Come, with the warmest speech your conscience will allow. Bring Mr. Mason and others of our friends. Bob, by *all means come yourself.* Write me an affirmative reply. Don't disappoint me and *neglect* your *own interests.*

---

[1] A Representative in Congress from Virginia, 1859–1861; editor of the Richmond South, 1857–1859.

LEWIS E. HARVIE TO R. M. T. HUNTER.

RICHMOND, [VA.], *June 16th, 1856.*

MY DEAR HUNTER: On my way back from Cincinnati I called to see you in Washington. I had much to say to you not only of the past but the future. I have thought much since we met last and now that I can look back calmly at all that has occurred I write the result of my reflections not without the hope that you may be somewhat influenced by them. You have heard and know how utterly Bright and Douglas disappointed our expectations and how false and hollow were their professions. That they were fair as long as it was their interest and false as soon as that bond was broken. And you must have come to the conclusion that the Presidency is not to be won simply by combinations and arrangements with men and that least of all are men seeking high place influenced by gratitude. It is only necessary to look to Wise to come to that conclusion. Even with the help of friends, such as few men have had, the battle has been lost. I am now coming to the object of my letter which is to urge upon you to *adopt* a different line of policy altogether from what you have heretofore pursued and which to some extent I know to be somewhat foreign to your tastes and nature. I want you my dear friend, to discard altogether, if possible, all thought of the Presidency from your mind, at all events so far as to be uninfluenced by it in your future course in the Senate. I want you to put yourself at the head of the South and where you ought to stand and strike hard and heavy and frequent blows and that at once.

The South has no leader and sadly wants one. It is a post that has been waiting your acceptance since Mr Calhoun's death. It is your duty to fill it and your interest too. Men say you are too timid, overcautious, that you wish nothing and thus it is that you have lost friends, power and influence. You must launch out into the sea of strife, your safety requiring it, your hope of renown depends on it, your own interest and that of the country demands it, and your ability to pay the just debts that you owe to Messrs. Wise, Bright, and Douglas and Co. is dependent on it. Leave the dull routine of your former Senatorial life, wean yourself from your Committee and throw yourself into the patriotick current and be as you ought to be the champion of the South in the Senate of the U[nited] States and you will have the power to control and make presidents. You can earn more true glory in the Senate, you can be more useful to the country, and wield a more powerful influence over the destinies of your race than in the Presidential chair. In addition to this I am confident that the course I recommend is the only one to lead to the Presidency. That must be won by you if at all, unsought. I have written to you more freely than any one else will, my dear friend, because perhaps I have been more enlisted in what has concerned you and your promotion. I know I write however, what all your true friends feel and while these are my decided convictions and therefore communicated, at the same time they are the opinions of all your friends with whom I have conversed and have been for years. Of such men as Seddon and Mr Old, whom you know I think the wisest, as he is the fairest, man that I have ever known. In order to take the position you are entitled to and ought to occupy you ought to launch out and strike so as to make your position, your .own peculiar property and give us a Hunter platform to stand on, in order to keep down the huckstering traders who have so foully betrayed you at home and abroad. Write to me upon the receipt of this and let us hereafter keep up a more uninterrupted correspondence. I will only add that your friends in Cincinnati did all that could be done and like me look to the Senate for a justification of their confidence.

James Alfred Pearce[1] to R. M. T. Hunter.

Chestertown, [Md.], October 17, 1856.

My Dear Sir: I fear that I shall not be successful in the money affair. There is a shyness about all investments not promising immediate returns and profits. Indeed money is scarce in proof of which I may mention that one of the wealthy men in Balt[imore] is taking deposits on call at 5 percentium One great difficulty is that the mortgage for the proposed loan is not preferred but comes in for paper with so much more. I will make one more trial and if that do not succeed will abandon any further effort.

I cannot give much hope of our political matters. There will be gains for B[uchana]n in some of our counties but the old Whigs generally swallow with a blind faith the resolves of the convention, Donaldson and all. They are besides confident that Filmore will be elected if not by the people at least by the H[ouse of] R[epresentatives] in which they say democrats and republicans will prefer him each to the other. The success of the former ticket in Penn[sylvani]a encourages them, they say that the Fremont men there will fall into Filmore's support being satisfied of their inability to elect a ticket of their own and consequently will nominate none. They say the proposed plan of " Thad " [Thaddeus] Stevens will not prevail but will be scented by the Filmore men and that the Black republicans will surrender at discretion to them, as they have to the K[now] Nothings. I have made several speeches and shall make two more but I do not think that I can accomplish much except to alienate old

<hr />

[1] A Representative in Congress from Maryland, 1835–1839 and 1840–1843 ; in the United States Senate from 1843 to 1862.

friends and make my social as well as political relations anything but pleasant. The Whigs here are talking strongly of Virg[ini]a as likely to go for Filmore.

The Florida election gives them encourage[men]t in the South and the Mayors election in Balt[imore] gives them exulting confidence of success in this State. Shortsighted they seem to me and blind to their own interests. What think you of all these calculations which I have mentioned? We do not know the condition of things at the West. Ohio is of course fanatical in the extreme and Indiana seems doubtful. Can you give us any hopes in that quarter. The most we can hope for with confidence is that the election will go to the H[ouse] R[epresentatives] and what then? There's the rub. It is a fortunate thing that the democrats have carried so many members of Congress in P[ennsylvani]a and the legislature and that some gains have also been made in Ohio. This will enable us to hold the moody heads in check in Congress until perhaps the delusion may abate.

I read with pleasure y[ou]r speech at Poughkeepsie. They called on me to report one of mine made in Worcester C[ount]y, [Md.], but I cannot remember a two hours speech made without notes and tho' I might write *a* speech it w[oul]d not be *the* speech. This state would I believe submit quietly to the repeal of the Kansas act and only growl a little at the essential modification of the fugitive slave law. If I were a young man I should sell my property here and look for a new home among a more southern people. The labouring men of our City sustain the Know Nothings because they wish to banish the competition of foreign labourers, So I am told.

Pray let me hear from you if you are not overwhelmed with correspondence as I suppose you are.

W. Grandin to R. M. T. Hunter.

New York, [N. Y.], *October 18, 1856.*

My Dear Sir: The glorious results of the elections of the 14th Inst in Pennsylvania, Indiana and even Ohio have made the calling and election of B[uchanan] and B[reckinridge] by the people next month "a fixed fact!"

Permit me to offer my hearty congratulations to one who will have contributed in such large measure to such "consummation devoutly to be wished"; not only by a long and brilliant career as a Statesman, but particularly by his masterly and profound exposition of national, democratic truths in this State. I sent you a copy of the *Daily News* (with which I am now connected) commenting upon this effort at Poughkeepsie.

Such has been the inspiriting effect upon the people of New York that truly I should not be surprised to find them following the example of P[ennsylvani]a and Indiana. The *Herald* in its leader gives up the contest!

JOHN PETTIT [1] TO R. M. T. HUNTER.

LAFAYETTE, INDIANA, *November 10, 1856.*

MY DEAR SIR: The smoke of the battle has cleared away and we are victorious. I congratulate you and the country on this glorious result and I sincerely hope that Mr. Buchanan may call you to the head of his Cabinet for I know of no man more worthy or better qualified. I expressed to you similar views before the formation of Mr. Pierce's Cabinet and do not wish to flatter you, but this is my honest desire. If I can serve you, intimate in what way.

We have carried our Legislature and shall elect two senators, Mr. Bright will be one, and I want and ought to be the other and can be if Mr. Bright will co-operate with me. Am I asking too much in asking you to write Mr. B[right] *at once*, urging him to unite his friends with mine for our mutual election? If so, you will pardon me for this intrusion, but believe me your sincere friend.

DANIEL M. BARRINGER [2] TO R. M. T. HUNTER.

CHARLOTTE, MECKLENBURG CO., N. C.,
November 11th, 1856.

MY DEAR SIR: I congratulate you and all true national men on the glorious result of the Presidential Election and especially on the decisive vote of the great mother of States and Statesmen. The "Old North" has also performed her duty nobly in this crisis, greatly increasing the majority of August last. Old *Mecklenburg* where I live has again vindicated principles as important to us, as those of the Revolution.

I read with the greatest pleasure your brilliant speech during the Campaign, at Poughkeepsie and had parts of it circulated in our papers, with good effect.

But, my dear Sir, the great struggle for us in the South is not yet finally ended. We must stand to our arms, Favoritism and bigotry, are even now again raising their heads. We must be always ready.

GEORGE BOOKER TO R. M. T. HUNTER.

NEAR HAMPTON, [VA.], *16th November, 1856.*

MY DEAR HUNTER: I have been thinking about this Southern Convention which is to meet at Savannah on the 8th [of] next month

---

[1] A Representative in Congress from Indiana, 1843–1849; a Senator, 1853–1855. He was not successful in his efforts for a reelection in 1856.

[2] A Representative in Congress from North Carolina, 1843–1849; minister to Spain, 1849–1853.

and it occurs to me and I suggest to you the importance of your going there, which may influence the action of the next administration of great importance to the south.

If we can succeed in Kansas, keep down the Tariff, shake off our Commercial dependence upon the North and add a little more slave territory, we may yet live free men under the Stars and Strips. Mr. Buchanan, if not committed to the "balance idea" is to the acquisition of more southern territory.

The next few years must be eventful ones in our history, may, probably will, decide the fate of the Union, at all events the destines of our section. Mr. Buchanan and the Northern Democracy are dependent upon the South, an extraordinary course of things here placed them and us in this attitude towards each other. Shall we use our power? or suffer things of such magnitudes to be controlled by our enemies, by accident, or any other causes? I repeat I want you to go to Savannah. Please tell me what you know of Dudley Mann and his line of steamers from the Chesapeake bay to Millford, is he a practical man and is his enterprise likely to be successful?

Who is to be in the Cabinet from V[irgini]a? Kindest regards to Garnett. Tell him I want him to examine and consider our Naturalization laws, as soon as he can. It does seem to me *time* to check this flood of emigration, the chief element of Northern power and ascendency. Tell him I would not only have him use K[now] N[othing] thunder but the thunder bolts of Heaven to crush the enemies of the South.

Ask him to tell me hereafter at his leisure why it was he ran ahead of Mr. Buchanan in every county at every precinct. Was it his eloquence? Was it Mr. Saunder's position? Was it Buchanan's position? Fillmore's position? What cause? What combination produced that striking result?

Tell him his district is proud of him and wishes him to grow in influence, in importance, in power fast as possible, but when he begins to grow "*National*" we shall begin to grow cold.

GEORGE W. MUNFORD TO R. M. T. HUNTER.

(*Confidential.*)

RICHMOND, [VA.], *November 22d, 1856.*

DEAR SIR: Feeling anxious that Virginia should be properly represented in Mr. Buchanan's Cabinet and believing that her interests and those of the South would be guarded with filial affection by you, it would afford me great pleasure to see you in a position where your advice would command the attention and respect to which it would be entitled and your talents be appropriated usefully to the Country. I know they are so already, but of course I mean in a different position from the one you now occupy. I think I am in a situation from which I may be of service to you and therefore do not hesitate to ask you in confidence and to be used in the same way, whether you would accept a seat in the Cabinet and would be satisfied with the post of Secretary of the Treasury.

Amid the general rejoicing for the great Victory achieved by the Democratic party and which we had hoped would have given us repose for at least four years longer, I cannot but regret that Mr. Buchanan should have done any thing to render less buoyant the feelings of his true friends. His letter on the Pacific Railroad in my opinion runs counter to all the cherished opinions and principles of Virginia on internal improvements and opens a wide door to a system of wild expenditure and extravagance that knows no bounds.

Please let me hear from you as speedily as convenient.

LEWIS E. HARVIE TO R. M. T. HUNTER.

(Confidential.)

[AMELIA Co., VA.], *November 23, 1856.*

DEAR HUNTER: I was in Richmond yesterday and saw Pryor who has heard from Washington that there is some effort being made there to get him selected as one of the two coeditors of the organ of the new administration at Washington. His circumstances and possibly his ambition would prompt him to desire this place earnestly tho' he says he is making no effort to get it. Dr. Garnett has written to him that he should urge Wise to apply to Buchanan for it on behalf of Pryor. On the other hand Beverly Tucker is struggling for it and says that Wise is committed to him. Thus much for that. I also found that Pryor thought that Wise would urge the offer of Secretary of State to be made to you and thought if so you ought to accept it. Reed [?] had heard Beverly Tucker say that Wise would turn you out of the Senate when the election came on. Now Pryor is a true man and true to you and moreover is under some obligations to some of your friends that he feels and wont disregard, but if he were to be the Editor of such a paper, you being of the Cabinet, would be what of all things he would desire and I am writing to you to warn and guard you in case such an offer be again and any advice he may offer by letter or otherwise. If it be made it will of course be for one of two reasons either because they know you will not accept it and thus get for Wise and his President the credit of having made the offer, or to create a vacancy in the Senate for Wise.

Now it is so clear to me that you ought not to go into the Cabinet and that you ought to remain in the Senate that I can scarcely think there is any occasion for writing. This Administration can't stand, at the end of four years; at all events there must be another and a

fiercer struggle than has just taken place and you ought to be in
the Senate preparing yourself and the country for it, sustaining the
administration in all measures calculated to secure our rights, leading the Southern men and forming and wielding them in a solid and
compact mass. You can and will have more power in the Senate
than if President. It is expected, it is conceded that you must take
the lead and it is not in the power of any party or partizans to arrest
your career. So confident do I feel of this, so clear does it seem to me
that I should think you mad if not criminal if you were to doubt or
hesitate. I write strongly because I feel so. There is no necessity
for the sacrifice there is no propriety in it. Your acceptance of this
offer if made would be laid to the account of timidity or mere love
of place and in either case your power and usefulness would be lost.
Don't then entertain any such idea for a moment. If the offer that
I just spoke of be made to Pryor, his poverty will make him accept it
and the power that he is exerting thro' the Enquirer will be lost to
him and that will be a great loss to us, but nevertheless you are invincible in the State and those who assail you will find it to be so.
I think he will write to you and it is as well that you have some
knowledge of his views beforehand. Of course all of this letter in
regard to him is strictly confidential.

Present my warmest congratulations to Garnett and say to him
that I am not only rejoiced at his success but proud of it. I don't
doubt but that his Excellency [Wise] will write to him to the same
effect and possibly that *he* secured his nomination and election. I
wish you would sometimes write to me without my forcing you to
do so in answer to my letters and tell me what is in the wind. I
should like to see you before you go to Washington but if not I will
see you then.

JOSEPH LEA, OF HECKER, LEA & Co. TO R. M. T. HUNTER.

PHILADELPHIA, [PA.], *February 23d, 1857.*

ESTEEMED FRIEND: Permit me to remind you, that four years
since, at your request, the Senate amended one of the Bills, by
which the small amount of duties collected on Flax Machinery,
within a specified time, was to be refunded, and such machinery
subsequently admitted free for three years. Kentucky, Virginia,
Penns[ylvani]a, and Ohio, raise more flax than all the other States
together, and we cordially concur in the Free admission of machinery, wh[ic]h will thus assist those States in the more rapid development of their agricultural resources, and add immensely to the
national wealth. We have associated with some of the most intelligent merchants of other cities in the first attempts at manufacturing Linens. At great expense have sent Agents and Circulars, thro'

the South and West; employed the public journals and spared no pains to direct attention to the best methods now adopted in Europe for the culture of flax. These efforts have not been fruitless, and we believe that Kentucky and Virginia will in a few years largely export flax, of wh[ic]h they are already the chief producers.

The manufacture of Linen goods has encountered at the outset great obstacles; our planters being unable to furnish the staple of proper quality, must gradually acquire the knowledge of preparing it, while the blockade of the Baltic during the late European war, greatly enhanc[e]d the price of foreign supplies, and entailed upon this infant interest, struggling for existence, serious and disheartening trials.

The Tariff which has just passed the House, and ere this may have been placed in y[ou]r hands, admits flax machinery free, hereafter, but we hope it will strike your honorable mind, that simple justice should at least be extend[e]d to those who have pioneered this branch of industry, by a refund of the trifling duties collected on flax machinery since Jan[uar]y 1st, 1850, to those now using the same; thus placing us on equal terms with our subsequent competitors.

I beg leave to assure you, that the refund of those duties, would in the present exigencies of the trade, do more to sustain and encourage the demand for American flax, than the remission of all future duties on flax machinery, while the suspension of this enterprise, and change of those mills to Cotton, must put back the developement of flax cultivation for several years, and long preclude our planters from realizing very profitable returns from their hitherto worthless fibre. The propriety of placing the first spinners of flax on as good terms as the last, we trust will obtain for them and this growing interest, your renewed favor, and if it be improper to give a Retrospective feature to the present Tariff Bill, may we ask you to make such amendment to one of the Appropriation Bills, as will authorize the Sec[retar]y of Treasury to refund to parties now in use thereof, the duties collected on Flax Machinery since Jan[uar]y 1st, 1850, the amount of which might be limited to the sum of $100,000 dollars?

We beg y[ou]r further consideration of the very great importance of having the new act, go into effect on April 1st next, so as to obviate an immense warehousing of goods imported for the fall trade. The postponement of the Act until July 1st, will make the market bare of many articles, now proposed for the Free List, and enhance prices to the detriment of the consumer, whilst its early enforcement will secure more regularity in the business, of the Customs, and occasion the least disturbance to commerce.

The policy of Sec[retar]y Guthrie, of approaching Free Trade by removing the imposts on all raw materials, meets the approval of all intelligent minds, and if now adopted must give the new administration a positive assurance of prosperity and success. To you, in the distinguished and most important position in which we now address you, more than to any other member of the Senate, is the public attention directed, relying on y[ou]r wisdom and experience to dissipate those clouds wh[ic]h now darken the financial affairs of our country.

Lewis E. Harvie to R. M. T. Hunter.

Dykeland, Amelia Co., [Va.], *March 11, 1857.*

Dear Hunter: Supposing that you will be at Washington during this week I address to you there. Pryor is very busy getting his paper under way and I confidently believe will get a large circulation very speedily. It is important that he start right and honestly. You should write to him or to me as to his course and particularly as to the Land question, about which his mind is considerably " exercised." It is Banquo's ghost to him and especially since the vote of some of our friends on distributing or depositing the surplus in the treasury. He desires conference with you on that subject and it seems to me important that his views and committals should be well digested before he breaks ground. I write to bring this about. Tell me what we are to expect from this administration. If coming events cast their shadows before I augur the worst. I am however for waiting for overt acts and against any such judgments founded upon conjecture or distrust, because of injudicious or distasteful appointments. I was almost led into opposition to Pierce by that and I am getting to be wary and cautious as my head is growing gray. Buchanan had no especial reason to confide in us that I know of and therefore we have no ground to complain that he didn't. At all events we can't make other people think so and there is no use in opposing him in anticipation, when in all human probabillity we shall be fully justified in it by his future conduct. He has been leading a loose life too long to become chaste all of a sudden. Tell me about the Cabinet and other appointments. I don't hear of or dread any opposition to you hereabouts. I got my Delegate to commit himself publicly and take some credit to my tact for it. You ought to write to Mallory. I did and found him true but not advised and I think sore over it.

Francis Mallory to R. M. T. Hunter.

Norfolk, [Va.], *April 21, 1857.*

Dear Hunter: I have just received your letter of the 15th and expecting to leave town in the morning I thought I would drop you a line before doing so to keep you advised of the state of things down here. And perhaps advices from this quarter may not be altogether without value being, *as it is*, one of the strongest outposts of your enemies. Their strength induces less of caution than may be observed elsewhere, and I know as well the condition of things at head quarters as if I were in communication by electro magnetism. Not that names are mentioned but from the tone of remarks indulged in by the initiated. *You may prepare for War next winter.* It will I fear be fastened on you and a few silly speeches of honest, but imprudent friends, will be the pretext, not the excuse but the justification. I cannot repeat all that I hear because of my peculiar relation to the two parties nor would I make mischief or widen the breach between those who stand towards me in the attitude of personal friendship. I am a well wisher of both and would hate myself could I be guilty of injustice to either. No selfish purpose have I to promote for declining health and energy forbid all aspirations. I aided somewhat in putting you in the way of going to the Senate and I am unwilling to see you "crushed out" without cause and guiltless of offence. Booker, who is really your friend, paid a visit to Richmond and when he returned I was on a visit to my farm. He rode over to see me and as I learned after he went away, for the purpose of consulting with me in order to try (if possible) if we could not bring about a reconciliation and better understanding between you and W[ise]. But several gentlemen were present and he left without the opportunity. This occurrence caused me to fear that hostilities which I had hoped were at an end, were about to be placed on a serious and enduring footing. Since then the weather together with my railroad engagements have prevented me from visiting the County.

Booker I suspect heard in person remarks which have been used in my presence here by W[ise]'s particular friends. Some of them speak freely before me and some half confidentially which embarrasses me much because while I am at liberty to speak or write of the first the last I would not communicate; and yet I may blend and mix them up together so as to be suspected of treachery where I am acting or mean to act in good faith. I have sought no mans confidence but sometimes it is thrust upon me, as if it were meant to commit me in a direction the very opposite of that I desire. To W[ise]'s more confidential friends my preferences are known, and his most intimate one in this town remarked to me the other night that I was the only man in Norfolk who could go to the Legislature by his consent who would not be required to pledge himself to go for W[ise] for the Senate if his name was brought forward. "His obligations to *me* personally would induce him to let me of all men in the city be a candidate of the Democracy without committing myself." They talk, freely in this way: "If H[unter]'s friends keep up their war on W[ise] we must carry it into Africa." "W[ise] is not to be driven off by threat." W[ise] says he dont want the place but, "by God, he will not yield an inch now." They (Hunters friends) will not let him (W[ise]) alone but force the issue on W[ise] and he and his party are ready to meet it. In other words they are determined not to be satisfied and will act over if they can the fable of the Lamb and the muddy water below the drinking place of the monarch of the forest. I write you about the imprudent speeches of your friends in Richmond I might have added Washington too. There is a constant fire kept up on Wise by certain parties in both places who chase him to madness and I do not blame him as much as I do them. I do not allude to Floyd for of his movements I know nothing. But maybe those whose peculiar relations to both parties should make them ministers of peace and not stirers up of stife and jealousy. A remark of Bocock in [the] presence of an M. D. in Washington reached Wise's ears and was repeated here in my hearing. This is a delicate subject to write about for I know not your feelings or relationship to the party and what I say is strictly *confidential* for I do not desire to be connected with that affair. I do not want to make mischief but to put you on your guard and thus checkmate those who would. How to remedy this state of things I cannot see. Peace could be restored if there was a *desire for peace* really entertained. When one is bent on insulting another it may be postponed but will come sooner or later.

How far an organized effort has been made to secure the Legislature I am totally in the dark but when men of a certain stamp could be secured without noise it has been done. Your opponents however feel secure and speak as if your destiny was in their keeping. Their forbearance alone, they think, can save you from annihilation, and if you go into the contest, you rush on certain defeat. They "cant sacrifice W[ise] for you." I know not what advice to give for I am not master of the ground but if I can in any manner be instrumental in bringing about a good understanding between you I should be most happy to do so. I hope the bitter cup of choosing between you and him will never be presented to my lips. I held no familiar or intimate correspondence with him. He understands me well and I do not know that he takes it unkindly. He has never sought to advance me, holding my abilities in low esteem but he is not I think unfriendly. I am not in his way and would not if I could harm him. If your positions were reversed I would vote against *you* to keep *him* in the Senate. I will see Booker and will write to you on my return. If not too late we may, if any *party* can, reconcile the difficulty. For the present you can only remain perfectly silent but if hostilities continue you and your friends have to enter on an active campaign. Mix about among the people in different portions

of the state, accept all invitations to make public addresses. You
have hitherto kept too much aloof from the masses relying on the
leaders. The people dont know you. Your love for retirement has
caused you to neglect those small attentions which tell among them.
Travel to the springs, come down to Old Point and make yourself
busy for you have work before you if these complaints of the other
party break out into open war. There is something going on here
about office. Loyall and Sawyer are in imminent danger. *You have
done enough for them.* Let things take their course. They would
not risk any thing for you, one because it is his nature, the other
because he is afraid. Their removal will do you no harm and you
could not prevent it. There are influences working against them at
Washington which you cannot counteract. I should not be surprised
if the next mail brought Simkins app[ointmen]t as Navy Agent.
W[ise] is in Washington and the first roll of Floyd's thunder has
been heard. I mean to take no action on the subject and you as I
said have acted your part. Strange to say the K[now] N[othings],
if opportunity comes, will sustain W[ise] against you on the principle that the Dog licks the hand that flays him. Dr. Robinson an
old tool of Floyds and a dirty one at that will be supported here
for the Senate by Wise men, tho' master and men have scorned him
as the vilest scoundrel in the land. He will vote for W[ise] against
H[unter]. Robinson after being refused admittance time after time
into the K[now] N[othing] Camp as too mean for their association
crept in thro' a North Carolina lodge, was ruled off in all his attempts
to obtain position, voted for Flournoy &c, apostalized and is now to
be a candidate of the Democracy of Norfolk and *gentlemen* have publickly vowed to vote for him in the issue between Wise and Hunter.
But let him alone. I dont think he can be elected and if he could his
vote will go with his interest and no where else. His opponent Mc-
Kenny is at least doubtful tho' I think I could control him. Segar
will go from Elizabeth City County. But on him no sort of reliance
can be placed. He speaks against you. I hear nothing from Muscoe
or of him. I think his election very safe. He will get the vote of
the W[ise] party but not their hearty support. They never speak
of him and seem indifferent about his success. I have written you
Hunter a long rigma role letter which when read burn. It is for no
eye but for your *own.* I have written freely and perhaps my letter
may prove an unwelcome messenger. It is kindly meant however and
I thought it due to our former relations. My own career has been
unfortunate as a politician. I never had the education or industry
to entitle me to a high position and I never aspired to one. As Wise
remarked of me " I have had quite as much as I could expect." But
if in quitting the field for ever I can be the means of contributing

but a mite towards rescuing an old friend from a conspiracy I shall at least have accomplished one good act.

[P. S.] Pardon this long letter. I will not soon repeat the dose. Of McClean I know nothing. Sawyer wont give him a place. He dare not. His paper could not succeed unless he bought one of the Demo[cratic] papers now established. Then it might. Both are for sale.

HOWELL COBB TO R. M. T. HUNTER.

(*Private*.)

WASHINGTON, [D. C.], *12th May, 1857*.

MY DEAR SIR: I reached here on yesterday and to day found your letter, which had been in the office for several days. I should have regretted very much to have seen any evidence of your approval of the conduct of Mr Merrick, conduct which in my judgment renders him unworthy both of private and public confidence. Neither Mr Clayton or myself believe that he acted under your sanction or Mr. C[layton] would never have addressed to you his first letter. It was under the full conviction that his conduct would secure your unqualified condemnation, that Mr Clayton called your attention to the subject.

I need not say for myself that I never for a moment entertained the idea that you either knew or would approve of the conduct of Merrick. It was not only inconsistent with our past personal relations but also with your own deservedly high character. I did not intend to make any suggestion to yourself on the committee in reference to the matter, as I felt assured that he would be properly dealt with, when the facts were brought to the knowledge of those who had the power to act, and I only regret that he has been permitted to resign and thereby saved himself from a dismissal, which would have properly characterized his conduct. I say to you frankly that I do not think that you had the power to remove him without the consent of the committee and do not therefore complain of your declining to exercise that power.

Your allusion to the merits of Mr. Thompson's claim, requires that I should say a word on that subject. I have never passed upon the merits of that claim. That duty was not devolved upon me. I have only decided in accordance with the opinion of Attorney General Black, that *the law* required me to pay it. If the authority was vested in me of reviewing the merits of claims allowed by Congress and by them *diverted to be paid*, I would save many a dollar to the Treasury, that I am not required to pay out. I do not however wish to justify my conduct by the opinion of the Att[orne]y Gen[era]l, for I say to you frankly, that I fully concurred in that opinion, and acted therefore not only upon his but *my own* judgement. I am quite sure that in my position you would have done the same thing, and I request as an act of justice to me, that you will read the opinion of Mr Black, which to any intelligent mind is conclusive and unanswerable not *upon the merits of the claim* but upon the duty of the Secretary of the Treasury, to pay it in conformity to the requirements of the law.

With yourself I regret the matter, not however on account of the public discussion which it has elicited, but that it should have embarrassed personal relationships. I do not however think that you will have cause hereafter to regret, that a timely exposure has shown the unworthiness of a man, who had enjoyed your regard and confidence.

WILLIAM O. GOODE TO R. M. T. HUNTER.

BOYDTON, VA., *July 21, 1857.*

DEAR HUNTER: I send herewith a letter to our friend Montague, which I must ask you to direct properly and commit to the mail. I do not know his p[ost] office. I very sincerely congratulate you on your speech at Lexington. I have read it with pleasure and admiration. I had occasion to pay a very hasty visit to the Rockbridge Alum (to take a daughter there and leave her) a few days after you left, and from all quarters your effort was greatly extolled. I hope I shall have it in pamphlet form.

What is to be the end of the Walker movement in Kansas? Will it not be made the *issue* next winter in the General Assembly of Virginia? or rather is it not *designed* to make it affect the election of Senators? I should like to know *your position* and views on the subject. In the present aspect of affairs, *what should we do?*

THOMAS S. BOCOCK TO R. M. T. HUNTER.

(*Private.*)

MARTINSBURG, VA., *July 23, 1857.*

MY DEAR SIR: Though I have ceased to take interest in politics, and hang on loosely to them for a while longer, somewhat as a matter of habit, and somewhat as a matter of necessity, I have promised a friend that I would communicate a few facts to you, and now proceed to redeem my promise.

While spending a few hours in Washington, a day or two ago, and since I have been here, I have ascertained that a good deal of maneuvering is going on in relation to the Senatorial election in Virginia. From what I have heard, I am satisfied that Gov[ernor] Wise is *very* anxious to be elected to the Senate. His hopes in that direction were a good deal chilled by the result of the Virginia elections last Spring, but within a few weeks past, they have been very much revived. He thinks that if he could place you, in a position of known antagonism to the administration, and stand forward himself as the administration candidate he would easily beat you. Therefore his friends are representing you as fully endorsing all that our good friends of "The South" have said about Walker and Kansas, and are endeavouring to produce the belief that hostility to Walker and his Kansas policy springs out of and indicates a spirit of settled hostility to the administration.

As I came through Washington the city was rife with rumours of your open and avowed hostility to Buchanan and his Cabinet.

Our friend Co[lone]l Orr of So[uth] Carolina who is a warm administration man told me that he heard with great concern that you had made a speech in which you attacked them fiercely. Since I came here, a friend of ours (Mr. John B. Hoge) has told me that the scheme has been worked with effect in *this* region, and is fraught with danger in the West at least.

I am clearly and openly hostile to Walker and his Kansas policy, but I do not think that either principle or policy requires it to be carried to the extent of opposition to the administration. They are acting badly towards us it is true, but they ought not to be permitted to drive us into opposition, except upon some ground which would be patent to the public. This is my view of the matter but it is probably badly taken. You can judge best of the course proper for you to take. I intended merely to give you facts.

The result of the elections in our region of the State was in this point of view, very favorable. So Edmundson writes me it was in his. I am nearly at the end of my race politically. I want however to see the true men in our State, prospered and advanced, and the intriguers thwarted and I will sing the "nunc dimittes" with full glad heart.

(P. S.) That "mendacious vagabond" who writes to the Herald from Richmond persists in declaring that the Parsons [?] Bill was gotten up by your friends to injure Buchanan's prospects in Virginia for the Presidential nomination.

A. D. BANKS TO R. M. T. HUNTER.

PETERSBURG, [VA.,] *July 24th, 1857.*

MY DEAR SIR: I had a letter from Letcher this morning. He, as other of your friends, sees the insidious attempts of the *Enquirer* and *Examiner* to strike at you over the shoulders of the *South*.

Nothing would gratify Wise more than to make up an issue with you on the Kansas imbroglio. Already some of his friends are striving to produce the idea that Pryor has been writing at your dictation and speaks your sentiments. This is roundly asserted in administration circles at Washington our friends can not be too careful. Pryor has gone too far and has already done mischief. The sooner he is checked the better. The policy of your friends is the strict line of defence, this renders your position impregnable. We are weakening the moment we set on the other task. The obvious course is to avoid all issues tendered by the opposition. Nothing will serve to foil them half as effectually. Wise is half dead for a hobby. I might say he would give his kingdom (not on this earth but in heaven (?) "for a horse." There is no special obligation that I am aware of on our part to furnish him one.

I saw Iverson of G[eorgi]a last evening. He gives a bad account of matters there. Several of the democratic candidates for Congress are in great danger. I met Kidwell[1] a day of two since. He gives cheering accounts from the North West. He says all the delegates are for you.

JOHN STRODE BARBOUR, JR. TO R. M. T. HUNTER.

ALEXANDRIA, [VA.], July 24th, 1857.

MY DEAR SIR: From all that I can learn the opposition in this State to your reelection next Winter are actively though secretly at work in getting up an organization against you in various parts of Virginia. I am told that Hughes of the Richmond Examiner is exceedingly busy writing letters in all directions to members elect of the Legislature. Floyd from his point of attack at Washington leaves nothing undone when an opportunity is presented, and Wise is using the power of his position to accomplish the same object. My brother James, who is well posted in these matters, has within a few days past expressed to me the opinion that he was satisfied there was a *formidable* opposition getting up against you in this way.

I have concluded from my own responsibility to drop you a hurried line upon the subject, to warn you of the danger in the distance, and to suggest that you give your friends throughout the State timely notice of these operations, and urge them to establish and perfect their own organization without delay.

So far as the Legislature stood in the beginning our Party certainly was largely in the ascendancy, but there is no telling what action an unscrupulous and unresisted organization may effect. If

---

[1] Prominent in local politics in northwestern Virginia.

we should be beaten next winter, the Southern Rights Party in Virg[ini]a will be hopelessly prostrate, never to rise again in our time. I shall continue to endeavor to keep a sharp look out upon the movements before referred to, and hope in my humble way to plant a thorn occasionally in their path, but would advise you, who have so much at stake, to telegraph your friends in different sections of the State and put them on their guard against the operations of the other side.

C. W. C. DUNNINGTON TO R. M. T. HUNTER.

WASHINGTON, D. C., *July 25, 1857.*

DEAR SIR: Having a few moments leisure, I have concluded to address you on the subject of the Senatorial election next winter. Not having the least doubt of your re-election, it has created surprise in my mind to hear some of the friends of Gov. Wise express themselves in the most sanguine terms as to the probability of his succeeding you. Gov. Wise and Mr. Faulkner seem to be on very friendly terms just now. It is said Mr. F[aulkner] is to help Wise to the Senate, while Gov. W[ise] is to use all his influence to secure Mr. F[aulkner]'s nomination for governor, and at the expiration of Mr. F[aulkner]'s gubernatorial term he expects to succeed your colleague in the Senate. It is well to be on your guard against the movements of these aspiring gentlemen.

Walker's course in Kansas has caused the administration much trouble. The cabinet, I have reason to believe are divided on the subject, and that the position of Georgia has rather weakened Mr. Cobb's influence.

Forney is causing much uneasiness. It is whispered that Cobb is concerned in the movement, and that the new paper will support him for the nomination next time. I know that the conductors of the " Union," are very jealous of the movement, and are of the above opinion.

The feud in Indiana between the friends of Gov. Bright and Gov. Wright has not been quieted by the appointment of Gov. W[right][1] and will brake out again at no early day.

There is no friendly feeling existing between Messrs. Bright and Douglas. Mr. D[ouglas] blames Gov. B[right] for the way in which the Indiana delegation voted at Cincinnati.

There is some talk of De Witt purchasing the interest of R. M. Smith in the Virginia Sentinel. I expect Gov. Smith will not favor the plan. Some of Gov. S[mith]'s constituents are blaming him for recommending a fellow named Wileman Thomas, from his district,

---

[1] Joseph Albert Wright, governor of Indiana, 1849–1857 ; a Representative in Congress, 1843–1845 ; Senator, 1862–1863 ; Minister to Prussia, 1857–1861, also 1865–1867.

for a high position here. Thomas is a notorious scoundrel, bankrupt in politics, morals, and purse. He was a know nothing, attended the Winchester convention, but was denied admittance, because he was self appointed. He procured the recommendation of several respectable gentlemen, and then obtained the endorsement of Gov. Wise to the genuineness of their democracy. I mention this matter for fear he may annoy you with his importunities. I should not be surprised if he received an appointment, as he voted for Mr. Buchanan, which absolves a man from all sins against the democratic party.

The Intelligencer of this morning contains a very handsome notice of your Lexington address, part of which it published. I would send you the paper, but suppose you take it.

JOHN S. BARBOUR, JR. TO R. M. T. HUNTER.

ALEXANDRIA, VA., August 1st, 1857.

MY DEAR SIR: When I wrote you some ten days ago I entertained much uneasiness from the efforts which I learned were making against you in Virginia, and which I feared, from the vaunting tone of certain parties, might be more formidable than I had conceived, or that you might be aware of. I was acting upon the wisdom of the maxim, ''forewarned, forearmed.'' With the exercise of ordinary prudence on the part of your peculiar friends I do not now think that you have anything really to fear. My brother Alfred has within a few days paid us a visit, and he assures me that his region is entirely sound. Haymond, Mortimer, Johnson, and the body of the North West (of the legislature elect) decidedly favour your reelection, and perhaps would not support Mr. Wise, if you were out of the way. I saw Dr. Graham (of Rockbridge Co.) a few days since and was informed by him that no opposition would be offered against your reelection, this of course depends upon the strength of the enemies. My brother James announced publicly his intention to support you, but neither he or Alfred deem it good policy to be too forward at present in this behalf. While you may rest assured that they will support you in good faith at the proper time, they conceive that more influence may be exerted by remaining quiet (unless called out) in the earlier stages of the matter. These views are communicated to me of course without any special expectation that I was in correspondence with you upon the subject.

I write in some haste, but if you will permit the liberty taken, I would suggest that you hold yourself free at present from any committals about this Kansas controversy. Every one knows where you will be found at the proper time, and you have nothing to gain by agitation now in advance of the action of Congress. Your enemies may endeavour to make capital of a different course on your part, and you have nothing to gain by the proceeding. Your policy I should think would be to remain quiet and let Pryor fight the battle through the South until next Winter.

In reply to your inquiry about De Witt I learn that he has abandoned all intention of taking the paper at this place. He is without means, and is very much under controul of the other side in Virginia.

JOHN LETCHER TO R. M. T. HUNTER.

LEXINGTON, VA., *August 1st, 1857.*

MY DEAR SIR: I received your letter of the 27th ult° this morning. I have been spending the past week at the Alum Springs, where there is a large Company, and where of course, I have met with a large number of persons from different counties of the State. I have conversed with many on the subject of the Senatorial Election, and I have met with but one man, who expressed opposition to your election, and declared himself for Wise, and that was Chapman of Orange Co[unty]. Kindred of Southampton told me that you would lose no votes in his section of the State, and from all he had seen and heard, he was entirely satisfied that you would be elected. I have no doubt of it myself, and do not believe, they can organize an opposition, that can defeat you. The vast majority of the people are just, and they will sustain you, against all combinations, that can be gotten up. I do not feel the slightest apprehension of the result.

The controversy between the South and Enquirer, at this particular time, and the temper with which it is conducted, is unfortunate. The tactics of the last named paper, are palpable. The object being to make the impression that all who were not for Buchanan as a first choice, are now inclined to embarrass his administration. I do not think however, that they can succeed in this, so transparent a trick.

I shall be on the alert, to see what is going on and to thwart the schemers.

WILLIAM O. GOODE TO R. M. T. HUNTER.

BOYDTON, VA., *August 4th, 1857.*

DEAR HUNTER: In reply to your favor of 30 July I have to say, that, at the time of the election, all the members elect from this Congressional District to the General Assembly were reported to be favourable to your reelection. I heard the members for Mecklenburg and Prince Edward severally pledge themselves in public speeches to vote for you against *any* other candidate. I made inquiries every where as to all the counties and was assured as to all.

In Charlotte, Wyatt Cardwell is returned, and he is an old line Whig—Know Nothing—and Distributuonist. I do now know his preference between you and any candidate who may be run against you. I suppose he would be controlled by party associations, Which I suppose cannot be expected to carry any one against you in favor of your probable competitor. As for me, I had not a doubt about my election. I told Meade before the Convention that I should receive more votes in the District than both of my competitors together if all three should run.

C. W. C. DUNNINGTON TO R. M. T. HUNTER.

WASHINGTON, D. C., *August 7, 1857.*

DEAR SIR: I received your favor and have made inquiry as to the position of members of the Legislature elected from Gov. Smith's district on the Senatorial question. I am assured they will vote for you. I had a short conversation with R. M. Smith, of the Sentinel yesterday. He is of the opinion that your reelection is certain.

Seymour Lynn, the newly elected delegate from Prince William, is very unfavorably disposed towards Gov. Wise. I do not know how DeWitt stands upon the question. From what I can learn, his negotiations for the purchase of the Sentinel have failed for want of funds.

Forney's new paper is out, and professes to be strongly in favor of Mr. Buchanan. Some say it is in the confidence of Cobb. The Editor of the Union is very " suspicious " both of Cobb and of the " *Press.*" The Treasury Department seems to be very much engaged upon the business of removing light-house keepers with salaries ranging from $250 to $500 per year.

The work on the Capital extension is progressing with great rapidity; but although the new chambers may be completed, it will not be prudent to occupy them next winter, on account of the dampness of the walls.

Hon. A. C. Dodge will return very soon to the United States, and will be the next democratic candidate for governor of Iowa. If he succeeds it will make him a prominent candidate for the Vice-Presidency, which, with the growing ill feeling between the friends of Messrs. Bright and Douglas may result in the selection of a Virginian. There is no possible chance for governor Wise before a *National* Convention. His denunciations of democratic *principles* and *men* in former days will not be forgotten, by the people, if they should be by politicians. They would not have been overlooked in Virginia, but for the extraordinary reasons then existing.

Gen. Rusk, had he lived, might have been a formidable candidate for the nomination; as he was deservedly popular. There is now no man in the East, North, West or South who can command the vote in the next convention that you will be able to obtain; and I think our Western friends will defeat themselves.

WILLIAM OLD, JR. TO R. M. T. HUNTER.

[PETERSBURG, VA.?], *August 15th, 1857.*

DEAR SIR: Doctor Harvie sent me two letters from you to Mr. L. E. Harvie, who is absent on a trip to the north, as he will be away from home for some weeks, and I do not know certainly at what point a letter would reach him, I will keep them until his return. As he is in the habit of giving me your letters to read, I have read these supposing that they referred to your reelection, a matter in which you are aware I feel a deep and friendly interest. I believe now, you will encounter a violent but not a formidable opposition as far as success is concerned. The alliance between Wise and Floyd is at present a close one, but as neither wishes to advance the other, and can assail you only, through your friends, I do not think they can seriously effect your election. They certainly cannot, if Wise is your opponent, he can get a certain but small vote. The danger is, in my opinion, that they may unite on Judge Daniel of Lynchburg, he is strong in the section of the state where you would get with his aid an almost unanimous vote, and he can array against us all of the old democrats, who have not abandoned their hate of the States rights portion of the party. The Enquirer has used its influence; and it is still strong, to impress the democracy, with the idea that your peculiar friends are resolved to assail Buchanan. I do not believe it has as yet, excited any feeling against you. I wrote Pryor, as soon as this Kansas controversy, assumed a decided character, urging him, to confine his attacks to Walker and his action, and as far as he could to separate Buchanan from the controversy. But Wise, who is editing the Enquirer (perhaps indirectly) has continued to produce an impression with many, that the "South" was established for the purpose of making opposition to Buchanan. Wise has as yet, suffered personally, in the contest, but I think he has managed to hurt you, and advance Floyd. In this last is our danger. I am on good terms with James Booker, but I know he is a warm friend to Floyd, and he will be very influential in the House of Delegates. I hear from various sources that he is in favor of your election. If he is so, not only as against Wise but as against any other, you will be in little danger. Your opponents, will have no really good leader in the House, and the Senate will be safe, unless the House overrules it.

The Northwest I hear from authority I consider good, is for you against Wise, it will be thoroughly for you against Wise and Floyd. If Mr Letcher can make Daniel stand firm and work and Layne the Senator from Roanoke, is true, we have little to fear from the Vally or the Southwest. Neither of these men can be relied on, but they have influence, and can be controlled by men in their congressional districts. I am so ignorant of the character of the delegation from Garnett's district, that I cannot form any opinion of the amount of Wise's strength in it. I look on Claybrook as most dangerous to you. Disaffection in this district and in the Lynchburg district, form our chief source of dread in Piedmont and Tide[water]. I will write to Barbour, and ask him frankly, what his position will be, he will tell me, I am sure; and if he is really for you against all competitors, he will fight the contest out and more adroitly and efficiently, than any man I know. There are men still in the Legislature over whom he used to exercise much almost entire control, and they are the class of men you have to dread. In reading your letter I see you suggest a plan of contest with these men which I hope may be used most advantageously. With it, we can certainly destroy Wise. Pryor can rally the old democrats, easily enough, for his services against the Know Nothings, and his difficulties as Editor of the Enquirer have given him a hold on the rank and file of the party, which he will not have, except by open opposition to the democratic administration. I think it would be well for the present, for him to show that his assailants are resolved to unite Virginia to the Northern States and sever her connection with the South. It can easily be done by extracts from the Examiner and Enquirer. Their assaults upon "secessionists," "Ultras," "Extremists," "opponents of the Manouvres of 1850" &c and their effort to show that we must be dependent upon the Northern democracy, can be so used as to show their intention to prefer allying the democracy to the party North, to granting anything to the Cotton States. If he would use this well, with the conviction now prevailing that Wise edits the Enquirer, and will keep back until just before the legislature meets, the proof he can bring to show that this is the scheme of Wise, we can utterly destroy him. Those who remember his conduct previous to the nomination of Pierce, know how easy it is to fasten this charge upon him.

But it is not desirable I think to kill off Wise early. When he is found too weak, and from what his weakness proceeds, they will take up another candidate, who is not so obnoxious. He is at present I hear sanguine, confident of your defeat, while he is so, they can not prevent his being your competitor. He has been all along disclaiming any intention to be a candidate, his friends say, lately he may be forced to be one. This and the course of the Enquirer and what I hear of Hughes lead me to believe he is more confident than heretofore. We can always defeat him, and send you to the Senate without disturbing the democratic party, but he and Floyd might put up another, whose defeat would be less certain, and an election over whom might add to the number of your opponents. There is another matter, which causes me some alarm, it is the action of the

Southern States, in the organization of the House of Representatives. Should the democracy of Carolina, Georgia, Alabama and Mississippi, unite and carry off enough Southern members, to defeat the election of the Administration Candidates for Speaker and Clerk, it may seriously effect us here. The threat of such action may frighten Buchanan, and its execution will prostrate him, but it will exasperate the democracy here, and throw off many from your support. This matter, of course, you and others better acquainted with its possible effects upon the democracy and the South, can judge of better than myself. I am for making no move, in the South, in which Virginia cannot be carried for her natural allies, unless it be forced upon us. And a contest which results in the election of a Black Republican however severe a blow to Buchanan, will react upon us not only in V[irgini]a but in States further South. These suggestions are offered with a full sense of my own want of information, as to the necessity, that may operate on representatives from States further South, and as to ultimate effect on the people there, of a conflict with the administration, which I believe by the democracy of V[irgini]a will be deemed preventable and perhaps utterly condemned by the mass of the people here. I have written to you hastily and frankly, and you will I am sure believe that I write impelled solely by desire to advance our common cause, and aid your reelection.

WILLIAM LAMB TO R. M. T. HUNTER.

NORFOLK, VA., *August 19th, 1857.*

DEAR SIR: The report that you sympathize with the attacks upon the Administration, made by certain journals in the South, having been industriously disseminated throughout Virginia, thereby embarrassing the mutual friends of Mr Buchanan and yourself, you will oblige me, if convenient and agreeable, by stating your position towards the Administration, which you contributed in a great degree to place in power.

R. M. T. HUNTER TO WILLIAM LAMB.

LLOYDS, ESSEX CO., [VA.], *August 23, 1857.*

DEAR SIR: I recognize in your letter a friendly spirit and I answer you with the same feeling. But my answer is for yourself alone, not for *publication*, or to become the subject of public allusion. I have never said or done anything against the administration nor have I any hostile feeling towards it. On the contrary I wish it success. What possible interest could I have in breaking it down or dividing the party? Nor am I responsible for the course of any newspaper. I do not see their editorials until after they are published nor am I consulted in regard to them. No one speaks for me.

I am responsible for my own sayings and doings and for nothing farther. Nor do I feel called upon to criticise the course of newspapers. If I have to commence with this there would be no end to it during the residue of my public life. In conclusion I must repeat the request that this letter is to be considered strictly private.

JAMES HUNTER TO R. M. T. HUNTER.

ELLENGOWAN, [VA.], *August 29, 1857.*

MY DEAR SIR: Suppose you accompany me to Kanawha, your going there may be of service to you. It will renew your impressions of the value of our property there. A Mr. Snead accompanied by five others went to Nicholas [County] early this month to see the lands with a view to a purchase and settlement. I have seen one of the party since their return, he is a very respectable gentleman, a magistrate of Hanover County. He reports that they are delighted with the lands and that they will purchase largely, probably 20,000 acres and form a large party and move out immediately and commence their settlements. These men will be bona fide settlers holding from 500 to 1500 acres each. I have not yet seen Snead, who is the principal man. He has not yet returned. As soon as I see him and have heard what he has to say, I will write to you.

Mr. Craig tells me that they do not go there with any hope of making more than a living for the first four years, but they are certain that by energy and industry they can make good estates for themselves and without leaving Virginia. This is the proper view.

I am expecting your letter in reference to the Elk River Coal lands and also the papers. There is now a great deal of inquiry about those Cannel Coal lands, and my last letter from Kanawha speaks of four new Oil establishments to be built immediately.

I heard from Phil [Dandridge] yesterday. He is at the W[hite] Sulphur and will leave for Kanawha about the 10th or 15th [of] September. He writes in pretty good spirits.

LEWIS E. HARVIE TO R. M. T. HUNTER.

[AMELIA, VA.], *September 4th, 1857.*

MY DEAR HUNTER: I find your letters at home after an absence of six weeks from the State. Just having returned of course I am not well posted in regard to current events. I am sufficiently so however to feel very confident that your reelection is safe. I came thro' the North West over the Baltimore and Ohio R[ail] R[oa]d and saw Judge Camden and Oldham who told me that you would get the whole vote of that section of the State. I heard from Alfred Barbour at the same time, the same thing. From Jack Willis and Jack

Barbour at the same time I.heard that from Alexandria thro' the red land country under the mountain *all* was right.· Lee alone preferring Wise and he not daring to misrepresent what he knows to be the will of his constituents. The Southside is all our own, I am sure. Powell's and Richardson's districts [are] all right. Your own county I suppose is sound. Still our friends should be alert and active, for we have fierce, unscrupulous and wiley foes. Write again and tell me all you know, what and where are the weak points and I will help to strengthen them. Your views and policy are all right and I and Wm. Old, Jr and Lewis [?] have been impressing them on Pryor warmly and earnestly before I went away. Pryor has been away from his post for a month leaving his paper in the hands of his assistant and his paper has lost ground and is losing it I fear daily. He had the Enquirer down and has now lost the advantage. I had urged Mayo to write to him to return at once and I think he will when he gets my message. In the mean time Wm. Old has sent a communication down to-day, which I presume will appear as an Editorial placing the paper on the true ground which is the same as that suggested in your letter. This he will follow up with others. I have written to Mayo to place the paper on it and not to drug it. To keep V[irgini]a in the Democratic party at the head of the South and not at the tail of the north and to appeal to State pride and urge upon him not to abandon her principles and natural allies for the purpose of getting broken victuals to feed her hungry politicians. I am and have been all along out and out against making war on Buchanan. It will be time enough when *he* does something not covertly but openly that will justify it. Any attack on him now only weakens his assailants and strengthens him. If we are to strike let us be clearly right and put him clearly in the wrong and then we can strike hard. Granting that we are able to pull down the pillars of the temple now cui bono. It crushes us as well as him. No I am for giving him full and fair play, supporting him until he drives us off, and to the end of the chapter. At the same time I have little hope that he will permit us to do it. I for one however will assail each in its turn every violation of principle and pledge, until forbearance ceases to be a virtue and then I will war on their authority, but not our Democracy, I am done with that. I wish to live and die in the Democratic fold and faith and shall fight enemies from without or false friends within under the broad shield and panoply of Democracy. Let us all take this position and be brave ourselves and we will keep these hungry curs in their proper places. I do not see any thing that you can do until the meeting of Congress. Then you should and I suppose will take the first opportunity to define your own position and not allow these gentry to make one for you. They can't put you against the administration if you don't choose to be against it, nor can they prescribe the mode and manner of your support or the extent of your opposition. In the meantime his excellency in his zeal for old Buck [Buchanan] or himself is as likely to run afowl of something or other in or out of his way as one that I know and his ex-excellency may be expected to protect the interest of Uncle Sam in other transactions as effectually as he is said to have done in the sale of Fort Snellings and be as implicity trusted by the people of Virginia as he is now. We have beaten these men before and can and will do it again. Keep me advised and trust [William M.] Ambler and Wm. Old implicitly. I name these because they are in the Legislature and should understand every move at once.

I sat up late last night on two strong cups of coffee to keep my eyes open in order to reply to your letters, as soon as I got them. That admirable narcotic having the effect of exciting my brain, may have prevented me from giving such a reply to your letter as it required and would have gotten when it ought to have reached me. Since then no doubt great changes have taken place in the tactics and perhaps in the views of the coalition. That they will crush us if they can is certain. If they can't they will say that they wouldn't if they could and perhaps one of them that he would " crawl to Washington to make you President." " Nous verrons " We will be more than a match for them. There is no doubt, that Wise is or has been at work. Write and tell me all you know.

EDWARD EVERETT TO R. M. T. HUNTER.

(Private and confidential.)

MEDFORD, MASS., *September 5, 1857.*

MY DEAR SIR: I was lately invited by the municipal authorities of Knoxville, to come there and repeat my Discourse on the character of Washington, during the recent session of the Southern Convention. A previous engagement in the State of Maine made it impossible for me to accept the invitation.

About the same time, I was invited and warmly urged by the ladies of the Virginia Association for the purchase of Mount Vernon to go to Richmond early in November, with a view to repeat my " Washington " during your State Agricultural fair. I have received similar invitations to go to Petersburg from the Executive Committee of the United Virginia and North Carolina Agricultural Society and from several other places in the Southern States.

The state of my family is such, as to make it very difficult for me to leave home, long enough for a Southern tour. I have accordingly not been able definitely to accept any of these invitations, and it is altogether possible that I may not.

Should I be able to overcome the domestic obstacle to the journey, there would still remain a ground of hesitation. The invitation to Knoxville above alluded to was made the subject, (so I am informed, for I never saw the article) of a severe attack upon me in the columns of "the South," in reference to the assault on Mr. Sumner. A visit to Richmond and an extensive Southern tour would probably produce new manifestations of Mr. Pryor's unfriendly feelings towards me. Coming as I should by the invitation of an Association of Ladies and upon an errand whose success depends entirely on the kind feelings of the community, such a course, on the part of an influential press, followed up as it would probably be by other presses which sympathize with "the South," would go far to defeat the object of my journey.

Nor need I scruple to add, that it must necessarily be a source of annoyance to me, to my personal friends and the ladies from whom my invitation to Richmond proceeds. I own I do not perceive any valuable political object which Mr. Pryor expects to accomplish, by these attacks upon me, for this is not the first. If I were in public life or intended to return to it, I might imagine a motive; at any rate I should have too much self-respect to deprecate any man's hostility, however formidable. But as things are, their only possible effect will be to deprive the Mount Vernon fund of a few thousand dollars, which I should otherwise earn for it at the South and so play into the hands of Horace Greeley and Wendell Phillips, who lose no opportunity of flying at my throat and barking at my heels; and who enjoy their greatest triumph when a Northern Conservative is abused at the South.

Supposing you to be in possession of Mr. Pryor's confidence I have concluded, after some hesitation, to request you to consider the expediency of advising him, to allow me to visit the South for the purpose of repeating my address for the benefit of the Mount Vernon fund, unmolested.

I need not say that, if any duty called me to the South, no man's hostility would prevent my going. But this is a voluntary and private errand, proposed by ladies, appealing to the kind feelings of the Community, of a patriotic but not a political character. I do not therefore feel obliged to subject my friends or myself to the annoyance of personal attack, perhaps of a bitter controversy, from a press conducted with so much vigor as "the South."

I make these representations to you confidentially, relying upon our friendly personal relations, my great personal respect for you and an opinion—perhaps the prompting of vanity—that a statesman of your comprehensive views would, even on general grounds, be inclined to discountenace such a warfare as Mr. Pryor seems disposed to wage on a person now in retirement, whose public life has perhaps been marked by nothing so much, as the unrelenting hostility of the enemies of the Constitution and the Union, in the Northern States. I may add that Mr. Pryor's recent attack upon me was made in entire ignorance of the material facts of the case.

C. W. C. DUNNINGTON TO R. M. T. HUNTER.

WASHINGTON, D. C., *September 7, 1857.*

DEAR SIR: An article appeared in the Virginia Sentinel on last Friday, which astonished me very much. I went to Alexandria next day and called on R. M. Smith, but he had gone to Fauquier. The article looked very much as if the editor desired to put Gov. Smith forward at your expense. Since then I have seen Col. Wm. F. Phillips, who was told by Mr. Finks that Smith intended to take ground for you against Wise. As soon as I can see him I will find out what he is after.

Dr. Tait says he never thought of applying for an office, until Rush Floyd wrote to him that he could get the appointment of 6th auditor if he would apply for it. It is a movement of Gov. Floyd to get his brother into the State Senate, that he may aid the Secretary of War in his schemes. Gov. Floyd told Harris of the Union, that you would be defeated. On the other hand, Gov. Smith told Col. Phillips last week that you would be reelected. Gov. Smith was here about ten days ago and says that in a conversation with the President, Mr. B[uchanan] said he supposed you would be in opposition to his administration.

Robt. E. Scott, of Fauquier, who defended the rioters here last July, told a friend, that he had been stopping with Wise, and that Wise was very anxious to succeed you as Senator.

I have no doubt demagogues and intrigues are endeavoring to poison the mind of the President against all who stand in their way. I repeat these items of gossip, picked up from authentic sources, in the hope they may be useful. Of course, I do not want to be known as giving them, as I do not know at what moment, or upon what pretext I may have the rotation doctrine applied to me, which, with a family of fourteen, would be rather inconvenient.

I met Mr. Montague yesterday. He is to come up to-day to talk over the position of parties in Virginia with me. He is a true friend of yours. It is said the Cabinet are all afraid of Mr. B[uchanan] and that he overhauled the Secretary of War the other day relative to the selling of certain lands owned by the United States. I do not believe the Cabinet will hold together until the adjournment of Congress.

JOHN W. FINK TO R. M. T. HUNTER.

WARRENTON, [VA.], *September 14, 1857.*

DEAR SIR: I have just returned from a trip through nearly all of the Western Countries and made it my business, as I passed through, in a quiet way, to ascertain who the Delegates would vote for, provided Wise was a candidate for a seat in the U[nited] S[tates] S[enate]. They may do their best between this and the election and you will get three Dem[ocratic] votes to his one, and all the Whig vote. To some extent I found opposition to your reelection among some of the people in most every county, but it will not amount to much. He is rather stronger in the State, than some of your friends put it at—twenty.

In the North West you will get nearly all the vote. In the Valley you will lose but one, unless Gatewood of the Tenth Legion goes over. He says he is for you, but at the same time, thinks you will have to come out and show your hand on Kansas. He is risky. South West is for Wise. In this section, from here to Lynchburg, I do not know but one vote you will lose (Kemper of Madison).

Col. Phillips, I understand, will be removed the last of this month to make room for Dr. Tait from the South West, which will make a vacancy in the Senate, to be filled by ———. I had a conversation with Smith, my partner, a few days since, and find I will have no difficulty in getting him to agree to come out, at the proper time, for you against Wise.

I have to be *very prudent* and must *ask the favor of you not to mention to a human being, that you received a letter from me on this subject.* If you do I am a goner.

ERASTUS T. MONTAGUE TO R. M. T. HUNTER.

WASHINGTON, [D. C.], *September 14, 1857.*

DEAR HUNTER: I have been here for the last week with but little to do except to pick up what political news I could find and I proceed to give you the result of my observations.

A few days since I learn that the President in a conversation with Gov. Smith remarked that he supposed he should have to regard you as identified with the opposition to his adm[inistratio]n. Smith replied that you were cautious prudent and sagacious and not likely to take any step without due consideration.

The efforts of the Enquirer to force from you an exposition of your views on Walker's Kansas policy occasion much talk here. Mr. Forney is the only high official with whom I have had any conversation on the subject. He says you should not notice the matter at all. That should a proper occasion arise during the approaching session " he doubts not you will define your position and that it will be found right as it has always been." Forney and Thompson are your only reliable friends in this concern.

Your friend Col. Phillips is to be removed from the 6th Aud-[ito]r['s] office and Dr. Tate of our state senate to be appointed in his place. The object is to remove Tate (who is your friend) from the Senate, and put Floyd's brother in his place. From all I can learn there is a regularly organized combination between Wise, Floyd, and Faulkner the object of which is to put Wise in your place make Faulkner Governor and bring in Floyd to succeed Mason. What a beautiful scheme!!! and to cap the climax old Buck [Buchanan] is made to play second fiddle to this immaculate trio. Hence the efforts of Wise through the Enquirer to identify you with the opposition to the Adm[inistratio]n. At every corner I am accosted with the enquiry what is to be the result of the conflict between Wise and Hunter in Virginia? My reply is there can be no conflict. The people of Virginia never change their public servants without cause. Mr. Hunter has served them faithfully, they are satisfied with his course, and desire no change. Wise's particular friends approach me with hypocritical cant professing to deplore the schism between Wise and Hunter. I ask them for the evidence of such schism they point to the opposition of some of Hunters friends to Wises oyster fundum and other crude and ridiculous absurdities. I reply that Mr. Hunter's friends are free and independent citizens who think for themselves, and that neither he nor any one else can properly be held responsible for their opinions and actions. That he should be judged alone by his own sayings and doings.

I give you these sketches that you may see how the Wise workers here and in Virginia would manage things if they could. But they are powerless. From reliable information from all sections of the state I am happy to learn that you were never so strong in the confidence of the people as now. I have seen Powell who tells me they can't get up a demonstration against you. That all these efforts of your enemies but kill their authors while they add to your strength. Bocock was here a few days since and declared publicly that they could not muster an omnibus load of Democrats in the Legislature who would go against your selection. Both of these gentlemen spoke from personal knowledge of the views and intentions of the members elect. I met with Daniel on Friday last and had a long conversation with him, he confirms the statements of Bocock and Powell and from all I can learn you have but to speak the word and Buchanan and all his friends are as dead as Chelsea in Virginia. I have been unusually cautious and prudent, said nothing but endeavored to learn all I could.

Cobb is laying his plans for the succession. Forney has commenced the movement by a complimentary republication of one of Cobbs speeches during the late canvass. This is to be followed up from time to time by similar compliments from others of the Northern Press, and thus clothe him with the habiliments of *National democracy par excellence*. Thus placed before the country as a Southern man with the greatest Northern popularity he hopes to secure the nomination. The removal from and appointments to office in his department it is thought will be made with exclusive reference to this object. Will the South be duped and gulp the bait? How will Wise relish this scheme which so effectively dash all his bright visions to the ground. Douglas too will be apt to rebel, rely upon it we shall have rare times here next winter and I sincerely trust that the old adage "When rogues fall out honest men get their dues" will be verified. But I will not bore you with speculations. I have hastily sketched what I have learned and leave you to make your own reflections.

WILLIAM W. CRUMP TO R. M. T. HUNTER.

RICHMOND, [VA.], *September 15, 1857.*

MY DEAR SIR: It is not my nature to witness unmoved, an unscrupulous and ingeneous effort, to crush or to injure a faithful, valuable and eminent public servant. Let this be my apology for addressing you upon a subject, which while it concerns you especially yet interests me as well, as one who feeling a sincere gratitude for past service, earnestly desires to retain you in the post you have so nobly filled. I am urged too by the recollection that an expression of mine last fall, was construed by the mischief making into a covert attack upon yourself, and I have had no opportunity to explain the matter to you in person, as I had hoped, if indeed it had attracted your notice at all. I have seen alike with pain and indignation the sedulous effort upon the part of Mr. Wise to bring about a controversy with you. I say Mr. Wise because Mr. Wise has no friends who are not guided, governed and absolutely swayed by him. Under the preposterous pretext that your friends are making war on *him*, he sets the Enquirer upon you, and assuming that your position towards the Executive is equivocal, it (or rather he) demands that you should speak obviously with the double purpose of either obtaining from you an answer which would place you in a position of hostility to the administration and so authorizing upon his part an open and undisguised war, or of displaying his power, in constraining an answer "though it might and no doubt would disappoint his hopes." That you will pursue the even and dignified tenor of your way I cannot doubt. That the same calm and manly firmness which has endeared you to the people of Virginia, will mark your course in this emergency I feel assured. And yet I could not forbear telling you, that one who is connected with you by no other bonds than those of esteem, watches with the deepest solicitude, in the present emergency, the course you may pursue and burns with indignation at the envious attempt to supplant you. I do not know that you feel as I do, our temperments differ so much that perhaps you may smile at my favour. It may be too that my own impulses are tinged by a cerbity which comes from the remembrance, that the only difference I ever had with your friends all of whom were mine was occasioned by my refusal to unite with them in elevating Mr. Wise to a position which would enlarge his (capacity I was about to write, but that is impossible) sphere for mischief. I was greatly displeased with them and except that they agree with me now in my estimate of him I should still express my displeasure towards them for their unhappy mistake.

I feel assured from what I have seen and heard that if the reins of the party are given to him, we shall have another Phaeton drive to lament. He must either rule or ruin. He cannot, *no man* thank God, can rule in Virginia and I greatly fear that he will, sow the seeds of discord which will bring disaster sooner or later upon our party. I write thus of him because he is now supposed to be the highest power in the State because he is said to be omnipotent in his influence with Mr. Buchanan and only because he is so do I thus speak of him. Power alone has no charms for me. And if he was in an eclipse I would not thus speak of him. I do not know or want to know, that you agree with me. I write in the fullest and most unstricting confidence to you and for your eye alone. It delights me to say, as I intended long since to have said that, all machinations against you will fail. I have learned that the Northwest, will be for you to a man that the tenth legion is sure, that little Tennessee, will stand by you and indeed I do not know any man of prominence in the Legislature who will lift his voice against you. Wise has not strengthened himself with the Legislature. I could see that he lost ground greatly with the last. No man can approach him and believe him fit to fill a statesman's place. He will lose ground yet more, before the next Legislature adjourns.

I cannot close without expressing the belief that the truce between Floyd and himself will be but short lived. In saying this, let me say at the same time, lest my intimate acquaintance with Gov. Floyd might lead to the supposition that I speak from information derived from him, that I have seen him but once, since he was Sec[retar]y of War and have never spoken of Wise to him or he to me. I reason in the abstract entirely. And from my knowledge of the men I feel assured that there can be no continued cordial co-operation between them. I have always deplored the estrangement between Floyd and your friends. Be assured he is your natural ally not in its modern sense, but he is a thorough States-rights man, he is a gentleman by education and by instinct and whatever deflections he has exhibited from the path of strict virtue he is still a gentleman, manly, generous, and brave. I know he did entertain a most exalted estimate of you and though he has never spoken to me unkindly of you, yet I believe there is some estrangement, which I should rejoice to see removed. Let me repeat that I am writing to you of "my own heart." I do not request a reply or want to open a correspondence and that no one knows or shall know that I have written.

A. D. BANKS TO R. M. T. HUNTER.

PETERSBURG, [VA.], *September 19, 1857.*

MY DEAR SIR: I reached home yesterday having been absent at the Springs and at Washington several weeks. From what I can gather I have now no doubt we are to have a contest for the Senate. Nothing will satisfy Wise but a good trouncing and he will get it for rely on it he means to run. The course of the *Enquirer* excites general disgust among the democrats every where and will greatly strengthen you. Some of your friends now desire you to "come out."

By the way cannot Ritchie be beaten for Printer. Say with the editor of the Wheeling Argus or of the Rockingham Register or Faulkners man Robinson? It would be a withering rebuke and I think we will have the strength to administer it. I merely throw out the idea for you to think upon it. Pryor could not beat him. He has been too ultra the other way. Better take a Western man and make a merit of it. Talk this over with Garnett and if he thinks proper let him correspond with Letcher on the subject. Cobb and Thompson assure me the administration will take no part in the contest. But I hear otherwise albeit they say Floyd is getting jealous of Wise. I met Powell in Washington. He says all is right in his country, also Albert Pendleton. Pendleton is enthusiastic says everything [is] right in the Central West, thinks it doubtful whether Rush Floyd can get to the Senate in place of Tait app[ointe]d 6th Auditor. Dunn of Washington has been gotten out by Hopkins' friends and they say will beat him. All right still on the South Side. You may lose Honerton Thompson and a man from Franklin but that will be all. All the information I get is cheering. What they base their hopes on I can not tell.

I met Judge Perkins in Washington. I was surprised to find him so warmly your friend. He promises to cut off the correspondence of Wise's man Keon and proposes to be one of two to bring out an edition of your speeches. By the way has it ever occurred to you that this ought to be done. It would do more to strengthen you over the country than anything I know of.

Albert Pendleton requests me to ask you by all means to come down to the Richmond fair in October. If possible you ought to try and do so. I wish very much you would try and come to ours also.

My prospects for next winter are as good as I could wish them. They will have hard work I think to beat me.

By the way speaking of Judge Perkins reminds me that Mrs. Bayly and himself are certainly engaged to be married. It will come off I believe in December.

P. S. I met Schell in Washington. He sends regards and the warmest wishes for your success next winter. He is your friend. Even Geo. Sanders is for you.

C. W. C. Dunnington to R. M. T. Hunter.

(*Private.*)

Washington, D. C., *September 20, 1857*.

Dear Sir: I received yours of the 12th inst. since which I have seen Smith of the Sentinel. I told him I was surprised at the tone of the article which referred to you. He said your friends secured the nomination of Wise, and were to blame for his present prominent position in the party; that he (Smith) had had his say, and at the proper time should take ground for you, in preference to Wise. His feelings towards you arise from you beating Gov. Smith for the Senate, not to anything else. To Wise he is opposed on both personal and political grounds. Smith is sound with the administration, and particularly with Gov. Floyd with whom he was particularly gracious last spring. I am told Gov. Smith has not much influence with the administration which accounts for it.

R. M. Smith is of the opinion that the weight of the national administration will be thrown against you, and that your friends are marked. Time, however, will show. Col. Phillips, 6th auditor, Brodhead 3d do., Streeter, Solicitor, and Anderson, Com[missioner] of Customs go out this month. Cobb sent for Phillips yesterday to notify him.

I understand a nephew, or cousin of Gov. Wise, is an applicant for the place made vacant by the resignation of Mr. Merrick. Mr. Montague's name has also been mentioned. The latter gentleman is reliable and a warm friend of yours. There is great dissatisfaction felt by the party at the course of the administration relative to appointments. The rule seems to be to proscribe the friends of the late administration; and reward knownothings if they preferred Mr. Buchanan to Mr. Pierce. The Postmaster General and Secretary of the Treasury are both known aspirants to the presidency, and I believe the present incumbent has hope of a reelection. With such a state of things existing, there will be trouble among them before the adjournment of the next Congress.

The coalition between Wise, Floyd and Faulkner for the purpose of placing Wise in your place, Faulkner in the gubernatorial chair, and Floyd in Senator Mason's place at the close of this adminis- tration, would be capable of much mischief. If they had confidence in each other; but I am told there is a jealous feeling growing up among them, each one being afraid of the other's cheating him.

I am told that Messrs. Bocock and Powell when here expressed the utmost confidence in your triumphant reelection. Mr. Montague says the people are all for you in his section; and R. M. Smith says the neighboring district will be represented by men a large majority of whom are for you. How is it in the West? It is said Rush Floyd cannot be elected without Whig votes, so that you may get an op- ponent of the triumvirate in place of Tate. As Hopkins can have no reason to like the Floyds, I hope he will aid you.

LEWIS E. HARVIE TO R. M. T. HUNTER.

RICHMOND, [VA.], *September 22, 1857.*

DEAR HUNTER: The skies are bright and brightening. I think I am informed of the sentiment of the whole state. You will be re- elected triumphantly and there will be *no opposition to your election.* Wise is [a] dead beat and the tone of his friends (he has very few) and of his paper shows that he knows it. Pryor says there is not a shadow of doubt about it. He has triumphed over the Enquirer, which is doomed and the South hereafter is to be the Democratic or- gan in Virginia. *Intra nos,* Hughes has told Pryor that there can be no difficulty between them and that your election is certain. Watch Floyd and meet any advances or indications. He has a good deal of sense and no great love for his excellency. Pryor will publish on tomorrow, all the Editorials favorable to your election throughout the State. He fears that you may think that he has been lukewarm in defending you from assaults &c and wishes you to know that it has been from a conviction that it was the best policy for you. This was my opinion and Seddon's and all of your friends hereabouts and he acted as we thought best. We did not wish you involved in the quarrel of the South with the Enquirer and told him to keep you out of it. I know that he is as true to you as steel and that he has the materials if it was prudent to put you in the contest to sustain you triumphantly. You stand now in the ascendent and if no mistake is made you are invincible. Those that have not heretofore been for you are now claiming to be for you against all comers. No man ever yet made war upon the State Rights party in V[irgini]a without being cast down, and several people who did not know it are now discovering it. I am writing in a great hurry and write of course without detail. You may rely however upon what I say. By the way I heard today that Beale is involved in some personal difficulty with one of the Brockenbroughs and that possibly a challenge may grow out of it. See Newton and stop it, if it be so. First because I think Beale a very valuable and worthy gentleman and secondly because he is your friend and ought to be in the next Legislature.

William L. McPhink to R. M. T. Hunter.

GLASGOW, [SCOTLAND], *3rd October, 1857.*

DEAR SIR: His Excellency George M. Dallas, American Ambassador in this country, having kindly undertaken to forward them to you, I beg leave to send, herewith, and to request your acceptance of, a volume entitled " Currency self regulating," and a pamphlet entitled " The true principles of currency."

The main design of these publications was to describe an arrangement by which (I believe it will, by and by, be acknowledged,) the thing as long dreamed of, a perfect currency without a standard, would be fully realised; but as I know there is a strong and general prejudice against abstract currency, originating, I daresay, in the utterly preposterous character of every other scheme of inconvertible paper money that has been proposed in modern times, the plan which I am desirous to bring under your notice is that of a paper currency convertible into the precious metals, according to the present law of the United States, with this difference, that the issuing of money should be so regulated that interest on inferior securities, such as commercial bills, should never fall below the return yielded, for the time, by securities of the highest class, such as the national funds.

On glancing over what I have just written, and observing how it jars with many of the principles laid down by masters on the currency whom we have been most accustomed to look upon as authorities, I am afraid that your final impression, as regards my plan, will be unfavourable. But I hope you will suspend your judgement till you have perused the details, which, as applicable to Great Britain, you will find on pages 333 and 338 of the volume, and at pages 67 and 76 of the pamphlet and I hope that when you have gone over these, you will be sensible that the plan is really sound, that under it interest could never become depressed as we have seen it in times past, and that the commercial prosperity of the American people would be very favorably affected by their being defended from such depression, and from the speculation excitement which it very rarely fails to engender.

From the small amount of your national debt, it is obvious that it would not afford a sufficient basis for the currency of such a large population as that of the United States: but it will, I doubt not, be equally apparent to you that title deeds of houses and lands might form an equally good security for repayment of advances made to bankers of the notes required for carrying on their business, *the really important feature in the proposed plan being that by which it provides that interest should be allowed on notes deposited at same rate as was charged on notes issued.*

I earnestly trust that you will consider it your duty to bring the subject of this communication under the notice of the committee on finance, over which you preside and should it appear to you that I can, either by correspondence or by personal attendance, afford assistance to you in arriving at a conclusion regarding it, you will be pleased to consider my services as being entirely at your command.

WILLIAM OLD, JR. TO R. M. T. HUNTER.

[PETERSBURG, VA.?], *October 5th, 1857.*

DEAR SIR: I received your letter a few days since and was much pleased at the information contained in it. Your explanation of the history of the Land bill prepared by you, would have been an absolute defence, had it been before the country at the time, so far as the democracy of this and the other Atlantic States were concerned. You are no doubt aware that, the proposition, not only gave an opportunity of assault to your opponents in the Dem[ocratic] party in the State but most unfortunately, made some of the warmest friends of State Rights, cold towards you under the belief that too much was yielded to the Northwest. Instead of comparing it with the Homestead bill, they took the bill as an original proposition and found large objections to its minimum. You allude in yours to the settlement feature of the bill. I have no recollection of the details of the bill and have nothing by me to afford me any information on it. You have just now clearly a majority so large in the legislature, that I do not apprehend, any serious opposition; still events may transpire which will strengthen the aspirants, and it may be the policy of your opponents to make an attack although an inefficient one so far as your defeat for the place of Senator is concerned. They have never been very confident of success in an effort to defeat you for the Senate, but to furnish evidence of strong democratic opposition to you in this state, will aid Wise as much, (almost as your defeat) in his objects. Hughes will be forced to assail you on this bill, if opposition is made to you and he is forced to concur in it, although now I think it will be no labor of love to him, he must cease his opposition to you on this bill. Wise is I think estopped from using it, if anything can prevent him from indulging his spleen and answering the appeals of his vanity. In case you are assailed, it would be well for some friend in the Senate and House of Delegates to be prepared with a defence; I am in a situation to assail Wise, and shall not fail to take advantage of it, if it is prudent to do so. But it may not be so, yet some of us should be in possession of the means of defence on this bill; no explanation of the bill has ever been made which we can make use of, that I remember. Can you furnish me with a copy of the bill, and any additional facts or reasons which I can use to sustain it, other than those contained in your letter to me.

Your situation now is such that I have refrained from sending Pryor some articles I had prepared. They were attacks upon the Enquirer, and I think the country press has rendered them unnecessary. The friends of Wise will now devote themselves entirely to preventing you receiving the support of V[irgini]a in the next Dem[ocratic] Convention. If they cannot succeed in raising opposition in the Legislature, we can treat their hostility displayed elsewhere, as the effect of disappointment and malice. I am writing as you will perceive in a manner the most disconnected, for I am at our County court and interrupted every moment or two. My only object in writing now is to ask you to furnish me with a copy of your bill, and with such suggestions in regard to it, as will enable me to meet an attack if one shall be made on it, and any assault made on you of any importance will be on that bill. Your position with regard to the Administration nobody really doubts, the only question being whether you will gratify the Gubernatorial editor of the Enquirer by yielding to his enquiry. I am with all of your friends with whom I have conversed utterly opposed to your noticing that paper. But I am disposed to think, that it would be well if some portion of the people or members of the legislature could elicit an expression from you. Such an exposition would certainly silence the Enquirer, and coming on the back of the united expression of the democratic press, would do much to complete its discomfiture in its efforts to represent the democracy. It is from the influence of this paper alone that the States Rights party in this state have anything to fear—any blow it may receive now will go far to destroy it. I am writing under such continued interruptions, it is impossible to continue.

HENRY E. ORR TO R. M. T. HUNTER.

(*Private.*)

PORTSMOUTH, VA., *October 6th, 1857.*

MY DEAR SIR: I have not written you since you were in Washington, because my presumption was that you would probably fail of receiving my letter at Washington. However, I now venture to address you at your home.

In the mail which conveys this note, I forward a copy of the "Transcript" and its views of the Senatorial question you may rely on as those of nine-tenths of the Democracy here about. The *Enquirer's* course, despite its denials, men will persist in believing to be stimulated by an *interested party.* How true my warning to Montague, some months since, as to the jealousy of Wise's friends towards you; and though censured by *some* of the presses of our party for intimating through my editorials such a fact, the justice of such a course is now fuly vindicated.

If the balance of the State does its duty as faithfully as will this section, your vindication against your foes will have a very desirable effect on future events. It is certainly very desirable that the South, through her public men, should indicate her true position as to the terms upon which the present administration may anticipate its support.

C. W. C. DUNNINGTON TO R. M. T. HUNTER.

(*Private.*)

WASHINGTON, D. C., *October 6, 1857.*

DEAR SIR: When I last wrote to you I thought before this I should have been rotated out. Dr. Blake opposed it with all his power, and some of my newspaper friends remonstrated in strong terms against it. The matter remains in statu quo.

Col. Phillips has been removed. Dr. Brodhead will go in a few days. It is said *every* member of the cabinet opposes Cutts' appointment; but the President is determined. Gov. Floyd told Dr. Blake, in speaking of Cutts, that Mr. Buchanan was different from Gen. Jackson; that Gen. Jackson could be *coaxed* from his purpose, but that Mr. B[uchanan] could neither be coaxed nor driven. Many little circumstances lead me to believe, that the President is getting suspicious of the Secretary of the Treasury. Mr. Cobb is evidently bent upon securing the next nomination, if possible; and one of Mr. Buchanan's Pennsylvania friends informs me that, Mr. B[uchanan] is aware of Cobb's movements, and is watching him closely. I believe the whole cabinet stand in fear of the President, who relies but little upon their advice. I rejoice sincerely that you are not in it; not only because of the policy of the administration, but because I do not think it will hold together long.

The agents of the New York Herald have great influence at the White House. One fact will show how the Herald stands. There are but three newspapers regularly preserved on the files, viz; The Union, the Intelligence, and the New York Herald.

I received a letter last week from Gen. Eppa Hunton of Prince William. He says our delegate Seymour Lynn, is for you, and Gen. H[unton] says "most everybody else." I do not believe Gov. Wise will be a candidate, for the reason that he has no chance of election. He is too wiley a politician to place himself in a position where he is certain to be defeated, and where defeat would be utter ruin.

I do not expect you to take the trouble to answer my gossiping letters about matters that are talked of privately here. When they become annoying, toss them into the fire. I hope to have the pleasure of congratulating you at an early day upon your reelection.

Gov. Bright has been very kind to me, and protested strongly against my removal. He is not very favorable to Douglas; and this appointment of Mr. D's father-in-law will damage him with Western men more than anything he could do. His opponents are already using Cutts' contemplated appointment against him.

SHELTON F. LEAKE TO R. M. T. HUNTER.

CHARLOTTESVILLE, [VA.], *October 10, 1857.*

DEAR SIR: I see that the "Enquirer" and its correspondents, continue to call upon you to "come out," on the Kansas embroglio; and, particularly, to say whether you are now friendly to Mr. Buchanan's Administration, and will support it, if you shall be re-elected to the U. S. Senate.

Now, while I have no doubt as to your position, yet as I hear, not unfrequently, your *friends,* (who constitute a large majority of the Democratic party of Virginia) express a wish that you would publish your views on these questions, not so much to satisfy them as to silence the cavilling of those who wish to defeat you in any event, I take the liberty, as an old friend, to ask your views, on the points suggested. It is needless to say that, unless forbidden by yourself, your answer will be published.

(P. S.) It is for you to determine whether you ought to publish in reply to a letter from *me.* You need not ans[we]r, as far as I am concerned. My name, *perhaps,* had better be suppressed. That, however, you may determine for yourself. For myself, I say that I have no concealments and wish none. I am fully convinced, *now,* that you had better write a letter to some *friend* for publication.

R. M. T. HUNTER TO HON. SHELTON F. LEAKE.[1]

LLOYDS, ESSEX Co., VA., *October 16th, 1857.*

DEAR SIR: I received on yesterday your letter propounding to me certain interrogatories, to which, without further delay, I proceed to reply. They are in substance nearly the same, with the questions upon which the Enquirer for some time past, has been demanding my answers. But to these last I have not replied, because they were either accompanied with threats, or what were so considered, which made answers on my part, inconsistent with self-respect, or else they were founded upon my presumed responsibility for the editorials of certain newspapers within, and without the State of Virginia, which were not only not authorized to speak for me, but which claimed no such authority. I was to be held responsible for the course of newspapers, unless I came before the public with a criticism of their course and a disclaimer of all sympathy with them; a responsibility, which I shall never acknowledge expressly, or impliedly, by any act of mine. To admit such a responsibility, would place it in the power of any third person who chose to impute to me a sympathy with the course of any newspaper within, or without the State, to call me out in a public criticism of its course upon any question of morals or politics which might be in discussion, or else fix upon me the charge of concurring in the views of that paper. No power could force upon me the office of censor of the public press. I certainly shall not assume it voluntarily. When any paper claims authority to speak for me, then it may be the time to question me in regard to it, but not before.

But to proceed with the answers to your interrogatories, I have to say, first, that the imputation of hostility, on my part, towards the administration of Buchanan, is founded upon nothing that I have either said or done. I voted for him as President, and not only entertain no feeling of hostility towards him, but I wish him success. He has only to carry out the principles of the Democratic party, as we understand them in Virginia, to command my cordial support. These, so far as applicable, will afford the test by which I shall judge his administration and support or oppose its acts, as they conform to, or depart from these principles. Nor shall I be disposed to apply that test in any captious, or unkind spirit, but as justly and fairly as I can. More I could not say for any administration or man. I never would commit myself to support unconditionally, the future acts of any man, but I will judge them as they arise, to sustain them when I believe they are right, and to oppose them when I think they are wrong. My opinions upon all the great political issues, may be known through my votes and speeches, to those who

---

[1] This letter can be found in the Richmond Examiner of Oct. 23, 1857.

feel enough of interest in them, to look into my past course, and these will afford the best evidence of the tests which I shall be likely to apply, in judging of the conduct of public affairs. Whilst I remain in the Senate of the United States, I shall stand there as the representative of the principles and interests of my State, so far as I can understand them, and in the pursuit of these objects, I should not scruple to differ, if necessary, with any administration. In saying this, it may be perhaps fair to add, that I hope and expect to be able to support Mr. Buchanan's administration in the main. Entire concurrence in the views of any man it would be too much to hope, or expect.

In answer to the other interrogatory which you propose as to the conduct of Governor Walker in Kansas, I have little hesitation in saying, that I disapprove. The Kansas-Nebraska act was passed under the hope that this, the last of the territorial questions, involving the subject of slavery, might be settled upon some common ground where a party could be rallied from the North and the South, the East and the West, strong enough to defend the Constitution against the assaults of its enemies and to administer the government justly upon other than purely sectional ideas. To rally a party which might be able to maintain the Union upon constitutional principles, was an object of high political importance, and justified some sacrifices of feeling, and even of interest. Accordingly, the bill was not such as would have been framed by the delegates of either section, if it had been submitted to them alone. Many, perhaps most of the Southern men, (of whom I was one) believed that property in slaves was as much entitled to the protection of law in the Territories of the United States, as property in any thing else; but whilst the Northern friends of the Kansas act would not concede this, they agreed to unite in repealing the Missouri restriction so as to remove the ban under which the domestic institutions of the south had been placed by Federal legislation. Accordingly, a bill was passed upon the principle of non-intervention, in regard to slavery, so far as the General Government was concerned, and which left the whole subject within the control of the people of these territories, when they should apply for admission as States. This, although not all that we thought the South entitled to, was a great advance upon the old order of things, so far as she was concerned, because it removed an unjust and odious discrimination against her domestic institutions, from the statute book. A moral triumph which was of vast importance to the South and to the institution of slavery itself. Nor could the North object to a bill which merely carried out a principle by which it had recently gained so largely in the series of acts, denominated as the Compromise Measures.

To all it ought to have been a subject of congratulation that a common ground had been found where a party might be rallied from all sections of the country to administer the government justly, and without sacrificing the constitutional rights of any portion of the Union. The sole hope of accomplishing so happy a result depended upon submitting this question of slavery to the people of these territories, when they came to form their constitutions as States, without interference of any sort on the part of the General Government. With the decision of the people themselves, so far as the character of the new States was concerned, the democratic party of all sections declared they would be satisfied. To fulfil, then, the conditions of this agreement, it was all important that there should be no interference on the part of the General Government, either through its Legislative or Executive influence. Any such interference was calculated to dissatisfy the one section or the other. Under such circumstances it was my opinion improper for the highest Executive officer in the Territory, the Governor of Kansas, to attempt to influence the decision of the people of that Territory, upon this question of slavery. Such an interference on the part of any branch of the Federal Government, was inconsistent with the principle of the Kansas-Nebraska act. Neither do I recognise his authority to declare that "if they (the convention) do not appoint a fair and impartial mode, by which a majority of the actual, bona fide settlers of Kansas, shall vote through the instrumentality of impartial judges, I will join you in all lawful opposition to their doing, and the President and Congress will reject their Constitution." If the convention itself was legally constituted and elected, the question of submitting their work to the people for ratification, was one of which that body had jurisdiction alone, unless indeed the act which called them into being, had required a final ratification by the people.

The practice of States applying for admission, as I understand, has been in both ways. Nor has the power of the convention to determine this question for itself ever been controverted, heretofore, so far as I am informed. The convention of Kansas, if legally constituted, has all the powers of any other convention to form a State constitution, and if Congress can limit this power in one respect, it may in all. If Congress can reject a State constitution for the manner in which the convention has exercised its undoubted powers, why not for the matter also of the constitution, even though it may be republican in its form of government? or, if the Governor of a Territory may attempt to overawe a convention of its people in the exercise of its powers in one respect, why not in another? With regard to the abstract propriety of the particular recommendations of Governor Walker, I do not feel called upon to speak. That is a matter for the decision of the convention itself, with which I ought not to interfere. The abstract propriety of these recommendations depends upon circumstances, of which the people of Kansas, acting through their convention, are the best judges. To them I leave it as their own affair. As to which course would conduct most to their peace and a fair settlement of the question, I should require a greater knowledge of the actual state of affairs in that Territory to enable me to decide.

With these answers to your interrogatories, I might here close this letter, except that I infer you desire to know how far my opinion in regard to Governor Walker's conduct may effect my course towards the Administration. What are the precise views of the President upon these questions, I know not; I await their development in the regular course. But should he differ how can any practical issue arise between him and those of his friends who entertain other opinions in regard to Governor Walker's course? I say, I do not see how any practical issue could arise out of this matter between the President and those who might differ with him in regard to these things, because I do not believe for a moment that he would aid in an attempt to reject the State, if Kansas should apply for admission, merely because its convention did not choose to submit the constitution to the people for ratification.

Upon such a question as this, in regard to the right of Congress to limit the power of a people to form their State Constitution according to their own pleasure, provided it be republican in its character, I should think there could be no division of opinion amongst the members of the Democratic party in any section of the Union. There could not be, if they remain true to what I understand as their profession of faith. To establish the great principles of the equal rights of the States to the enjoyment of the territories of the United States, which no act of federal legislation can constitutionally abridge or destroy, and of the right of the people of each State to determine the character of their own domestic institutions without prejudice to their claim of admission into the Union, the Democratic party has submitted to losses and sacrifices, which could only have been justified by the successful accomplishment of a great object. To obtain a common ground upon which all might rally for the defence of the constitution and the peace of the country against the enemies of both, did constitute such an object. And now that the position has been conquered, after so arduous a struggle, who supposes that the Democratic party would volunteer a retrograde movement, and renounce the fruits of a hard-won victory? To abandon either of these positions now by a retrograde movement, would be an act of felo de se in the party, and not merely a folly, but a crime for which posterity would never forgive it. For these reasons, I do not believe that the Democratic party, or the President whom it has chosen, will aid in any attempt to restrict the power of the people of Kansas, acting through their convention, to form a constitution according to their own pleasure, both in manner and substance, provided it be republican in its character.

Having now answered fully your interrogatories, I need proceed no farther; but as you are kind enough to say that you question me not because you doubted me yourself, but to save me from misconstruction by others, I feel that I ought not to conclude without thanking you for your generous motives. To those who are disposed to misconstrue me, I have only to say, that if the past course of one who has served the State in a public capacity so long as I have, affords no sufficient guaranty as to his future conduct, it is idle to seek for further security in professions of faith. My past course affords the best evidences of my principles of public action, and these are the tests by which, as an honest man, I am bound to judge every administration. If, therefore, I should be blamed, if blameable at all, not for the act of differing with a President, but because of the false principles by which I am to judge him; so that it is by these that I am to be tried, after all. It is true, that when new questions arise, one may be fairly and properly questioned as to his opinions. But what is there new here? The principles of the Kansas Nebraska act, by which I have been just testing Governor Walker's conduct, and the right of the people, acting through their convention, to form a constitution of republican character, according to their own pleasure, without prejudice to their claim of admission as a State in the Union, have all been discussed heretofore, by myself and others, far more fully than would be consistent with the limits of this letter. Nor have I expressed any opinion in regard to those questions, to which I have not been committed long since. If, then, I repeat sentiments which I have before declared, you will excuse me, as I do it in deference to your request.

LEWIS E. HARVIE TO R. M. T. HUNTER.

RICHMOND, [VA.], *October 21, 1857.*

MY DEAR HUNTER: Y[ou]rs of last week was duly received and I dare say that you have adopted the best course under the circumstances. I take for granted that you will demur to the right of the Enquirer to demand any reply to its arrogant assumption of authority. I would rather however rely upon any conclusion to which your own judgment would lead you, than upon the soundness of the opinions of either Leake or Chapman. Tho' both of them are at present (no doubt) your very good friends neither of them is particularly sound or trustworthy in my opinion. Your election is certain and

has been clearly so for some time and your reply even to a friend
will to some extent break the fall of Wise and be attributed by him
and some others to your fear of his power. As I said tho' it is probably the best course and could not well be avoided. The union of
the Enquirer and Examiner under Hughes is abandoned, and Hughes
I understand will wage no further war on you, but in due time will
advocate your reelection. This I learn from Irving. I was also
prepared to learn from him that you and Floyd had been brought
together by Crump, for when I was in Washington I saw Floyd and
his reception of me and his conversation and manner altogether was
exceptionally cordial, and I was satisfied that my opinion as to his
future course and policy was correct. He requires *your support* and
is willing to pay for it. He is not and never can be in your way and
will be useful as long as you can hold him, which will be as long as
you can be of use to him and no longer. *With this always before you,*
you can safely trust him. He does not forgive nor forget. And is
ever true—to himself. Hughes demanded the *control* of the Enquirer and would take it on no other terms. This was refused, all
of which was a corollary from Floyd's change of tactics. Don't
make any entangling alliances but receive all well wishes with open
arms. You see I write like your mentor and if you doubt the wisdom
of my counsel you will not distrust its sincerity. To be forewarned
is sometimes to be forearmed. I saw Finch, the mail Ag[en]t, who
has just returned from the North West and says that you will not
lose more than 2 or 3 votes in all the Northwest and from the Potomac
to Charlottesville. Pendleton told me yesterday that you would get
all in his district. A man named McDonough, said to him that you
might lose the Tazewell man and Finch said a man named Dunn from
Barbour would vote against you if you did not answer. From Norfolk to the mountains, on the South Side, you will lose no vote.
Will you come to the Fair? The whole state will be represented
here and there is no good reason why you should not come, if you
choose. You are a poor hand in cultivating personal intercourse
with the sovereigns and lose by your neglect of them. But I have
told you this so often without any amendment on your part, that I
fear you are incorrigible. You ought to desire to be loved as well
as admired by others besides your intimate friends and it would
strengthen them and you too.

LEWIS E. HARVIE TO R. M. T. HUNTER.

RICHMOND, [VA.], *October 21st, 1857.*

DEAR HUNTER: Since I mailed my letter of to-day to you, I fear that
the information that I derived from Irving is not to be relied on. I
have seen Loyd of the Examiner, who is utterly averse to its amalga-

mation with the Enquirer and is litigating with Hughes in order to prevent it. And he thinks that Hughes is determined on it, if he does not prevent him, which he thinks he can do. He will if he can. He called to see me and let me into many of the secrets of the Prison house. Intra nos. Irving can't be relied on after he takes twenty or thirty drinks and liquor has a wonderful effect on his imagination. I am disposed to think that nothing that he told me last night can be depended on. I write therefore to prevent you acting on anything that I got from him.

RICHARD K. CRALLÉ TO R. M. T. HUNTER.

"MEADOW BLUFF," GREENBRIER Co., VA., *October 24th, 1857.*

MY DEAR SIR: I met with Gen[era]l Chapman, Mr. Echols, and others of your friends on yesterday and had with the former a pretty full conversation; especially in reference to the course you ought to pursue in regard to the factitious issue raised by your opponents on the Kansas matter. Their design is very obvious, and needs no remark. The question is whether, on the score of *duty* or *policy* you ought to stand, or permit others to force you on your *voir dire.* I am constitutionally opposed to compliances with a vicious public sentiment at all times, and more especially when demanded by still more vicious Leaders, as they would be called. Under existing circumstances, however, I do not well see how you can avoid the expression of your opinions. The matter is one of public interest; and one which, as a Senator, you are, I think bound, when called upon, to answer,—be the motives of the interrogation what they may. As to the merits of the controversy I am ignorant, or at least, so slightly informed that I shall not venture an opinion. After the base calculating treason of 1850, I gave up all hopes that the Southern States could ever secure an acre of the public domain over which to extend their institution. Whenever such a question shall arise, there will always be found traitors enough to dispose of their rights and honor, for a consideration, as in the case of California. I never doubted no, not for a moment—that such would be the case in respect to Kansas. I *infer* that such is the fact, from what curiosity meets my eye in glancing over the newspapers; though I have read no article in connection with the subject. I know we have been hitherto *sold out* by our own Representatives,—and feel the fullest assurance that we will continue to be *sold out* to the end of the Chapter. Even if Texas should consent to carve out of her area, two or more States, they will only be admitted into the Union under Yankee Constitutions. I therefore, do not trouble myself with the miserable platitudes of the political jobbers who traffic in treason. *In the Union,* our Institution must stop where it is. We shall, however, get some secretaries of the

Treasury, of War &c &c in exchange for our *rights* and our *honor*, and these, perhaps, at the market value, or a pretty fair equivalent. Damaged goods cannot be expected to command a full price when exposed at auction.

But viewing the question in reference to yourself particularly, my opinion is that you ought not to give your enemies the advantages which your silence is expected to afford them. At the same time I would never compromit my dignity and self-respect so far as to respond directly to their malignant and impertinent inquiries. Chapman will write to you for your opinions on the subject. As a personal and political friend, you can give him a frank and dignified response, allowing him to use his discretion, as to publication. Be these views in accordance with those of the Administration or not, I do not think they can hurt you, as much as your silence might. The chief aim is to cut you and your friends off from the administration; and thus to bring the weight of its patronage to bear against you. The movement, I think, will fail. The question is one of the deepest interest to the country, the people have examined it with no little feeling, and Mr. Buchanan is not Gen[era]l Jackson. I have neither seen nor heard of any unfavorable demonstrations; tho' your opponents are active and indefatigable. I fear not the result, if the election be brought on at an early day in the Session, and such is the purpose of your friends. Delay might be attended with some danger, as Wise is a most adroit manipulator. I have no time to talk of general matters, and write this in compliance with a promise made yesterday to Chapman, and simply to express the opinion that you ought to place your views before the country, in the manner suggested, be they what they may.

I did not receive your favor of December last, until the *16th of May ensuing* and therefore did not reply to it, as the matters were by-gone. The Administration is undoubtedly losing ground in the State and *justly.*

P. S.—I suppose the rumored transfer of Yancey to the Supreme Court Bench, is to deprive you of all Cabinet connections.

I have a few moments at command, Floyd is your determined enemy. I am told he says publicly, that you "*must be defeated.*" Can you not get some *Whig* friend in the lower House, to move an inquiry into the sale of *Fort Snelling?* There are some *dirty facts* in the chapter, and I can (in profoundest confidence) refer you to *persons* and *papers.* He deserves to be exposed naked to the world. I may be mistaken, but, *entre nous,* I believe there might be facts elicited which might subject him to impeachment. This, however, is *strictly confidential.* He is a bad man, and tho' once on terms of the greatest intimacy, I have found sufficient reasons to break off all intercourse with him. My situation is, however, a delicate one; and to be of service, I must be utterly unknown in the matter. He is shrewd, wary, and adroit. Wise, who would use him *for the nonce*, has still his eye upon him. He will prove treacherous in *the end.* Mark the prediction: His object, for the present is the Vice Presidency, and he has no further interest in the fortunes of Wise, than to make him your opponent; and thus divide the state on the *Presidential* nomination, which will open a fair chance for himself as a candidate for the Vice Presidency. Is not Douglas playing a similar game? I fear so. But, as you know, I am cut off from all active participation in public affairs; and speak as from some hollow tree in the forest. I wish I had a better field, but the time is past for me. There is but one situation in the Country that I covet, the Secretaryship of the Senate, and this not for itself, but for exterior usefulness. I wish to be near a good Library, in order to complete satisfactorily to myself, the Memoirs of Mr. Calhoun and to contribute my mite to the cause of the State Rights Party. This, however, I cannot get, and I am reconciled to my lot. Mr. Buchanan, who once offered me all the favor I desired, and much more, is now become something more than a stranger. "*Honors*," says the old French proverb, "*make men forget names.*" I am content. I shall, however, have a letter from him shortly.

R. M. T. HUNTER TO SAMUEL T. WALKER, JOHN T. HARRIS, JOHN H. WARTMANN, M. H. HARRIS, E. A. SHANDS.[1]

LLOYDS, ESSEX CO., VA., *October 28, 1857.*

GENTLEMEN: I have received your letter, enclosing me the resolutions adopted by a Democratic meeting in Rockingham, on the 19th October, with a request that I would respond to them. The subject matter of these resolutions is so fully covered by my letter of the 16th of this month, to the Hon. S. F. Leake, which was not published at the time of your meeting, that any other answer, on my part, is, perhaps, unnecessary. But as there seems to be a difference of opinion between us with regard to your fifth resolution, a farther explanation may be proper. If I understand your resolutions, we agree in the principle that the people of Kansas alone have the right to form their State institutions according to their own pleasure, provided they be republican in their character. I extend too, the limitation upon the power of Congress, in regard to a State applying for admission even farther than you do; for I maintain that upon this issue it can raise no question in regard to the Constitution, should it be republican in its character, if the people of the new State, acting through their Convention, have made and adopted it in the manner prescribed by these, their authorized representatives. But from

---

[1] Copied from the Richmond Examiner of Nov. 10, 1857.

your fifth resolution I dissent entirely. That the people of Kansas have the same rights with the people of any other State in this Union with regard to the formation of their State Constitution, we must all admit; that they can delegate to a Convention, called for this purpose, the same powers which may be delegated by the people of any other State, is also clear. That they might limit the power conferred on such a Convention by allowing them only to form a Constitution to be submitted to the people afterwards, for ratification or rejection, or that they might elect a Convention with a general authority over the subject, can hardly be denied. It is for the people of the territory, about to become a State, to say in which of these ways they will constitute the Convention. Such, I understand to be the intent and purport of your third resolution, in which, with that understanding, I cordially concur. If, then, the people of Kansas have these rights, the question arises as to what they intended by electing a Convention with general powers, and without any limitation imposed by themselves.

The practice of the States and the reason of the case both prove that it is to be treated as a general delegation of their sovereignty, under which the Convention may submit the Constitution or not, for a popular vote, according to its own views of propriety. If the people of Kansas, acting as an inchoate State, imposed no limitation on the trust, it is not for any third party, outside the Territory, to undertake to affix it. If they can in one case they might in all, and Congress, as it seems to me, might exercise the very power which you so properly deny to it, in your fourth resolution. As has been well said by a distinguished statesman of Pennsylvania, "Either this Convention is clothed with sovereign power, or it is a nullity." If it be a legitimate Convention, it is the people who speak through it; and it is for them to say what action is to be final in regard to the Constitution which it forms. To say otherwise, in my opinion, is to unite the power of the people of Kansas, whose plenary jurisdiction over this subject we all admit. But this fifth resolution does not stop with requiring the application of Kansas for admission as a State to be rejected, because the Convention did not submit the Constitution to the people, it goes much farther, and claims for Congress the power of prescribing who are to exercise the right of suffrage, when the people pass upon the question of ratifying their own State Constitution. Here it is in totidem verbis:

"Resolved, That Kansas, in forming her Constitution, ought to submit the same to the bona fide inhabitants thereof, for adoption or rejection, and the failure to do so is in violation of the spirit and letter of the act creating her Territorial Government, and ought to be returned by Congress to the residents of Kansas for endorsement."

Congress thus undertakes to say, not only that the Constitution shall be submitted for a further vote, but to whom. If then, the Convention of Kansas should submit its Constitution to a popular vote, but establish a qualification for the right of suffrage different from that which you say Congress must require, the State must be rejected, and the Constitution, although thus ratified, is to be returned to the " residents of Kansas for endorsement."

The most significant act of sovereign power is, perhaps, the regulation of the right of suffrage, and the power over this subject must be exclusive, wherever it resides. If Congress possesses it, then the people of the inchoate State cannot have it; and if the people of the new State cannot say who are to pass upon its own Constitution, then its equality with the other States is disparaged and destroyed. But this is not all; if its right to equal powers and privileges with the other States be denied, and if Congress can regulate the highest of its political rights, I mean that of suffrage, what is to prevent it from regulating all the other political rights and relations of its people, slavery included? If Congress may exercise this right of sovereignty over a people in the very act of forming its State Constitution, what is to be the limit to its power? When we have admitted so much, by what arguments, so far as constitutional power is concerned, can we resist an attempt to reimpose the Missouri restriction over these Territories? A restriction which, it must be remembered, goes much farther than the Wilmot Proviso; for the latter only applies to the people in a Territorial condition, whilst the other is extended over them when they are acting as the people of a State. And what sort of suffrage is Congress here required to prescribe for the good people of Kansas? It is to be returned " to the residents of Kansas for endorsement." Who are the " residents of Kansas?" May not aliens, Indians and negroes be included in that denomination? How, too, can this resolution be consistent with the third, which preceded it in the series? If Congress may prescribe the right of suffrage for a people acting in their highest capacity of sovereignty, that of forming a State Constitution, and say who shall pass upon it, how can " we recognize the right of the people of a Territory, in forming a Constitution for admission into the Union, to establish such local policy as to them may seem right and proper?" Surely, we do not confound the power of Congress to prescribe the right of suffrage for a free people acting in a territorial capacity, with the power of Congress to prescribe that right for those who are acting as the people of a State in the formation of a Constitution.

Congress can make the organic act for the people of a Territory, but it has no such power in regard to the people of a new, or inchoate State. It may prescribe the qualifications of the electors of the

Territorial Legislature, which calls the convention to form a State Constitution; but when that convention is assembled, having been legally elected and constituted, it must be treated either as the representative of the sovereignty of the people, so far as the formation and adoption of a Constitution is concerned, unless the people themselves have prescribed otherwise in the act creating it, or it must be treated as a nullity. We must take the one horn or the other of this dilemma, as it seems to me.

It may be said that no such conclusions are intended as those which I have drawn from the fifth resolution. I have no idea that there was any such design, but in my opinion these inferences are to be deduced from it, not only fairly, but necessarily. That it was the opinion of your meeting that the people of Kansas ought themselves to do the things recommended in that resolution, I do not doubt; but there is a wide difference between what the people of a State, new or old, should do, and what Congress can constrain them to do. The people of Virginia, doubtless, ought to do many things which Congress cannot force them to do. But even if the fifth resolution had been confined to a recommendation to Congress to reject the application of the State for admission on the ground that the Convention had not submitted the Constitution for ratification to the people, the matter would not have been much helped; for, after all, the two resolutions would have been nearly identical in principle.

Suppose that the people of Kansas had elected a Convention with the authority expressly delegated to them to form and adopt a Constitution; suppose, farther, that Congress, in the spirit of these resolutions, had rejected the application for admission, and sent back the Constitution, because it had not been ratified by a final vote of the people. Might not the people of Kansas well say, " You have rejected our Constitution because it was not ratified, as you affirm, by the people; now, as you claim to be the judges in this matter, you must designate whom you mean by the people, whose ratification by a farther vote, is to be the condition of our admission?" But if Congress undertook to prescribe who should vote it would claim this very power of regulating the right of suffrage for the people of a new State, of which I have been speaking, as it seems to me, all the consequences would flow from that assumption of power which I have already depicted. If we permit Congress to control the Convention in the exercise of its delegated powers in one respect, it will be hard to resist its inference in another. It is far safer to leave the whole matter, as your third resolution seems to design, to the people of the new or inchoate State themselves, for otherwise we shall be embarrassed by difficulties at every step that we take. If we begin to make such retrograde movements as these, must we not prepare our minds to lose all that has been gained for the Constitution and the South by the Kansas-Nebraska act?

I have given you my opinions in this letter and that addressed to the Hon. Shelton F. Leake, upon the subject of your resolutions, because they were asked, and I express myself freely but with great respect for those who may differ from me. But it seems to be the sentiment of the Democratic party of the State, if I may judge by the general tone of its press, that they ought not to divide upon these recent Kansas issues, as they probably will be temporary, and it is uncertain whether they will ever become practical in their character. In this, as it appears to me, they were wise. When the Democratic party established the principle of the Kansas-Nebraska act, and obtained common ground upon which all its members might stand in regard to a disturbing question, it overcame the greatest difficulty. Its success in this respect encourages the hope that when the time for action arises, and its representatives get together, they will be able to reconcile satisfactorily any differences which may have arisen in regard to the application of their principles. I say this for the good of the party and the country, but not for myself. So far as I am personally concerned, I shun none of the responsibility which attaches to me individually for the opinions which I have expressed.

In this connection, too, I must return to you and those whom you represent, my thanks for so much of good will and confidence as you express in the resolutions which relate to myself personally. To win fairly and justly the trust and confidence of the people of Virginia, has been the highest object of my political aspirations. There is none other which I place in competition with it. But it is their trust and confidence, and not the office, that I value. If I have not the first, I do not desire the latter. Office, unless it is bestowed in that spirit, can have no attractions for me. Entertaining these sentiments, I have been reluctant to appear before the public in any communication which might wear the air of solicitation, or place me in the apparent position of advocating my own claims and interests. I hold no such position—I prefer no claims—I make no solicitations. If my past course has failed to sow the seeds of confidence in the public mind of Virginia, it is my misfortune, perhaps my fault. Nor are the people to be blamed for the fact, or for exercising their undoubted right and duty in bestowing their offices where they place their trust. Assuredly, they will not be disturbed by me, either with solicitations before their decision is made, or by complaints to be uttered afterwards, because of the manner in which they may have exercised their powers, according to their own sense of duty. Neither do I purpose to trouble them farther by any public communication in regard to my sentiments and opinions, as I have answered as fully as I am capable of doing, upon the various subjects of inquiry. I will not conclude, however, without venturing the prediction that, if any serious attempt should be made in Congress to reject the application of Kansas for admission as a State into the Union, because the Convention did not submit the Constitution for a further ratification by the people, it will only occur in the event of the adoption of a pro-slavery organic law.

Is Virgina, then, prepared to reject the application of a sister slave State to be received into the Union, merely because its Convention has exercised its undoubted powers in the same manner with many other States, which have acted similarly, without prejudice to their claims for admission into the Confederacy? I do not believe it for a moment, and I am sure that in such a contingency, the gallant Democracy of the time—honored Tenth Legion, which has never yet hung. fire, nor asked even for time to " peck the flint and try it again," will be amongst the first to cry out, " Never! no, never ! "

A. D. BANKS TO R. M. T. HUNTER.

RICHMOND, [VA.], *October 31st, 1857.*

MY DEAR SIR: Within the past ten days, I have gathered some information which it is important for you to know. While in Washington I had occasion to meet with the President and several of his cabinet. Buchanan is evidently dissatisfied with your letter, and is imprudent enough to express himself. Brown and Cobb I think really want your election. The former is cordially your friend and desires me to say so to you. Floyd I did not see, but hear that he is non committal. At the Fair I had conversations with leading men from all parts of the State. Never have I seen such an exhibition of universal support and approbation. You ought to have been here. It would have done every heart good to have seen the results of the machinations of your enemies. I saw at least twenty members of the Legislature all for you, men even from whom I did not expect a committal, such as Lee of Orange and others. If there ever was any doubt of your early election (and there never has been) it is all dispelled now. The opposition is dead. You are stronger by two hundred per cent in the State than you ever were. The course of the Enquirer has done more to build you up in the confidence and affections of the people than all your friends together. The opposition will attempt to postpone the election, but it will not avail them. You will be elected the first week of the session. I saw Caperton, Renold, Paxton, Jones and others, they say everything is right and that you were never stronger with their people, never 1/3 as strong.

My matters continue changing. When will you be in Washington.

JOHN SEDDON TO M. R. H. GARNETT.

FREDERICKSBURG, [VA.], *November 4, 1857.*

DEAR MUSCOE: Your kind letter of 2d Inst is just received. After reading and taking a copy of the " Veiled Prophet," envelope and all was consigned to the fire. Your wishes had in part been anticipated. When in Richmond it was decided by Mr. Hunter's friends that the " mark " must be taken from the incognito editor of the Enquirer and Charles Irvin wrote an article which appeared in the Whig of Oct[ober] 31st. Pryor could not publish it because he had incautiously, but from generous feelings, promised secrecy when engaged in his first difficulty with young Wise. All of our friends thought that he could not publish without signing his name to it. As yet the Enquirer has not noticed this article. To-day I headed Irvin's article with a few *borrowed* sentences and it will appear in the Recorder of next Saturday. This I think will bring him out. I know positively that O. J. Wise is the incognito, he acts as amanuensis to his father, and their joint labor is sometimes relieved by the man Friday—Geo. W. Munford.

Many of Mr. Hunter's friends met at the Fair. They are exultant in his assured prospect of reelection. There is not a doubt of it and it will be done quickly as in J. M. Mason's case two winters ago. Many of Wise's fast friends condemned the course of the Enquirer as heartily as do we. Geo. Booker, Dr. Simpkins, William Taliaferro and his brother Warner &c were among the denunciators. I did not see or hear of anyone who expressed an opinion to the contrary. All were delighted with Mr. Hunter's letter, the occasion of it and its contents alike gave pleasure. We have resolved to carry the war into Africa to defeat the Enquirer for public printing. If strong enough we want to unite a Western man with Pryor and elect him. If not we will split the enemy by electing the Examiner. On this subject we will be perfectly mum until after [the] Senatorial election and then be governed by our strength to avenge.

Old Crutch [1] told me to day that Wise was working to defeat his election to the Speakership. His weapons, as usual, are concealed. The special inuendo is that Old Crutch is partial in the appointment of committees especially the committee on Internal Improvement. This discloses Wise's intention to War upon all who are opposed to him.

Write soon and excuse the haste of this letter.

---

[1] Oscar M. Crutchfield, Speaker of the House of Delegates of the General Assembly of Virginia, 1852-1859.

R. M. T. HUNTER TO JAMES ALEXANDER.

(Copy.)

(Private.)

LLOYDS, ESSEX CO., [VA.], *November 9, 1857.*

MY DEAR SIR: I send you by the first mail since I received your letter the copy of Mr. Leake's letter as you request. I suppose he wishes to publish the letter and not the postscript. That however is for himself to decide and for that reason you had better show him the copy before you publish it. All that I wish is that it should appear to be published at Mr. Leake's instance and not at mine. It is his letter which he has a right to publish or not as he chooses. Personally it is a matter of indifference to me whether it be published or not. I only desire that it should not even seem to be published at my request. I must not conclude without returning you my thanks for the efficient support you have given me in your paper.

R. M. T. HUNTER TO S. F. LEAKE.

(Private.)

LLOYDS, ESSEX CO., [VA.], *November 9, 1857.*

MY DEAR SIR: Our friend Alexander has written me for a copy of your letter which I have sent as he said it was your wish that I should do so. I have written him not to publish it until he has shown you the copy, as I presume it is the letter and not the post-script which you wish published. That however must be as you wish. I have no wish on the subject except that it should appear in the paper to be published by you and not by me. This is necessary to save me from the imputation of being forced into publishing your letter by the Enquirer. I certainly should never have asked you to publish it. Not that I have any care about the matter. It can do no harm to any one to publish it unless it should be thought that I had requested you to do it.

I received a letter from Clarksburg this evening informing me that mine to you was entirely satisfactory in N[orth]Western V[irgini]a, "the Enquirer" to the contrary notwithstanding.

D. H. WOOD TO R. M. T. HUNTER.

WASHINGTON, D. C., *November 11, 1857.*

MY DEAR SIR: I have thought it would be agreeable to hear the opinions of your friends respecting your letters, and your prospects of re-election to the Senate.

On the first head, many of your most discreet friends think as you had preserved so long a dignified silence *under* the lashings of the " Enquirer," that it would have been best to have *persevered* in this respect; and have said to your true friends in reply to their queries the substance of your last paragraphs to the Rockingham constituents.

But, the matter is done, and I may say without dissimulation, " *Well done*," to quote King George's reply to Dr. Johnson, especially the *last* letter. The first letter did not measure up to your accustomed felicity of style; but the last, has even evoked the praise of the *National " Intelligencer."* Your positions are impregnable, and will be sustained by the mass of the democracy of our State. You will pardon my suggestion, I hope, when I venture to say, that your *omission* in both letters to refer to the very manly and patriotic reply of President Buchanan to the Connecticut Clergymen, has been construed into a cold admiration on your part of its contents, or of your want of personal or political allegiance to his administration. I say the mere *absence* of approval has implied a dissent.

Gov. Toucey [1] says that *he* has no doubt of your faithfulness to prinicples, party, or the Administration; and that he supposed you would not be induced by mere newspaper squibs to define your position, but wait until a proper opportunity offered on the floor of the Senate. As one of the humblest of your friends *I* had hoped this would have been your course. But of course you knew best.

There is a rumor that because of the " Enquirer's " *faux paux* in respect to the Senatorship, that Gov. Wise has avowed his intention, recently, not under any circumstances to allow his name to come into competition with yours; also, that the friends of that newspaper, seeing there is no probability of defeating you, and that a further opposition may jeopard the interests of the paper, will soon cease its childish hectorings, and be reconciled to your success under the plea of endangering democratic supremacy in the State if further war shall be waged! *What a pity!!*

Dr. Kidwell, and others assure me that there is now not a shadow of doubt as to your re-election. All my correspondence looks to this result.

So *mote it be!*

Rumor assigns Mr. Orr is most prominent for the Speakership. Forney's paper thinks he will have no serious opposition. But I learn that his own colleagues will not support him. He is looked upon as the Administration candidate, *which may defeat him.* If the Southern Rights men will go into Caucus they can control its nominee, and give it to Bocock, or any other as popular a member.

---

[1] Isaac Toucey, Representative in Congress from Connecticut, 1835–1839 ; governor of Connecticut, 1846–1847 ; Attorney General of the United States, 1848–1849 ; Senator in Congress, 1852–1857 ; Secretary of the Navy. 1857–1861.

But the fear is that the S[tate] R[ights] members will not be here promptly, nor go in a body to the Caucus.

If the Virginia delegation presents one of her members for Speakership, the strong presumption is in favor of success. Bocock, Letcher, and Hopkins are spoken of in this connection. The first can command the united S[tate] R[ights] strength and is besides very popular personally. Have you heard any expression of opinion from Mr. Garnett, or any of the Members?

SIDNEY WEBSTER TO R. M. T. HUNTER.

BOSTON, MASS., *November 11, 1857.*

MY DEAR SIR: I venture to write to you of the enclosed article in relation to yourself. It is cut from the Boston Courier, a paper formerly Whig in its politics, then a Webster paper, so called, subsequently betrayed into wrong paths by public sentiment in this state upon the Nebraska-Kansas Bill, but now under new editors conservative in tone and supporting the democratic party in the issues between it and the republican organization.

Its present editors, Mr. Hillard and Mr. Lamb, formerly Whigs, are accomplished men, able writers, and excellent lawyers. Mr. George S. Hillard, is one of the worthiest men in the state, and the person to whom Gen[era]l Cushing alludes in his Faniuel Hall speech. Mr. H[illard] informs me that he sent to you a copy of the paper although he had not the pleasure of your personal acquaintance.

I am sure that you will appreciate the purpose of this hasty note and pardon the intrusion.

General Pierce is with me in this city on his way to Madison with Mrs. Pierce.

WILLIAM FRANCIS McLEAN TO R. M. T. HUNTER.

ALEXANDRIA, VA., *November 18, 1857.*

DEAR SIR: According to promise, I send you my prospectus. The erasure made in the printed form, was done at the suggestion of the President, James Buchanan, for which I am much obliged, for I believe it will have the effect of giving the journal a more national character and strength amongst all parties, at the same time, it shall not make me forget the duty that I owe Virginia the south and yourself; for if there is any one object above another, that I have a preference for, it is your advancement to the highest political fame known to our Republic.

This may have the sound of sophistry, not so, for you have given me evidences of your friendship in an unmistakable form; and for which I only hope that I may have an opportunity of convincing you, that it has been properly appreciated by me.

I have never asked any other person to intercede for me, in obtaining what I asked of you, (an office) and I do not intend to ask others, but let it remain until I see you in person. Were I to attempt to detail all the questions that has been asked about the probable prospect of your *election* and the sources from whence they came, it would make this note too tedious. But I will tell you what I said to Gov. Brown, when he asked me, what was your prospects for selection; my answer was this; that the combined opposition in Virginia backed up by the administration could not possibly defeat his (your) election. The next interview I had with him he stated to me, that he regretted to see the course the Richmond Enquirer was taking for it was only calculated to cause a division in the ranks of the party. I said nothing but thought a most material change had come over him. I stated in a previous note that I discontinued the publication of the Southern Statesman. It was, because Mr. Baker P. Lee, the late acting editor of the Richmond Enquirer sold me the old News office in Norfolk, and from all the information obtained from him the office was not in debt, or what was due, they were of a personal character and he would settle them. He no sooner found that I was and intended to be your friend in the Senatorial Election, than he caused a levy to be made upon all the material, not only what I had bought of him, but all the new material that I had carried there, for the payment of nearly one years house rent due by the said Baker P. Lee, while I was absent in the upper part of Virginia on a visit to my sick wife. The distraint was made and the things sold the very day I arrived home, at least a sufficient quantity to satisfy the demand about $1000 worth sold to pay $300. So finding myself placed in such a dilemma, the paper not paying, and your election reduced almost to a certainty in my opinion, I concluded to incur no more expenses and cease opperations in that quarter. I publically denounced Mr. Baker P Lee and his attorney in a note sent them for the advantage taken in my absence but without effect, they stating I could get redress through the court.

I say to you now what I have said about the columns of the Statesman, you can command them. The gentleman whose name is appended to the prospectus will have no controll over the columns unless with my consent and approval.

CHARLES MASON TO R. M. T. HUNTER.

ALTO, [VA.], *November 18, 1857.*

MY DEAR SIR: I know the opinions of an humble individual, like myself, are of no moment in matters of public concernment; but in

view of our former relations, I am constrained by a feeling of gratification, experienced in perusing your two letters, to congratulate
you on their happy conception, and the influence their manly and
independent tone must exert on all honorable men, and it is to be hoped
the world is not made up altogether with ingrates. At first I thought
you could not, well, break the dignified silence you had properly
assumed without detrement, but under the circumstances, I do not
see how you could have avoided a reply, and how you could have said
more or less, or said it better. The only doubt in your position is,
at what point or period of adolescence (if I may use the term) does
sovereignty attach to the new state?

What a "trump" Leake is! You will remember, in the early
part of this controversy how much importance, I attached to his
friendship. I saw him on my visit to Albemarle in Sept[ember]
and was pleased to find how warmly he had espoused your cause. He
is mistaken in the paternity of the Rockingham resolutions. They
are unquestionably the eminations of Smith's brain, and develop
completely all the combinations of the hellish plot against you.
Deneale is Smiths first cousin, and I know this is not the first time
he has attempted to use him for his purposes. He is made of such
suple stuff that I would not now, even, dispair by proper management, of converting him to our side.

You should counsel some of your friends to prudence, whose own
zeal has, heretofore worked no good; but I do not think you ought
any longer to restrain them from letting loose, the "dogs of war"
upon the *chief* of sinners.

R. M. T. HUNTER TO SHELTON F. LEAKE.

[WASHINGTON, D. C., 1857?].

MY DEAR SIR: I received your letter yesterday evening just as I
was going out to dinner so that I could not attend to it then. To day
is Sunday and the libraries are closed which prevents me from
searching out the speech which you desire to see. On tomorrow
however I will find it and do myself the pleasure to send it to you.

As you have complimented me so far as to express a respect for
my thoughts upon this subject I will venture so far as to submit them
in a somewhat different form for consideration. The power to acquire
Territory and to govern it has been derived from three different
sources, the War, and the treaty making powers and the right to
admit New States into the Union have each been referred to for the
origin of the jurisdiction of Congress over the Territories. I have
always been inclined to refer to it to the last which I think was
the view generally taken in the debate on the K[ansas]-Nebraska
bill. The implication from this last is more immediate and less re-

mote than it would be from the other sources. It is too a more necessary implication from the first than the last, you may make treaties and carry on war without making *premanent additions* of Territory when you have implied the right to acquire territory from this source you have to resort to another implication for the power to govern which involves an implication upon an implication. Not so with the power to admit new states into the Union. There you have the direct grant of the power to acquire Territory and the implication is necessary that Congress may and must govern it whilst its society is maturing and progressing to the condition which fits it for a state. That this power to admit new states into the Union looked directly to Territory then without the pale of the Confederacy is proved by the history of the Convention which sought to keep open a way for the admission of Canada.

It is not to be supposed that any government was ever formed without some view towards the acquisition of Territory, and if such view was entertained it is no where so directly expressed as in this entire section. If this power of altering the boundaries of old states and of fusing or dividing them with their assent, was given for the purpose of forming or erecting new states all the objection to it might arise which could be urged against the right to admit a new state formed out of Territory at that time foreign. If state necessities justified the one they might also the other and if in the last case it should be objected that the equilibrium of power might be disturbed by such means then the same powers ought to have forbidden the exercise of such a right in the first case. But be this as it may from whatever source the power is derived it is clear that it must be exercised under the limitations and restrictions imposed by the constitution upon the action of Congress. Congress is a trustee created and called into being by the constitution of the United States for certain purposes and trusts declared in that instrument. It is the creation of that deed. There are certain things which it cannot do because it is directly prohibited from doing them and there are certain just ends and purposes which constitute the very design of its being. By its foreign action it must preserve the peace and existence of the states by its internal operation it must secure their equal enjoyment of all the benefits of Federal legislation. Its legislation was designed to operate equally upon the states and individuals. Everywhere in the constitution we find Congress fixed around by prohibitions to do certain things which might operate unequally upon the states or commanded to act upon considerations which more fully look to equal justice to all. I will not enlarge upon this here as I have elaborated this in the speech upon the Kansas question which I sent to you. But that the general purposes and end of the makers of this Federal Government were such as I have described I think there can be no doubt.

This right then to govern the Territories must be so exercised that on the one hand Congress shall do none of these things which it is prohibited from doing, as enforcing a title of nobility for instance, whilst on the other its action must conform to the general efforts of the Trusts for which it was created. That its powers in the Territories are limited by the constitution has in effect been decided by Judge Marshall in regard to the District of Columbia. This is a case with which you are doubtless familiar. I do not now remember its style but can find it if necessary. If however it had never been so decided, it is so clear that I am surprised at the necessity for arguing it. That Congress may exercise some powers in the Territories that it cannot in the states I admit but not for the reason that the constitution does not limit it in both cases. The reason is to be found in the different nature of the cases. When there is a dispute between the General and the State government in regard to a power which might be exercised by either then if it be an implied power the implication must be short by which the former can claim it. Because in such cases the constitution raises the presumption in favor of the states by declaring that all powers not delegated to the U[nited] S[tates] by the constitution nor prohibited by it to the states are reserved to the states respectively or to the people.

But when the power is one which must be exercised by the Gen[era]l Gov[ernmen]t, if exercised at all, it may be implied on a more liberal measure or rather it may become necessary because the citizen could not otherwise have the protection of his government. Thus the power to regulate Commerce with Foreign nations and amongst the several states is given in the same terms and yet under this power by a necessary implication the Gen[era]l Gov[ernmen]t exercises a jurisdiction over the persons and property of its citizens above which it could not assume within the states. If the Gen[era]l Gov[ernmen]t did not exercise this power alone the states could not do it and thus a power necessary for the protection of the citizen in the pursuits of freer commerce would be in abeyance if it were not used by the Gov[ernmen]t which alone has jurisdiction over his affairs abroad. Within the states however no such necessity exists as there is another jurisdiction there adequate to his relief. So in the government of the Territories Congress takes jurisdiction over subjects which it would not touch within the states. Not because it governs in the Territories without the constitution but because powers necessary & proper to be implied in the one case are not so in the other. But it could not act in the Territories or anywhere in opposition to the great ends of the constitution or in defiance of its express prohibitions. It could not establish a religion in the Territories because it is expressly prohibited to do so.

Nor could it establish a lower rate of duties upon imports in the Territories than it exacted within the states because such a law would disturb the equality of citizens and of states which is the fundamental condition of the Union. "Vessels bound to or from one state shall not be obliged to enter clear or pay duties in another." This applies to the states alone, and yet every one feels that Congress could not require it to be done in the Territories either, because it would operate unequally upon the states and thus be contrary to the just objects of the constitution. So too Congress would allow greater privilege within the Territories to the citizens of Massachusetts than to those of Tennessee, or deny to the citizens of the several states the privileges granted to the inhabitants of the Territories.

It could not do these things because they are contrary to the general spirit and purpose of the constitution which so completely seeks equality amongst the states and the citizens of these states. And yet if Congress governs in the Territories without the Constitution it might do all or any of these things. I might multiply instances in which it would shock common sense to suppose the exercise of power within the Territories which were against the spirit of the constitution, but to do so would be unnecessary. The supreme court has declared that the "United States" is a term which embraces territories as well as states and that the constitution of the United States covers all. If this course of reasoning be right then the United States cannot use and govern these Territories for the good of a part and not of the whole of the citizens and the states. It cannot say that the free states may settle and colonize vacant territory the common property of all whilst the slave holding states are to be debarred from the same privilege. The great value of vacant Territory to states consists in the outlet which it affords to their surplus population and the means which it gives for promoting their growth and increasing their power.

These considerations far transcend in importance those which may be implied [?] with property in the land and yet none would pretend that the money arising from the sale of these lands might be given to the Free States alone without regard to the others. And why? Because this would be to deal unequally with the States of the Union. And yet in the distribution of advantages and benefits of a far higher nature it is gravely asserted that such a discrimination may be made. It will not do to say that the prohibition of slavery within its boundary does not prevent the white citizen, who holds slaves, from emigrating to a Territory. We all know that it does because it involves the breaking of what, in some sense, may be called family ties. Lot parted with Abraham to follow his herdsmen. But be this as it may as to the citizen, the State itself has the deepest interest in keeping open an outlet for all its population, black and white, and, further, it is a matter of deep concern to it to preserve all the means for promoting the growth of its political powers which are enjoyed by the other States of the Union. To deny to the slave-holding States equal rights in these respects is to disturb the equality of the States in a most vital point. This is to say that the most valuable of the advantages which flow from Territorial acquisition are to be confined exclusively to ourselves and to be denied to another. Let us see how how such an exclusion would operate on the equality of the citizen. On the high seas, where the jurisdiction of the United States is exclusive, an undeniable obligation rests upon the United States to protect the citizens of all the States in their property and rights. Nor can Congress discriminate between citizens and States in this regard. Whatever is property in any one of the States must be so considered under this jurisdiction which is common to all. The right of the United States to the enjoyment of the high seas is a right which belongs equally to all of the States and the right to transport his property upon those seas is the equal right of the citizens of all the States.

To discriminate between the citizens and the property of the several States in regard to these rights would be a plain violation of that equality which the Constitution ordains. Congress could not, therefore, destroy the property of the master in the slave upon the high seas because its jurisdiction was exclusive there unless it acted upon the assumption that there could be no property in slaves even in the States themselves. To do the one it must affirm the other. To argue such a question is unnecessary here. This right is acknowledged in too many ways by the Constitution and the laws to be questioned here. If, then, it would be a violation of the equal rights of the citizen which have been secured by the Constitution of the United States to destroy his property in the high seas because the jurisdiction of the Gen[era]l Gov[ernmen]t was exclusive, then may not the same be affirmed of any attempts to destroy his property in the common territories of the United States because the jurisdiction of Congress is exclusive there? These high seas are the common property of man, the General Gov[ernmen]t is the trustee to secure the enjoyment of that right to its States and its citizens and the Constitution requires it to deal equally by all. The territory of the United States are the common property of its States and its citizens and the Gen[era]l Gov[ernmen]t is the trustee for all. Does not the Constitution assume in this case also that it should deal alike with all? It is admitted by all that Congress could not give to some of the States a greater proportionate share of the pecuniary or commercial advantages to be derived from the Territories which are the common property of all. Must not the same principle be applied to the political advantages to be derived by the several States from such common possessions? The last are of a far more transcendent importance than the first.

HOWELL COBB TO R. M. T. HUNTER.

(*Private.*)

WASHINGTON, [D. C.], *July 26, 1858.*

MY DEAR SIR: I had already spoken to Governor Toucey in behalf of your friend. He did not say what he would do, but I let him know your great desire on the subject. I will repeat to him what you now say. We have not yet received full returns from the customs for the last fiscal year, but I have made an estimate for the few posts not heard from. I give you the general result.

From Customs	$41, 800, 725
" Public Lands	3, 461, 734
" Miscellaneous	1, 243, 445
	46, 505, 904

The gross amount is a little over $46,000,000. The falling off is from public lands. The receipts from customs for the present fiscal year have been very encouraging. From New York the accounts are quite favorable. Last week averaged $140,000 per day. A letter from Mr. Schell this morning says as the opinion of well informed merchants " the business will be good though not large and that the improvement already shown will continue." With these indications " I feel confident that we shall fully realize if not exceed the calculations in your speech on the loan bill." I hope to be able to get through the first six months of the year with the ten millions of the loan already advertised for. If I can do this, I feel certain that there will be no further call for loans. To do this, we must make up in customs for the *great* falling off from public lands. From the 1st of this month to the 24th inclusive as far as heard from, our receipts from customs amount to $3,203,524. The receipts of the whole month from all the posts will probably reach $4,500,000. I give you these items as a basis for any calculation you may have the time and inclination to make. If we can keep clear of deficiences I feel confident that we will not be disappointed in our expectations. I am struggling hard for such a result, but have my fears of the P[ost] O[ffice] and War Departments. The estimates will be brought below $64,000,000, *unless* this last mentioned cause should prevent it.

The political news from the north is favorable. The greatest trouble will be in Illinois produced by Douglass' course, and in Pennsylvania on account of the tariff. The slavery excitement appears to be over. The result of the vote in Kansas cannot seriously effect the counts. I regard that vote as very doubtful. Denver when here so considered it. He tells me, that there is no excitement in the territory on the slavery question, but that the decision will turn upon other points, such as their inability to support the State Government &c &c. As evidence of this fact Denver says, the strongest slavery and anti slavery men are for the admission and vice versa.

Pardon this hasty note, but I thought it might be interesting to you to know all that we know here about this matter.

P. S. Leake's brother will go into office on the first of next month. I have so notified him.

JOHN L. DAWSON TO R. M. T. HUNTER.

BROWNSVILLE, [PA.], *August 17th, 1858.*

DEAR HUNTER: Gov[erno]r Bright and myself made a contract with Moore and Robbins of Superior for the making of a road to Medary on the Mississippi and to Mille Lace. The aggregate distance is about 71 miles and the price agreed to be paid is $300 per mile. The contract is conditioned that a majority of the original share-holders approve the same and sign the enclosed paper. Gov[ernor] Bright has obtained the signatures of Corcoran, Wallridge, Forney and Cass and has gone to St. Paul to see Rice and others in that direction. If you approve the arrangement please sign the enclosed paper and return the same to me without delay. Robbins one of the contractors came down with us and is now awaiting our action. I think the arrangement a good one. Superior wants relief, and these roads will do much. The town is dull and lots no sale at present. The point is a great one but has been prejudiced by the legislation of Congress.

I will send you the contract or a copy of it as soon as Breckenridge returns it to me. I enclosed it to him together with the paper for his signature.

WILLIAM M. BURWELL TO R. M. T. HUNTER.

LIBERTY, VIRGINIA, *August 22, 1858.*

MY DEAR SIR: You will I hope excuse an invasion of your quiet so far as to offer some suggestions upon the present state of party and sectional politics, especially when I promise that my letter will need no reply.

I think your conference bill has settled the Kansas question for two reasons;

1. The land holders in Kansas are unwilling to furnish any longer the lists upon which the sectional battles are to be decided.

2. The Coalitionists cannot revive the slavery dispute without destroying all chance of Union with the Americans of the North.

It may be added, that if the right of Kansas to adopt a constitution without an enabling act should come in question, it will not involve the subject of slavery except incidentally.

But if the Freebooters can effect a coalition upon the sole basis of dividing the prey, the prospects of the Democratic party for continued rule are gloomy.

In this state of things I think some new issue indispensable, but before stating what I think that issue should be, I will say that [there] are two preliminaries to the next Presidential campaign which I think important.

The first is that the Democratic candidate should be a southern man. If it has come to this: that no democrat can be elected unless he be a northern man, and if the power of the opposition lies in the north, it must follow, that we are to have none but northern Presidents. This sectionalises the Confederacy.

The second suggestion upon this point is that the Democratic party should make its own reforms. This government is extravagant and corrupt. Its expenditures will render necessary an established protective tariff, or a national debt, perhaps both. Neither are Democratic. Let then the Democratic members of Congress at the next session acknowledge the wasteful tendencies of the government and endeavor to restrain them. The people then will have no motive to take the Government out of the hands of one set of reformers to place it in the hands of another.

But a new issue is needed to counteract the clamor now raised against the Administration.

What *think you of the acquisition of all Mexico?* As I do not belong to the school of ethics which believes any political advantage will atone for a moral wrong I will endeavor to show that this measure is eminently right and judicious. And this not only in a national but in a sectional view.

I know your apprehension of expansion. You look upon it as a necessary evil. But " out of this nettle danger, we (must) pluck the flower safety."

You apprehend danger from the embodiment of States having a mongrel population into this Confederacy. The people of Mexico are divided by the Statisticians into 3/4th natives, industrious and peaceful, 1/5 Mongrel, and 1/7 White. If the States of the Mexican Republic shall be admitted into our union it would become the duty of the Federal government to suppress insurrections, repel invation, and guarantee a Republican government to each of the States admitted. *This* would protect the native race, and control the governing class. The equal right of our citizens to settle in the Mexican

States, and the great inducement to them to do so, would in a short time carry a sufficient population across the gulf to control the present governing class of Mexico, and we might expect to impress upon their interests and institutions the doctrines established amongst ourselves, as we have already done in Texas, Louisiana and California. In each of these cases the argument of an incompatible population has been urged as a reason against union.

It is unnecessary that I should expatiate upon the extraordinary inducements offered to our people to emigrate to Mexico. I will only mention therefore the facilities for doing so. We have now completed that great system of physical development by Rail Roads which was so indispensable to the political power of the South. We have now Railroads which connect the gulf states with the Atlantic. We can now bring the great grain states of the South into full production and we can employ the ports of the South to export its staples.

We have now a Mail route from Washington to New Orleans which supersedes the Ohio river and the Coast lines; in October next, there will be a mail and travel route opened across Tehuantepec which will save 3,000 miles of ocean risk and ten days time between New York and San Francisco; this will transfer the gold and passenger business from Panama to New Orleans. But this will also bring the Southern States within four or five days of the Mexican States. It will bring the city of Mexico within ten days of the City of Washington and within instantaneous communication by a cable across the Gulf.

When we acquired Louisiana, New Orleans was twenty six days mail time from Washington, and this is the mail time of St. Francisco now. With even present facilities the States of Mexico are nearer Washington than Tennessee and Alabama were twenty years ago.

I cannot then see how the character of the Mexican people can infect our own for they will not come amongst us, but we shall go amongst and reform them. Nor can there be any impediment in the distance, and want of commercial facilities between the two countries.

There is one obvious risk which the South has to run in such a union. We must agree of course upon the number of Mexican States to be admitted, and the territories to be held in pupillage. We must agree also upon the rule of political enumeration to be applied to the Mexican people. Of course we should wish to apply the 3/5ths principle as far as possible, and diminish at first the senatorial and popular representatives of Mexico in Congress.

But these people are in theory free, they might side with the Abolitionists and thus control the American government and the South also. This is an obvious consequence of a wholesale confederation with Mexico. Whether this consequence can be guarded against or counteracted if it occur, or whether it will precipitate a sectional collision, I will not consider. As *a Southern Statesman you have no alternative except to encounter them.*

You have been turned out of Kansas, upon the application of your own principles. You have neither the inducement nor the slave population to go further north. But you have two invaluable advantages. You have secured the equal admissibility of the slave with the free states. You have given to the North a region in great part uninhabitable and incapable therefore of being divided into numerous and populous states.

Upon your part you have within your grasp a country accessible, abounding in all the metals and staples which civilised man most values, and a territory so extensive as that you can by only promoting the existing communities of Mexico to an equality with the present members of the Union preserve the balance in the Council of States, and so guarantee the peculiar rights of those States of which you are one of the guardians and representatives.

Here then is an opportunity to place the rights of the South upon the impregnable basis of equal or superior political power in the Confederacy.

I repeat the admission that the success of this plan will depend upon the established ascendancy of Southern principles within this new acquisition. But suppose you refuse to admit Mexico into the Union lest she be the wooden horse of the Greeks. Will she not be as well indoctrinated with free soil ideas out of the union? Will not our enemies seek to environ us with an abolition cordon and will we not be safer if we have the right to send into Mexico the army of Southern youth that would go there under the Confederation?

And if the worst should befall us could we not cut loose from the Union throw an emigrant army into Mexico and make it as safe as Texas?

You have I repeat no alternative. The North has more states and more territory than the South. It has the immigration of Europe to aid it. Your subjugation is as certain as the unrelenting operation of these great causes can render it.

Your only chance to secure the good will and forbearance of the world is to seize upon all the territory which produces those great staples of social necessity which the world cannot go without. Do so and you are safe. Fail to do so; you will be slowly and certainly enveloped in the coils of an avoricious and ambitious power, and your subjugation will be perpetual.

I can not in common civility extend this letter, so as to embrace all the reasons why, in my opinion, the South should advocate the immediate acquisitions of the Mexican States. It would task your eyes and good nature too much to read them. But I will add a few words upon the practicability of such a measure.

The success would depend upon negotiation. England wishes to secure her debt and develop a market for her manufacturers. *She would have to manage Mexico and make the treaty for* us. I infer she could do so from the recent change in her policy toward us.

The Southern States would advocate the measure. The manufacturing interests of the north would favor this Extension of our Home market and these interests detached from the coalitions would continue the government in the hands of the Democracy.

You see I have dispatched the practicability in very few words. It is unnecessary to do more with you than suggest the reasons upon which I rely, you can judge better than I can what weight they should bear.

Again I apologize. Should any point in this letter appear of sufficient interest to you to render it proper for me to elucidate, or defend it, I could of course do so otherwise my end will be attained by submitting it to your consideration as a suggestion intended for the success of principles important to us both as natives of Virginia and citizens of the Union.

ROBERT SELDEN GARNETT TO R. M. T. HUNTER.

FORT MONROE, VA., *October 17th*, [*1858?*].

MY DEAR COUSIN: It was my expectation to have visited Essex this fall and to have seen you before the meeting of Congress. I am disappointed in this expectation. On Monday last I got an order to go to Fort Washita, Arkansas, as Judge Advocate of a Gen[era]l Court-Martial to meet there on the 20' prox. I shall endeavor to get off from here on Saturday.

There are many matters of general interest to the Army and the public about which I wished to speak to you before Congress met; but as I shall not be able to see you before Jan[uar]y, I will state them by letter.

And, first, about the *vacant Brigadier Generalship*. Should a nomination for this office be presented to the next Senate, I hope you will cause it to be understood that whosoever he may be, he is destined at no distant day to be the *Commanding* General of the U[nited] S[tates] Army. Gen[era]ls Scott, Twiggs, and Wool can not last much longer, and this officer will thus soon find himself the Senior General of the Army, and, therefore, best entitled to the chief command. Who he is to be I have not the remotest idea, but whoever he may be his qualifications for the command of the Army ought to be closely examined by the Senate. The appointment will not be merely that of a Brig[adier] Gen[era]l of the Army, but that of the future Com[man]d[e]r Gen[era]l.

Some say that Col. Davis wants it himself. I don't believe this unless he stands no chance for election to the Senate. Of all the aspirants for this office from *civil* life he is, perhaps, the best, or at least as good as any. In the Army, Gen[era]ls Smith, Harney, Garland, Col[onel]s Lee, Mansfield, Smith, C. F., and Bragg are spoken of by their various admirers. In my opinion Col. Lee is infinitely superior to all of them together. Since the Mexican War Gen[era]l Smith has shown himself to be utterly deficient in administrative capacity and, in my judgment, entirely unqualified for the position of Com[man]d[in]g General of the U[nited] S[tates] Army. Garland and Harney are entirely out of the question, both in private as well as professional character, and their appointment would be exceedingly distasteful to the Army. I will not say that Col. Lee would make a better Com[man]d[in]g Gen[era]l than Gen[era]l Scott, but he would make unquestionably fully as good a one. I believe he is Gen[era]l S[cott]'s equal in professional knowledge and ability, while he is infinitely more equable in temper and uniform in conduct. He is a man of the highest tone of character, of the most scrupulous integrity, and the highest sense of honor and justice. Of all the officers of our Army below the rank of Col[onel] he is, beyond any doubt in my mind, the best suited for the place, will give the most satisfaction to the Army, and reflect the highest credit on the country. Upon inquiry among officers of the Army you will not find that I am alone in these opinions.

2d. *The merging all mounted troops into one corps.* This was recommended to the last Congress, and the two New Mounted Reg[imen]ts received the designation of "Cavalry" in accordance with that recommendation; but Congress failed to direct that the 2 old Reg[imen]ts of *dragoons* and the Reg[imen]t of *M[oun]t[e]d Riflemen* should be known by the same designation and constitute one general corps of cavalry. You recollect I expressed myself in favor of this last spring when I was in the cavalry and when it was of the highest importance to me that these corps should be kept distinct. In an Army there ought to be but three general corps—infantry, cavalry and artillery: and the promotion in each of these corps should run throughout the corps whatever may be the equipment of the various regiments of which it is composed. Thus under the general designation of Infantry we may have heavy and light Inf[antry], Foot riflemen, and under that of Cavalry we may have Heavy and Light Dragoons, Lancers, Hussars, Chassons &c &c, but the promotion should run from one reg[imen]t and Inf[antry] to the other whatever may be its particular equipment and designation; and so of all the Reg[imen]ts of Cavalry. Let us have but *three* arms of service—Infantry, Cavalry and Art[iller]y, and give the Pres[iden]t the power to arm and equip them as the wants of the service or the improvement in the profession of arms may require. This arrangement would compel officers to keep themselves informed of all their doubts which can be required of any officer of his arm of the service. The off[icer] of foot riflemen would thus have to keep himself informed of the drill and duties of heavy Inf[antr]y, as it might be his fortune to be promoted into a reg[imen]t of heavy Inf[antry].

3d. *An increase of the corps of Cadets*, by having a cadet for each Senator.

Previous to the addition of the four New Reg[imen]ts the Mil[itar]y Acad[em]y barely graduated enough cadets yearly to fill the vacancies in the army. This year when the first class graduated there were 40 vacancies in the Army. *They were all filled by Mr. Pierce from civil life*, and those cadets who had been four years preparing themselves to fill these places were attached to the reg[imen]ts below the Civilians as *brevets*. Hitherto a theoretical *fourth* of the corps of cadets have graduated every year. But this year the five years' course of study has gone into operation and we shall soon have only a theoretical *fifth* graduation, or about 25 men. These will not begin to supply the vacancies of the increased army. They would not have done it, before the New reg[imen]ts were added. The consequence will be that each year before a class graduates there will be 15 or 20 vacancies in the Army, and they *will always be filled from Civil life*. The Civilians will be made full Lieut[enant]s & the Cadets, brevets, for the law does not allow the President to appoint a citizen a brevet. These cadets after five years toil, hope & expectation, will find themselves, as they did last June, ranked on the very day on which they graduated by men who couldn't tell a gobien[?] from an apple-basket. The result of all this will be that the graduates will resign and the army will soon lose the distinctive character which it has derived from the Mil[itar]y Acad[em]y, and which has reflected so much credit on it and the country. I wish I was able to explain to you fully the importance of this thing. The present Barracks at West Point could accommodate this increase.

4. *Increase of pay and a retired list.* These subjects you already understand. There is no one measure which could now benefit the army more than a retired list. But the Retired list of the Navy has raised such a dust that I despair of anything for the Army in that way for the present. With regard to pay I have but one remark to make. It ought to be enough to make an officer feel that he can devote his time and talent exclusively to his profession, and to exempt him from all anxiety as to his means of living both for the present and in his old age. If this is not the case men will turn their

attention to other pursuits & neglect their professional duties. A principle of self preservation prompts it. If Congress thinks the present pay sufficient to protect the off[icer]s of the army from want & anxiety, then nothing more can be said. For my part I do not think so.

5. *The superintendency of the Mil[itar]y Acad[em]y.* Since Col[onel] Lee's promotion, the engineer corps, to which the superintendency is confined by law, is unable to find an officer in it of sufficient rank to make a Sup[erintenden]t, Capt[ain], and Br. Maj[or] Barnard (wholly unfitted for the place) is now acting Sup[erintenden]t, while Maj[or] and B[rigadie]r L[ieutenan]t Col[onel] Walker, his superior, is commandant of cadets. They have been obliged to put Barnard temporarily in his brevet rank. When Maj[or] Delafield returns from the Crimea, it is said he will be sent back there as Sup[erintenden]t. He is the best man in his corps at present of any rank for this position, though there are many better men elsewhere in the army. The great objection hitherto urged against throwing the superintendency open to the whole army, is that the appointment would soon become a matter of political favoritism. This is probable. The position of Com[man]d[e]r has already become so. But could not the law throwing it open provide that the Sup[erinten]d[en]t of the Mil[itar]y Aca[dem]y should hereafter be appointed by the President from any corps of the army, upon the recommendation of the Inspector of the Acad[em]y and the Com[man]d[er] Gen[era]l of the Army? Or let the app[ointmen]t be so made from a number of persons so recommended. I have hitherto been opposed to throwing it open to the army for the reasons above stated but I am not so now if it can be done with the conditions I have mentioned. The engineer corps can no longer in my opinion supply a suitable man. I have reason to believe that Gen[era]l Scott's opinion has undergone a change on this subject similar to my own. He wants to see Lee sent back. To use his own expression he wants to see him "throttled and dragged back." I should be glad to see this also if they do not make him the New Brig[adier] General.

JOHN RANDOLPH TUCKER TO R. M. T. HUNTER.

RICHMOND, [VA.], *November 6, 1858.*

MY DEAR SIR: What are we to look for in the North? If Seward has carried N[ew] York upon the basis of his *pronunciamentos,* what in 1860?

EPPA HUNTON TO R. M. T. HUNTER.

BRENTSVILLE, [VA.], *November 8th, [1858?].*

DEAR SIR: Some months ago I was informed that John Letcher who has always been understood to be a warm friend of yours had urged H. A. Wise to become a candidate for the Senate against you. That he was the first person who wrote to Gov. Wise [on] that subject and that he wrote as far as three letters all urging upon him to oppose you. I was referred to Mr. Garnett your nephew for the truth of this charge. Will you be kind enough to inform me whether this is so or not.

I am not pleased with the Ruffner business but that would be more tolerable than conduct such as I have mentioned above, because he could not be relied on if the above charge is true. Please give your views fully on this subject at as early a day as practicable.

PHILLIP A. ROACH TO R. M. T. HUNTER.

SAN FRANCISCO, [CAL.], *November 20, 1858.*

DEAR SIR: I have taken the liberty of forwarding you via Panama, a communication on questions affecting the revenue and showing to what an extent they affect articles of Southern growth. It might be supposed that the balance of trade for certain regions would be against us for articles we do not raise and for which our productions would be the natural exchange. Such however is not the case. Our indebtedness to those regions is not for coffee and tea which we do not raise, *as for them* we *ought to consider* our *exports* of *certain kinds* as the fair exchange; but for sugar, rice, molasses, hemp, tobacco &c. I had the honor of presenting you an introductory letter from Gov. Weller and have to express my warm thanks for your kind influence in my behalf. I have just rec[eive]d letters from the Governor. He is in the enjoyment of good health. If I can be of service to you here, in any way, be pleased to command me.

P. S.—When in Washington, I mentioned to Mr. Clayton the effect of allowing Spanish dollars to be our standard of value, also the necessity of coining Silver Dollars, U. S. He informed me that the matters were before Committees, hence I have addressed you.

R. M. T. HUNTER TO ———.[1]

[*1858?*]

MY DEAR SIR: I have received the letter from Mr. Randall to Mr. Randolph and can well appreciate the anxieties of the Biographer. You ask my opinions as to his true course in dealing with Mr. Jefferson's opinions upon slavery. He sums them up fairly that is as I understand them, and I think he proposes to treat them properly, that is to say " independently, justly, and manfully " to use his own words. Truth ought to be the first object of a historian and without it history is worse than truthless. Truth told in the *spirit* of truth

---

[1] Henry S. Randall's Life of Jefferson occasioned this correspondence. The book appeared in 1857.

injures no man or at least he suffers less in that way than any other. But there is yet another view of this subject. Mr. Jefferson published his opinions because he desired them to be known and every man has the right to present his own view of his own character so far as that character is to be affected by his sentiments and opinions. It is by these last that a man often desires not to be known to posterity. He would be a rash man indeed who would undertake to judge for Mr. Jefferson and pronounce against his wishes in such a matter as that, one in regard to which he was especially anxious to stand truly and as he thought rightly before posterity. I am no relative of Mr. Jefferson but I feel a deep interest in the reputation of that good Virginian and if I were the historian I would not take the responsibility of concealing any opinion of his which he had thought it fit to publish. I do not say the same however of opinions which a man breathes to a friend in the spirit of confidence and which he obviously did not wish to be published. A biographer has no right to publish them or to use such materials, he can have no more right to do this than to receive stolen goods.

This is a matter in regard to which biographers have sometimes made sad mistakes or more perhaps have committed unpardonable errors. You see I wish Mr. Randall to speak the truth but much depends upon the liberty and spirit in which it is told. Macauley can take the skeleton outline of a truth and so color it as to produce the falsest impressions. This is very apt to be the fault of these picture writers when they deal with history. Whether Mr. Randall be one of that class I know not but the taste for such writing is becoming too prevalent now a days. Mr. Jefferson is one of those great men who must appear before the bar of posterity to receive its judgment on actions as good or ill in his services or character. I say let him speak then for himself and present his own view of his case for I know not who else can perform that office so well for him.

JAMES G. BURET TO R. M. T. HUNTER.

WASHINGTON, [D. C.], *May 18, 1859.*

MY DEAR SIR: The article which I sent you on Neutral rights was written by a Brother-in-law of Gov. Marcy. As he is a democrat, this is, of course *entre nos.*

I think you are entirely right, in declining at this time, the trip proposed by Mr. Pruyn[?], who is a clever gentleman and friendly to you. His wife was the niece of Hon. Erastus Corning, and not related by ties of kindred to Gov. Marcy.

I cannot resist the conclusion that Mr. Buchanan is looking to a second term, yet it is only a few evenings since he disclaimed in my presence any such purpose, and spoke of the approaching termination of his official life (which he counted by months) with apparent sincerity.

It is thought that Appleton will soon retire from the Department of State, and has left for Maine to look after Delegates for the Charleston Convention who are to be chosen next month. He will encounter Peter G. Washington who preceded him to New England having an eye to Mr. Guthrie's interest in that quarter.

Douglas has visited New York twice since the adjournment of Congress, and left here yesterday for New Orleans on private busi· ness, and at the same time is likely to take care of his political inter ests. It is so much the habit of New York City politicians to flatter every Democratic aspirant for Presidential honors who may chance to visit them that he in all probability was greatly encouraged by their professions, and if induced to expect Southern support his friends will push earnestly for a nomination at Charleston. I am hopeful that he will see his true position, and urge the North West to go for a Southern candidate, which I cannot but believe he will do before the meeting of the Charleston Convention.

I do not see that Breckenridge has any positive strength, yet he is well spoken of by leading party men, and on his recent visit to New York City and Philadelphia, doubtless received strong assurances of support from the business politicians of those cities.

The name of Gen[era]l Lane is frequently mentioned as a compromise candidate, while Slidell and Bright are understood to be figuring for themselves.

The administration, through the office holders will make an effect to secure the New England Delegates, and thereby hope to control the nomination, but they are not likely to succeed to any very great extent.

If Virginia, North Carolina and Alabama should at any time present an unbroken front at Charleston, which your newly established paper at Richmond can greatly aid in bringing about, by keeping your own State firmly united, I do not fear the result, as New York will surely unite her fortunes with the " Old Dominion " in good season after the Convention assembles. It will give me pleasure to confer with Mr. Harvie of Amelia County personally, or by letter and I hope you will write him to that effect.

Lewis E. Harvie to R. M. T. Hunter.

Richmond, [Va.], October 18th, 1859.

Dear Hunter: I have been expecting a letter from you for some time past. And I write now to know whether the correspondence by your friends hereabouts has been politic and prudent and such as you approve. The fact is that without hearing from you frequently, we feel at a loss how to act. As to Douglas, for instance, it was necessary to take action and we did so, upon reflection unaided by our friends elsewhere. Was our course good or bad? Now in regard to this Harper's Ferry imbroglio, in its political bearing or that which it will be made to assume by designing men, we should like to hear your views. Of course we will stand up to and by our section " at all hazards and to the last extremity," but we do not desire nor design that this outbreak should be used to subserve the selfish purposes or schemes of profligate and unprincipled politicians.

We have been very still and quiet of late, thinking that it was best; on me rely to write freely and fully, you know that you can do so unreservedly. Wm Old's eyes are still too bad to be used. He is now staying with Frank Ruffin and can give more active supervision to the paper than he has been able heretofore to do. Jack Barbour thinks that things are moving well and that quiescence now is the best policy. He is very hopeful. He has been North and East as far as Boston. He thinks Douglas is done and you rising.

Thomas S. Bocock to M. R. H. Garnett.

(*Confidential.*)

Appomattox, Va. *November 8th, 1859.*

My dear Garnett: I received your letter last evening and return many thanks for your kindness. I shall leave here for Martinsburg, about the 20th and soon afterwards expect to be in Washington.

I shall be very much gratified if you would, as you propose, go on some days before the meeting of Congress. Though I have not allowed myself to become much interested about the speakership I will affect no indifference on the subject. I consider my chances for election it is true very poor. The elections of this year have resulted very adversely to Democratic prospects. Parties are so balanced as to invite combinations and they are always controlled by management. In this sense I am not and do not desire to be a manager, because I am unwilling to create false expectations and will not make improper committals. Under all the circumstances however, I would be glad to receive the endorsement of my political friends, whatever might be the result of the election. The Richmond papers circulate mainly in my District as well as in the State, and they seem always to fall into the hands of men who ignore my existence.

The Examiner, (I suppose through the influence of Aylett) ignores me as completely as "*The Enquirer.*" On this account I would like this endorsement as well as on others which I need not give but which you will appreciate.

23318°—18—vol 2——18

As to the chances for the nomination I know but little positively, but I think they are good. A large number of the members of the last House voluntarily tendered me their support, a tolerable proportion of whom are reelected.

The views of the South Carolina gentlemen are known to you. I regret however that only one or two of them attend our nominating Caucuses. I hear through reliable sources that all the Democratic members from Ohio are for me. I have reason to think that the Illinois Democratic delegation, will be found to be so likewise with the exception of Mr. Morris. Craige, Branch, and Ruffin of North Carolina, Crawford of Georgia, Curry, Stallworth, Cobb, and Moore of Alabama, Lamar and McRae of Mississippi, Stevenson and Burnett of Kentucky, Kunkel of Maryland all I think more or less decidedly declared the same preference. Rust of Arkansas is an old friend and a very true man. I have no doubt of him. John Cochrane of New York intimated friendship but was non-committal. I know nothing of the views of that delegation, nor of the Pennsylvania, nor of the Indiana. In relation to my colleagues I feel sure of Edmundson, Millson, Clemens and Jenkins, besides yourself. I think I may safely count on Pryor also. Our good friend W. O. Goode was warmly enlisted in the matter. He wrote me a note not long before his death saying that he hoped to be in Washington at the opening of the session with the view to aid in this object. Smith, Leake, De Jarnette, Harris and Martin I have no reason to count on. Gen[era]l Clark of Missouri expressed favorable intentions, but I suppose that all Missouri will be for Phelps.

Gen[era]l Reuben Davis said he was for Barksdale first and for myself second and I *duly* appreciate the compliment. I have gone thus into detail, to put you in possession of the field. You might consult freely with South Carolina, Craige of N[orth] C[arolina], Vallandigham and Pendleton of Ohio. Carey, Stallworth, Lamar, Rust, Kuntel, Stevenson and Burnett and of course with my Virginia friends. Give my best regards to Hunter. Two friends of his will be sent to Charleston from the Lynchburg District.

JOHN LETCHER TO R. M. T. HUNTER.

LEXINGTON, VA., *December 9th, 1859.*

MY DEAR SIR: I received your letter of the 6th (postmarked 8th) this morning.

We are in the deepest distress, in consequence of the death of our second son, under the most afflictive circumstances. A week before his death he got a splinter in his hand, only a part of which as it turned out had been extracted. He attended school the entire week, and never complained of it. On Saturday last he was playing throughout the day. At supper he ate heartily, and remarked when we were leaving the table that it pained him to open his mouth. After supper he read until bed time, without further complaint. Twice during the night he complained that his neck was stiff, but after getting up and placing the clothing over him, he slept until morning, and we supposed he had taken a slight cold. At ten on Sunday morning, the first symptoms of Locked jaw appeared, and in spite of all that could be done, he died in fifteen hours. He was ten years old, sprightly, intelligent, noble hearted, and a universal favorite with old and young about the Town. His death makes a sad breach in our family circle.

My general health has greatly improved, but I still suffer from Erysipilis. I fear I shall never get clear of it. I have intended to visit Washington to consult Doct[or] Garnett before going to Richmond, as I have more confidence in him, than the physicians here, who are divided in opinion about it.

It really looks to me, as if the days of the Republic were numbered. All the indications seem to me to point to a dissolution of the Union, and that at an early day. There must be a speedy and a radical change in Northern sentiment, or we cannot remain a united people. They can save the Union, and it rests with them to do it. If I am to have a stormy administration, so be it, I am prepared for it, and will meet any issue that may be tendered promptly and with that decision which a Virginia Executive should exhibit. I know what my friends·expect of me, and they shall not be disappointed.

I think I will be in Washington next week, perhaps on Wednesday.

FRANCIS W. PICKENS [1] TO R. M. T. HUNTER.

(Private.)

St. Petersburg, [Russia], December 10, 1859.

My dear Sir: I wrote Mason a week or so ago and enclosed him his letter which I had published in the leading paper of this city, and you will now pardon me for enclosing you a letter in the same paper, the leading court paper, written from N[ew] York, and I would most respectfully call your attention to it, as it embraces exactly the current ideas that now prevail throughout Europe as to the weakness of the South and the general belief that the North are about to " Conquer and subjugate the South." We are looked upon and studiously represent as being in the condition of Mexico and the South American States. And I would cautiously suggest, that one leading object of McLain [?] in travelling in England and the Continent this last

---

[1] A Representative in Congress from South Carolina, 1834–1843.

summer, was to spread these ideas, and most particularly to ascertain the feelings of the public men in England in reference to a rupture which he anticipated as certain. I will not say this certain, but it is my firm impression from various sources of information. We are certainly on the eve of very great events and I do not wish to be so presumptious as to advise any one in your distinguished position, but it does seem to me that it would be more impressive for Virginia to say less through newspapers and through them, to use more calm language and a firmer higher tone. She is a great state and has a great name. She made the Constitution and the Union, and she has a *right to be heard*. Under the circumstances in which she is placed, if the *Legislature* were, by a unanimous vote, to *demand* a Convention of the States, under the forms of the Constitution, and propose new Guarantees and a new League, giving security and peace to her, from the worst form of war, waged upon her, through the sanction of her border states, it would produce a profound impression. And if the South were to join in this *demand*, unless the Northern people immediately took *decided* steps themselves to put *down forever* the vile demagogues who have brought the country to the verge of ruin, a convention could not be resisted. And if after a full and truthful hearing, new securities and guarantees were refused, then the Southern States stand *right before the world and posterity*, in taking their own course to save their power and independence, be the consequences what they may.

Under the old articles of Confederation the Union had practically fallen to pieces and the wisest men thought it could not be saved, and yet in Convention of able and wise men, face to face and eye to eye, disclosing truthfully the dangers with which they were surrounded, the present Constitution was formed for a more perfect union and adopted by the States. So too now, when new dangers are developed, a full and manly discription in a Constitutional Convention of all the States, may develop new remedies, and even a new league or covenant suited to the demands of the country. I merely suggest these things most respectfully, for I dread to see any hasty or ill-advised, ill conceived measures resorted to, which will end in bluster and confusion. Every thing ought to be done by the state as a state, with a full comprehension of the gravity of the matter and the momentous consequences involved. I think we ought to endeavor *faithfully* to *save* the Constitution and the *Federal* Union, if possible, and if not, then it is our duty to save ourselves. Even if the two sections were compelled to have separate internal organizations and separate Executives, still they might be united under a League or Covenant for all external and foreign intercourse, holding the *free interchange of unrestricted internal and domestic trade* as the basis of compeling peace and union by *interest*. I merely throw out this idea, as I know your philosophical mind will readily comprehend it in all its details and bearings. It is a subject that I have thought of before, and it is forced up by the present unfortunate condition of affairs in our country. At this distance from home, I am filled with pain and apprehension for the future. I know and feel that we have arrived at a point where we will require stern and inflexible conduct united with thorough *knowledge* to carry us through safely. There is no time for ultraism of factious moves. There mus; be firmness and wisdom, and it must come from the States, and especially from Virginia moving as a state determined to protect her people and their rights, without the slightest reference to partizan contests of any kind whatever. Excuse me for writing thus freely, but our former relations justify it, and I sincerely desire to know the councils of wise and true men of the South. True I am here, but at the first tap of the drum I am ready for my own home and my own country.

WOOSTER SHERMAN TO R. M. T. HUNTER.

JEFFERSON Co., [N. Y.], *December 10th, 1859.*

DEAR SIR: In your debate in the Senate you speak of the apparent indifference of the great masses of the north at the sympathies with Brown. I think you cannot be aware of the true feeling of the Democracy on this subject or of the action which has already been taken in this matter.

In order to show you what was done here I mention that immediately after the news of the attack at Harpers Ferry, as chairman of our Dem[ocratic] Cent[ra]l Com[mittee], I called a public meeting of the County which was promptly and heartily responded to by our people. I addressed letters of invitation to Gov. Seymour, Hon. John A. Dix, Hon. Danl. S. Dickinson and others from whom letters were received denouncing in the strongest terms the outrage in Virginia. Mr. Dickinson appeared in person before the meeting (which was very large and enthusiastic) and in a splendid speech of two hours exposed the act and its abettors in a manner which would have satisfied the most ultra Southern man. Genl. Dix's letter, which was also very strong and decided, was read before our meeting by Judge Hubbard and also, at another meeting at Adams, with decided effect and afterwards published in our Democratic paper here. I notice it was republished in the Journal of Commerce of New York City on the 8th inst from which paper I clip it and enclose to you herein.

I assure you the Democracy are not sleeping in regard to the interests and the rights of our brethren at the South, they are active and decided and feel certain of a powerful reaction in their favor:— look at the movements in Philadelphia, Boston, and New York. In the language of that sound and conservative paper "the Journal of Commerce" let us understand each other". You will not then doubt the good faith and integrity of the true northern Democracy towards the institutions of the South.

I have great hopes for the future, the republicans have overdone John Brown, and their acts will recoil upon their own heads if Southern men will treat the present excitement with moderation. I fear for the sentiments expressed by Iverson in the Senate and a member of the house who threatens to hang Seward as well as Brown if they get hold of him. Such sentiments do us more harm than good. Seward will hang himself, politically at least, if let alone. I notice Messrs. Trumbull and Corwin have already repudiated him simultaneously, one in the Senate and the other in the house. This looks well. I congratulate the country upon this good beginning. I wish they would now do the same in regard to Sherman their candidate for Speaker and that the good sense of the house would unite upon Mr. Bocock or some other good conservative Democrat. Can I entertain such a hope with any prospect of realization?

I wrote Hon. Lansing Stout yesterday, member from Oregon (and a native of our county) in regard to the remarks of Senator Wilson on your Colleague's resolution (Mr. Mason) in which he said he travelled in New York and New Jersey just previous to the election and *heard no one sympathising with Brown or words of that import.* It is well known that this statement is false, as Wilson himself made a sympathising speech on that Subject at Syracuse and his very language was copied into the papers at the time (last of October I think) and I wished the Virginia Senators to know of the false assurance of this great abolition gun. The republicans and their leading papers have all gone too far in this matter and will be retaliated upon, but the democracies are all right as you will see.

WILLIAM OLD, JR. TO R. M. T. HUNTER.

RICHMOND, [VA.], *December 16th. 1859.*

MY DEAR SIR: I have received some papers forwarded by you, and had extracts incerted in the Examiner.

The feeling in Virginia is so strong on the sectional question, and Wise so prominent in connection with it, that, I am unable to form a guess just now, at the complexion even of the legislature. Before this he was excessively [unpopular]. I do not hear of any of our active men who have been influenced by recent events, but there is certainly a strong reaction among the people. You can aid us very much, by a strong speech in the Senate. To have any effect it should come at once, and certainly before the Christmas holidays. An elaborate speech on the state of the Union would give great confidence and endear you to our friends, and in candor I must say they are very lukewarm throughout the state so far as I can see. They are anxiously waiting to hear from you. And the feeling of distrust of all Northern men is so strong that I do not believe Douglas could get one electoral district in the South out of L[ouisian]a, and Dickinson could not carry one in Virginia by a popular vote. In such a condition would it not be best to take a most prominent Southern position, for a candidate nominated by Northern votes, however true unless very prominent at this time, will have opposition from the Northern democracy. The nominee must have a thorough Southern endorsation in the Convention, not a nominal or formal one, to get the popular vote. This at least is the view which has been impressed on my mind, by what I hear from the different quarters of the State. I have been compelled by every view that I have taken of this affair to make the course of the Examiner accord with and lead if possible the feeling which has been awakened, in' the State. My own judgement and feelings work together it is true. The vote of this state unless there is a reaction will be cast for the man, who is more distinctly with the popular sentiment on the slavery question. I do not think Wise will maintain his present position, he will certainly be looking Northward and eulogising the Union in a month or two. If he does, this event is lost to him. You can make our position very strong. Such at least is the opinion of your warmest friends. I hope to be in Washington in a day or two.

DABNEY H. MAURY TO R. M. T. HUNTER.

RICHMOND, [VA.], *December 17, 1859.*

DEAR SIR: I only rec[eive]d yours 1st Dec[embe]r enclosing your bond, as stated for which thank you.

It gives me pleasure to inform you that a vein of Cannel Coal, the best yet found for oil, has been found on our Kanawha property and from the information I have, do not doubt that we have the most valuable Coal property in all that Country, and that to make it very desirable as well as valuable only need the completion of the Covington and Ohio Rail Road and the improvement of the Kanawha River. The Edwards Suit is progressing with the usual *speed* of such matters. Our Counsel have succeeded in having a Surveyor appointed to *run* the lines and he will commence work sometime in January. So we may look for a decision of the suit at the *June term* of Kanawha C[our]t.

I have the best reason for believing that the Hill Lands also abound in Cannel Coal, but of this you will be informed in due time. A survey of this Land has been ordered. The *Caveat Suits* [are] not yet tried. We ought to sell these Lands this winter or the next Spring. Think you there will be a chance of doing it? Or will this Sectional agitation keep persons from embarking in enterprizes of this sort in our State.

FREDERICK W. COLEMAN TO R. M. T. HUNTER.

RICHMOND, [VA.], *December 21, 1859.*

DEAR SIR: I suppose you have heard, before this, that the State Convention will come on the 13th of February. It was important for your interests that it should take place at as late a day as possible, as the Gov[ernor] had made no small capital out of the Harpers ferry affair, and time was needed to let its effect die away. Your friends, accordingly, went for the latest time in Caucus.

As to the temper of the two houses, and the state of the districts, I cannot with certainty inform you, though I see no indications that your popularity in Virginia is not as great now as it ever was. It grew up so gradually, and is so well cemented, that it is not easily overthrown. The Gov[ernor']s, on the contrary, is of hasty growth and speedy decay. It has even now been much impaired by his proposition to commute the punishment of Copper. I think it probable that, if your friends will be prudent, and not oppose the Gov[ernor] with too much bitterness and too little discrimination, long before the Charleston Convention, you will be as decidedly the choice of Virginia as you were before merely accidental circumstances gave him a prominence, in my opinion, transient. The maner in which you pitched into Hale, did you great service in Virginia. He richly deserved it, and caught it most effectually. As to your remark that I am one of the friends on whom you think you may safely rely, you do me but justice. There is no man whom I should be so happy to see President of the states as yourself. But this is not from any personal feeling. I most conscientiously believe that, at the present time, your election would do more to save this country than any other event that could transpire. I shall, therefore, do everything in my power to bring about a result so desirable.

JAMES A. SEDDON TO R. M. T. HUNTER.

ST. JAMES PARISH, LOUISIANA, *December 26th, 1859.*

My DEAR SIR: I have only now on my return from a distant plantation received your very interesting letter of the —Inst. Despite my great disinclination to obtrude upon your valuable time, I had just determined to write you for counsel and information on the emergencies of the time and am both relieved and flattered by your overture to confidence. I am spending the winter here partly from considerations of health but mainly from the claims of imperative private business. I left Virginia with great reluctance just as the Harper's Ferry Raid had occurred for I knew it to be a crisis of great moment to our State and Country and of deep interest to your political fortunes in which as a sincere friend I always cherished a lively concern. It was too early however to judge the effects of the events occurring or of the feelings they would excite, and since, I have been so engaged in affairs and so removed from sources of correct information, rarely ever seeing a paper from V[irgiñi]a or the North, that I feel real diffidence in forming or expressing opinions on the aspect of public affairs. I must venture however to say that in my humble opinion the train of events and the course of public conduct and opinion upon them, especially in V[irgini]a have been injudiciously and alarmingly mismanaged and misdirected, and I hold the unsound judgment, insatiate vanity and selfish policy of our fussy Governor mainly responsible for them. The Harper's Ferry affair ought to have been treated and represented either in its best light as the mad folly of a few deluded cranks branded fanatics, or, more truly, as the vulgar crime and outrage of a squad of reckless desperate Ruffians, ripe for any scheme-of repaine and murder, and they should have been accordingly tried and executed as execrable criminals in the simplest and most summary manner. There should not have been the chance offered of elevating them to *political* offenders or making them representatives and champions of Northern Sentiment. Indeed, our Honorable Governor, seduced by the passion of oratorical display, commenced by a picturesque description of them as heroes and martyrs, and, by insisting on holding them as the chiefs of an organized conspiracy at the North, has provoked and in a measure invoked the sympathy and approbation of large masses and of established organs of public opinion at the North (who might otherwise have been frowned and rebuked through a correct estimate of public opinion as to the base criminality of the fanatics and their deeds into shame and silence) to them as veritable heroes and martyrs, exponents and champions of the North immolated for their love of liberty and aid to the oppressed to the Molach for Southern Slavery.

In V[irgini]a and throughout the South with corresponding policy, all possible representations have been made and agencies adopted to make these infamous felons grand political criminals— to hold the whole North or at least the whole Republican party identified with them and to spread the greatest excitement and indignation against that whole section and its people. In short, for I can't dwell, with his favorite policy of swaggering and bullying, Wise has *exploited* this whole affair to his own selfish aggrandizement, to aid his vain hopes for the Presidency and to strengthen the fragment of a Southern party he heads. And as the result, has conjured a Devil neither he nor perhaps any other can lay, and, arraying the roused pride and animosities of both sections against each other, has brought on a *real crisis* of imminent peril to both. Of course, I do not mean that the Harpers Ferry outrage was not a fact and indication of deep significance, and that it ought to have awakened earnest reflection and timely preparation for even the worst at the South, but it ought to have been viewed and met calmly and firmly, and made a means of added strength to us both North and South, not a cause of irritation and prejudice in the one and of excitement and depression in the other. The point I fear is too that the feelings of the South is too much more excitement, a sudden storm of indignation soon to pass and I predict that in any real shock of sections, any practical disunion of which he is not the *stulting* hero, Governor Wise will be among the first to recoil and betray. However the mischief has been wrought. The peril is, judging from your letter and your known sobriety of judgment, even greater and more imminent than I had imagined. The question then of practical statesmanship is in the crisis, what ends are to be aimed at, what courses to be adopted? If the permanent continuation of the Union, consistently with the safety and institutions of the South be, as I hope, still practicable, then all my convictions and my feelings *turn* earnestly to that. But if the Union is only to be *temporary*, amid growing strifes and deeper discontents, then I think its speedy disruption certainly not to be avoided, if indeed it should not be schemed for and courted. I had rather the responsibility of innitiative action should not be on us and our section, that results so doubtful and beyond all human ken should come from resistance to wrong, from those courses of self defence, but the spirit not the forms of things must be regarded and *we* must not be wanting to an emergency, or a necessary *coup d'etat* from timid dread and an *overt* act. In this connection and in answer to one of your enquiries, I am bound to say that in my deliberate judgment, based on the maturist reflection I am capable of the election by the North of Seward, or any confessed representative of his opinions, that slavery must be overthrown by the powers of the general government, under the constitution, and that its legislation, its influences and agencies must be directed openly and insidiously against the pean and institution of the slave holding states ought to be the signal of *immediate* Disunion. We would be *fools* and *cravens* to submit to such insults and meditated wrong. *Fools* if we waited till all the sanctions of legality and all powers and resources of the Government were arrayed against us. *Cravens* if we cowered to favors and waited till the [?] were duly set to entrap us. In essence and spirit, the North and the day of such election has rent and trampled the common constitution under foot, and we must haste to defy them as foes and be ready to battle for our homes and families, at least that will be counsel of my vote, my voice and all the little influence I can exert. If this were the real purpose of an united South and known as such to the North there would .be *now* and probably for some time no danger, but the leaders and demagogues of the North do not or affect not to credit such feeling, and indeed make its alleged existence only an added means of rousing the pride and passion of their section. Thus blinded and hurried on, there is very great danger, even probability of such election. And is the South united and prepared for action in such emergency? I doubt and fear. Your suggestion of the proposed action of the Southern Legislatures is very well as a means of rousing and acting on the Northern Mind in time to avert, but w[oul]d be a mistake and disappointment as a means [of] concerted action in the event of such election. It is too cumbrous and slow. It would distract and divide each state and give a chance to the timid, Union lovers to rally and canvass. The President would be inaugurated before decision and action. No! In such event to aid at all, the first impression of indignation and dismay at the South must be seized. A few and the boldest either of private men or of the States must at once *strike* and then there will be no chance but for the others to rally and unite. A *single state*, if prepared, would suffice and be clearly best, but if even a state collectively can not be commanded in sufficient time, a few daring spirits if willing to peril life and honor, might *leap the trench* and *fire* the *magazines*.

I hestitate to counsel, yet I believe this to be [the] only feasable plan of action. Perhaps a few public men of highest reputation and position from the South concurring on such an election in a public recommendation of disunion and immediate action might suffice to put the ball in motion, but I doubt. But to divert such evil, at least for the present, can't the Republicans be divided, the Democrats be united on a great public diversion given by some foreign shock to the slavery agitation. It may be rather Macheavillian policy, but it seems to me some mode might be divised of casting an apple of discord in the Black Republican Camp. They have many aspirants, no real principles or measures, nothing but a prejudice and fanaticism, unless it be lust of power to unite them. Could not some [person] of influence be lured or frighted or led by patriotism to make diversion and schism. The South should always aim to divide the North and win Northern patriots and while wise, so far in resting on and courting the Northern Democracy, it might have been better in the past to have been somewhat considerate of acceptable Republicans too. This you will remember was a favored idea of our great leader, Calhoun.

Of the Union of the Democrats and of their success I still have strong hope. Wise is a marplot by nature and of purpose, but unless unaccountably strengthened since I left V[irgini]a powerless for much ill.

On Douglass mainly rests the prospect. What a noble chance, that man has to achieve and deserve a Fame which is infinitely above, tho' in the future it would bring the Presidency. If he would only soar above self and party, cast aside the rankling petty animosities of the past, leap forth from the morass of a false position and the meshes of a delusive Sophistry on the territorial question, and renouncing a candidacy, at present vain and mischievous, rush into the arena of the North to confront and crush this Hydra of abolitionism with all its kindred isms without suspicion of interest, sustaining some sound Southern man, he might wield the club of a Hercules and win the honor of indeed saving the Union and his Country. I have thought sometimes of making the direct appeal to him, but he would most probably smile at and discard the thought. He will be forced though to retire before the convention if not sooner (for how could either he or Wise be nominated without plain ruin to the party) and I mistake much his judgment and feelings, if among Southern men, he does not decidedly prefer you. Backed warmly by your own State (and when I left there was *no* doubt of that) you I candidly thought had the best chance of nomination. The North I believe would prefer you to any Southern man, and on the part of the South there would be satisfaction and a disposition besides just now to take a Virginian. You *must* however have your own state first, then a decided manifestation of willingness to take, if not prefer you from the North. With these cards, the game may I think be won and with it, for four years at least the turning away of all dangers and calamities which wisdom and patriotism may avert. I regret greatly it is so little in my power to aid and forward a cause which from both friendship and patriotism I have so much at heart. I shall make it a *point* to be at Richmond should my services be required in Charleston but I cannot return to V[irgini]a before spring. Here I am thrown little in association with politicians but I loose no chance to present your claims and I should be happy to be brought into acquaintance and cooperation with your friends. I need not say, I shall be most happy to hear from you and to put at any time my poor thoughts or pen at your service.

WILLIAM OLD, JR. TO R. M. T. HUNTER.

[RICHMOND, VA.], *December 30th, 1859.*

MY DEAR SIR: As I hear that you made some remarks in reply to *Wilson* some days since, and have not seen them I write to ask you to send them to me if they are either reported or written out.

The legislature having adjourned and no one renominated here, we are in the dark. Buchanan's message seems to me a bad one. I have been constrained to comment on it with dissent. I consider this effort to draw off attention from our domestic affairs, by a war with Mexico and Central America, as the most dangerous movement against the South, and a high and I fear a strong bid for the nomination. I have had no one to counsel with, and have had to take my own position. I am striving to give the Examiner the position of the leading Southern journal in V[irgini]a and I cannot do it without risking something in our old party organization. I had no idea that this old man had hopes until I went to Washington but I am confident he has now. I should think it best to discontinue any comments on him after opening the fire unless forced into it. Mr. Harvie will be in Washington. Our friends think you have the strength in the legislature. The county meetings are doing harm, but they will not be made longer, for Wise's speech here to the medical students, has injured him, and as his friends have found out no Southern strength before, they will not be in spirits now. I have been waiting to see his friends who left here with the news as I heard of a compromise. When they return I will know more. Send me anything I can use.

WILLIAM OLD, JR. TO R. M. T. HUNTER.

(Private.)

[RICHMOND, VA.], *January 1st, 1860.*

DEAR SIR: I wrote you a note on yesterday, since writing it I have seen Letcher. He has a message, the important points in which are two. He suggests that our sectional difficulties, have reached such a point, as to *require* a final settlement, that if not settled now on some permanent basis, they must produce eventually a dissolution of the Union. That these difficulties, have their origin, in the construction given to the Constitution and in ideas of the objects to be attained by a Union, which control the legislative and general political action of the Northern People and States. This difficulty he contends can only be removed, by an authoritative adjudication, of all questions depending upon such a construction, and upon such an estimate of the objects, for which the Confederacy was formed. He contends that the majority does not acknowledge the Supreme Court as an arbiter, and suggests the proposal of amendments to the Constitution settling these questions of construction and defining distinctly the powers and duties of the government on all the issues involved in the sectional controversy, to be submitted to a convention of the States. This is the first suggestion. He also advises the appointment of either one or three commissioners by the legislature to visit the Executive or legislatures of all states, which have passed laws, hindering the execution of the fugitive slave law, to ask the repeal of such laws, and to request a distinct enunciation of the purpose of such states, either to allow and aid its execution, or to retain their present legislation on the subject. On the rejection of the proposed amendments or a refusal to go into Convention, he thinks the Southern States should call a Southern Convention authorized to act as they may deem necessary, to protect rights which the Union will not, arming the militia, and sustaining our own commerce, and preparing the state for independent action are generally recommended.

I am anxious to have some distinct course of action, advised by the Governor, and some indication of a favorable reception from the Legislature. Any course which recommends distinct measures of independent state action, will aid us in Virginia, and I believe is essential to our success at Charleston. If we place our Southern Candidates, on ground which looks, to protecting the South, by the agency of the federal government or by the operation of the Union alone, Wise will be a great gainer. If we have a candidate who is known to approve State action, and to ask for and require additional guarantees, he, Wise, loses Virginia. We can beat him before the legislature, the democratic convention or the people. Whenever we have these issues distinctly made up, he must fight them and we have him. At present he cannot be assailed, directly, without injury to his immediate assailants, for while we may injure him, those who have gone to him under this Harper's Ferry excitement have no distinct policy on which to make issue with him and no candidate identified with a distinct Southern policy on whom to rally. His supporters are mostly men who are ready for action and although they do not like his position they will not quit him, unless they have a man to attract them or a policy on which to contend. The newspapers cannot force this issue, although they can direct and carry it when once started. And with it we can certainly carry Virginia and the South I think. If you make a speech on any such issues as are likely to affect these matters, I should like to be in Washington at the time and I hope it will be before the middle of this month.

RICHARD H. COLEMAN TO R. M. T. HUNTER.

BOWLING GREEN, [VA.], *January 6th, 1860.*

MY DEAR SIR: I have just returned from a visit of four days to Richmond. During the visit I had conferences with many of your staunch and influential friends, among them, James A. Seddon, Lewis E. Harvie, Frank Ruffin, Paxton of Rockbridge, John Seddon, Wm. B. Newton, and my brother Frederick. The result of these conferences was highly gratifying to me. With the exception of Mr. Harvie all of your friends seemed to be sanguine of V[irgini]a. Mr. Harvie too thinks that you will have a majority of the delegation to Charleston, but he has some fears, and says that our friends, to ensure this, must be very energetic. My brother has no doubts; he says that all of the Democratic members of the Senate with but one or two exceptions, are for you.

I am pleased to say that all of your friends in Richmond are very active. James A. Seddon had just returned from Louisiana, and was compelled to hasten to his home from which he had been absent for some time. He promised however to return to Richmond in a few days, and devote all his energies to your cause. He is deeply interested, and can and will exert a greater influence in Richmond than any other man in the state. This much is certain, you are gaining every day and Wise is losing. Wm. B. Newton told me that the Wise men in the legislature were evidently *under the hack*.

I formed the acquaintance of many of the members, and endeavoured (with some success I think) to impress on them the fact that Wise was utterly without strength beyond the limits of this State.

I shall return to Richmond in about ten days to hold a special court for Judge Meredith. Fortunately the character of the business will be such as to leave me disengaged during the evenings, and I shall avail myself of every opportunity to advance your interests.

JAMES S. RITCHIE TO JOHN C. BRECKINRIDGE.

SUPERIOR, LAKE SUPERIOR, [WIS.], *January 17th, 1860.*

DEAR SIR: After reading this letter and accompanying address please hand them to the other Washington Proprietors of Superior.

The population of Douglas Co[unty] is now less than 750, many houses and stores unoccupied and some of our people financially ruined. The "Proprietors" are directly *responsible* for this state of affairs. They made certain representations to settlers. Are these promises fulfilled? Let the uncompleted Military and Crow Wing and other roads answer. Six years have elapsed and a stage cannot come through St. Paul in summer, and if the taxes are not paid up, *Six* more will elapse and no road to St. Paul. 25 miles of uncompleted road between the lake and Mississippi. The City of St. Paul on one side and the great Superior Company on the other, and the *$5,000* required cannot be raised unless Douglas Co[unty] does it! Can we expect settlers if there are no roads, and can roads be built if we do not *pay* our Taxes? I acknowledge that an assessment of 3 pr ct. would be more suitable to my limited means instead of the 7 pr ct. But I am not so blind to the future. What are my 2d Street lots worth without roads? *I advocated this Tax*, it is hard to pay up just now, but I am going to. The Laws of Wisconsin are very strict, 25 cts a *lot* charged for delinquent advertising &c &c. This *counts* when one owns a whole share. The U[nited] S[tates] Court decided recently in the matter of the Alleghany P[ennsylvani]a Bond's case, that taxpayers must pay up. So did the Supreme Court of Penn[sylvani]a and also that of Wisconsin. In either case, *We*, the Tax payers suffer. Can any one at present sell a town lot or even rent one? Navigation opens in a few weeks, *shall cattle, flour etc. be brought from Minnesota to Superior for shipment by the first steamboat, or will we have a Lawsuit, depreci*ate property, confidence, County orders, stop road building and other improvements, and *have to pay* lawyers fees, and also the County Indebtedness? Shall the attention of the Legislature be called to this attempted violation of the late law for the collection of Taxes &c?

In a few weeks an important case will be brought to trial viz: Wilcox vs the Proprietors. The property at stake is some of the best in Superior. Suppose Wilcox gains the suit, would not each Proprietor or share holder be held individually responsible to the bona fide settler, and on a very serious charge? This law suit should be well attended to, it is important!

In conclusion, permit me to add, that if the Vice President, and the Washington Proprietors *can afford* to wait for their property to improve, and not pay Road and other Taxes, it is more than myself and others in Superior can! I left Philadelphia in April last for Superior, determined while I staid here to *push* the Town along, and if these roads are not completed and that pretty soon I am *determined* to proceed to *extreme measures*. The question for the new Board of Supervisors, shall be *Roads* or *No Roads*. And if my opinion of the Vice President is correct, he agrees with me in this matter. And the reason of my addressing this letter is that report said that Hon. Mr. Breckenridge had *at last* agreed to contest this tax with the others.

LEWIS E. HARVIE TO R. M. T. HUNTER.

RICHMOND, [VA.], *January 24th, 1860.*

DEAR HUNTER: I think it probable (after consulting with several of our true and staunch friends) that Mr Benett had better defer his visit here until some of our friends go to Washington. I do not believe that he could come on now without his purpose being known. And I doubt whether the manifestations of any active, or aggressive policy would not be injurious. Wise as a part of Harper's Ferry is now in Virginia, unassailable. The current is too strong to be controlled. We must be content for the present to wait for the subsidence of the waters. Our policy now is to prevent any expression of preference by the State Convention and after it to struggle in the Districts for our men if we can get them and cool sound ones when we can not. This we can do, I believe. To attempt to do more would be ruinous. Even this is difficult, if not more than doubtful without help from you. Men, some of our own truest, are complaining that now, when all men in the State are excited and aroused, by the outrage upon the State and the manifestations out of it that you remain quietly, calm and apparently indifferent. I have heard remarks of this kind quite frequently—more than once to-day. I know the difficulty of your position but present the unquestionable fact before you. I do not know that a different line of policy heretofore or now would avail to change the condition of things, but it is and has been a stumbling block in our way and is used with great effect against us. I do not *wish* you to understand that I despair of the State, or of your success even if the vote of V[irgini]a should be given to Wise in the first instance. But I am confident just now that the popular sentiment is here about with him. Edmundson's District from what I learn from French is for Wise. Paxton thinks that the tenth Legion is for you. With Leake's aid you can carry his district. Powell is all right and will keep the counties around him straight. If Leake can so arrange with Goode in Bedford as to prevent that Delegation from going in Convention for Wise Delegates to Charlestown, the district will be for you. Goode is stated to be for Wise as I see from the papers, but I am under the impression from what I have heard that he would not like to make issue with Leake in view of ulterior results.

Either Wm. Old or some of our friends will be in Washington soon. Every day is presenting new aspects and in a few days we will know what to do.

Gordon says the Louisa meeting was composed of some twelve or fifteen persons who were nearly equally divided. This district is safe I think, so is Bocock's in the Lynchburg part of it. So I think is ,the Halifax and incline to think Pryor's, Petersburg is also. Campbell and myself won't clash. If you do speak, do so at once and decidedly. It is necessary I think. It is right I know.

George W. Loyd to R. M. T. Hunter.

New Rochelle, [N. Y.], *February 4th, 1860.*

Dear Sir: Allow me sir to congratulate you for that masterly speech of yours in the Senate lately. Account for it as we may, the Southern man is the great defender of the rights of the *white man*, for which Service I will as a working man of the North, work for the man for President of the United States who will give the best proof of being true to the interest of the Glorious South. Again Sir, let me say, that if ever it should take place, that a Southern man of your opinions should even come North to free us from the "Irrepressible Conflict" of capital he would find more friends than Brown did in trying to put the Negro on an equality with the White man. Again sir, let me say, that I think it is misfortunate to our Dear Country, that the true National Democrats did not allow Shurman to become the Speaker of the House. Pennington will give them a longer lease of Political life, but then, if the National Democracy can triumph at the next Contest, I will content myself for awhile. It seems to me, *that you of the South cannot possibly yield one* inch more, and Sir let me assure *you*, that you have friends in the North, friends Sir, that will contest every inch of ground with the enemy of our country in the North!! I hope *all True men* will live to see the enemy of our country fall *one* by *one* on the field of battle, and that the gallant Democratic *few* the *Square unbroken!!*

Be so good Sir to send me all the Documents that will help the cause. I will use them for the *cause*, to the best of my ability.

P. S. Give my *very best respect* to Hon. J. H. Hammond.

W. H. WINDER TO R. M. T. HUNTER.

PHILADELPHIA, [PA.], *February 4th, 1860.*

DEAR SIR: The sketch, by telegraph, of the speech made by you, in the Senate, on Tuesday last, was such as to cause me to desire to read it extenso. If you have it in power to gratify me I will be very much obliged to you. If you could agree with me in regard to the propriety of the administration causing, so far as lies in its power, the *immediate publication in extenso* in all the Democratic and Independent papers such speeches as the one delivered by you on Tuesday, the result could not fail to be very perceptibly beneficial, in correcting much of the gross misapprehension which prevails in regard to the issues between the parties.

I took the liberty on Monday last of sending you the Pennsylvanian of that day containing an article prepared by me on "Sherman and the Impending Crisis" and the one of to day having another article on "Dough faces" which contains some home truths.

It seems to me there is a lamentable want of discipline in the Demoortic Ranks, which contrasts most unfavorably with that manifested by the Republicans under the wand of that master spirit, Thurlow Weed. I do not like the action in the Legislature of the State of Maryland upon the South Carolina communication. It seems to me a proper reception would have been, to admit the *undeniable truth*, that many of the Northern states had broken some of the vital links of the Union, and that a wide spread feeling or disposition to break more, was manifested to a dangerous, to an alarming extent at the North, but that Maryland relying upon the native patriotism and conservatism of the South, would look to it, to correct the present wrongs and provide against future ones, and that until this hope should be extinguished, she did not desire to take a step towards imitating the conduct of the north, by herself breaking the remaining ligements. The discussion in the Legislature of M[aryland], as reported by the telegraph, gives aid and comfort to and strengthens the hands of the Northern aggressionists.

GIDEON D. CAMDEN TO R. M. T. HUNTER.

CLARKSBURG, VA., *February 14th, 1860.*

DEAR SIR: I have read with care and much interest your speech in the U[nited States] Senate, on the subject of protecting the States from invasion and which you was pleased to send me. You clearly show, that whilst the South has kept in good faith the compromises of the Constitution, that the North has failed to do so, but has constantly encroached upon the rights of the South, and that the time has arrived when the South should take a firm and decided stand against any farther encroachments. Situated as we are on the borders of two free States, we have some trouble to keep a proper sentiment on the slavery question. We have a mixed population, many coming from free states bringing with them in many cases strong anti-slavery feelings. My situation prevents me from taking an active part in public matters. I was forced to make a few speeches at public meetings soon after the outrage at Harpers Ferry. In general our people are all right, but the elements of danger to which I have refered should be looked to, and another which I should have mentioned, the news papers from the free states and also some published in our state. We have the Northern methodist church to encounter, although the members and ministers in general are sound on the slavery question. Yet their associating with the Northern Conferences and getting their religious papers from the free states tend to create among them an anti-slavery feeling. We have the Southern branch of that church also. Its ministers and members take strong pro-slavery grounds, justifying and sustaining it by the precepts of the Bible and common humanity to the slaves. It was a great error in many of our best revolutionary men to denounce it and it seems to me that our Eastern friends in Congress especially the Senators, should aid us as much as they can by furnishing documents, to keep the border region right. East of the Alleghanies all are sound and need but little attention. Our Southern methodist preachers who find their way into every neighborhood should be furnished with documents to enable them to maintain their position before the people. Not that they should become noisy politicians but should be well informed as to the controversy between the North and the South and in a quiet way infuse it into the minds of the people. I would suggest that the Senators and Eastern members of Congress be furnished with suitable names to whom documents might be sent. If you desire it I will get my son on his return from the Democratic Convention at Richmond to furnish you with a list for this section. Our member of Congress, Mr. Jenkins, will no doubt be active in supplying his district with suitable documents, but the district is so large that we can not do so to the extent that is required, besides there is a freshness in new names in matters of this sort that ensures a reading of the documents &c.

JOHN H. NUTTING TO R. M. T. HUNTER.

CANDILL VILLAGE, ROCKINGHAM CO., N. H.,
February 15th, 1860.

DEAR SIR: Menston, Edwards, and others are sending abolition or *Black Republican* documents into this State with great profusion. I wish you would please send to my address, some documents of the pure *Democratic Stamp* that I can distribute in this town, as I believe that it will be the means of doing much good to such men as are a little undecided on some of [the] main questions of the day.

JOHN BLAIR HOGE TO R. M. T. HUNTER.

MARTINSBURG, [VA.], *February 19th, 1860.*

MY DEAR SIR: I have, until within a day or two past, expected to go to Washington and proposed to answer in person, the inquiries in your letter of the 14th. This will explain the delay in its acknowledgement.

I had concluded *not* to go to the Richmond Convention for many reasons, but had your letter reached me in time to do so, I would have changed my arrangements and gone. I am as yet, unadvised of its action beyond the telegraphic reports, but if they have made that body the vehicle of any Presidential preferences, I am satisfied the District Conventions will rebel and resist its right to express an opinion upon questions belonging exclusively to them. It is very difficult to say, at this time what are the Pres[identia]l preferences of this electoral district. In one sense, the answer is easy enough—the great mass of the party neither feel nor have expressed any preference, being perfectly content to abide the action of the Charleston Convention. Thus at the largest meeting ever held here, at the last November Court, it was resolved that no expression of opinion should be made, the Democracy of Berkeley merely asking that a sound, loyal and true man should be nominated by the Con[ventio]n.

Prior to the Harper's Ferry affair, there would in my judgement, have been no difficulty in obtaining an expression of opinion in this district, favourable to your nomination or, at least, the delegates to Charlestown would have been left entirely unembarrassed. The effect of that affair has been to give Gov. Wise what he had not before, a party in the District, advocating his nomination. How strong it may be, I have no means of knowing, but thus far no county meeting except in Page, has avowed a preference for him.

It is proposed, I learn, very generally to send me to Charleston. I have been very prudent about expressing my own opinions and feelings, beyond the declaration that I would not go trammelled by instructions and I have reason to believe the Convention will not instruct its delegates, though I apprehend that if I were to declare myself openly for you, I might arouse an opposition which would defeat my appointment.

The usual defect in the organization of political Conventions, is to be observed in those of our region. The best and most thoughtful men will not take the trouble to attend them, and the action of a whole district is left to a few, many of whom are nothing more than noisy and irresponsible politicians, actuated solely by motives of selfish interest and guided by some vague hope of personal benefit to result from their action. Our district is peculiarly cursed with these small politicians and they often succeed in forestalling public opinion and thereby preventing its full and true expression.

My own belief as to Gov. Wise is, that he has not the ghost of a chance for the Charleston nomination even with a united delegation from Virginia. There are serious personal objections, in the minds of the masses, to the election of one whom, they regard as erratic and impulsive, in a period like this. The popular demand is for calm, grave, and conservative statesmanship, and while all just tributes are freely accorded to him, the judgement of the people is conclusive, that he does not possess those sound practical qualities which are required in an Executive in a crisis as delicate as the present. I believe this to be a fair representation of the sentiments of a majority of our people.

I think too that your position, as shown by your speech of Jan[uar]y 30th, meets precisely the true Virginia sentiment and 1 wish from my heart, it could be more widely disseminated.

I would be very glad to distribute some copies of it in quarters, when I am sure, it will do good.

I hope to be in Washington in a short time and will gladly avail myself of the opportunity to present more in detail, such information as I may possess touching public sentiment here and elsewhere in the state.

In the meantime, if there be any way in which I can serve you, I trust you will not hesitate to point it out; for I can give you the assurance, that nothing would afford me greater pleasure than to exhibit in some useful mode, my high personal and political regard for you.

WILLIAM T. YANCEY TO R. M. T. HUNTER.

LYNCHBURG, [VA.], *February 21, 1860.*

DEAR SIR: I avail myself of this mode of tendering to you my thanks for the Copies of your speech which you were so kind as to send me, having previously read it with feelings of pride and pleasure I have distributed those copies among your friends of whom you have many in this part of the State. I consider it the ablest, grandest, most masterly view of the whole subject which now convulses the union and menaces its destruction I have seen any where, and would be glad if you would send me some additional copies for distribution. While I was unable to attend the democratic Convention in Richmond I done what little I could to have Campbell properly represented in that body. While I regret to see the confusion and disorder which seemed to " reign supreme " in that body I rejoice that the Wise party were defeated, and are of opinion, that the course pursued by his friends will tend to consign him forever to seclusion from public office. I neither want to see or hear any more of him. There can never be any peace or harmony in any party which he undertakes to lead. All the injury to our party resulting from the disorder, and disgraceful scenes enacted both in the Petersburg and Richmond Convention, is imputable to his dictation, and to a selfish and vaulting ambition which must rule or ruin. Restless, unstable, indiscreet, selfish without judgment, I regard him with all his brilliant genius as a mill stone around the neck of our party which will sink it forever unless it can be Providentially relieved from the intolerable incubus.

Prior to the Harper's Ferry Raid he had been well nigh if not thoroughly used up by his ridiculous letters and speeches, and his ceaseless and contemptible electioneering and demagoging for the Presidency. But the prompt and decided course he pursued in that affair, while it produced a great reaction throughout the South in his favor has only retarded I trust his political destruction. Availing himself of the temporary popularity produced by this affair he has not hesitated to insist through the columns of the Enquirer and the editorials of his own son, that the democratic convention should, contrary to the usages of the party in V[irgini]a declare himself as the favorite candidate of V[irgini]a for the Presidency. That a man who has tossed the political compass and whose whole life is a tissue of political inconsistency and folly should thus most indelicately and arrogantly attempt to foist himself upon us as our first choice for the presidency and the exponant of our principles to the exclusion of others more modest and meritorious than himself, and that too against the usages of the party was well calculated to arouse a spirit of their resistance, and to invite a war to the knife on the part of those who are opposed to his pretensions. Did not he and his friends know that this would be the result of such a course. But what cares he for the success of the party or its principles, or for all those noisy and disorderly scenes which disgraced the convention, and which he knew would be the inevitable result of his course provided he could be in the ascendant? Not one fig. I shall go down to the Farmville Convention and do what I can in the way of sending delegates to Charleston who will only vote for him in one improbable contingency and that is in case he is the nominee of the party. But I have written more than I intended, which was what is embraced in the first nine lines of this note.

RICHARD H. COLEMAN TO R. M. T. HUNTER.

BOWLING GREEN, [VA.], *February 22nd, 1860.*

MY DEAR SIR: Your letter was not rec[eive-]d by me until several days after it was written. I went to Richmond the day before the Convention met so that I could see the Delegates as they arrived. The Wise men were at first in high spirits, and your friends somewhat discouraged. We resolved however to bear up, and fight to the last, and the result has been a victory. All that we desired was to prevent an expression of a preference for Wise and in that we succeeded. But for the unfortunate absence from the convention, at the time the vote was taken, of a number of your friends (representing three or four thousand votes) the resolutions offered by B. B. Douglass of King W[illia]m would have been carried. Montague, (the Lieutenant Governor) who is a close and accurate observer told me that not more [than] 500 or 1,000 of the Wise votes were for the resolutions of Douglass, and had these votes been cast differently and all of your friends here present, the majority would have been with us. Your friends are much pleased with the result, and have returned to their homes resolved to make every effort. They fought nobly in the convention; they had a great preponderance of talent and tact. It is difficult to say to whom you are most indebted, but when you are President, B. B. Douglass and Lewis Harvie should have a *carte blanche.*

In the Accomack district we have I fear but little choice. Your friends should endeavour to send Booker of Elizabeth City. He prefers Wise, but will go for you at any time at which your name may be presented.

From the Richmond district James A. Seddon will be sent, and probably Alexander Jones of Chesterfield. Jones does not desire to go; I urged him to consent; he promised me that with Seddon should be sent some person opposed to Wise and not unfriendly to you.

From this District we shall send Wm. A. Buckner of Caroline, and some one from the Northern neck. I prefer Col. Henry T. Garnett. He is a much more efficient man than Beale.

From the Fauquier District we shall send two. I do not know whether our friends have agreed on the men. This will be regulated by John S. Barbour, Gen[era]l Eppa Hunton and John Seddon. In Gen[era]l Hunton you have an invaluable friend, with one or two such men in each District, I would guarantee you the state. There will be a close contest in the Albemarle District. Our friends had not decided on their man. I think that it would be well to send Paulus Powell, and to leave the choice of the other to Shelton F. Leake. Powell, I learn from Wm. T. Early (Senator from Madison) does not wish to go; he should be written to on the subject at once; if he will consent to go, by combining his strength in the upper part of the District with that of Leake in Albemarle and Green, we can carry both. Early promised me that he would go home in a few days, and see that a delegation favourable to you should be sent from Madison to the District Convention. Leake's views should be entertained, and he should be urged to go to Albemarle and have suitable delegates appointed.

The Norfolk District is against you. From the other two districts on the South Side you have, no doubt, been informed by Mr. Harvie.

In the Rockingham district there will be a close contest. Massie of Rockbridge (a member of the last legislature) assured me that you should have the two delegates. He said that you had nothing to fear from Harris, the member of Congress. I called twice on yesterday to see Gov. Letcher and urge him to exert all his influence in that District, but he was too unwell to see me.

All will be well, if your friends will *work hard* and *work* right. Tact is worth as much as zeal. The few Wise men in this county had formed a plan to pack the Delegations to Richmond and Tappahannock but while they were consulting, we called the meeting, put Edmund T. Morris in the chair, and appointed proper men to both conventions.

I regret that my official position trammels me, but for that I would visit some of the counties in the adjoining districts, and urge your friends to greater efforts.

Work, work, work is all that we want. We triumphed in the Convention; can't we triumph in the Districts! We *can* and we *must*.

I shall visit Richmond again in a few days and will write to you.

P. S.—All of Wise's appointees were at the Convention—Colonels (without regiments), bank directors, visitors to the different institution &c &c; and of course many of them represented entire counties. Their influence at the district conventions will not be great.

GIDEON D. CAMDEN, JR. TO R. M. T. HUNTER.

CLARKSBURG, VA., *March 2, 1860.*

DEAR SIR: At the suggestion of my father (G. D. Camden), I send you a list of suitable persons, in several counties in this region, to whom documents in favor of Southern rights should be sent. I also enclose a list of the preachers of the Methodist Church South in this region, to whom documents might be sent.

They have taken a strong stand in favor of Slavery and they traverse the whole country and it is important they should be well informed as to Northern aggression upon Southern Rights.

I will send you a list of persons in other Counties if desired.

N. B. HILL TO R. M. T. HUNTER.

RICHMOND, [VA.], *March 2nd, 1860.*

DEAR HUNTER: Old Wise is here and has been here for several days. God only knows what he is after.

There is a time in the affairs of men which taken at its flood leads on to fortune.

You must come here and make us a big speech, come as a guest or friend to see me or some one else and we will bring you out. Let me hear from you and that you will come.

Your friends are in fine spirits.

Tell Leake to go to Charlottesville and get his friends to vote for Powell to go to Charleston.

W. H. WINDER TO R. M. T. HUNTER.

PHILADELPHIA, [PA.], *March 3rd, 1860.*

DEAR SIR: I have already mentioned to you, that I had some 2000 of your speech printed, for my own distribution; of these I distributed 1000 in N[ew] Jersey, 500 in the interior of this state and 500 in this City. I have had occasion to hear the opinion of a number of persons who had received copies without knowing who had sent them and who therefore in speaking of it to others in my presence undoubtedly expressed their sentiments. I was much gratified at learning my anticipation of its effects confirmed. While in company with Mr. Meredith (late Sec[retar]y of Treas[ur]y) at his house, Benj. Gerhard, Esq., son in law of John Sergeant, called in on a visit and in the course of conversation referred to your speech asking

Mr. M[eredith] if he had seen it, saying it was well considered, well timed and well calculated to make a favorable impression on the northern mind (such were about the substance of his remarks); he made particular reference to your significant observations on labor and capital saying there was much in it for reflection. Mr. M[eredith] had not received the copy I had sent to him, but he went on to say that he had no doubt the speech deserved commendation; that the Senator was an honest and honorable as well as able representative of the views he advocated, and as such entitled to the confidence of all entertaining their views. He is himself, unhappily most decided in opposition to the Democracy. I might enumerate the incidents connected with the announcement of opinion by other readers of the speech, but I feel I have no right thus to trespass on your time. I regret now that I had not ordered a larger number and had distributed them entirely in the large cities, for the speech is most pertinent to such circles. If a million of copies of this speech had been promptly circulated, as in the case of Sewards speech, in N[ew] H[ampshire] Conn[ecticut] and other Northern States, I firmly believe that at the spring election we should sweep these two States. As it is (and this is my apology for this intrusion on your attention) too many copies *cannot be too soon* circulated.

Mr. Ashe (of N. C.) left for Washington yesterday morning promising me that he would not forget to urge the matter at Washington on the Committee for Distribution. If the Committee would order it, here I could get 10,000 and over printed for $8.00 per 1000 and the speech again in the Pennsylvanian. More than 75,000 copies of Gov. Sewards speech were *instantly* printed and distributed and it has been copied into hundreds of papers. *Why* do not the Democrats take equal pains to throw their great speeches broad cast, while public *attention is alert and eager for the information?* They are delayed until public attention has become not only cold to impressions, but indifferent, unwilling even to read a stale speech unless a different course be pursued, we shall have a perilous fight. I wish to get down to Washington when I would, at the hazard of being deemed importunate, urge incessantly and upon every one, the importance of *instant and widespread* circulation of proper documents. Your speech is received with less reserve, because of the great confidence of considerate men in your personal and political integrity, sincerity and ability: and if your views only allowed a discriminiting tariff, or specific duties, or even home valuation, your influence even at the North would be second to scarcely any other: these last being my principles of political economy is the divergence where my judgment fails concurrence with your views, while the boundless elements of wealth and prosperity embosomed in the soil of Virginia, if they had a voice would say that such principles acted on by Virginia, would have added to Virginia some of the hundreds of millions of dollars expended in other states, some of the millions of population drawn to other states and many of the improvements which facilitate travel and commerce in other states.

Pardon me for having insensibly (and beyond original intention when I began this letter) entered upon a subject upon which I differ, perhaps presumptuously, from you. But I am sure your candor will not take offence and I therefore send this rather than rewrite or leave out what I have thus said.

If there can be any of your speech which can be spared for distribution, I will personally take care that all which may be sent to me, shall be advantageously circulated.

BENJAMIN H. BREWSTER TO R. M. T. HUNTER.

PHILADELPHIA, [PA.], *March 5, 1860.*

DEAR SIR: The State Convention has selected as a candidate for Gov[erno]r a most worthy faithful and capable man.[1] No one in Penn[sylvani]a would have answered better. The means by which it was done was most irregular, and if adopted as a precedent will lead to most violent results in future Conventions. It was done by a preconcerted trick. Genl. Foster had nothing to do with that. Indeed I doubt if he did not rather decline to have his name used. From all I can learn, the two factions, the rebels and the regulars— i e. the Forney Packer and Press party outwitted the Custom House. The plan of the regulars was on the *real* ballot to spring the name of Judge Strickland on the Convention and call for its adoption by unanimity: of that plan the other party got wind and the others who were outside of both connections, and they started out at once with Genl. Foster and adopted the policy of the regulars and so now the game!

It was a gross departure from duty and principle: but in this case it has been a lucky act. Genl. Foster is staunch and conservative and manly. The people will be with him and he can carry the State.

The Delegates to Charleston are made up of a medley. The Administration men had the most to do with making them, but when they get to Charleston they can not be controlled wholly by the Custom House power. Bigler was the result of arrangement, so Baker, the Collector, Dawson and Montgomery of necessity and compromise. Dawson to reconcile Irwin for his defeat for Gov[erno]r. The Congressional Delegation here, are all of them the choice of the Custom House but the *first* and that is represented by Mr. Riely a worthy plain man and a Mr. Cassidy a Quarter Sessions lawyer and

---

[1] Henry Donnel Foster, a Representative in Congress from Pennsylvania, 1843–1847, and again from 1870–1873. He was an unsuccessful candidate for Governor.

rather a low person who was ousted from the District attorneyship because of fraudulent returns. He owes his influence wholly to his connection directly with the five boys and gamblers of Fir Points of Philad[elphi]a. His original tendencies were Anti-Lecompton and a little Anti-Slavery but as to that I think he has changed. He will be open to various influences, he has no fixed principles and is eager to get a place to make money, but is easily led away by his vulgar excitements or resentments.

Mr. Phillips is a retired Quarter Sessions lawyer and rich by such practice. He is a Jew and feels a restless desire to be noticed and conspicuous. He is noisy for Mr. Lane of Oregon. He fancies he is a great regulator and so he is in a little way—meddling. His alternate is N. B. Browne, the Post Master, wholly under the command of Mr. Baker, Mr. Robert Tyler and Mr. Phillips who are the triumvirate that rule us here by the permission of the Power they hold from the President. In fine no one can say that the Delegation will do this, or do that, and no one man can command them. There is not a man on the list who is the equal in knowledge of public affairs or in mind to Mr. Bigler and he *can not* dispose of them as an unit. They will *follow* faithfully any nomination that shall be made only anxious to be seen shouting the loudest for the successful person. They want nothing but a man who will carry and then they all want places. The politicians and not the people have acted.

P. S. I have the honor to ackn[owle]dge the recept of y[ou]r letter. The public rumor is that Mr. Bigler's hope is that he shall be the nominee for V[ice] President. He is "too weak in the knees." Had it not been for his feeble camp when in our State Senate and when candidate for Gove[rno]r in yielding to the outcry for the Wilmot Proviso, Penn[sylvani]a would have been free of doubt and cleared of all reproach in giving aid and comfort to the heresidials who have bewildered the people with their false doctrines.

JOSHUA A. LOWELL TO R. M. T. HUNTER.

EAST MACHIAS, ME., *March 12, 1860.*

DEAR SIR: Having had the honor of some acquaintance with you during the sessions of the 26th and 27th Congresses, of which I was a member, and as the Democracy of Maine have now no Representative in either branch of Cong[ress], I take the liberty to request you, to send me a Pamphlet copy of your excellent speech delivered in the Senate Jan[uary] 31/60, on the Resolution of Mr. Douglas.

Our Convention in this (the 6th) Cong[ressiona]l Dist[rict] for the election of Delegates to the National Convention, was held on the 22d ult. It was the largest Convention ever held in the District.

Col. P. S. J. Talbot of East Machias and Col. John W. Jones of Ellsworth were elected as Delegates; and the Conv[ention] unanimously adopted the resolutions reported by me as Chairman of the Committee, a copy of which I send you herein. The Delegates elected are friends of the present Admin[istration] and friends of the *Union* and of the *Constitution*, willing and desirous, that all the states may be sustained and protected in their *Rights under the Constitution;* and having been elected without any *pledges* as to Candidates for the Presidential nomination, will consult the interests of the *whole Party and of the whole country.*

WILLIAM H. OLDHAM TO R. M. T. HUNTER.

MOUNDSVILLE, VA., *March 16th, 1860.*

DEAR SIR: I have just returned from Fairmont where on yesterday we held our District Convention to select Delegates to the Nat[ional] Convention. You are already advised that we selected Mr. Russell, your warm personal and political friend, and the Hon. Wm. G. Brown of Kingwood, Preston Co., who is also a political friend of yours and with whom you are no doubt acquainted.

On Mr. Russell no contest was made. We were a unit for him from the River Counties; what is called the Mountain Counties were somewhat divided and Mr. Jas. Neeson, our State Senator was nominated, and was only defeated by Brown, because he was known to be an uncompromising *Wise man.* Mr. Neeson is personally far more acceptable to the District than Mr. Brown and but for his Wise proclivities would have been selected with great unanimity. Some of your political friends, to wit: Drinkard of the Virginian, avowed openly, whilst he was voting for Neeson, that such vote was not an endorsement of his position in favor of Wise, but remarked that " Wise had no more chance than he (Drinkard) had, and Mr. Neeson could see that, and properly reflect the will of the District." Many others no doubt voted for Neeson upon the same conditions of mere personal preference over Brown and yet Brown beat him nearly 3000 votes. I have no doubt but that in the Parkersburg District, they will instruct for Wise. Wm. L. Jackson is working that thing and unless Johnson of Clarksburg and others watch he will succeed. The feeling I believe here generally is the South ought to have the nominee and you are the choice, perhaps Brenckenridge next. If we go north, for myself I prefer Douglass. I was on the Com[mittee] on Resolutions in our Convention and succeeded in preventing anything more than a re-affirmation of the Cincinnati platform, lest we might be passing resolves that would be, one day, troublesome.

T. E. NORRIS TO R. M. T. HUNTER.

ST. PAUL, [MINN.], *March 17th, 1860.*

DEAR SIR: I am unknown to you but send you some copies of my writings over the signature of " Kasota " in the Henderson Democrat, the editor of which is from the same town as myself, Baltimore. In [one] of those numbers the editor takes occasion to pay a handsome tribute to me. I had previously written some articles for the Winona Democrat and that editor [has] done the same. I am not a *professional* writer. I am a private gentleman and never sacrifice my private position for any purpose as I *wish* to preserve a pure record politically, morally and religiously. My father's family are from Harford Co[unty] State of Maryland, about 18 miles from Baltimore and date their residence in that locality *anterior* to 1650. My brother wrote a digest of the Laws of Maryland and the date 1650 I give you is from an accidental reference in that digest, a deed drawn by Jno. Norris of Harford Co[unty], the deed in question being cited to prove what constituted a valid deed. My mother's family are equally ancient in their locality in the same State, Worcester Co[unty], though I have no particular dates to refer to.

Some short time since a gentleman in this city, Dr. Thos J. Vaiden, mentioned to me in conversation he had been a class-mate of yours in Virginia, he himself being a Virginian. As I intended to forward you to-day a newspaper in which you are nominated for the Presidency it occurred to me that Dr. Vaiden might in some measure give me a line or two stating *generally* my character. I *know* he has no *particular* information on that subject. I have only been here about 10 or 11 months, though the Reverend Mr. Neill, the author of the History [of the] State of Minnesota and a gentleman the most prominent of all others here in the literary circular, is a relative of mine. Dr. Vaiden thought my being spoken of by the Editor of the Henderson Democrat was sufficient to satisfy you that the gentleman now addressing you was a *gentleman* of character. On the 11th of June 1840 I rec[eive]d a commission in the U[nited] S[tates] Navy as Purser which I resigned in about five years afterwards. I was *unanimously* approved by the Senate, all the *Whigs* coming to my rescue as there was [an] effort among the Democratic Senators to induce the President to withdraw my name in order to have some of their particular friends provided for, but the attempt signally failed.

I also recollect some circumstances which lead me to conjecture that you were in some measure aware of these movements, at that time generally, as I heard it stated a gentleman of y[ou]r name, a brother or a cousin, was an applicant at the time for a commission as *Purser* and the gentleman in question no doubt knows and perhaps yourself, the *rush* made by Senators for their respective applications for the position referred to.

This is to advise you that I send you per to-day's mail a copy of the Henderson Democrat 10th inst., nominating you for the Presidency and Caleb Cushing for the V[ice] P[residency] and if I can obtain another copy which I expect to I will forward it to Mr. Cushing if I can find out his address.

I know it is contrary to *etiquette* to write hurried letters but when time presses on us we have to do the best we can.

[P. S.] It gives me pleasure to say that Dr. Vaiden expresses gratification at the commanding position you now occupy in public estimation.

PHILIP P. DANDRIDGE TO R. M. T. HUNTER.

WINCHESTER, [VA.], *March 18th, 1860.*

DEAR HUNTER: I was so broken down by the long session of the Convention on Friday (not reaching home until Two o'clock in the morning) that I could not write by yesterday's mail. I presume however, you rec[eive]d my despatches on Friday or Sat[urda]y and Sherrard promised me to write to Col. Mason, to let you know how we were progressing. We succeeded better than I expected. The friends of Gov Wise, made a desperate fight with what seemed to be a thorough organization, but it soon became apparent, that your strength was decidedly in the majority, about 4000 of 6500 votes, not two thirds, but showing "the same to be in our hands" if we could command patience enough to worry out the determined resistance of the opposition. Hoge was elected with many doubts by our friends, and only upon my assurance that *you*, and Mr. *Mason* had written to recommend it. I could give no personal pledge of his reliability, because I could get none from him, and did not want to go beyond the assurances rec[eive]d from you and Mr. Mason in answer to the many questions about his position, otherwise he would have been placed in a most awkward position towards the Wise men, who voted for him under the most positive assurances (from his friends) that he would certainly support Wise in the Cha[rle]ston Convention. As it is: he has been elected by the votes of both parties, each satisfied with their assurances. (Our friends voting almost under protest). I don't like such proceeding and would doubt the fealty of any man who under the circumstances would receive his election from the hands of those whom he must have determined beforehand to disappoint. I trust to your assurances, and with many doubts upon my own mind, because his sponsor. Many of your friends have decided and positive objections to *him*, but were true enough to *you*, to waive them and do whatever you thought best. You and Mr.

Mason are responsible for his loyalty. I only represented you. Ran. [Randolph Tucker?] could have been elected I think beyond doubt, but Alf [Alfred Powell] withdrew his name so absolutely, "by authority," that I could not venture to interfere. In Funsten, Parsons, and Duckwall, I have every possible assurance, that you may rely to the last extremity. They are *for* you, not to furnish any other candidate for nomination, but "first, and last, and all the time" *for you*. And ready to work hard and constantly for your nomination. This I get from Funsten's and Parson's friends and from Duckwall personally, and think it may be relied on.

I have no doubt, that Hoge will redeem his obligation (whatever it may bè) and will support you, at first. The only question to my mind, is whether he will remain constant, if your chances at Charleston seem at any time to waver, and whether he may not leave you then, for a more promising candidate, as Meade did at Cincinnati. One account says that Funsten will be at home next week, another, that he will take Charleston in his way, and not return until the 1st of May. If he comes sooner, I will try to see him immediately upon his arrival and urge upon him the importance of his presence at Cha[rle]ston, and I think Mr. Mason and Ran' had better write to him *at once* (at home) to insist upon it. I understand Parsons will go, and I think he will recognize no alternative to your nomination. Duckwall is very poor but seems so much in earnest that I suppose he will certainly go too. With all three at Charleston, *all four*—must continue faithful through every trial.

I found myself placed in a much more conspicuous position than I had desired, or supposed necessary. But our friends met, without a shadow of organization, and with nobody to act as referee for you. With a general knowledge of my connection with you, naturally I was obliged to assume the position, and everything that was done, was done at my suggestions and concurred in, as being acceptable to *you* (except Ran's withdrawal). I hoped we might have carried out the letter of your recommendation, and have no doubt we could have done it, but for the interference of an almost ridiculous timidity. I don't think we have made a mistake, and trust the result may be satisfactory to you.

Write to Hoge. He will be *flattered* by any indication of [his] personal importance! And to me, if you have time.

[P. S.] In the Convention, you were *stronger than the Delegates*. The Wise men *begged* hard for "even an alternate" which I did not feel at liberty to concede. They are disappointed and mad at me. They managed adroitly and obliged many of us, to ignore the claims of personal friendship, in our votes for Delegates or Alternates. If I can, I will be in Washington the last of this week. I am pretty well again. Be particular in long civility to *Jos H. Sherrard*. He deserves it. I mean, send him Doc' &c &c.

I was surprised, when early in the day, Palmer of the " Winchester Virginian " and Beale of the " Spirit of Jefferson " came to me (at different times) saying, " Mr. Dandridge whichever way you vote, (knowing your relation to Hunter) I will vote too." As they did, *dont neglect them* in your distribution of Documents &c.

R. TANSILL TO R. M. T. HUNTER.

U. S. FRIGATE CONGRESS.
MONTEVIDEO [S. A.], *March 22, 1860.*

DEAR SIR: We continue to receive news here of the miserable state to which the abolitionists have brought our country.

Their recent treasonable and murderous expedition into our State proves, if proof is needed, their cruel character and barbarous intentions towards the South. They are the most detestable creatures that ever existed, and are truly a curse to the Republic. They will yet force the Southern people to seek that safety out of the Union, that is denied them in it.

I blush, Sir, for the unfortunate condition of the country, and sigh at the remembrance of the happy time when we believed that national liberty had firmly established herself upon our favored land, and our glorious Union would last forever.

But alas, how vain are the hopes and expectations of man. We only hope to be disappointed. Indeed, I have lost all hope of the preservation of the Union. It is already virtually dissolved. When the great laws of necessity and self-preservation shall implore the solemn duty of a formal separation upon the South, we must act like freemen who know their rights and are determined to maintain them, let the consequences be what they may. We must not hesitate or cavil about legal forms, but " cut the Gordian know " of abolitionism at once, and " provide new guards for our future security," and bid defiance to our enemies, against whom we are invincible, if we act wisely. Should the National Democracy succeed in electing the next President and I believe they will, and fondly hope that you, Sir, will be their choice, the Union will exist a few years longer. Yet, the catastrophe is certain to come sooner or later, and the South ought to prepare for it. To fail in this, would be highly criminal.

I have written to His Excellency Governor Letcher, that whenever Virginia shall withdraw from the Union, I will at once resign my commission and return to my native State, and then he may consider me as subject to her orders, in whatever capacity her Governor may think proper to command, to assist in defending her honor and rights. At first I intended to write you, Sir, a long letter upon this unfortunate subject, but the thought of the wrongs the South has already endured, and the calamities with which the whole nation is threatened, "maketh the heart sick," and disqualifies me for the task. Besides, it would be useless for me to recapitulate the injuries we have sustained, and dangers which now threaten us, as you are doubtless already too well acquainted with them.

There can be no real reconciliation with the abolitionists, et al at all. They are alike incapable of reason or justice. They are ever ready to cast away the garb of humility, and grasp the staff of power, and show their barbarous appetite for blood and murder. Trust them not, they always "nurse the dreadful appetite of death." If the South should ever be so unwise as to submit to the election of an abolition President, her degradation will be complete; her end that of St. Domingo. Mark the prediction.

CHARLES LINSLEY TO R. M. T. HUNTER.

RUTLAND, VERMONT, *March 26, 1860.*

DEAR SIR: I take the liberty of addressing a line to you, a line upon politics though a stranger. As to my sincerity and respectability any of our members of Congress or Senators will inform you. My only object is to do you a service if I can, though I am not very certain I can do so.

I am a democrat who supported Jackson in 1828 and every democratic candidate since and you know enough of Vermont to know that being a democrat in such is not much to a man's advantage if a professional man, unless an office holder.

Now I assume that the Presidential candidate must be nominated from the South if *demanded by them.* This is too plain for debate, as you command nearly all the certain votes. You will then virtually make the nomination. I dont for a moment believe that Judge Douglass can be nominated. Thus far in the history of the country the democrats have not been guilty of the folly and weakness of running a man for President who was not thoroughly with them. Now our danger and weakness at this moment grows out of the course of Judge Douglass in relation to slavery. He not only abandoned our standards on the floor of the Senate (the battle field) but he has traversed the whole country to divide the democracy and that, against the United South; always, a Gibraltar for Conservative democracy, but he attacks the President and his cabinet and stands in opposition to the Supreme Court.

Now there are a good many true men in Vermont, that Judge D[ouglas]'s sophistry does not deceive. They would have carried the

State if the President had been disposed to remove a few of the leading official hypocrites from important offices. I mean they would have sent delegates, who would have been ready to cooperate with the Senate. But at the start they adopted the absurd idea of voting by towns, instead of by numbers so that a town with fifty inhabitants has the same power as one with 10,000. By this miserable trick they carried the Convention through the P[ost] Masters. The post masters in Vermont are nearly all Douglass men, because they have been mostly appointed on the recommendation of Judge Smally and Mr. Bawdish [?] Collector. At Washington I am told they profess to support the administration. But here they are undisguised friends of Douglass and using every effort in his favor by which the President and the P[ost]master Gen[eral] are deceived.

Now we have two delegates from the third District who were carried against the Douglass men and against Smally and his friends. The leader will be H. E. Stroughton, now U. S. District attorney who resides at B. Falls. The other delegate will be apt to go where Stroughton does. Stroughton has a brother in N[ew] York, a lawyer .of some eminence, who might perhaps influence him. He is a democrat. Unless he is for Douglass I can think of no influence that will carry H. E. Stroughton out of the way in which he ought to go.

Charles G. Eastman of Montepelier is one of the delegates, who may go right. He was elected against Smally and Bawdish's influence and is now in a bitter quarrel with them. This leads me to think that he will go against them as he knows if Douglass were to succeed that Judge Smally would control every appointment in Vermont.

Now I think no Southern man has been named who I think would be so acceptable to us as yourself, though there are many others we should cheerfully support if nominated. I do not want this made public, but you can use it with any friends you choose and if you are a candidate you have friends who might act in this matter in your behalf.

HENRY FITZHUGH TO R. M. T. HUNTER.

KANAWHA C[OURT] H[OUSE], VA., *March 26, 1860.*

MY DEAR SIR: By way of experiment, I have been circulating many copies of your late speech among some very intelligent acquaintances I have in Ohio, some of whom are Republicans. From one of these gentlemen, prominent in his state and the country by his efforts for Mr. Fremont, I received the following acknowledgment for your speech: " While on this subject let me say that I read with the greatest pleasure Mr. Hunter's great speech upon the slavery question; and I return you my thanks for sending me a copy. It has given me some new ideas: and I frankly confess that upon the platform laid down by him, I would not greatly object to his election. Indeed under some circumstances likely to occur, I could cheerfully vote for him. Another matter may interest you. I have for the last ten days been in various parts of this State (Ohio), part of the time attending the Legislature at Columbus, and I find many influential democrats and others, are looking to your friend as the best man for the Charleston nomination."

I hope very much that the Charleston Convention may nominate you; and present to the gentleman from whose letter I quote, and others in like predicament, a choice of which they may avail themselves. I shall be at Charleston, acting cordially with your friends, not to cast a vote for you and feel discharged from the duty, but with a sincere desire to secure your nomination.

Asa Biggs[1] to R. M. T. Hunter.

WILLIAMSTON, N. C. *March 27th, 1860.*

My DEAR SIR: Although I have escaped from the corrupt and corrupting atmosphere at Washington, and the strife of politics, and feel relieved by the escape, I feel a deep and abiding interest in the success of our government and a heartfelt sympathy for you and others: a small Spartan band it is true, who I believe are endeavoring to guide the state safely in her driftings to ruin. It has been evident to my mind for a long time that a large number of our Statesmen of all parties are being corrupted, the evident tendency of which is to lead to centralization and disaster; and my great hope has been on the masses, who although frequently misled yet I believe had an honest purpose to do right. Recent measures however in the name of protection, grand plans of internal improvements, homestead laws and pension laws &c have been inaugurated, well calculated to diffuse and infuse among the people the same corrupting influence that we see so lamentably operating upon the politicians; and if these measures are successful, which I greatly fear, this great hope of mine is taken away. The dangerous rock upon which we are threatened with shipwreck (slavery) in my opinion has been seized upon by the suggestions of political ambition to obtain power and place induced by the extravagance of the government and our departure from the economy and simplicity of our fathers who organized the government. All things however seem to be tending to centralization, corruption and ruin, and I admire the more those statesmen, few in number though they be, who have the moral courage to resist the evil spirit of the times and who if calamity befall us can truthfully say "I advised and warned against these influences and did not yield to the seduc-

---

[1] A Representative in Congress from North Carolina, 1845–1847; a Senator, 1855–1858.

tions to falter from pursuing the path of duty and safety." But it is not my purpose to write you a letter on the corrupting tendency of the times for I know with your experience I am far behind you in a knowledge of the dangers that beset us; but it is to enquire whether there is hope for our escape. I am decidedly of opinion that we need and ought to have a Southern man for the next President and I am, as decidedly in favor of your nomination. We must have some one who has the courage and ability to stand in the breach and who will fearlessly exercise his power to discountenance and denounce the corrupting measures of the day or we cannot escape the ruin which threatens us. Although I know I differ from the generally expressed opinion, yet I believe a Southern man of the right kind, will be more generally and cordially sustained by the Northern Democracy than one of the many Northern aspirants and expectants who are rivals to each other. I am aware of the difficulties and improbabilities of your nomination but recently I have entertained some strong hope.

I know that it will be impossible for you to reply in full, if at all, to the numerous letters you receive on the subject, but if you can find time to drop me a line, *entirely confidential* if you please, give me your opinion as to the prospect of your nomination or if that is not practicable or probable who at present bids fair to obtain the nomination I shall be greatly obliged to you.

Lest I bore you with too long a letter I conclude. I have many pleasant recollections of Washington and particularly of those with whom I cooperated in the public service in endeavoring to keep the administration of the government within the Constitution.

Thomas L. Kane to R. M. T. Hunter.

[Philadelphia, Pa.], *March 30, 1860.*

My dear Sir: I did not think when we parted that I sh[oul]d wish to write to you so soon, but a paragraph in the Herald correspondence of this morning giving additional currency to reports which have been some days upon the street here, I am led to remark upon the rumor that friends of Mr. Hunter have been arraying a coalition with Mr. S. A. Douglas.

In the course of an imperfect canvass wh[ich] I have been making of our Delegation, I have had occasion to communicate with several of the Douglas men, who are more numerous than I supposed, if we include under the designation all who are unsound upon the slavery question. As far as I am able to ascertain, Mr. D[ougla]s' adherents incline to consider it their chief's interest to support you, and, what is more, I suspect one individual of having taken his cue to this effect directly from the Illinois Senator himself. They have no difficulty in understanding that, if their candidate must look to another Convention, it is his interest to have the Presidential chair filled till '64 by a Southerner, to have a platform adopted which it will not humble him or his men to stand upon, to have an opportunity of conciliating the South by contributing to nominate its accepted favorite. I defer of course to the superior discernment of your supporters who are in Washington, and nearer Mr. Douglas than myself; but an item of intelligence from the provinces is not always without significance; and, as things look with us, there w[oul]d certainly seem to be no occasion for going half way to meet the gentleman.

I am pleased to believe that I have written thus far quite unnecessarily. I hardly doubt that your friends unite in looking upon any arrangements with Mr. Douglas as to say the least, premature. Will you permit me through you to direct their attention to a quarter in which they have it in their power to render us in Pennsylvania essential service?

Baker (the Collector, a gentleman with whom I have no personal influence) McKibber (late of Pittsburg), Hugh Clark, and a number of other delegates under their influence have been determined Cobb men. Their eyes, as you will understand, are directed to signals expected from the White House, yet they are all at present up in the wind, so to speak, since Mr. Cobb's withdrawal, and are all in the best possible mood to be influenced in your favor. If Governor Cobb will really exert himself, I do not hesitate to say that he can effect a change of from 15 to 20 votes in the Delegation. Should not this be attended to at once? I am at a loss to see what better disposal the Governor can make of his followers.

I am tempted to write to you at great length, but it is my intention to visit Washington next week. I hope to have the pleasure of calling upon you on Wednesday evening or on Thursday morning after breakfast. I cannot help being very sanguine. The phenomenon particularly to which I adverted in conversation with you has become more strikingly apparent. Our waiters upon Providence, you may depend upon it, continue of opinion that the tide is rising.

C. G. BAYLOR TO R. M. T. HUNTER.

(*Private.*)

NEW ORLEANS, [LA.], *March 31st, 1860.*

MY DEAR SIR: We have started an organization here to bring your name before the public as the proper man for the Charleston nomination.

I have to day sent a communication to the "*Constitution*" on the subject. It ought to be published by the Editor and I presume it will be. I shall start at once for Washington and hope to arrive in a few days.

You must not consider this a liberty Mr. Hunter, because it is the duty of every man who has a stable in the country to do something to save it. Your nomination is in my humble opinion the only one with which the party can succeed. Believing so, I have taken the liberty of giving an impulse to the idea in the Southwest and shall follow it up.

GEORGE FISHER TO R. M. T. HUNTER.

MORRIS GRUNDY CO., ILLINOIS, *March* —, *1860*.

DEAR SIR: I have received a packet of your speeches, for which please accept my thanks.

The New York Tribune, edited by Greeley, has done more for the success of the Black Republican cause, than is generally admitted; the Tribune is scattered profusely over the Northern States. The dispersion of the Black Republican ideas among the people, through Greeley's paper is the principal cause of their success. We should fight them with the same weapons. I beg leave to suggest that a news paper be published, in the city of New York, with a first class editor, having correspondence all over the world, giving all the interesting matter at home and abroad, commerce, agriculture &c. The political page to be National Democracy. To put such a paper into full operation is no small work; it can be done and made profitable, in this way. The Senators and Representatives, at Washington. resolve to establish such a paper, select the Editor or Editors, give them the creed political; then send agents over the Union to procure subscribers, (send no circulars, because they are not attended to). These agents to call on all the Post Masters of the larger Post offices, and urge them to procure subscribers for the National paper. We have over 29 thousand Post offices; they can be made average *four* subscribers to the post office, this will make over one hundred thousand. Our chance is better, take the Union over than Greeley's, because he is confined to the North, our field would be the whole confederacy. It would take a large sum of money to start, but if persevered in would succeed and be profitable to the owners. We have been losing ground in the North, for the past few years, this ground must be retaken, but it will require a powerful effort to accomplish it. I can conceive of no better plan than in scattering our opinions broad cast over the land, by a well conducted paper. We have too many superficial notions to be successful, our opinions should be one. We should advocate nothing but what is right and constitutional. Make the paper so cheap and interesting that every person would wish for a copy.

I am a stranger to you, but you are [a] Democrat of the true stripe and this is my excuse for communicating my opinions to you; I consider all true democrats of one family. I should be pleased to have your views on the propriety of establishing a National paper. To be certain that you are not writing to an enemy, I refer you to President Buchanan.

A. G. HOLMES TO R. M. T. HUNTER.

PHILADELPHIA, [PA.], *April 3rd, 1860.*

DEAR SIR. The conservative portion of the people of the north want the agitating question of slavery put at rest, but which can only be effected by throwing the agitators of this question into a hopeless minority. The doctrine, that the constitution carries slavery into the territories, and that it can only cease there by the power incident to a sovereign State, when [the] territory shall have assumed that legal form, is just as acceptable to them as any other theory or interpretation of that instrument, and hence, their moral and political views are not offended by it. But there is another question of vastly more importance to them, and that is, adequate protection to American labor; and that is the question, with the practical direction given to it by Southern influence in our legislation or policy, which has induced the antagonistic feeling toward the South, that has existed and now prevails.

It was this issue, the affirmative of which was taken by Mr. Clay, that arranged so strong a party for forty years, under his leadership. It was what during that time they contended for, and it is the only issue or question that interests them now. They will go for protection to American labor by whomever presented, though the declaration of the Northern democracy, so faithless heretofore on that question, are merely viewed as the tub thrown to the whale. And if, therefore, it is upon the banner of a Seward, looking not beyond it for the time being, they will vote for Seward, even though they despise the doctrine that contemplated any restoration upon the South in relation to slavery, trusting as they will, for an antidote to such a bane to some subsequent election, when a party that is constitutional, shall cease to occupy an antagonistitc position to their life blood interests, believed to be as essential to their protection as is slavery to the South.

The black Republicans are anxious to keep the issue on this question open notwithstanding their present manifestations, and hence, if it is settled by enacting into a law Mr. Morrill's Tariff Bill, it will withdraw from the opposition hundreds of thousands of votes, their interest in that organization having ceased, and then, the next Presidential contest will give you some idea of the strength of those devoted to the Constitution and Union.

Expediency, when not inconsistent with the general interests of the country, may be adopted. To weaken abolitionism or fanaticism, by yielding to the demand for protection to home labor is a case in point.

In taking the liberty of addressing you, I seek neither notice nor answer; as I have no aspirations, political or social to gratify, except that of a constitution loving citizen of the American Union; and, therefore, I trust you will give this communication considera-- tion.

GEORGE DENNETT TO R. M. T. HUNTER.

BOSTON, [MASS.], *April 3rd, 1860.*

DEAR SIR: I feel a great interest in the national election that is soon to take place. I also feel that our success in that election depends very much on the standard-bearer selected at the Charleston Convention. We ought [to] nominate a Southern statesman for our candidate, to be successful. I am about fifty years old, and have always voted and exerted my humble influence in favor of the Democratic party. As long as Mr. Calhoun lived, of all men, he was my choice for the Presidency. Since his death, my preference has been very strongly in your favor. With you as our candidate we can succeed. Make New York the battle ground, and I think you can whip Seward without any doubt. New York City alone would give you 40 to 50,000 maj[ority]. I did not think of going to Charleston, as I am not a delegate, and I am unable to incur the expense still, some of my friends insist on my going, saying that I can do much good. If you think I can be of any service to yourself I will go. We have had three northern Presidents since we had one from the South, I say three, because Gen. Taylor was ruled by Webster and Co. If our Presidents during that period had been Southerners, our party at the north, would now be as sound, and in the majority as it was during the administration of Mr. Polk, and prior.

As I am not personally known to you, I will get some mutual friend to give me a line to enclose with this.

JOHN M. JOHNSON TO R. M. T. HUNTER.

QUINCY, ILLINOIS, *April 4th, 1860.*

DEAR SIR: I send the enclosed paragraph which I cut from the Missouri Republican of the 2d Inst, that you may give it a prompt contradiction, as it is calculated to do you great harm with the friends of Judge Douglass in the North West, of whom you are almost invariably the Second choice.

I have seen a good many of the Delegates from this State and Iowa to the Charleston Convention, since I left home, and I am sure they will aid in your nomination, should Judge Douglass not be the nominee.

J. Cook to R. M. T. Hunter.

CHICAGO, [ILL.], *April 4th, 1860.*

DEAR SIR: I have just paused to notice the rumor, started by the St. Louis *Republican*, a paper devoted to the interest of Judge Douglas, and, I may say with truth: almost the only one favorable to him in the State of Missouri, "that you have written to a prominent National Democrat of this State, that you wish the National Delegates from Illinois to be sure and go to the Convention, and that, if it is necessary, you will supply them with funds to enable them to go." I also notice, by the Telegraphic reports, in the papers of this morning, from Washington, that you deny having written such [a] letter as above indicated. Of course the whole thing has been gotten up by the Douglas-men for a fling at both yourself and the National Democrats. No one will believe for a moment that you have particularly interested yourself to induce the Delegates from this State to go to Charleston, and any one, who knows the National Delegates from Illinois, will also understand that they can pay as they go, and are now as they have always been, self sustaining, and relying upon nothing but their principles to carry them through. Permit me to add, that they could not be better pleased than they would be in supporting your claims to the Presidency.

CHARLES LEVI WOODBURY to R. M. T. Hunter.

BOSTON, [MASS.], *April 4th, 1860.*

DEAR SIR: Allow me to introduce to your acquaintance George Dennett Esqr., a gentleman who has always been a consistent democrat and was last year a candidate of our party for State Treasurer. Mr Dennett was a great friend of the lamented Calhoun in his life time and enjoyed much of his confidence, as I well know. You will find him a reliable and particularly sound democrat on constitutional points and well affected to the administration although he had the misfortune to be removed by Mr. Collector Austin at the beginning of this term.

WILLIAM OLD, JR. to R. M. T. Hunter.

(Confidential.)

[RICHMOND, VA.], *April 5th, 1860.*

MY DEAR SIR: You will have seen the result of the proceedings of the Convention in this district. The vote was stronger against us than it should have been, but they really had a majority in the Convention. The unfortunate action of our friends in Chesterfield defeated Mr. Seddon. He could have been elected but it would have been because of his great strength in the district. You now have the

State, but we will need our strongest men to be in Charleston with the delegation to make them really work for you. The Wise men will be there and every effort will be made, to get the delegates to drop you after a complimentary vote, they desire your defeat, to be followed by the nomination of Douglas, as an excuse and an incentive to independent action in Virginia. Seddon's presence would aid us very much there. You ought to have as many true friends from every district in the State as you can possibly get to go there. I have not the least faith in Hoge, I never did have any. He cannot fail to vote for you, but he can be persuaded to attempt to drop you early I believe. And I am not sure that he will not let it be known, that he intends to do so early and before any action is had. He wrote to Duckwall to see me and induce me as I understood him, not to class him so decidedly with your friends. I will not cease to claim him publicly, until he denies his conversation with Duckwall and denies his letter to Tucker, and satisfies me too that he never had the one or wrote the other. I hope Duckwall has told him my determination. I do not wish to assail him but I will expose the whole facts if he is encouraged by Barbour's conduct to make any publication—he got his position from your friends by assurance made to the warmest and most intimate of them, and he ought not to be allowed to shuffle out of it.

I write with some feeling, because he and Barbour are making our hard won victory of as little value as possible. For Barbour; his position I have always considered to be publicly what he defines it in his cond.[?], but the assurances of his brother made to others both in writing and orally convinced them and me that his election would be more beneficial to you, than that of a more decided and avowed friend. I know he will give you an earnest and active support unless some influence is brought to bear on him stronger than any I can anticipate. his cond. will hurt us beyond the State. The defeat of Seddon is a severe blow too in the same direction. I see Washington makes an effort to count something on the gain of the democracy in Connecticut. We should count it as a decisive defeat if we wish to unite the South on a Southern candidate at Charleston. Nothing but the conviction that a Northern candidate can get strength enough in the free States to lose some Southern States can gain Douglas the nomination. We ought to make the nomination rest on making such a one as will unite the entire South. This will prevent you from losing a Southern State in Convention, and the North must yield to the pertinacious vote of the United South. Every calculation favorable to democrat success in the Northern States weakens you in Convention. We should in my judgement, make the impression that we intend to meet the Black Republicans, in their sectional character and in their most Northern aspect, that we mean to make the presidential election one of the issues with the antislavery party, and to make them all distinctly, and that we do not want a victory won by any means that cast doubt on the character of the contest, and that if we leave them the platform unchanged, we will insist on the candidate, as the only means of making the election of any use to us.

We should make this issue with the Northern democracy at once, I think in time for the Charleston Convention to see and understand it, and thus the Virginia delegation could be made to do more with such men as Seddon then to look after Hoge and Crockett. I cannot prevent this effectively through the paper for I cannot now afford to make a distinct issue with the friends of Douglas in or out of the state. I have not full proof of their intrigue in this state, although I am convinced they are carrying on one, and that its object is to make use of you to get a delegation, nominally for you but prepared to drop you early and take up every body else, not Douglas in particular, but any one to get you out of the way. A few good articles written, presenting the Southern claim to this nomination, and stating distinctly the necessity of giving us the candidate if we leave the platform as it is, would decide the fate of Douglas in this state. His strength is over-rated here. Lyons attacked him last night in the Convention and if he had made the same assertion in full convention which he did when it was but a skeleton, he would have defeated the resolution pledging the district to the Charleston nominees. It was a bad resolution, and though I voted for it, as I intend to vote for such nominee against any Union candidate or Black Republican, the people are not going to do it. Lyons asserts that Douglas still occupies the postion that the Dred Scott decision does not effect the right of the territorial population to exclude or destroy slave property. I do not believe he does, but it is not my game to relieve him from the imputation now, and his friends did not. If I believed he and his friends were playing a fair game, I would let them have the use of the columns of the Examiner, to defend him—but as I do not, I will not aid him untill, the interests of the party and country require it. I believe he is working harder and more exclusively against you than Wise or any man in the South or North, whether through himself or his agents I do not know, but certainly his friends in V[irgini]a understand that this is their task. These views I submit to you, and wish to know whether they are yours. And if they are how can I get them presented to the public without making a direct attack upon Douglas which I will not do as I may have to support him, and do not wish to make his friends implacable.

JOHN LETCHER TO R. M. T. HUNTER.

(Private.)

RICHMOND, VA., *April 6th, 1860.*

MY DEAR SIR: I received your letter of yesterday, this morning, and reply to it, at the earliest moment.

I have regarded the result in this district as doubtful—not from any knowledge I possessed, but from such information as I could pick up, from casual conversations, with individuals. The Wise party were exceedingly active, and spared no effort to rally their friends, in the several counties, and secure their attendance at the Convention. Besides, Seddon has been much absent from the State, and has had very limited intercourse with the people of the district. To retain influence, a man must mingle with the people, and keep himself prominently in the public eye. This is the great disadvantage to which Seddon has been subjected in this contest, and it is rather surprising to me therefore that he ran so well.

The result in the Petersburg district disappointed me, and I am wholly at a loss to understand how it was, that Harvie was elected by so large a majority, and that Thompson holding directly opposite opinions was chosen as his colleague. I have heard no satisfactory explanation of it.

From all my information from my old district, I think there is no doubt we shall carry it. Mr. G. Harman was here last week, and told me, that he was satisfied that you had the state, and he would resist all factious movements, to injure you. He said also, he would vote for Paxton, and he had no doubt of his election, and he believed you would get the district. This is in conformity with all my information from other well informed sources. And besides, I know that some of the most ultra of the Wise men in the district, have said that they now believed it was best to take Douglas which I regard as an admission of their impotency, under their old leader.

I am satisfied that you have the State, and the only danger I apprehend is, that Wise's tools will seek to defeat you, by linking their fortunes, with some one candidate, who will provide for his late Excellency. The man cannot live out of politics, and as he has nothing now to hope for, from the State, he must direct his attention to the Federal Government. What the move will be no man can tell, but we may look out for something, that promises to embarrass you and your friends.

At the Convention here, a proposition was introduced, pledging the members to the support of the Charleston nominees, which was opposed in speeches by Lyons, and others of the Wise party, and although it was carried, nearly all the Wise men voted against its adoption. Lyons I hear stated that he would not vote for Douglas, if he were nominated. This looks significant, as these men doubtless know the views of their leader, and speak and act by the Card.

As to Col Hubard's letter, I had heard very much the same things from himself, when he made his application for the appointment. The scuffle between Clay and himself embarrasses me, as they are both valued friends, personal and political, and about equal in their qualifications for the position. I have the matter under consideration, and when the time to act shall arrive, I will do what I think right. They ought to relieve me from this position, but if they will not do so, I must meet it, and take the consequences.

W. H. WINDER TO R. M. T. HUNTER.

PHILADELPHIA, [PA.], *April 9th, 1860.*

DEAR SIR: In conversation, this morning, with a distinguished politician, and speaking of the prominent names for the nomination, he expressed the belief that a potential influence would probably defeat the nomination or election of Senator Hunter. He referred to the corruptionists of all parties, who make common cause to exclude those who they expect to find inexerable towards them. He said while it was a cause of shame and regret, yet it was a fact which could not be overlooked. That such a state of affairs can be supposed to exist as to render unbending integrity a disqualification for the presidency, is a burning shame. And while I do not admit it, to the extent claimed, yet it has become a power, this corruption, and is yearly increasing to an extent to justly alarm every patriot mind. I object to it, because it is tantamount to saying of all candidates, nominated by any party, that they will not see the corruption existing under them. Such depreciation of a man, is his highest honor, and I believe also, that if your views should be deemed consistent with the interests of Pennsylvania, that your election, if nominated, would be certain.

In regard to the proper action at Charleston, I am in a fog, and wish to get to Washington to learn something definite. My own personal predilections, are in the first instance, for parties from whom I differ on the important subject of the Tariff, while the safety and harmony of our Union being at stake are our primary care.

I have thought it might not be altogether amiss to acquaint you, with one of the elements used to remove your name from before the Convention. I do not do it as a partizan of yours, but as simple justice to a most distinguished and most honorable Senator.

G. BAILEY TO R. M. T. HUNTER.

INTERIOR [DEPARTMENT], *April 9th, 1860.*

DEAR SIR: I enclose the draft of a bill to reorganise the Indian service in Cal[ifornia], it has been submitted to Mr. Thompson and received his approval. I have condensed it as much as possible supposing it was to be offered as an amendment to the appropriation bill. Should it be determined to introduce it as an independent measure, some changes would be advisable.

You remarked to the Secretary, in my hearing, the other morning, that something ought to be done towards reviving the Intercourse law &c. Allow me then to call your attention to a bill, prepared by me in 1858, in reference to reservations, printed with Senate amendments to House bill No 557 1st Session 35th Congress. Nine tenths of the troubles with the Indians, on the Western frontier, grow out of the attempts of speculators to get possession of their lands. The law in relation to Indian titles has to be collected from a mass of contradictory statutes and precedents which it is impossible to reduce to anything like a system. And the evil has been aggravated by the indirect aid, afforded to the speculators by Congress, so that each case instead of being settled *upon a fixed principle*, has been decided according to interests or caprice. I am satisfied that the passage of that law would put an end to speculation in Indian reserves, and remove one of the principal objections on the part of the Indians, to attempting to support themselves by agriculture. This was the opinion of Genl. Denver,[1] the then Comm[issione]r, and Mr. Sebastian,[2] at whose instance the bill was prepared. As you seem to manifest some interest in the matter I trust you will excuse the liberty I take in alluding to the bill.

THOMAS L. KANE TO R. M. T. HUNTER.

PHILADELPHIA, [PA.], *April 13, 1860.*

DEAR SIR: I asked for you twice at your lodgings on my recent visit to Washington, and hoped your public duties would have permitted you to call upon me before my return home. Perhaps I exaggerated the importance of some of the points which I desired to bring to your notice; they have also in a measure been attended to here.

I ought not however, I think, omit to communicate a suggestion which is not my own, and which it is not in my power to carry out. Mr. N. B. Browne (Postmaster), one of our own delegates suggested

---

[1] James Wilson Denver, a Representative in Congress from California, 1855–1857.
[2] William King Sebastian, a Senator in Congress from Arkansas, 1848–1865.

to me in conversation yesterday the importance of procuring a member of the Virginia delegation to take his passage with the Pennsylvanians. They leave here on the 18th in the Keystone State which has been chartered to convey them to Charleston. Mr. Browne, who is [on] the Committee of Arrangements, will keep a berth in the steamer vacant as long as possible.

I need not offer my own services. Mr. Garnett or any other of your friends can communicate directly with Mr. Browne who will be glad to hear from them.

I regret to say that Mr. John Robbins, Jr. who will probably be prevailed upon to remain in Philadelphia to see to the interests of the party in respect to the Mayoralty for which he has our nomination. You will in this case be without your best friend in the Pennsylvania delegation. Next to Mr. Robbins, Mr. Browne is perhaps your most sincere well wisher. He is also a perfectly safe man, and may be corresponded with as such.

THOMAS S. BOCOCK TO R. M. T. HUNTER.

[Telegram]

CHARLESTON, S. C., *April 25th, 1860.*

If Southern States remain in convention Douglas nomination impossible. If they go out he is certain. Virginia goes for reasonable change in platform.[1]

THOMAS S. BOCOCK TO HON. WM. P. MILES.

[Telegram]

CHARLESTON, S. C., *April 25th, 1860.*

If platform not satisfactory, Mississippi, Florida, and Texas will go out with the anti-Douglas men of Alabama and Arkansas. No nominations sooner than Saturday or Monday next.

LUCIUS QUINTON WASHINGTON TO R. M. T. HUNTER.

[Telegram]

CHARLESTON, S. C., *April 25th, 1860.*

Improvement since yesterday. Virginia and New York voted against the gag.

---

[1] The above telegram was endorsed on the envelope "Honorable Howell Cobb present."

WILLIAM WATSON WICK [1] TO R. M. T. HUNTER.

INDIANAPOLIS, [IND.], *April 27, 1860.*

DEAR SIR: I have just read the dispatches of last night. What a painful picture they present. The Southern people have not slaves enough to meet their demands, not enough to perform the labor of their country, as is admitted by candid men among them, and as is proved by the greatly enhanced prices of slaves. The right of having their property in slaves, in the Territories protected by Congressional legislation is a mere abstraction; because they, on emigrating to any Territories *now* existing, will not take any considerable number of slaves with them. Yet, as appears from the proceedings at Charleston, they are ready to risk *everything* rather than fail in obtaining a *direct* affirmation of the power and duty of Congress to protect their right *within the Territories.* On the other hand, while the north would, without doubt, concede an extension of the fugitive slave law for the benefit of slaveholders *in* Territories to enable them to welcome slaves escaping from Territories, deny the power of Congress to provide for the protection of slave holding *within* the Territories. Considering the very limited number of slaves which will be taken into Territories, this also is an abstraction. There is, in fact, nothing at issue except abstractions. Yet on these abstractions, deduced from the K[ansas] and N[ebraska] bill and the Dred Scott decision by two different constructions thereof, it would seem that the Democratic party is likely to fail of action, either united, or tolerant, and undecisive.

Were it not that the masses are wiser, cooler, and better politicians then variant opinions about an abstraction, wholly impracticable in its character, I could not see how the unity of the States and the people are to be maintained. I see Gov. Wise thinks Virginia would go for Judge McLean over Douglas. While I apprehend that Indiana may go for the same man over any one but D[ouglas], and am very sure it would do so over any one who is committed to Congressional Slave Codes, to operate *within* the Territories.

The conclusion of my mind is that we (the Dem[ocratic] party) are to go under. Hoosiers will say every thing good of you, save only one thing. Hoosiers do not know what Mr. Guthrie and others think; and without a platform offensive to them would give them their votes. And although clouds gather around us here, I would hope to carry you, on the Cin[cinnati] platform and the Dred Scott decision, *unconstrued.* In my ward we have an immense pole ready to go up the moment we have a standard bearer and I am set down

---

[1] A Democratic Representative in Congress from Indiana, 1839–1841, 1845–1849.

23318°—18—VOL 2——21

for a speech when the flag unfurls at the top.   God grant it may be raised.   But I fear.

Note.   I hope you will appreciate my voluntary notes.   I love Democracy.   I love the Democratic party, albeit I am bound to admit that corruptions are rife within it.   And I love my country.   Mental ebullition must find scope.   So I write to you. Excuse me, if my notes trouble you.   Your ambition is chastened and moderate, as I well know.   Mr D[ouglas] is *not*, as I well know ambitious of the Presidency, *just now;* but is convinced that his ideas are right, and that unless they be adopted formally or acted upon informally we can no longer carry the North West.   I wrote to him sometimes formally, but not lately, as there is no reason for writing. If either you or he were haunted by such ambition as characterises many men, I would never think of writing to either of you.

CHARLES MASON TO R. M. T. HUNTER.

[FLORENCE, S. C., *April 30th, 1860*].

MY DEAR SIR: I have not ventured to add any thing to what I last wrote you, because I have been unable until this morning to discover any material change in our prospects.   Early in the day, I thought them brightening.   There is a decided *back down* on the part of Douglas' friends and a stern determination to allow no third party to slip in.   But yesterday a sort of Southern conference was held, at which the chairman of each delegation was present (including Virginia).   Russell took a conservative, or rather neutral position and the idea now is, that the seceding states, Al[abama] G[eorgi]a S[outh] C[arolina], Texas &c having induced us to unite with them in demanding a protection resolution (which the sequel will prove was a great mistake) threaten to desert us, unless we will agree to retire from the Convention with them, on the adoption of the minority report or any thing like it.   God only knows whether they are in earnest.   If they would but stand firm, your nomination w[oul]d be certain, if any at all is made.   There is a threat of adjourning the Convention over, which the Douglas men have the power to do, as it is understood, they command 153 faithful followers.   The idea is that Jeff [Jefferson] Davis proving unavailing they will take up Guthrie or Jo Lane [Joseph Lane of Oregon]; but as you suspected, there is an outside preference for Breckenridge.   I still hope for the best, but the game is too well played, for unsophisticated men, like the Virginia delegation, to stand a fair chance of preventing the cards from being packed on them.   You are too calm to be effected by the result, one way or the other.   If you should not succeed, you will come out of the fight damaged neither in honor nor popularity, and are young enough to make a good fight four years hence.

This may be no news to you, or perhaps better things may reach you before this. My earnest, heartfelt prayer is, that it may be so. If any thing good turns up, I will telegraph.

WILLIAM WATSON WICK TO R. M. T. HUNTER.

(*Confidential.*)

INDIANAPOLIS, [IND.], *May 6th, 1860.*

DEAR SIR: We in the north did understand the K[ansas] and N[ebraska] Bill and the Cin[cinnati] platform as guaranteeing to all future Territories perfect sovereignty and independence in reference to all municipal questions and matters. We understood Southern Statesmen, even Mr. Yancey in Cincinnati in 1856, to concede the same, and to glory in non intervention. We find nothing in the Dred Scott decision, not even in the obiter dicta of that decision, to justify an abandonment of our past position, on this point, nor to justify Southern States and Statemen in presenting any other idea. We *know* that our people are thoroughly indoctrinated into the dogma, or Truth above stated, and that to change our ground is to break up and destroy the Dem[ocratic] party *with us*. We think we know that the Dem[ocratic] party can serve us in the South without the direct assertion of the right of Slaveholding protection from Congress in the Territories in reference to the infinitessimal interest which exists (if at all) at this hour and which interest owing to the scarcity and high price of slaves, and to the character of the last of all the Territory which is now ours, cannot be increased till we make further acquisition. We look for defeat if the Southern platform or a candidate who favors it be forced upon us. We have scarce a hope to the contrary, aggravated as our people are by the efforts to force upon us the President's "*Lecompton policy,*" contrary to all our preconceived ideas, and expectations derived from the columns of all our local prints, and from *all* our Orators, and by the other disappointment named in my last. Mr. Bright thought he had all fixed when he compromised with Joseph A. Wright, and sent him to Berlin. It is his way to suppose that if leading politicians agree on anything, the people will assent as a matter of course. In this he is in error, especially when those leading politicians have lost caste, as both he and Joseph A. Wright have here at home. A hundred thousand Jos. Wrights have sprung from the ashes of his weak and dispised *self immolation.*

If the Dem[ocratic] party should be defeated we in Indiana shall despair of its restoration for a long series of years to come, in Ind[iana]. With our platforms and candidate we shall tremble for· the consequences should the same man be nominated at both Balt-[imore] and Chicago; but not truly totally discouraged ·we shall toil and expect in hope. Suffer me then to appeal to such Southern men as I can reach (and I wish I could reach all of them) to not take *this time* to make their useless demand—useless, because if their platform, and their candidate could be adopted and elected, not five northern members of the lower House would even under existing circumstances, vote for a law in accordance. I beg for the sake of my country (which will probably before two winters more be mine no longer) that, even if you are sure you are right, let no *definite* declaration of that right *now* be asserted. When Tamaulipas and Vera Cruz shall be ours, our people will find a way to favor the views of the South. But for God's sake let us have our platform and our man once more, till scars are effaced. Discredit witnesses who testify concerning us and our opinions, under the influence of extreme prejudice and malignity, and who will never again share public favor. I swear to you, by the living God that our Indiana witnesses are mistaken or testify falsely. Neither of them could this year be chosen to any office in Ind[iana] or in any county or district thereof, because in *almost all matters* they have disregarded opinion at home.

You may think me indelicate and impertinent; and I confess I would be so, but for the fact that I am assured that but little of Truth from Indiana has reached you.

I made a written appeal to J[ames] B[uchanan] just after his inauguration. He has suffered terribly in our State from a total disregard of my suggestions, and I ruined myself with him I suppose. My notes may ruin me with you. If so I cannot help it. I would be a traitor to my convictions of duty were I to be silent. God commands it and I obey.

Note. What feelings of personal hostility actuate the President, both our Senators, our most corrupt Governor, and others, I think cannot be held from a man of your powers of observation, and judgment. Why then rely on their testimony, concerning public opinion? Why consult their preferences? Be indulgent to the Northern Democracy *at this crisis*, and we can come through. The time for a Southern Candidate, and for the presentation of Southern views is not now, but will come with future Territorial Acquisition if not precede the same. Even if I were to minister to *your* personal ambition, I would say *now is not the time*. I do not however believe your Ambition to be other than decidedly modest, & moderate. Save the Dem[ocratic] party and it will yet again save you of the South. I pray God to give you & others the wisdom which all Human beings need to derive from a Divine power.

I am the same man now that I was when I spoke upon Giddings, in the House, except that I do not now hold a "*professional Slave trader as an unmitigated brute beast.*" But I am perfectly aware of a concerted effort of Bright, Robinson & others to depreciate me in 1847 & onward. I know too that I have suffered much from it abroad, but not here at home where my unsuspecting disposition, generosity, and artless *unguardedness*, are known, and my blunt honesty appreciated.

WILLIAM OLD, JR. TO R. M. T. HUNTER.

[RICHMOND, VA.], *May 11th, 1860.*

MY DEAR SIR: After leaving you I remembered a conversation I had with Mr. Washington in which I approved his intention to write out some reminiscences of the Charleston Convention. I have great confidence in his judgment, but our fight with Douglas, if one is necessary, requires most delicate management. It must be carried on as a state affair. The Virginia democracy must be the arbiters. Our course towards Douglas and his friends must be borne in mind, we built him up in V[irgini]a, or *rather prevented his destruction.* We must wait for action by his friends before we commence hostilities in that State. Every feeling I have impels me to assail the man and his friends, but we must be careful in doing so. Can you present some such views to Mr. Washington? Excuse this short note as I am very tired.

CHARLES W. RUSSELL [1] TO R. M. T. HUNTER.

WHEELING, [VA.], *May 13, 1860.*

DEAR SIR: Since my return home I have seen a good many of your friends in this part of the State. I have found them unshaken in their preference for you over other candidates for the presidency, although recent events have caused them generally to take a desponding view of the prospect of your success. I am sure that nothing will be done about here to embarrass you in any course you may be inclined to adopt with reference to your own position as a candidate.

Upon the latter subject my impressions are about as they were when I last saw you. But I think you ought to do nothing and to resolve upon nothing for the present. The future is still too doubtful to justify a hasty decision and, whatever may be your decision, it may be made with as much propriety hereafter as it can be now. Events will certainly take place within a few weeks which will make the path of duty more clear.

It has been my opinion for months that the nomination must fall upon yourself or Judge Douglass. Between you of course I could readily choose. If you should be withdrawn, I am inclined to prefer

---

[1] A prominent local politician from northwestern Virginia, now West Virginia.

him to all others who have been proposed if he will stand on a proper platform. But, in spite of weighty reasons for that inclination, I find myself yet unable to decide that a Southern man ought, in any event, to promote his nomination. A single obstacle always interposes. But for that, I should say that it is clearly the interest of the South to nominate and elect him, unless you can be nominated and elected. The South, now falling into a minority, ought to bind the North-West to herself with hooks of steel. The alliance is natural and almost unavoidable, unless we repel it. It is the only alliance between the South and any part of the North which is likely to be permanent, apart from mere government connections.

As to the "platform," there ought to be no changes in it, unless Judge Douglass is to stand on it. If he is to be the candidate, the South must protect herself against an affirmation of his doctrine of "Squatter Sovereignty." But no more ought to be asked than is necessary for that purpose. Whatever we gain in that direction will be gained by a sacrifice of other interests of the South and at some risk to the Union. Even in the Territories, a sound Democratic president would be worth more to the South than any "Slave Code." But we in Virginia have a more immediate interest in turning the hostile governors and legislatures of neighboring states out of office.

You know it would best comport with my first opinions if we could elect you and let the platform alone. This we could have done but for the conduct of Southern men who professed to be your friends. They have done more to injure the South than all her enemies could have done during this year. I wish I could accord to them *all* the merit of good intentions. Possibly through all this confusion we may get back to the goal for which we first started. But if Southern leaders intend to renew the contest at Baltimore and to make an ultimatum such as Alabama made at Charleston, or the Senate resolutions or anything of that sort, I do not desire to be a member of the Convention at Baltimore. I am not willing to separate from the South. Neither do I wish to participate in measures which, in my judgment, will be ruinous to the South and disastrous to the country.

I should have added with reference to Judge Douglass that most of the Democrats whom I have seen in this part of the State begin to look upon his nomination as a sort of necessity and are prepared to acquiesce on proper terms, rather than break up the party. But the disposition to take him up as the "available" man under the circumstances is less decided than I expected, although rather generally diffused.

The length of this letter, I trust, requires no apology as it is written in fulfilment of a promise.

[P. S.] The speech to be made by Douglass tomorrow may change some of my views.

THOMAS D. SUMTER [1] TO R. M. T. HUNTER.

STATESBURGH, [S. C.], *May 14, 1860.*

DEAR HUNTER: I went down to Charleston to the convention to see what I could do for you, but I am sorry to say that I was unsuccessful. The N. Eastern and Western men, were immovable. They stuck to Douglass to the last and will still do so, unless they are *bought* out. The course the Virginia delegation has taken, if not amended in June, will cause her to lose irretrievably the influence and prestige she has heretofore held in the Union. The North are *exacting* without a prospect, or a very slim one, of giving a single electoral vote, and we look upon it, as a piece of impudence and an attempt at bullying that they should require us to give up to them, upon the mere *chance*, of obtaining one or two votes. If we meet at Richmond, which I think we will do, pass the majority platform and nominate candidates, it is probable most of the states will wheel into line. There is now no other course for us to pursue. I think we will send from this state to the Richmond Convention our *best* men. All the Districts are up and doing and what is better, all the ultra State rights men in the State join in the movement and are willing to participate in it. If my hopes are realized, that is, if the Richmond Convention will act uncompromisingly and with energy, I think yours is the best chance. At all events you have luck, which is something in political as well as in other matters. I will endeavor to be at Richmond and Washington. I saw our friend from Virginia, Hubbard, and expressed my views to him. I knew a great many men from various parts of the Union in the Convention, with all of whom I broached the subject of your nomination, as the only satisfactory one that could be made for the South. They all agreed, that you were perfectly acceptable to them, but no reliance can be placed upon the Northern and N[orth] Western men. Woods delegation, if it had been admitted would have gone for you. It may possibly occur that they will be admitted in Richmond, however, every thing is just now very uncertain. In this state, we have now fortunately got clear of a subject of disagreement, that is Convention and anti Convention. More than two thirds of our people have been heretofore opposed to Conventions, but now they feel no hesitation in being represented at Richmond. I am sorry we have not more time, to perfect this arrangement, however, as it will be a game of chance, I go for luck. Dont write a line on politics, " keep your bowels open and ride with a snafle-bit."

P. S. Send me some interesting document, in acknowledgment of my letter. Now the old Boss is dead (Calhoun) we States rights men have to look to you to keep us straight.

---

[1] A Representative in Congress from South Carolina, 1839–1843.

CHARLES W. RUSSELL TO R. M. T. HUNTER.

WHEELING, [VA.], *May 19th, 1860.*

DEAR SIR: I have read with much care the " address to the National Democracy " published in the Constitution of the 17th Inst. over the signatures of yourself and some other members of Congress. I regret to find it so different from what I had expected. Owing to the relations between us, I feel obliged to state with friendly candor the impression it has produced on my mind.

In this paper the course pursued by the " Seceders " at Charleston is applauded with emphasis; while that of your friends who remained in the Convention is approved in cautious and measured terms. If the former were "compelled to withdraw" in order to escape "a burning imputation upon the honor and patriotism of the party," they doubtless deserved your applause. But I expect to be called upon to defend myself and others against the attacks of those in Virginia who take that admiring view of the late secession.

This paper also encourages the Seceders to believe that, if they return to the Convention, we will follow their lead in a course of conduct which will "proudly vindicate the action of the seceding delegates." That course is repugnant to my convictions of duty, as I have partially explained them to you already. I have yielded to the seceding delegations the utmost that my judgment would sanction and, in return, they have recklessly spurned the counsels of Virginia, ruined the prospects of her candidate, put her material interests at hazard, broken the harmony of the Democratic party and imperilled the Union, without a sufficient justification.

The Alabama delegation were compelled to withdraw. The others acted under no compulsion except that which resulted from their own imprudence. I believe the most of them acted with the best intentions, but under a pernicious influence. Whatever their motives may have been, however, I cannot " vindicate their action " or put myself under their guidance.

I need not tell you how much I regret to discover such a divergence between your views and my own in this crisis. Although, it may prevent me from being further useful (if indeed I have been at any time useful) to your political interests in the present canvass, it does not diminish my admiration of the qualities which have attached me to your cause and to your person. I shall be compelled to vindicate my conduct, even against the publication to which you have lent your signature.

O. H. BERRYMAN TO R. M. T. HUNTER.

U. S. S. FALMOUTH, ASPINWALE, N. G., *May 19, 1860*.

DEAR SIR: I had the honor some time ago to address you a note upon the subject of a bill before the Senate for my relief, and had the great pleasure since of noticing your remarks, on its coming up and final passage.

At the same time another bill from the Court of Claims for my relief was put before the Senate, and was postponed at the suggestion of Mr. Pugh of Ohio. I beg leave to say to you that I think there is not a more just claim before Congress than that very one.

When I was on the Coast of Brazil in 1848 in command of the On-Ka-hy-e I captured a Slaver having on board *$25,000* in Specie. I sent the ship home to the district to which she belonged. She arrived safe, was delivered according to law to the Marshall of the District. The case was duly tried, the vessel, cargo and appurtenances sold by order of the proper court. The Specie being a part of the Cargo I delivered in person to the marshall of the district and took his receipt for it in quantity and kind. That is the last I have seen of it. The officers and crew of the On-Ka-hy-e *by a law* of the land are entitled to a portion of that money, as well as the proceeds of sale of ship and cargo. Now sir the only money which was paid from such proceeds has been the fees, amounting to upwards of $4,300.

I beg Sir in the name of justice that you will give me one single glance at this case, and I am sure you will readily perceive how illy the Captors of that Slaver have been used. It has now been upwards of twelve years since that capture occurred, and I have been at great expense endeavouring to get a bill passed for the relief of that faithful and deserving little crew.

CHARLES W. RUSSELL TO R. M. T. HUNTER.

WHEELING, VIRGINIA, *May 24th, 1860*.

MY DEAR SIR: How came Hunter the cautious to be so inconsiderate as to sign that circular? It has unquestionably lost him every vote from our delegation. I have only had letters from three, but I have no doubt they speak what will prove to be common sentiment.

Come back to the Convention, the platform will be modified to suit you, if not, your choice for a candidate will prevail and failing both you still have the resource of secession left you and you will have power then to carry out other conservative states with you.

Now you know the temper of the Convention well enough to understand that whilst there was every desire on the part of the majority to conciliate as to those who *remained*, there was a clear manifestation that no effort would or could be made to harmonize with those who undertook to dogmatize in the convention, and failing there endeavoured to demoralize the party by Secession. They failed to drag Virginia at their chariot wheels as a captive and thus their own movement a total wreck, they desire to come back and to smooth their way Mr. Hunter has to throw his body in the rut.

Not content with that the circular goes on by implication to argue that those who constitute the majority are not democrats, and that their love for the plunder of office will be sufficient to induce them to yield.

What would you think of a man who was a candidate for your support and who would thus speak and advise in regard to you.

It seems to me that the manifest tendency, if not the intent of the circular was to defeat the object of the adjournment, a harmonious nomination by the democracy.

CHARLES W. RUSSELL TO R. M. T. HUNTER.

WHEELING, [VA.], May 29th, 1860.

MY DEAR SIR: It did not require your assurance to satisfy me that in signing " the address " you did not intend to disparage the course of your friends. If I had thought you did I could not have professed, as I have done very sincerely, that my attachment to you remained and remains undiminished. Lest you should misunderstand my feelings, I will make no further comment upon the address. But, I fear, its effect upon the public in some quarters of the country has been unfortunate. I enclose a copy of a letter which I have received within a day or two from a friend in the Ohio delegation. One of the links of association between him and myself for some years has been his admiration of you as a public man. But he is now for Douglass on the score of availability. The letter was written in the freedom of private freindship and I might not be warranted in giving you his name. But I send the letter as a means of enabling you to judge of public sentiment; supposing that such information must be desirable to you at present. About here the impression produced by the address was that you leaned to the cause of the "seceders." Your friends, however, believed that your purpose was worthy of you. I sincerely wish that I felt competent to give you advice, as you request. In the confusion that prevails it is almost impossible for me to form an opinion satisfactory to myself as to the course which you ought to pursue. If you can yet be nominated with a reasonable chance of election, that is what I still desire to accomplish. But I confess that I am greatly discouraged. Unless we receive decided encouragement from other States, North and South, you ought not, I should think, to let your name be used again in the Convention. But I see no harm in deferring a final decision until the time for the meeting of the Convention.

If you retire I shall be as much perplexed to decide upon the choice of another candidate as I am now to advise about your course. In this part of the State there is a pretty general inclination to take Douglass. But I am not yet able to see how that can be done. Nor has any other name been suggested which offers a reasonable hope of extricating us from our present difficulties. I enclose a copy of an address which I have felt constrained to publish in vindication of my course and that of our delegation so far as I was concerned in shaping it. I have said some things which, I fear, you will think had better been left unsaid. I observe what you say in your letter about our conversation of the subject of seceding. As the address which you signed only expressed an opinion that we will secede in a certain contingency, I can not say that it was not authorized in that regard, if the contingency had been more precisely described and it had not been intimated that we would go to Richmond with the former seceders. I requested Mr. Garnett not to *commit* the delegation to any course in the proposed address. I did not know what they would do. I knew the most of them would have seceded at Charleston if our terms had not been agreed to. I intended myself, when I saw you, to retire if the Tennessee Resolution should be rejected at Baltimore. But if we had seceded at Charleston we would not have joined the convention of seceders. Nor will I if I am constrained by any event to secede at Baltimore. I am totally opposed to the separate movement organized by the seceders. When I leave the National Convention I will go to no other unless it be a State Convention. The leaders of the seceders have objects in which I do not concur. Their policy, which led to a disruption at Charleston, was opposed to my judgment. If their combination grows to a head in Virginia, I expect to fight it.

H. C. TIFFEY TO R. M. T. HUNTER.

SIOUX CITY, IOWA, *June 4th, 1860.*

DEAR SIR: I am a Virginian, from King Geo[rge] Co[unty], am a Hunter man. I am surrounded by Douglassites and Republicans. Please send me any Speeches or other documents in defense of the Southern Views of democracy and with much success in your glorious future prospects.

JOHN LETCHER TO R. M. T. HUNTER.

RICHMOND, VA., *June 4th, 1860.*

MY DEAR SIR: I am obliged to you for your prompt reply, to my enquiries respecting the Japanese, and their future movements. The information you furnish, will satisfy my friend Colo. Smith.

The present condition of political affairs, bothers and annoys me excessively. I do not see how the divisions and dissensions in our party are to be adjusted. The complications and embarrassments seem to me rather to increase than diminish. Davis' resolutions and the discussion they have created, has tended only to increase the trouble and difficulty of a settlement at Baltimore on the 17th instant. For the first time in my life, I cannot to my own satisfaction, work out the results that are to follow the existing condition of public affairs.

I had almost despaired, when I saw in the papers, a day or two since, that Rhett was placed at the head of the South Carolina delegation, to the Richmond Convention. Since that time I have had hopes, that union and harmony might yet be secured. I do not think it possible, that any party can survive the leadership, of two such politicians, as Rhett and Yancey. The result now I think will be, that all sensible, practical, conservative men will seek for some ground, upon which they can unite, to defeat the objects of these ultras. Their purpose is the disorganization and overthrow of the Democratic party, and the country must see it, and understand it.

I have regretted to see Benjamin's speech in the " Examiner " of this morning. It is calculated to hurt you, by exciting Douglas and his friends against you, and I see no possible good its publication can accomplish. An article in the "States " a day or two ago looked hostile, and I fear this may induce other attacks upon you. I hope it may turn out otherwise, but I have my fears.

The folly of General Houston in announcing himself a candidate, is another movement, that tends to add to the complications, and will have the effect of further distracting the South. I suppose that he will take off Texas, and thus weaken us, to that extent, even if we shall harmonize at Baltimore on a ticket.

It really looks to me, as if the Democratic party, was going to pieces, and if it shall be dissolved, I regard the future as gloomy indeed. With these divisions we may hope for, but we shall have no power to secure, a practical result, against the Republican organization, under the lead of Lincoln and Hamlin.

FRANKLIN MINOR TO R. M. T. HUNTER.

CHARLOTTESVILLE, [VA.], *June 5, 1860.*

MY DEAR SIR: The appointment of a successor to Judge Daniel is of very little less importance to the South than the election of the next president. One is for life, the other for but four years. There may be no danger of a wrong appointment, but still I am filled with solicitude by a rumour, which I have just heard, that Jas. Lyons is the favorite of Mr. Buchanan.

Our friends here all believe Wm. J. Robertson of the Court of Appeals is the very man for the place. True as steel and firm as a rock the South may rely on him with the surest confidence. He is, moreover, in the prime of life, and may live to serve us long, even until the stormy and the evil day come, as it surely will come, if we cannot break our bonds, which I fear we cannot yet. To incorruptible fidelity, and unflinching firmness, Robertson adds vast stores of legal learning, which will make him a great judge.

The ardent wish of many of your friends here is that Robertson may be appointed, but, of course, we are very far from wishing to embarrass you in the least. If you can help us in this thing we shall be very glad; if you cannot, we know it will be for a good reason.

HENRY S. ACKER TO R. M. T. HUNTER.

" DEMOCRATIC STANDARD OFFICE,"
POTTSVILLE, PA., June 8, 1860.

DEAR SIR: Permit me though a stranger to you to address a few lines to you upon a question of vital interest to the Democratic party of Pennsylvania. I am the Postmaster of this place and am the editor of an administration paper, so that you may know that I am a friend and no enemy in disguise. I also refer you to Gov. Bigler. Having said this much by way of explanation as to my position in the Democratic party, I will refer to the subject upon which I believe so much depends. It is this, you are aware that the Democratic party in the North is in an almost hopeless minority, except perhaps the great states of Pennsylvania and New Jersey. They have always been conservative national and patriotic. The waves of fanaticism have dashed against them only to be hurled back by her sturdy and Union loving people. These are facts with which you are conversant. Pennsylvania has on almost all occasions decided the Presidential contests. *She will decide the next.* If so, and I think you will not doubt it, it must become apparent that if the Democratic party of Pennsylvania is successful, that the next President will be of the same faith. Can this be accomplished? I answer sir, beyond the possibility of a doubt that it can. Its solution rests with the United States Senate of which you are an honored member. I refer to the Tariff bill now under consideration in Committee of which you are chairman. With its solution depends the success or defeat of the Democratic party, nay more—I verily believe that it will defeat it for years to come, and may indeed result in influencing the destruction of our glorious Union by elevating sectional discord. If a proper Tariff bill passes the United States Senate it will make a difference of 20,000 votes in Pennsylvania, to the Democratic Party. If it is defeated we cannot hope to succeed. This is conceded by all who know the feelings of the people.

With this view of the case, and it is not an overdrawn one, cannot you, sir, who represent the Southern idea upon this question, sacrifice your principles a little, and save, yes *save* the Democratic party of the Keystone state, that has so often battled side by side with the Mother of Presidents. You sir, can save us, or consign us into the hands of sectionalism that will keep us in the minority for years to come. The present opportunity is one pregnant with anticipation. Now the blow must be struck for our weal or woe. Now the question must be met? Again, shall our honored Senator Bigler be the last of Democratic Senators from this state. Language sir fails me to express the sentiments my heart would utter. But let the appeal not be in vain. You sir, have the key to the solution. You sir, must remember how often the victorious columns of a Pennsylvania democracy have sent a thrill of joy to your heart. With all these recollections of the past can you fail to be impressed of the necessity of saving our party from annihilation and defeat. The masses of this state think and speak of nothing else but the Tariff. It is a question sir, that rises up from every fireside, and all, *all* are looking with anxious eyes to the democratic Senate for its solution.

But sir, I am perhaps trespassing too much upon your time, and will bring this hastily written letter to a close. But while I do so I am trembling with anxiety, not for that bill only, but for the Democratic party and my country. Oh sir, fail not to appreciate the position that the Democratic party of Pennsylvania, occupies on this question, I hope and trust that you may be induced too look favorably upon it, and once more give power and success to the democracy of Pennsylvania.

WILLIAM M. AMBLER TO R. M. T HUNTER.

LAKELAND, [VA.], *June 11th, 1860.*

DEAR SIR: The vacancy on the Bench of the Supreme Court, has caused almost every man of sound (state rights) principles to turn to my friend Wm. J. Robertson, now of the Court of Appeals. My attachment to him is very strong, and I think I make all proper allowance for the effect of my feelings towards him. But if I had the choice of any, and every man in the South, to fill a position so important to us, to be rightly filled, I should unhesitatingly take Robertson. He is so pure, morally and intellectually and far abler than (high as he stands) he is yet known to be, that I break through my rule of not pushing my opinions upon you, to *urge* you, if you can consistently with your own opinions, to use your influence in obtaining for us the services of such a man, on the last line of defence which it seems is now left to us.

JOHN RANDOLPH TUCKER TO R. M. T. HUNTER.

RICHMOND, VA, *June 12, 1860.*

DEAR SIR: I have just written to Mr. Mason. Please see his letter. I prefer Robertson of course. My warm personal regard and high estimate of his ability, with confidence in his opinions on political subjects determine me.

Judge Lee I know well, and respect highly, my personal regard for him is strong not only from early association, but from recent intercourse. He is a good lawyer, and a clear headed judge, and of studious habits.

I should hate to lose either from V[irgini]a. As I have said to Mr. Mason I fear the result of this Convention. The impression is they are set upon a rupture. Nothing then can save us from Douglass but the fear of defeat on the part of the North with his nomination. What is to be done?

T. APOLION CHENEY TO R. M. T. HUNTER.

CHERRY CREEK, CHAUTAUQUA Co.,
New York, *June 13, 1860.*

DEAR SIR: I will beg permission to say, that the very able manner in which you have sustained the principles of Democracy during the present session of Congress, not less than throughout your long and eminent public career, has awakened my deepest interest and admiration. I will here express the conviction that, a glorious triumph now awaits the efforts of the patriotic men who have so eloquently maintained the great ideas enshrined in the Constitution. I had anticipated that the late Democratic National Convention would finally place your name upon its standard, the rallying watchword to battle and to victory, and, if upon assembling at Baltimore it shall judiciously adopt this course, all of the conservative elements of the country would be united in enthusiastic support and I believe we should achieve a national triumph almost unparalled in our political history. In the auspicious event of *your* nomination, we should indeed expect to carry this state. New York will again take her proud position, as of yore, in the ranks of the Democracy.

Permit me to enclose an extract from an article of mine. In its reference, however, to your senatorial career it but inadequately gives expression to the sentiments which I have long entertained. I shall hope that the loftiest political honors may continue to gather around your path.

It will afford me, I beg to say exceeding pleasure, in being allowed, indeed, as an especial favor, the honor of *hearing from you*, at your early convenience.

JOSEPH S. WILSON TO R. M. T. HUNTER.

GENERAL LAND OFFICE, *June 14th, 1860.*

DEAR SIR: In reply to your oral inquiry of this morning, I have the honor to State, that we estimate, that of Warrants issued under the Bounty Land Acts of 1847–50–52 and 55, there are outstanding at the present time about 72,054 Warrants, embracing an area of 7,319,370 acres.

JACOB THOMPSON TO R. M. T. HUNTER.

DEPARTMENT OF THE INTERIOR, *June 16th, 1860.*

DEAR SIR: I observe from the recent proceedings of the Senate and House of Representatives that it is proposed to authorize the Executive to contract for the return to Africa of such recaptured Africans as may be brought into the ports of the United States, and for their support for twelve months thereafter at a rate not exceeding one hundred dollars for each individual. I also observe that an appropriation of $250,000 is proposed to be made for the return and support of those now officially known to be at Key West.

It is not improbable that other Slavers will yet be captured, and, indeed, it is reported, not officially but upon respectable authority, that such is already the fact, in which event additional expenditures must be incurred and the means therefore should be supplied at the present session.

How much may be required it is, of course, impossible to conjecture as it must depend entirely upon the number of persons for whom provision will have to be made.

I have the honor, however, looking to the contingent nature of the Service, to recommend an appropriation of two hundred and fifty thousand dollars with the remark that even this amount may fall below what will be required for the service of the next fiscal year and that Congress may be called on to meet the deficiency at its next session.

——— TO R. M. T. HUNTER.

PHILADELPHIA, [PA.], *June 22, 1860.*

DEAR SIR: Will you allow me to trespass upon your valuable time so far as to ask you to read the enclosed and reflect upon its contents? It is one of a series of letters addressed to a free holder and anti slavery editor of New York, but it might with equal propriety have been addressed to the Enquirer or the Whig. Southern policy, as you will have seen is rapidly forcing all the trade of the country through Northern cities and more and more North at every step.

Southern policy is creating an entire monopoly of manufacturers in the East, and the monopoly becomes more complete with every year. The men and the States to whom the South is most opposed, are thus enriched and strengthened while the men [of] other cities, and other States, to whom the South is accustomed to look for help are becoming impoverished and enfeebled. Boston and New York are becoming stronger every hour, while Phila[delphia], Baltimore, and Norfolk are becoming weaker. When is this to end? Is it not likely the Southern man should see and understand the great fact that they are always *aiding* the ones whom they regard as enemies while punishing those who would wish to be their friends?

The interests of these States, Maryland and Virginia, are one and the same, and if they could be brought to act together for the development of their just resources, they could guide and direct the entire Union. Divided as they are, they are little better than mere instruments in the hands of extremists of the North and South. Could they not be brought to act in harmony with each other? The man who could bring this about could do more for the Union than has been done by any man since the days of Washington.

R. M. T. HUNTER TO JAMES R. MICOU, THOMAS CROXTON, AND OTHERS SIGNING THE CALL.[1]

December 10, 1860.

GENTLEMEN: I have had the honor to receive your letter inviting me to fix some day previous to my departure for Washington upon which I would address the people of my native county, at Tappahannock, upon the present state of public affairs. I regard it as both a duty and a pleasure to respond to such a call on the part of my friends and fellow-citizens of Essex and were there time enough before the day of my necessary departure to convene the people, I should have been gratified to have addressed them as you propose. But as there is not sufficient time for this, I have thought that I should comply substantially with your wishes by responding in writing to the call which you have made upon me. I am not surprised that you should desire to take counsel, not only with your Representatives, but with all who have a common interest with you, in the present perilous conjuncture of public affairs. Never in the whole of my public life, now not a short one, have I known a period when the destiny of our beloved State, and the fate of the Union, were involved in so much of doubt and uncertainty. If there be a remedy for the catastrophe, which now seems so imminent, it rests chiefly with the North to provide it. And yet there would seem to be but little

---

[1] Copied from the Richmond Enquirer of Dec. 12, 1860.

hope in that quarter, when we behold the strange unconsciousness in the Northern mind of the imminence of the danger and its almost entire insensibility to the state of public sentiment in the South. So far, the attempts made to rouse and inform it on these points, have only served to provoke taunts and menaces, which were calculated to embitter the feud, whose fires were already blazing high enough without this new fuel for the flame. And yet it ought to be obvious to all that the present state of things in the United States is unparalled in our previous history. For the first time since the Union was formed we have seen a President of the United States nominated and elected, so far as the popular voice is concerned, by a sectional party, a party founded in hostility to the institution of African slavery, which exists in nearly half the States in the Union, and composed of members, all of whom believe it to be their duty to war upon the institution whenever a legal opportunity is afforded them; the difference being that some of them profess a respect for the restraints of the Constitution, as they construe it, whilst others openly avow a contempt for all such restraints in regard to the subject of slavery. The man who, more than all others, seems to make the issues for that party, Mr. Seward, of New York, has declared that upon this subject of slavery there was a law higher than the Constitution, which should govern him, despite the provisions of the latter. And, as if to practice upon such theory, many of the non-slaveholding States have, in effect, nullified the fugitive slave law, and nearly all of them have practically made the provision of the Constitution, upon which that law was founded, a dead letter and of no avail. All of them deny to the slave States that equality under the Constitution to which we are entitled by the principles of a fair construction of that instrument, and by the decisions at different times of all the departments of the Federal Government. This sect or party, for it seems to be as much of one as the other, where it bore the rule in the co-States, has failed, and in the case of Ohio, I believe, refused to discharge in our behalf the duties which were not only common to humanity, but which, as neutral and independent States, they would have been bound to have performed towards us. Notwithstanding the assault made by John Brown and his confederates upon the State of Virginia, and the excitement produced by it, none of the non-slaveholding States have passed any law to prevent or punish such armed combinations for the purpose of making war upon the slaveholding States. On the contrary, the leading State in New England has just elected as its Governor an open sympathizer with Brown in his assault upon Virginia. For purposes of exasperation, what this party has said is almost worse than what it has done. Nearly an entire generation of men in the non-slaveholding States must now have grown up in the constant habit of hearing such denunciations of slaveholders and slaveholding States as were calculated to infuse into their minds a spirit of hatred towards the South. The seeds thus sown have already borne their bitter fruits in the division of churches and parties North and South, and who can now say that the final result of such teachings will not be found in a disruption of the Union itself? It is true that there are numbers in the non-slaveholding States who have fought the battle of the Constitution, and of justice, when we were the objects of assault, with a fidelity, an ability and an intrepidity which have earned and won our warmest gratitude and admiration. But, alas! for the cause of the Constitution and the Union, they have been overpowered by their adversaries, and it must be a work of time with them to recover—if, indeed, they shall ever effect it—their former ascendancy. If time could be given them, I should still hope for good results. Such is my faith in the power of truth, and such my confidence in the men. But, unfortunately, events have occurred to bring the two sections into presence upon the fearful issues which divide them, and there seems to be no voice now powerful enough to still the tumult or quiet the storm which has been raised. And yet we see around us daily that preparations are being made which look to the possibility of an appeal to the arbitrament of the sword. No man can doubt but that the time has arrived when the people should consult together and look around them for the remedies—if there be remedies—for the evils with which we are threatened.

It is now almost certain that one of the slaveholding States is about to secede from the Union, and the probability is that four more of them, lying near her, will soon follow her example. Believing, as they do, that their social systems and the peace and safety of their people will be endangered by the advent of this mischievous sectional party to power, that this party, when in power, will pervert and change in its practical operations, the Constitution, which is identical with the Union, as it was formed by the fathers, and that the General Government, in such hands, instead of providing for the common defence, will be used as an instrument of hostility towards the slaveholding States, they are already taking measures to withdraw themselves from its jurisdiction, and to form another, to which they may look with some confidence for assistance in the protection and defence of their rights. In this state of things, who amongst us does not ask, what is to be the final result of these movements, and what is the practical mode of healing the breach between the sections? We already hear from the stronger party threats of coercing the seceding States, by force. But if, unfortunately, such an experiment should ever be tried, even the stronger section would find the remedy worse than the disease. Suppose they could succeed, which result I regard as being in the highest degree improbable, what sort of Union would that be which could only maintain itself by dragging along after it five or more of its members in captivity and chains? Our political system is founded on the idea of self government, and how is that principle to be maintained when a part of the States are bound to the Union, not by voluntary association, but by force, and are ruled, not by laws which they have assisted to make, but by the sword? You commence by governing five States of the Confederacy by the sword, and having set aside the Constitution, as you must do to effect it, how long would it be before the whole system became one of force? First, we should have the absolute control of a sectional majority without restraints from the Constitution, which hereafter would be whatever they wished it; and then as sure as the day follows the night, would come another change. The majority would find it necessary for the efficient and convenient exercise of its power to concentrate it in fewer hands, and the minority for some protection from the human sympathies of one master, would gladly seek any escape from the proscription and tyranny of the soulless corporation of a sectional party.

What, then, would become of the remaining slaveholding States which had aided in the unworthy application of force to the others, who were bound to them by common interests, common sympathies and common wrongs? What security could they have in such a position for their rights or their peace and safety? A helpless minority, declared to be inferior, and voluntarily accepting that position, to whom could they look for protection, and from whom could they command respect? From themselves? Alas, that would be the worst feature in the case, for who can command respect from others, when he has lost his own? But the border slave States, in my opinion, would not permit the use of force to coerce the seceding States without taking part in the contest. The attempt to do this would kindle a general civil war, and one which, in the end, might draw within the vortex other parties, for almost the whole world has now an interest in the great staple of cotton, of which certain of the slave States are almost the only producers who make a surplus beyond their own wants for exportation. What would become of the interests of the non-slaveholding States themselves, who are so largely concerned in the employments to which cotton gives existence, whilst such a war was in the course of prosecution, or, indeed, after its conclusion, with the waste and destruction which it would occasion, if, unhappily for themselves and others, these States were successful in such a contest?

But in the case which I am discussing, I hold coercion by force to be almost impossible. It would fail if attempted, and would never be attempted, unless madness ruled the hour, and passion raged where reason ought to govern. But how would we stand if we would attempt to rule by force five States of th Confederacy, who declared our Government over them to be a ,. .anny, and claimed the right of governing themselves? Is it not the great American principle, that legitimate government rests on the will of the governed? Was it not in behalf of the sacred right of self government that we appealed to the world for sympathy and assistance in our struggle for independence? Is this General Government to play the very part towards some of the United States themselves which was taken towards us by the British Government under Lord North? Is this General Government of ours to resort to the British statutes to search after the Boston Port Bill, and other coercive measures used against us in our struggle for self-government, as precedents of the means to be directed against some of our States, who are engaged in asserting that same right for which we all contended then?

It would, indeed, be an instance as ruinous as it was melancholy, of the instability of human opinion, and of the mutability of man, if a portion of the old thirteen States should be found searching the political armory of Great Britain for models of the engines of oppression and coercion, and send them against another part of the States which constituted the glorious old Confederacy. But, in my opinion, there is no rightful power in the Government of the remaining States to coerce a return to the Union, if States acting in their sovereignty capacity had seceded from it. They could not derive such a power from either the law of nature or the Constitution of the United States. The Convention which framed that instrument refused to give the power to coerce a State to the General Government. The very nature of the compact of government into which the United States entered, implies the right, I believe, to secede from the Union which it formed, when the conditions and obligations upon which it was made have been violated and annulled.

I believe in the truth of what was "explicitly and peremptorily declared" as its view in the General Assembly of Virginia, in one of the immortal series of resolutions, and drawn by James Madison, in 1798, to wit:—that "the power of the Federal Government results from the compact to which the States are parties, as limited by the plain sense and intention of the instrument constituting that compact, and no further valid than they are authorized by the grants enumerated in that compact; and that, in case of a deliberate, palpable and dangerous exercise of other powers not granted by the said compact, the States who are parties thereto have the right, and are in duty bound, to interfere for arresting the progress of the evil, and for maintaining within their respective limits the authorities, rights and liberties appertaining to them." Or, to express the same idea more fully and explicitly, I will borrow the words of Mr. Jefferson, the reputed author of the Kentucky Resolutions of 1798, in which it is affirmed, "That the several States comprising the United States of America are not united on the principal of unlimited submission to their General Government, but that, by compact under the style and title of a Constitution for the United States, and of amendments thereto, they constituted a General Government for special purposes, delegated to that Government certain definite powers, reserving each State to itself the residuary mass of right to their own self-government," and "that to this compact each State acceded as a State, and is an integral party, its co-States forming, as to itself, the other party; that the Government created by this compact was not made the exclusive or final judge of the extent of the powers delegated to itself; since that would have made its discretion, and not the Constitution, the measure of its powers; but that, as in all other cases of compact among parties having no common judge, each party has an equal right to judge for itself, as well of infractions as the mode and measure of redress."

In other words, I believe, with these high authorities, that the Constitution of the United States is a compact of goverment between parties, and that the several States constitute these parties. And farther, I think, with them, that in case of a dispute between the parties as to the mutual conditions of this compact, there is no common judge. As evidence to sustain the first proposition as to who constitutes the parties, it is enough to refer to the fact that the Constitution of the United States was formed by a convention, in which the States were represented, and voted as States; that it was afterwards ratified by the people of the several States, acting each in its separate capacity; that the provision for the amendment of this instrument requires the concurrence of three-fourths of the States, each acting in its individual capacity; that the powers reserved from grant to the General Government were reserved to the States, and thus the Constitution-making power is recognized as residing in the several States, which are considered as the units of which our Federal system is the multiple. That the Federal Judiciary is not, as is contended by some, a common judge in cases of disputed powers between the parties to the compact, is, I think, conclusively shown by Mr. Madison, in his report on the Resolutions of 1798, which was made in 1799, and adopted by the Virginia Assembly of that day. In that report he says:

"However true, therefore, it may be that the judicial department is, in all questions submitted to it by the forms of the Constitution, to decide in the last resort, this resort must necessarily be deemed the last, in relation to the authorities of the other department of the Government; not in relation to the rights of the parties to the Constitutional compact, from which the Judicial, as well as the other departments, held their delegated trusts. On any other hypothesis, the delegation of Judicial power would annul the authority delegating it. And the concurrence of this department with the others, in usurped powers, might subvert forever, and beyond the possible reach of any rightful remedy, the very Constitution which all were instituted to preserve."

Whilst I do not dispute the right of the Federal Judiciary to decide the law of the case, so as to bind parties within its legitimate jurisdiction, whether that law is drawn from the Constitution itself, or a statute passed in pursuance of it, I do deny, for the reasons given in the above extract, that this Federal Judiciary can make an authoritative decree in cases of disputes growing out of the Constitution between the parties to that compact. If, then, this Constitution be a compact, between the States, as parties, and consists, as it does, of the mutual obligations, stipulations and conditions, and if there be no common judge in cases of disputes between the parties as to infractions of that compact, it follows clearly that each state may decide for itself whether the compact has been broken and whether the breach be of such a nature as to justify its withdrawal as a party to the compact. Should it determine these questions in the affirmative, then in my opinion its political right to secede is demonstrably clear. Such must have been the opinion of the Convention of delegates of the people of Virginia, when, in the very act of ratifying the Federal Constitution, they did, " in the name and in behalf of the people of Virginia, declare and make known that the powers granted under the Constitution, being derived from the people of the United States, may be resumed by them whensoever the same shall be perverted to their injury or oppression; and that every power not granted thereby remains with them and at their will." Indeed, Mr. Webster himself, 1851, when his judgment was fully ripened by experience, is reported to have said, at Capon Springs, Virginia:

" I do not hesitate to say, and repeat, that if the Northern States refuse, wilfully and deliberately to carry into effect that part of the Constitution which respects the restoration of fugitive slaves, the South would no longer be bound to observe the compact. A bargain broken on one side is a bargain broken on all sides."

As I understand it, the Union, as it was adopted and formed by the fathers, and the Constitution of the United States are one and the same. To sustain the one you must maintain the other. There were no formal articles of Union between the States, but each acceded to the Union by ratifying the Constitution; the members of the General Government are sworn to support, not the Union, but the Constitution. The Constitution has two great purposes in view— one to create the machinery of a common government, the other to prescribe the conditions and limitations under which it was to operate, and the ends and purposes of its action. Now, if one section

should get possession of this machinery, and not only destroy the
limitations and conditions of its action, but direct that action to ends
and purposes not only different from, but hostile to, those for which
this political organism was created, they destroy the Union as it was
framed by the fathers, and seek to substitute another for it. The
States which secede for such a cause, and refuse to contribute to the
farther maintenance of this machinery of Government, are, in fact,
refusing to aid in the destruction of the old Union and the substitu-
tion of a new. The Union-breakers are those who destroy the Constitution; the Union-savers are those who preserve that instrument
or compact in all its parts. Those who would maintain the existence
of the machinery of a common government, although it was acting
without regard to the restraints of the Constitution, and for unconstitutional purposes, plainly prefer the means to the ends, and
acquiesce in the exercise of unlimited power by a sectional majority
which may have possession of the machine. The plain statement of
such a proposition is enough to condemn it, at least in the opinion
of Virginians, who have always been distinguished for a jealous
regard for their rights and liberties, and by an anxious desire to preserve the limits imposed by the Constitution upon the action of
government.

For all the reasons which I have given, and for others not now
enumerated, I believe that each State, acting in its sovereign capacity,
has a political right to secede from the Union, when it believes that
there has been a palpable and dangerous infraction of the Constitution or compact. But whilst I recognize its right to judge for itself,
I am also of opinion that the act is morally justifiable only when the
infraction is of such a character as to make secession the only remedy, or when the danger of such an infraction is so imminent that
secession must be immediate to be a remedy at all. Therefore it is
that when I was questioned during the recent canvass to know
whether I would regard the election of Lincoln, by constitutional
means, as a just cause for secession, I replied, that for such a cause
I would not advise Virginia to secede, but that if any State did deem
it just cause, and for that reason secede from the Union, I hold that
she had a right thus to act, without question from me, and that there
was no rightful authority anywhere to force her back within the
jurisdiction of the General Government. In the case of Virginia,
where, as a voter and a citizen, I have a right to speak, I would say,
that although such an election, in my opinion, affords just cause for
serious apprehension, and makes it prudent to prepare the means of
self-defence, in case of the worst results, still, I would not desire to
break up this Union, without at least an honest effort to preserve it,
upon terms consistent with the rights and safety of the South. To
preserve the Union of the Constitution I would be willing, I trust,

to make any personal sacrifice. I therefore desire and advocate a conference amongst the Southern States to consult and agree upon such guarantees as in their opinion will secure their equality and their rights within the Union.

These might be found in constitutional amendments, which either declared the construction of the Constitution to be such as we now give it, or which still more explicitly defined and protected that equality and those rights, or, better still, if it could be had, which made a new distribution of power, so as to give each section the means to protect its rights. That the circumstances of the case, and the condition of the times are such as to justify the Southern States in demanding new securities, or a re-institution of the old ones, would be allowed, I think, by the Northern mind itself, if we could have the decision of its reason, uninfluenced by passion. If the Southern States could obtain terms which would secure their rights within the Union, then they ought, as I think, to stand together, to maintain and preserve it. My own opinion is, that the Southern States have a common destiny, and ought to stand together, either to preserve their rights within the Union, or, if that cannot be done, then to defend them without the Union; for in either move they would be able to protect themselves. Should, however, the Northern States refuse either to give the South new securities, or to re-institute the old ones, then the question presents itself in a new form.

In that event it is hardly to be doubted that at least five of the cotton producing States will withdraw immediately and irretrievably, to be soon followed by all, or most of those, engaged in the production of that staple. The question, then, for the border slaveholding States will be, not whether the Southern States would have been safe if all had remained in the Union, but to which division of the Confederacy they ought to attach themselves now that it was severed. In such an event, I have not the shadow of a doubt as to what ought to be the course of Virginia and the other Southern border States. If they united with the other slave States they would confederate as equals, and with those whose population was homogeneous, and whose interests were identified with their own. If they united with the North under such circumstances they would constitute a helpless minority, in an association with States whose population was not homogeneous with theirs, and whose interests would be considered as different and hostile. They would be treated as inferiors by the dominant majority, and considered as having acquiesced in that position by the choice which they had made. In the Southern Confederacy they would find an outlet for their surplus population of slaves, not only in these co-States, but in whatever Territory might be acquired by the Union. Under that Government, too, they would find effectual protection for their property and institutions. In the other Confederacy their slave population would indeed be " penned in " and " localized " within their own borders.

The dominant party in the North looks to this object as the cardinal principle of their association, and they would be able to pursue that end without the show of an opposition. This negro population would then be penned up, not only by restrictions from the Northern majority, but by restrictions from the neighboring slave States also, who would probably hold it to be their interest to force the border States to hold on to their slaves, not only for political reasons, but also from a desire to interpose an obstacle to the escape of their fugitive slaves. What then would be the position of the slaveholding States in the Northern Confederacy? As their slave population increased there would be a tendency to fall in wages. The white laborer, by emigration, could better his condition by removing where his labor was more productive, but the slave, by the circumstances of his position, must remain and work for the home rates of wages, whatever it might be. In this state of things, the white laborer would emigrate where he could work on better terms, and the slave would remain to increase his hold upon these States, and to become the governing element of their population. Whilst the new territory of this Northern Confederacy would be given to the white man, according to their theory, the old territory of the border slaveholding States would be given to the negro. The consequences of such a process would soon reduce to such an extent the number of whites in these States, that they would lose their only, but slender means of defence, which they had enjoyed through the little political strength with which they had entered that Confederacy. Indeed, how long would it be before the non-slaveholding States would increase to the mark requisite to enable them to abolish slavery within the States by a constitutional amendment? Would they wait for that progress, if they did not know it to be both rapid and sure? With the principles and feelings of this sectional party, which would wield the power of that Confederacy, how long would the institution of slavery endure in the five or six slaveholding States which were attached to that Union? Is there one of the slaveholding States which would voluntarily incur such a risk, with the fate of the British West Indies before their eyes? .In a Union with a Southern Confederacy, they would encounter none of these dangers. In that connection, the slave population operates as a safety-valve to protect the white laborer against an unreasonable or ruinous decline in the rate of wages. The law of profit moves him to a theater where he will earn more for his master, and yet more for himself, whilst the labor market which he leaves is thus gradually relieved from the pressure, and the white man remains in the land of his birth, to enjoy the profits of remunerating operations. As a proof of the truth of this view, I ask if the average rate of wages of the white laborer of the South is not higher than in any other settled portion of the globe?

But I have not done with the view of the relative advantages of an association on the part of Virginia with either of these Confederacies. In the Southern Confederacy, the border States would soon derive all the advantages which the non-slaveholding, and particularly the New England States now derive from the markets of the cotton States. With Virginia, this would especially be the case. Under the incidental protection afforded by a tariff, laid without other views than those for revenue purposes, there would be an unexampled development of her vast capacity for mining, manufacturing, agricultural and commercial production. Nor would a great navigation interest be slow to spring into existence within her borders. Falling heirs, as she and the other border States would do, but Virginia principally, to the profitable occupations and rich markets of the Cotton States, where they would find customers mainly, and not rivals, and of which hitherto the Northern States have enjoyed the almost exclusive monopoly, their development of all these sources of material wealth would be greater, probably, than anything that has been witnessed in the North, or West, or East. If the Northern States are mad enough to throw away such advantages, in their insane war upon slavery, to the existence of which institution they chiefly owe them, would not the madness of the border slave States be even greater than theirs if they should voluntarily shut themselves out from such a field of adventure? But this is not all. The most profitable commercial relations of Virginia are with the South and South-west. The manufacturing, mining and agricultural productions of North-western Virginia, if we look down the Ohio, find their chief markets in the South and South-west; or on the Chesapeake, if we look Eastward. The great railroad connections of Virginia almost all look to the South and South-west for their profits.

The connecting links of the great South-western line are so nearly completed that Norfolk and Richmond may be said to have already locked arms with Memphis and New Orleans. When we look to geographical position, who can doubt but that in a separate Southern Confederacy, composed of all, or nearly all, the slaveholding States, there would arise in or about the shores of the Chesapeake a great and commanding centre of credit and commerce. With the completion of the central line of railroad, and above all with the completion of the great water line of the State, there would grow up some city on or about the Chesapeake, which would enjoy immense and commanding advantages for the interchange of commerce, and for the distribution of the commodities of the world over a vast area filled with rich and profitable consumers. Indeed, through this water line a large portion of the great North-west would stand towards some place in Virginia as the Canadas do to New York. But this is a subject to which I will barely allude, as to treat it fully would swell this letter far beyond its proper dimensions. Suffice it so say, that for these great advantages, we could find no compensation in an association with the non-slaveholding States, where we would find more rivals than customers, and where these great interests of Virginia would probably be exposed to hostile legislation.

So far I have dwelt upon the relative political and material advantages to be derived from an association with the one or the other of these Confederacies. But there is yet another point of comparison, which weighs more with me than all the others. I mean the social effects of a union with either. We should enter the Southern Confederacy as equals. The roads to honor, office, and profit would be alike open to all. We should enter into a government whose constituents are bound together by common interests and sympathies, and who treated each cther with mutual respect. But, above all, our social system, instead of being dwarfed and warred upon by the action of the Government, would receive all the assistance and means of development which it is proper for a Government to render to the society which it represents. If it be the individual culture which develops the man, it is the social culture which regulates the progress of the race. This social culture depends much upon the system of government itself. The difference is wide between the measure of progress of a social system, when the government aids and promotes on the one hand, or assails and seeks to prevent its development on the other. But what would be the operation upon the social system of these few slaveholding States in the Northern Confederacy? Declared to be inferiors by the dominant majority, and forced by weakness to submit to the position, they could not enter with equal chances into a competition for the honors and profits of Society. Who would voluntarily place a son in such a position? Humbled by the stamp of inferiority placed upon him by his government, conscious that he was attached to a political system from whose honors he was excluded by the circumstances of his position, and a member of a social system which was assailed and dwarfed by his own government, then it would not be long before he would lose, together with his sense of equality, that spirit of independence to which manhood owes its chief grace and its power.

I have given at some length my views as to the relative advantages to the border States, in case of a dissolution of the Union, to be derived from an association with the one or the other of the two Confederacies which will be formed at first. I have done so because I see much reason to fear that it is in this form that the practical question will present itself. For myself, I would much prefer to see the whole South remaining in the Union upon such guarantees as would secure their rights and safety. My own opinion is, that the non-slaveholding States would do wisely to give that security, and thus preserve the Union and peace. I cannot, however, shut my eyes to the fact that these guarantees may be refused, and that in such an event a part of the Southern States will secede. A portion of the slaveholding States would probably prefer to remain in the Union, and make yet a farther fight for their constitutional rights, if they could make that fight with a united South. But when a part of the Southern States had left, it would, as it seems to me, be a hopeless contest for the residue. Whether it willed it or not, the Union would have been divided, and the slaveholding border States would have to decide, not upon the question of Union or no Union, but to which division of the Union, now that it was dissolved, they would attach themselves. That question must be decided, should it come, upon considerations of reason rather than of feeling.

I know that it is said by some in the border States that it is hard they should be dragged out of the Union by the other States. On the other hand, the Cotton States might say, it was hard for them to be held in the Union by the border States if they thought their peace, safety and prosperity required them to withdraw from it. The question, if it arises, ought to be decided upon considerations of moral, social and political advantages, and not be approached in the spirit of anger or crimination. The time has now come when Virginia ought to be acting. It may possibly be within her power to mediate the differences and save both the Union and the rights of the South. There ought to be a conference of the Southern States to see if they cannot determine upon some common course of action in this regard. If this cannot be done, and the Southern States cannot obtain such guarantees as would retain them all within the Union, then comes the other question upon which Virginia must decide in her sovereign capacity, and that is, with which confederacy will she unite her destiny. Such a decision would not necessarily occasion war.

If all the slaveholding States were united in one Confederacy, and the non-slaveholding States in another, the consequences of war would be so disastrous, and the consideration in favor of peace would be so strong, as probably to prevent a resort to force, unless, indeed, the passion engendered by the occasion should be so high as to gain the mastery over reason. Indeed, if there were two such Confederacies, each standing upon a Constitution, the same, or nearly the same, with that of the United States, I could conceive of a league between these two, whose bonds not being so close as those of the present Union, would avoid the exciting subject of dispute, and which might yet embrace enough of the objects of common interest to place them in the position which Mr. Jefferson assigns to the United States under the existing Constitution, which, he said, made "them *one*, as to the rest of the world, and *several* as to each other."

But it is idle to propose remedies unless we know the temper with which such proposition would be received by the non-slaveholding States, with whom it lies to save the Union, if it is to be done at all. If we judge of that temper by the past conduct of the party which now wields the political power of that section, we can hardly expect either reason or moderation from them. It is consoling, however, to know that the issues of our destiny are in the hands of Providence who makes and unmakes, the prosperity of men and nations at His own good pleasure. It may be that with His aid, some scheme of deliverance may yet be worked out. The Southern States, I believe, can preserve not only their rights and domestic safety, but also the peace of the country, if they will stand together. It is time, however, that some movement was made for conference and consultation amongst those States, and I do not see why the Legislature of Virginia may not initiate such a movement at its approaching session. If, however, nothing can be effected in the way of conciliation and adjustment and a separation of the States should take place, it will be for the people of Virginia, acting through a Convention, and in their sovereign capacity, to determine with which of the two divisions they will unite themselves. Of that choice I do not permit myself to doubt. We have now reached a period when this controversy must be settled. All the great interests of society require it. The business relations of the country are obstructed by it, and if the Union holds together without an adjustment of the dispute, the same difficulties will recur with each succeeding Presidential election, shaking the foundations of credit and property, and filling the public mind with anxiety and uncertainty, until the people will accept any change of government which promises to give more stability and security to their peace and their property. These quadrennial agitations seem to increase the intensity, and must inevitably break down the government at no distant day, if something cannot be done to quiet them. If this state of irritation between the sections should become chronic, the question will be not how to preserve it but how to get out of it. When the future which lies before us is so clouded by gloom and uncertainty, we all must feel that the time has come for Virginia to put her house in order. No man can now tell what a day or an hour may bring forth. An accident might fire a train, whose explosion would part the Union asunder. But, be the issue what it may, peace or war!, and no man desires the former more earnestly than I do, may the noble old Commonwealth be prepared to play the part that becomes her. Certain I am that I speak the common voice of nearly all her sons, when I say, where she leads we will follow; and should she in her sovereign capacity throw her banner to the breeze, we will rally to it as the emblem of our allegiance, whether it bears upon its fold a single star, as the representation of her undivided sovereignty, or a whole constellation to mark the numbers of a confederated system. When she speaks, her voice will be heeded at home, and, I trust, respected abroad.

But I fear I have already exhausted your patience by the length of this letter, which must be excused by the magnitude of the crisis to which it relates; and I will conclude with the expression of my thanks for the confidence you have reposed in me, and subscribe myself, with assurances of respect and regard.

CHARLES G. HAYSINE TO R. M. T. HUNTER.

NEW YORK, [N. Y.], *April 14th, 1861.*

DEAR SIR: Enclosed is a sketch in which you may find some interest. It is designed to be fair, though hurriedly drawn and without quite sufficient data.

[Written expressly for the N. Y. Leader.]

PEOPLE WE MEET; OR, UP AND DOWN THE PLAZA ON THE SHILLING SIDE.

Number XLVIII.

Not often seen on our Plaza, but very conspicuous and attracting much attention whenever visible,—this broad-shouldered, thick-set, middle-aged and middle heighted man, handsomely but plainly dressed, and with features a good deal suggesting traces of Pocahontas lineage; this rather slow, steady and courteous gentleman, with masses of thick brown hair, silky and straight as an Indian's; dark and large brown eyes of a somewhat sleepy tendency; dark eyebrows, handsomely arched and sharply defined at the base of a full, broad forehead; regular and very pleasant features; shaved cheeks, oval and olive colored, with a developing double chin and rather animal contour;—such is the outer man of Hon. Robert M. T. Hunter, one of the clear-grit F. F. V.'s— a public man of prominence before the country during the last three and twenty years—many times re-elected to the Senate of the United States, and holding in that body the most laborious and responsible Committee Chairmanship—to wit, that of Ways and Means. Run Mad Tom Hunter, as he was once nicknamed, was first elected to the lower house of Congress in the year 1837, running on an independent ticket and in opposition to the regular Democratic nominee. That was the year of the famous Broad Seal Controversy—so-called from the fact that Speaker Pennington, then Governor of New Jersey, had given the Broad Seal of State-Certificate to a Whig delegation, whose seats were contested by Democrats claiming to have received clear majorities of the popular vote. What part the independent Mr. Hunter took in this fight, it would be difficult to say; but certain it is, that in the Broad-seal struggle for Speakership of the House—after almost as many weeks of ineffectual balloting as we have lately witnessed,—the Conservatives, led by ex-Senator Talmadge, Reeves, Wise and Company, coalesced with the Whigs; and as the result of this, the independent R. M. T. H. was elected Speaker as their compromise candidate. Serving several terms in Congress after this, he was first elected to the Senate, nearly twenty years ago, by a coalition between the Whigs and bogus Democrats of the Virginia Legislature. It is but justice to Mr. Hunter to add, however, that notwithstanding his first election to the Senate in this manner, he has ever since been re-elected as the regular Democratic nominee; and that on every occasion when his name has been presented to Virginia, the solid and responsible men of that Old Dominion, have thronged in mass to express their confidence in his abilities and their high estimate of his character. On the return of Henry A. Wise in 1846, and ever since that date, there has been a rivalry on the part of Wise against Hunter—the fiery and gallant ex-Governor sometimes carrying with him for a brief season the sympathies of the lower strata; but the upper-crust old families, always standing like a wall of granite to buttress the fortunes of the Pocahontas Senator. So far as regards personal repute and habits, we hazard nothing in saying that Mr. Hunter is one of the purest and most fortunate men that has ever lived so many years in the National Capitol. In all our recollection we have never heard his name breathed except in accents of respect; and foes dare not deny the boast of friends, that in all his official acts—dealing, as he has done, with the whole finances of the country during the past ten or fourteen years— no shadow of suspicion as to the absolute integrity of his motives, has ever rested on the name of Robert Hunter. A laborious and faithful man, persevering, quietly ambitious and with all his desires under most admirable control,—the subject of our sketch is more free from faults than any public man within the range of our experience. His appetites are moderate; his style of living handsome, but largely within his means; every hour in his life seems to have its allotted mission, and he is of that cautious, indefatigable temperament which works and progresses without cessation, and yet without betraying any of the jar and racket which accompanies the spasmodic industrious-fits of less persevering men. True all this—and the praise is rather under than over what we feel to be due,—it is no illogical consequence that a man so correct as Hunter should lack that popular, vitative force, which more frequently surrounds men of more decided, but less perfect characters. It is not the mere negative angel that masses of men will bow down to reverence; they are too faultless for popular sympathy—too cold to make allowance for the hot fancies and passions which sway the multitude. At some calmer period of our history, such a man as Hunter would be a resistless candidate for the Democratic party to put in national nomination;—but in the present inflamed and illogical condition of sectional and factious feud, the mild virtues which we have described would count for nothing, and a more positive man of some kind must be our standard-bearer, if we hope to win. As to the present Virginia Delegation, Wise undoubtedly expected, and made strong efforts to carry it for himself; but the solid men of the State prevailed, and there can be no doubt that the first vote of the mother of Presidents at Charleston will be cast for Hunter. That such a vote can amount to a mere compliment and nothing more, we feel convinced; nor as friends of R. M. T. H. could we wish to see him put up for popular slaughter at such a time. Should he be nominated, however, it would puzzle his enemies to find a blot, personal or political, on his escutcheon; and it might also puzzle his friends to find any " Cry," or popular watchword of sufficient potency to make his name successful. He might, however, we suppose, reckon on the very earnest support of his old " Conservative " friends in this City—such as Francis B. Cutting, Chas. O'Connor, Jerry Towle and others of that class—who have, since 1837, aspired to be ranked as the only original

Simon-pure Democrats of Manhattan Island! We think the best policy for Mr. Hunter—he being abundantly young yet—is to stand back for the present and pursue such a course towards Douglas as will form a claim of gratitude on the friends of that candidate—to be used for Mr. Hunter's benefit·in the Convention of 1864.

R. M. T. HUNTER'S SPEECH BEFORE THE CONSERVATIVE CONVENTION.[1]

December 13th, 1867.

Mr. Hunter said he could claim the merit of impartiality for the counsels which he was about to give his countrymen, as he had no interest in the proceedings of this or any other political body except those which every citizen has in the good government of the country to which he belongs. He had a sentiment, however, which was stronger than any interest could be, and that was for the promotion of the welfare and preservation of the honor of his native State, which was dearer to him now in her misfortunes than in the palmy days of her prosperity. He had no political aspirations, and if he had, there was no possible public career before him. He said this not by way of regret or complaint, for whilst he held that no man had a right to throw away any opportunities of usefulness which had been bestowed upon him, yet if they were taken from him he might rightfully turn aside to domestic pursuits, which were far more congenial to his tastes than the stormy career of public life. He had, however, a difficulty in offering counsels now which he had never experienced before. He had been a member heretofore of public meetings which had the welfare and honor of Virginia under consideration. But then, there were always some general principles of justice or considerations of expediency upon which he could reason and form some theory, which, whether right or wrong, was satisfactory to himself at least. Now, he was not to consider the questions before us in that point of view, but he was to ascertain, if possible, what would be allowed to us by those who controlled us, and to choose amongst these things what would be best for Virginia.

Even in this limited view of the question he was at a loss as to what was before us. If he were to take the recent elections as a test of the feeling of the North, he could hope that the cup of universal negro suffrage would pass from us; but if he must take the reconstruction act as the ultimate and final decree of the Congress which must rule us at least for the next two years, then he had only to choose between military government or the control of the colored race. Between these alternatives he had no hesitation in saying that he preferred the military control. Under military government he was controlled by men of his own race; educated men who acted

---

[1] See Richmond Whig, Dec. 13, 1867.

under the responsibilities of their commission and in some degree under the control of a President who we know to be disposed to do us justice, and accord to us, as far as he could, our constitutional rights.

If we were to be placed under the control of the black race, in the country between the Potomac and the Rio Grande, it was not difficult to divine the results. We had the experience of Hayti and Jamaica before us. There was no doubt but that it would result in the formation of a black man's party, which would persecute the white man in all possible modes. In Hayti they were suddenly emancipated as in this country, and without adverting to the scenes of atrocity which occurred when they had the control of public affairs, it is enough to say that the result was to destroy all the elements of material prosperity and moral progress. A black man's party was formed and the whites were persecuted until most of them were driven from the country, and he had the authority of an intelligent observer, who has recently been amongst them, that they not only exclude all white men from office, but deny them the privilege of holding real estate. The black men themselves only work by compulsion, and the culture of sugar, of which they made 120,000,000 of pounds in 1789, has disappeared, so of cotton, and so would it have been of coffee if it were not that the trees planted long ago still continue to bear. In Jamaica we have the same history as far as was compatible with the control of the English Government. The same hostility to the white man, the same decadence in agricultural production.

Could any one doubt but that we should see similar results in the Southern States if the whole country between the Potomac and the Rio Grande should be submitted to the rule of the colored race? The Radical party seemed to think that they would thus secure the support of the whole Southern country so long as the black man should rule. They would find themselves mistaken in this after the first election. The blacks would form, not a Radical, but a black man's party, and we know, from the history of party welfare, that all parties would bid for them. They would act for the benefit of themselves and not for this or that party of the whites, and can there be conceived anything more demoralizing than a party consisting, in the language of one of the resolutions, one third of the Senate, and a fourth of the House of Representatives who would thus hold the balance of power between the two parties of the white race, and act only for their own good. As Free Lancers in the field, they would determine all disputed questions in reference only to their own interests.

He said this in no feeling of hostility to the colored race, but in accordance only with the history of the past. On the contrary, he

felt kindly towards the colored race, but thought their welfare was
to be promoted in a mode which was contrary, perhaps to their own
view.   But there were dangers ahead of them in their present
course to which they had not adverted, and which had been carefully concealed from them.   Suppose they could assume the control
of the Southern States for the present, how long would it last?
Would the white race in the North long endure a state of things
in which the blacks, though a minority, would control, by holding
the balance of power in all contested political questions?   Would
they consent to see the material resources and productions of the
South wasted and perhaps destroyed which used to yield them so
large a harvest of wealth?   Would they contribute to the result
which was to restore the cultivated field to the wilderness and
jungle, and leave the wild beasts and the alligator to reign supreme
over those plains and bottoms, which heretofore had been the seats
of a refined civilization, and of a production whose profits extended
North as well as South?   Would they stand by contently and see
the moral, material and social elements of strength and happiness
wasted and almost destroyed to maintain the supremacy of the
colored race, which would seem to be the present policy.

Every consideration of self-respect and national interest would
forbid it.   The extreme western limit of agricultural settlement east
of the Rocky mountains has already been attained.   It cannot be
long before the tide of agricultural immigration must soon tend
Southward.   The colored race will not be allowed to hold these
immense resources in abeyance.   This country belongs to the white
man, and they will claim its control.   To subject the white race in
Virginia to the government of the black race, when it is superior in
numbers, wealth and intelligence, would be to commit one of the
highest of all sins, a sin against nature.   Would any party in the
loyal States permit the blacks to give the power of the government
to a minority amongst themselves when they had only to call into
action their own strength to avert it?   Was there ever a race superior
in numbers, wealth and intelligence to those who governed them
who tamely submitted to be so ruled?

I throw out these considerations not merely to encourage my
own fellow-citizens and brethren, but for the black race itself, for
whom I have kindly feelings.   I was not only reared amongst them
and feel the kindly ties of early association, but I acknowledge the
obligation which rests upon us to give them all the opportunities
of progress and development which we can afford them in justice
to ourselves.   That the reaction will come, I have no doubt, but
I fear it will come in a mode which I should regret as a friend of
civilization and humanity, and to the black race itself.   And suppose for the sake of a brief period of control which is given them,

not for their own sakes, but to secure the supremacy of the Radical party they should thus get up a contest between the races and incur the hostility of the whites, what will become of them when the re-action comes? I shudder to think of the result. If the Radicals appeal to the black race to sustain them, will not the other party invoke the aid of the whites, who are so much more powerful in all the natural elements of strength in the country in which they may be brought into competition? I speak not only in the interests of the white, but also of the black race, when I protest against any system of laws which seeks to place the weaker and inferior race in control over that which is superior in wealth, numbers and intelligence. After all, the citizens of any community have more interest in its good government than in the question of who shall direct it. I will not offer the advice, because it will not be received in the spirit in which it is offered, but far better would it be for the blacks to leave the government of the country where they found it. If they do not provoke the hostility of the white race, they will be treated not only with justice but generosity. If they are made equal in the eye of the law and protected in all their rights, would they not be in a far better position to leave the government to the whites, who are best fitted for it? I am sure I speak not only my own feelings, but those also of the white citizens of Virginia, when I say that at present we would tolerate no government which did not respect not only their freedom, but their just rights of person and property.

But, Mr. President, it may be that they will heed no advice which I can give them. The Radical party which now controls Congress may retain that for two years yet to come, and they may force on us a state of things contrary not only to justice, but sound policy. There will nothing be left to us then but patience and endurance until the reaction comes. That it will come I do not doubt for a moment, and if it should bring consequences to the black race which we shall all deplore, we shall not be responsible for it. Mr. President, I know what I recommend when I counsel patient endurance and manly for-titude to the people of Virginia, if this state of things should occur. It will be best for our beloved State that it should be so. The present generation has suffered, still suffers, and perhaps may continue, for some time to come, to suffer. But what is the life-time of one gen-eration in the existence of a State. Virginia will revive, and fulfil a destiny as bright probably as her most ardent son ever wished for her. Trials, difficulties and sufferings constitute the discipline by which individuals and States are trained to moral and heroic excel-lence. What individual ever attained greatness who was reared in the lap of ease and luxury, and was not trained, for some part of his life, in the school of adversity? What nation has achieved excellence in greatness which was not disciplined in the same school? England had what is called its rebellion, a period of some cruelty and much suffering, and yet from that rebellion sprung some of those acts which are the proudest monuments of the liberty of the subject, and more than all, the resolution in which were laid broad and deep the foundations of British freedom and prosperity.

The revolution of France was far more terrible. The wisest men trembled for her future, and yet from that revolution sprang that equality of all men before the law, and the throwing open of all the pulses of life to the free and equal competition of all, which gave a new impulse to the energy of the nation, and placed it at the head of the European powers. Who shall say that the present period may not prove a new seed of progress and a new germ of growth in the career of Virginia? I think I already see its effects in the rising generation. The times are teaching them habits of self-denial and self-reliance, which contributes so much to give strength of character and self-respect. The feeling of patriotism is intensified by the present condition of the good old Commonwealth, and every true son feels a redoubled desire to redeem her from her present depression and to reconstruct her morally and nationally. Mr. President, they will do it! The young men of Virginia will do it. Let them meet their present difficulties with a manly fortitude, a noble constancy. The State has been dismembered, it is true, but she is still a great State, large in territory and abounding in resources. To speak the language of flattery in these times would be vain and wicked. But the past justifies my confidence in my fellow-citizens; they have been equal to all emergencies in the past, they will meet the difficulties of the present in a proper spirit. We are poor, very poor, it is true, but our hands, I trust, will be endued with a patient fortitude and manly constancy.

There is wealth in the earth, let us plough, dig and mine for it. There is wealth in our falling waters and running streams. They will turn the mill and build up manufactories. There is wealth, too, stores of wealth, in our black diamonds; they will make the steam which drives the car, propels the boat and turns the wheel. We have streams to bear away the fleets of commerce as far as the tide may flow, and we have forests to build those fleets. It is for the people of Virginia to say whether we have not the men to develop those resources. I believe that we have. I have confidence in my fellow-citizens. I believe that there is great and glorious destiny yet in store for Virginia. I have given, I think, a reason for the faith that is in me. But, Mr. President, I confess that I, too, have my moments of despondency. When I think of what Virginia has been, of all that she has done for the Union, her sister States and for mankind, and then reflect upon her present condition, I may say, in the eloquent words of another, that thoughts, feelings and emotions crowd upon my mind which I cannot altogether repress, and yet which in humble submission to divine Providence I dare not express. But I thank God that this is not my permanent state of mind. I do not despair. The present hours of darkness and despondency will soon pass away, and Virginia, if not exactly her old self, will be a great State again. The time must come when she will hitch on to the Federal train as great as any in her constitution of freight and passengers; and who shall say that the trumpet of leadership may not be placed once more in her hands.

Mr. President, every man has sometimes a belief for which he cannot exactly account and which seems to come to him more from intuition than reason. Such, perhaps, is in fact the foundation of my faith in the future greatness and prosperity of Virginia. I believe, Sir, that the seeds of Anglo-American civilization was first sown on the silent banks of the James for some divine purpose. It is now nearly three centuries since the Anglo-Saxon came, the master builder of forms of government, with his compass and square to lay the foundations of the immense social fabric which we now see around us, embracing almost every variety of climate and race which are known upon earth. From that seed sprang the "Old Dominion", the mother of States and of statesmen. The "Mother of States", for every State South of the isothermal line of the northern line is numerously stored with the descendants of Virginia sires. Kentucky was her eldest daughter, and under the great pioneer, George Rogers Clark, acquired the territories which now comprises most of the Northeastern States, already the seat of empire freely bestowed by Virginia upon the Confederacy for purposes of peace and harmony. The mother of statesmen, all acknowledge her to have been. It was she who gave the author of the Declaration of Independence, and the long line of Virginia Presidents under whose guidance the beginnings of empire were laid which are the most painful steps in a nation's progress. Her great mission seems to have been to promote individual liberty as far as was consistent with the existence of democratic republican government. We appeal to history to sustain the assertion that whenever the Federal Government was under the influence of Virginia principles the people were harmonious, prosperous and happy, and so soon as that government departed from those principles trials and discontent have arisen. The old state of things has passed away; concentration and consolidation are now the order of the day. Time will make up the issue between the old state of things and the new; history will record that issue, and impartial prosperity will pronounce the verdict. I will not undertake to predict what it will be, but, as a Virginian, I do not fear the result.

Mr. President, I hope for better things, but still I will look to the future in its worst aspect. Suppose that a temporary supremacy of the black race should be forced upon us. We must meet it with a manly fortitude, a patient endurance; we must do nothing inconsistent with our self-respect or wound the honor of our people, which to nations is the pearl of greater price. Patiently we will bide our time until the reaction comes, as assuredly it must. The interests of the North will not endure the waste of so much of the sources of its wealth and prosperity, and may I not hope that its feelings will also forbid our subjection to such domination. Such a state of things cannot last. We would not even be treated with such a danger if the passions and bitterness of the contest had not obscured the judgment of those who now govern. These passions must subside before long, and the volcano will burn it. For this, I trust not only to natural causes, but to Providence, which will not permit the destiny of such a State to be marred or leave its tale " half untold."

In conclusion, fellow-citizens, as Lord Elder said amongst the best of his utterances, " I submit the cause of my country to that Great Being who can say to the madness of the people as he can say to the raging waves of the ocean—Hither shall thou come, no further."

R. M. T. HUNTER TO BEVERLEY B. DOUGLAS.[1]

LLOYDS, ESSEX CO., VA., *June 14, 1869.*

MY DEAR SIR: I hasten to respond to your letter received a short time since, in which you suggest that some interest is felt by yourself and others in regard to my opinions upon the gubernatorial contest and the issues upon which the people of Virginia will soon be called upon to vote.

If the expression of my opinions upon these subjects will gratify any of my friends, it will give me pleasure to make it. In regard to the gubernatorial contest, I feel no hesitation in choosing between the candidates. I know that they are both Republicans, and that it is sometimes a most unpleasant task to be forced to choose between evils. But nevertheless, it is often a positive duty to do so, and in this instance we are not responsible for the issues on which we are called upon to decide, but which are forced on us by circumstances and a power that we cannot control. There is nothing left us but to deal with the circumstances in which we are placed not by ourselves, but others, so as to make the most of them. We are not responsible for doing the best in the abstract as we might be if we were a free and equal State in the Union; but for doing the best which is

---

[1] Copied from the Richmond *Enquirer*, June 23, 1869. Beverley Browne Douglas was a member of the State Constitutional Convention of Virginia, 1850–1851; represented Virginia in Congress, 1875–1878.

possible in the situation in which we are placed. Neither can we justify ourselves for inaction by saying there is nothing left us but a choice between evils, which we refuse to make, if by doing so we can render a service to our State, which, in my opinion, we can and ought to do in this case. Many of the most important steps in the conduct of life, and particularly of government are after all a choice between evils. No great question exciting bitter strife between parties, if not settled by the absolute submission of one of them is ever adjusted, except by compromise, which, by its nature, involves some sacrifice of opinion on both sides. It was so in the great acts of the British government, which are considered as monuments of their liberties; it was eminently so of the constitution of the United States, and it will always be so of questions between great and opposing parties who have a voice in their settlement. To say therefore, that we will do nothing which involves a sacrifice of opinion is simply to assume an impracticable position. Under this view of the case, I should not hesitate to give my vote, if I had one, to Walker for Governor, for a Conservative State government and for the expurgation of the constitution submitted to the people of Virginia for a ratification.

We are to choose, as it seems to me, between what is called the Underwood constitution, simple and pure, with Wells and his party to administer it on the one hand, or the same constitution so expurgated as to leave the power of governing and representing the State in Conservative hands with Walker and his friends, the Conservatives of Virginia to administer it. Who can hesitate as to his selection between such alternatives, or refuse to make a choice in which his State and all whom he loves have so deep an interest? That the issues are such as I state them to be, I do not for a moment doubt. That either Walker or Wells will be elected as Governor nobody denies, and that the constitution in one shape or the other will be adopted by the people of Virginia everybody seems to believe, and if it were not so, who will guarantee us that the Congress of the United States, as at present constituted, will not force it upon us in its most obnoxious form? That body has shown no great consideration heretofore either for our rights or feelings, nor does it seem to regard much either the constitution of the United States or even simple justice where we are concerned. That the election of Wells and the adoption of the Underwood constitution, as it came from the hands of its framers, would ensure the ruin of our State and consummate the degradation of our people, there are few Conservatives who will deny.

On the other hand, although I have no personal acquaintance with Mr. Walker, I am induced to believe by friends in whom I rely, and by what I have seen of his course, that he would exercise the power and duties of his office, if elected, in the manner which he supposed would redound to the interests and honor of the State which he represented. The constitution, if expurgated, as we may do if we choose, will throw the political power of the State in the hands of the Conservatives, who would administer it with a just and proper consideration for all. Can we refuse to accomplish such results for our State, which has suffered so much already, because we care not for Mr. Walker, who acted once with the Republican party on issues which are now past and gone?

If there were still a question as to negro suffrage and negro eligibility to office I might see how opposition might be made to him upon these grounds. But all must see that these questions are settled against our opinions—I mean those of the whites, by a power greater than ours and from which we at least have no appeal. Upon those questions which, as I said before, are now gone and past dispute, he did differ with us it is true, but upon the issues which are yet to come, and which are now before us, it is in every way probable that he will act with the Conservative party from sympathy as well as from principle. Shall we sacrifice the living to the dead? Shall we take no part in the real and the practical, because we are too much absorbed with the memories of questions now decided and gone, to do so? God knows those memories are as dear to me as they can be to any man; my interest, too, in those questions when they were before us and living was as keen as that of him who is most sensitive in regard to them, and continued to be so whilst there was any hope of accomplishing their defeat. But the necessities of our State are too pressing, and her suffering too great to justify us in pausing upon matters which are no longer the subjects of action, when by striking at once we can secure even a partial relief, which though partial and not entire, will yet be felt as great in every nerve and fibre of the body politic. There are sometimes great national emergencies in which the necessity for immediate action is so great that we must follow the scripture injunctions and let the dead bury the dead. We can find ample employment for all our energies in dealing with the real and the living. Let us not then refuse the assistance of men in the present and future, who are willing to give it honestly, because they were unwilling in times past to act with us on questions which though near and dear to us, are now finally decided. The more of such men we get, the more we enlarge the basis of the power of the Conservative party, which is now a matter of much moment with us.

So much for the gubernatorial contest, but there is another question which I confess has occasioned me more doubt, and upon which I have had more difficulty in forming an opinion. I mean the course proper to be pursued in regard to the constitution if expurgated of those clauses which disqualify so many of our white citizens. This constitution is indeed so bad in nearly all its parts, that there is hardly any expurgation which can reconcile me to it. Those who framed it, seem to have looked more to the punishment and to the humiliation of a large majority of the white race, than to the ends of justice and good government, a scheme of government devised for the injury of a decided majority of those to be affected by it, cannot be made acceptable to that party, unless indeed it be so amended as to transfer the moving power of the government to them, or unless it is plain that they have to choose between the instrument with amendments or without them.

After some reflection I have come to the conclusion that such is our case at present. If we can so amend the constitution as to strike out those clauses which disqualify and disfranchise so many, the whites will have a decided majority of the voters, and thus wield the political power of the State. If they administer that power, as I trust they will, with justice and a proper consideration for all, the Conservative party, of which the whites constitute so large a majority, will continue to increase. When the blacks perceive that their rights as now established will be respected, and themselves treated with justice and proper regard, they will open their eyes to their true policy and, in time, act with us, when they will perceive that in Federal legislation our interests are the same.

This process will be slow, it is true, but we ourselves may probably make it sure. At present they are misled by improper influences exercised over them by those who are looking only to office, and by a distrust of us, who they are made to believe would use political power unjustly and to their injury. It will not be long before they learn the true motives and character of those who now deceive them, and in time I trust they will dismiss their fears of us. Should this state of things be brought about, society will move more harmoniously and happily. But whether it does or not, with the removal of the two great disqualifying clauses in the constitution the whites will wield the political power of the State, a power to which they are entitled by the tests of intelligence, numbers and propriety, whether considered separately or together. The Underwood Constitution administered by the Conservatives will be a very different thing from the same constitution administered by.Wells and his party. I do not go the length of saying that the government which is best administered is best, but I believe that very much depends on the administration, so much that a bad government may be so administered as to become tolerable, and a good government may be so badly administered as to be intolerable. The operation of the county organization clause itself, will depend very much on the character of the men who fill the offices. If the constitution be expurgated as proposed, the whites in most of the counties can protect themselves. A Conservative Governor and Legislature can do much in a legitimate way to mitigate the mischiefs of this and some other provisions of the constitution. But the whites, if they have the majority, can amend the constitution, and after there is some experience of the operation of this instrument, I think it probable that many of the blacks will unite in a call for the change. Those at least amongst them who hold property and understand their interests.

But there is yet another consideration which makes me desire to rehabilitate the State, and restore her to the exercise of political power. I wish to see the representative seats of Virginia in Congress filled by men who will represent her truly and honestly; who will look to her honor and interests, and not sell them out to cater to the avarice or animosity of her enemies. Let the power to which she will be entitled under the constitution as it now stands, be wielded by such men in her defence, and they will find the means to protect her. She will no longer be treated as the cheap subject of every political experiment which it may please red republicans or New England Radicals to try at her expense. Here is the true " brazen wall " of our defence, which will be worth more to us in the way of protection than all the good feeling toward us which exists in all the North, even if we had unlimited power to draw upon that capital. It is a work of difficulty I confess for the present, but if we can so administer and manage our State governments as to produce harmony and good feeling between the races, it may lead to a common pursuit of common interests. Should it happen that this invention of negro suffrage, conceived as it was supposed for the injury of the South, should be so returned as to plague the inventor, it must be remembered that we are not responsible for such a result. We did not originate the measure, but against our earnest remonstrance it was forced upon us.

So far I have considered to enforce my views by considerations special to Virginia herself, but I confess that there are others of a more general nature which have weight with me. I believe it is a matter of general interest that the influence of Virginia should be once more felt in the government of the Union. Her worst enemies will admit that it was an honest influence, and all must feel that such an element was never more needed than now in the conduct of national affairs. When I reflect upon all that she did to delay the establishment of the despotic powers of a mere majority of numbers, I cannot but think that there may yet be some potency in her voice to check abuses and restrain oppression. When I remember, too, how long she maintained her gallant struggle with no other weapons than reason, the constitution and the moral influence bequeathed her by her mighty dead, and that she held her line until overwhelmed by the corruption of the times and the vast odds against her, it seems to me that she must have discovered the true line of defence against despotism in every shape. Even though it should appear in its last development and final form of imperialism, whose coming many secretly believe and some openly declare to be inevitable. Should that time ever arrive, those to whom its approaches are unwelcome, may rejoice in the assistance of her who has been ever ready to resist unlimited power in all its forms. Weapons that are now rusting from disuse in her political armory may again come into play, and she may be called upon for hands skilled in wielding them. It is true that in the past she failed to commend to the favorable consideration of her co-States a democracy with limited power, but her voice may be better heeded when it becomes a question as to the limitation upon the power of a monarchy, should that be ever established, an event upon which it used to be thought almost sacrilegious to speculate, but which now somehow seems to have become a familiar topic in the mouths of men.

If Zisca's dead skin, when stretched upon a down, could give forth a sound, as fabled, to awe even the haughty Turk at the height of his pride and power, the voice of what yet lives of Virginia, like "the shout of a king amongst them", may once more rally the hosts who are called upon to repel the approach of oppression with the tramp of its iron heel or of despotism with its merciless and all-absorbing grasp. I could wish that the country might be saved from such trials, but what nation, what government, and especially what republic, has ever escaped them? But I am approaching a subject which would take me too far from the matter in hand. I have given the reasons which, in my opinion, make it proper for Virginia to accept even the Underwood constitution if it should be so expurgated as to bestow the political power of the State upon the white race, which constitutes the majority of its people. I would accept almost any constitution which would have that effect. I would do almost anything to see a State government composed of Virginians who would respect her honor and represent her interests. There may be worse things, I know than even military government, but it was reserved for these extraordinary times to force that conviction on the mind of one trained up in the enjoyment and tradition of social and individual liberty. I confess, however, that I am weary of seeing the sword of the conqueror in the scale of justice. I can live under arbitrary power, I know, because I have done it, and still do; but it is comparatively a new thing to me, and I can never be reconciled to it. I shall take the first fair mode of escape from it which is open to me. I think the opportunity is now afforded in the issues presented by the Conservative party of the State. They do not offer, it is true, all that I would like, or all that I think we are entitled to, but it is all that they can give. I am for taking every step towards self-government for which an opportunity may be afforded me by the majority that rules us. Concessions may be forced upon them by the necessities of the times, or may be made from a slow returning sense of justice. I will take them as they come, be they little or much, without inquiry into the motive which prompts them, if they enable us to take another step towards the restoration of our State to the rights of self-government. I will not only accept them, but accept them promptly, for I believe this Congress to be capable of resuming to-morrow what they may have granted to-day.

Should we fail to ratify this constitution after it has been expurgated, I feel by no means sure that the party in power will not force it upon us as it came from the hands of its makers. Let no hope be entertained to the contrary, because the constitution of the United States forbids them to do so. When has that instrument stood in the way of accomplishing any purpose which they cherished? Did it restrain them in their dealings with the President or the Supreme Court of the United States? Has it been respected by them in their conduct towards us? On the contrary, it seems to be the most approved theory with them that we are beyond the pale of the constitution, and subject to their arbitrary power and absolute control.

I will not fail to do anything which may help my State for the present, because I hope they will do something better for her hereafter. I do indeed hope to see a returning sense of justice at some future day, but that time is probably distant, and I dare not wait. The white people of Virginia have now an opportunity to restore the State to the right of self government, and to obtain the control of its political power at home and in the general government. If they fail to do· so, it will be their own fault, and owing to their apathy and indecision. Before they lose such a result, let them consider in time what a loss that will be, let them remember too that their majority, though decided, is small, and to secure such relief as is possible, every Conservative voter should cast his vote, and unite in the common cause. I know that our position is difficult, and that even if we obtain the victory we shall require wisdom, forbearance and energy to reap its fruits; but I have faith in my fellow citizens, and when I see Virginians ruling Virginia, I shall feel that the first great step, which costs more than any other, has been taken towards the restoration of her rights and prosperity.

R. M. T. HUNTER TO LEWIS E. HARVIE.

March 7th, 1876.

DEAR HARVIE: I see you so seldom when you come to Richmond that I have concluded to write you in relation to a matter upon which

I want your advice. Since I last saw you I have received another letter from the gentleman in So[uth] Ca[rolina] of whom I spoke to you.

It seems that some months ago Mr. Calhoun's friends and relations had a meeting and nominated me to write his life and add the remaining papers which Crallé did not publish. Mr. Clemson, his son-in-law, wrote to communicate this fact to me. I did not receive that letter and could not answer it. After waiting sometime without an answer they wrote to Miles and requested him to undertake the work. This Miles declined saying that his knowledge of Mr. Calhoun and his political history was not sufficient to qualify him for the undertaking and that he knew no one so well fitted for the purpose as myself, upon which Mrs. Clemson who was then living said that was also her opinion. She is now dead and was the last child of Mr. Calhoun and had more sense than any of them whom I have seen. He writes to urge me again as he says that I am the only person who can write it as the nominee of his children. What shall I do? If I undertake it my book is postponed for a long time if not indefinitely. If I can complete it, the book would sell for something and in my circumstances I feel bound to eke out my scanty means of subsistence by the use of my pen. On the other hand no life of Mr. Calhoun which I could write would sell, so much is he maligned and misunderstood at present. Yet I am not willing that his life and works should be presented to the world by an indifferent or unfriendly hand. In presenting him fairly to the world I should be able to do something for the party with which I have acted and in that way to my own political character. Moreover, I think I could do that book better than the other. If I were not poor I should not hesitate a moment. It is possible that I should get through with the life in a year and then take up the other. I have written to my wife about it. She is more interested in my doing something to make money than any one else. I think I shall determine according to her wishes but I am anxious to hear from you about it. I am anxious to vindicate myself and my friends especially Mr. Calhoun but if I do I shall die as poor as I am living and very unpopular. Please let me hear from you as soon as convenient. Amongst all my companions you are the only one living who would give me friendly and considerate advice. I am not very old, 67 now and soon to be 68 but if my age is to be reckoned by the friends I have lost I am old indeed.

INDEX.